GEPIDS

LOMBARDS

BULGARIANS

CRIMEA

Cherson

BLACK SEA
(Pontus Euxeinos)

DACIA   Danube R.   MOESIA
  • Naissus

DALMATIA

ILLYRIA
ILLYRICUM   • Serdica   Sykae (Galata) *Bosphorus*   PAPHLAGONIA   PONTUS
Vederiana   Constantinople • Chalcedon
Durrës   MACEDONIA   THRACE   *Propontis*
  Thessalonika   *Sea*   BITHYNIA   A N A T O L I A
                          Cyzicus Prusa   CAPPADOCIA
APULIA Apollonia   EPIRUS   PHRYGIA GALATIA   • Caesarea
                THESSALY   AEGEAN   LYDIA   PISIDIA   CAPPADOCIA
                          SEA   Ephesus   LYCAONIA   ISAURIA
IONIAN   GREECE   • Philadelphia   CILICIA   Tarsus Antioch
SEA   *Ithaca*   Smyrna   CARIA   PAMPHYLIA   Seleucia
      ACHAIA   • Athens   LYCIA
                                                  Laodikeia   SYRIA
CRETE   CYPRUS   Apamea •   PRIMA
                                            Berytus •
      N   SEA   Tyre •
                                            Nazareth
            Cyrene   Caesarea •
      Ptolemais • Apollonia   PALESTINE Jerusalem
      Teuchira • Barka   Bethlehem   *Dead Sea*
            CYRENAICA   Alexandria   • Pelusium   ISRAEL

TREBIZOND

ARMENIA
              Dara
MESOPOTAMIA   Nisibis •
      Edessa •
            Euphrates R.
            Palmyra •
SYRIA
SECONDA
  to PERSIA →
  • Damascus
  to BABYLONIA →

ARABS

ARABIA

LIBYA

EGYPT

Nile R.

THEBAIS

RED
SEA

NUBIA

Adulis •

ETHIOPIA

© 2004 Jeffrey L. Ward

THEODORA

Empress *of* Byzantium

THEODORA

EMPRESS of BYZANTIUM

PAOLO CESARETTI

Translated from the Italian by
Rosanna M. Giammanco Frongia, Ph.D.

A MARK MAGOWAN BOOK

THE VENDOME PRESS

First published in the United States of America by
Magowan Publishing LLC and The Vendome Press
1334 York Avenue
New York, NY 10021

ISBN: 0-86565-237-6

Library of Congress Cataloging-in-Publication Data
Cesaretti, Paolo.
  [Teodora. English]
  Theodora : empress of Byzantium / Paolo Cesaretti ; translated from the Italian by
  Rosanna M. Giammanco Frongia.
    p. cm.
  "A Mark Magowan Book."
  Includes bibliographical references and index.
  ISBN: 0-86565-237-6 (alk. paper)
    1. Theodora, Empress, consort of Justinian I, Emperor of the East, d. 548 2. Empresses–
  Byzantine Empire–Biography. 3. Byzantine Empire–History–Justinian I, 527-565. I. Title.
  DF572.5.C4713 2004
  949.5'013–dc22   2004043528

Jacket designed by Lisa Vaughn
Interior designed by Francesca Belanger
Maps by Jeffrey L. Ward

S E P S

SEGRETARIATO EUROPEO PER LE PUBBLICAZIONI SCIENTIFICHE

The translation of this book has been funded by SEPS.

Front cover: detail of mosaic of Theodora and her attendants from the basilica of San Vitale,
Ravenna. Back cover: detail of mosaic of Justinian from basilica of San Vitale. Both
© Cameraphoto Arte, Venezia

Printed in the United States

To Clara

tutusque sacerque

Contents

Foreword

The original Italian version of this volume was published in the autumn of 2001, before I read Clive Foss's article about Theodora published in 2002. In addition, James Allan Evans's book on Theodora, *The Empress Theodora: Partner of Justinian,* promises to add significantly to the literature on this important historical figure. My text would certainly have benefited from my having read these works, but I don't think I would have changed my basic concept, which is reflected in this edition: I have tried to build a real narrative out of the facts of this great woman's life and give the story a certain rhythm. This element of artifice is ultimately the most important part of any biographer's work (as Hans-Georg Beck, the great scholar of Theodora and Procopius, has noted). Because the same few sources are (almost) all used by every one of her biographers—mute sources that leave themselves open to all sorts of interpretations—I have sifted through and reorganized them into something new. A friend of mine described the result of this effort as "not a fictionalized biography but a biographical novel." I like the expression and I hereby adopt it.

I am deeply grateful to Vendome Press and particularly to Mark Magowan for being interested in my book in the first place, and for his great care in producing the best English edition possible. I have Rosanna Giammanco to thank for translating the text, and Abigail Asher for her editing: I cannot praise her enough for her patience with knotty Italian word problems, and for her rigorous treatment of the

Greek and Latin terms I used in the original edition, and which, when appropriate, are used here.

Thanks to Peter Garlid, Emanuela Canali, and Isabel Venero, who all helped to bring this edition into being. The editions in English and Greek (the chief language spoken by Theodora and Procopius) were both subsidized by grants from the European Secretariat for Scientific Publications in Bologna (Segretariato Europeo per le Pubblicazioni Scientifiche, or SEPS). I'm happy, of course, about the grants for personal reasons, but I'm even more gratified by their cultural significance: this biography, with its interpretation of the sources and its various literary devices, is considered to have its roots in "science." My thanks to Chiara Segafredo on behalf of all her colleagues at SEPS.

With each reprint of the original Italian edition, and each publication of foreign editions, information and facts are updated or modified to reflect local differences or new information uncovered by recent research, but the intent and the basic structure of the work remains the same. I emphasize this to introduce my readers to the idea of the divergent interpretations of the texts used to study Theodora: these issues are relevant here because they have always influenced the image of Theodora provided by historians and other writers. So what is the real "truth" about Theodora? That's a question that cannot be tackled in this foreword—that is part of our story.

Paolo Cesaretti
Milan, December 2003

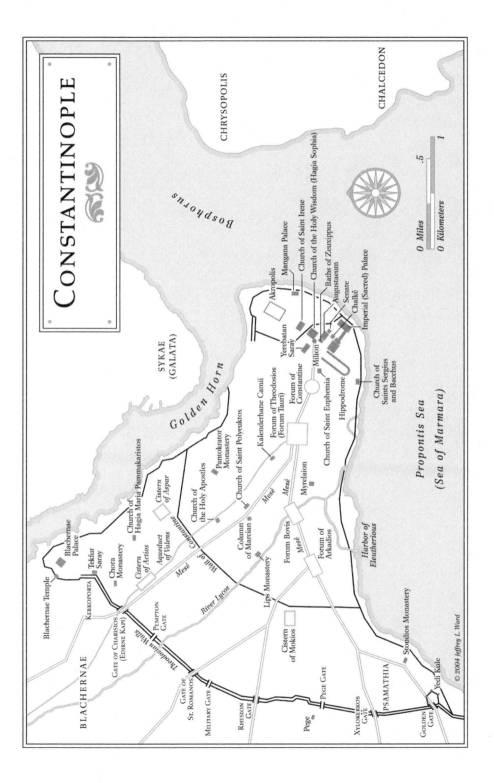

CONSTANTINOPLE

CHRYSOPOLIS

CHALCEDON

Bosphorus

SYKAE
(GALATA)

Golden Horn

Akropolis

Mangana Palace
Church of Saint Irene
Church of the Holy Wisdom (Hagia Sophia)
Baths of Zeuxippus
Augustaeum
Senate
Chalkè
Imperial (Sacred) Palace

Yerebatan Saray
Milion

Church of Saints Sergius and Bacchus

Hippodrome

Church of Saint Euphemia

Forum of Constantine

Forum of Theodosios (Forum Tauri)

Kalenderhane Camii

Pantokrator Monastery
Church of Saint Polyeuktos

Church of Hagia Maria Pammakaristos

Cistern of Aspar

Church of the Holy Apostles

Mesè

Mesè

Myrelaion

Column of Marcian

Forum Bovis

Forum of Arkadios

Mesè

Harbor of Eleutherious

Propontis Sea (Sea of Marmara)

Blachernae Temple

Blachernae Palace

Tekfur Saray

Chora Monastery

Cistern of Aetios

Aqueduct of Valens

Constantine

Wall of Constantine

Lips Monastery

River Lycos

Cistern of Mokios

Studios Monastery

BLACHERNAE

KERKOPORTA

GATE OF CHARISIOS (EDIRNE KAPI)

PEMPTON GATE

Theodosian Walls

Mesè

GATE OF ST. ROMANOS

MILITARY GATE

RHESION GATE

Pege

PEGE GATE

XYLOKERKOS GATE

PSAMATHIA

GOLDEN GATE

Yedi Kule

© 2004 Jeffrey L. Ward

0 Miles   .5   1
0 Kilometers

FAMILY OF THEODORA

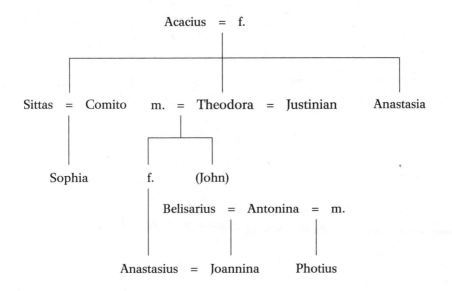

Note: Greek and Latin words that are particularly relevant are translated in the text and their definitions may be found in the Glossary, together with other technical terms relating to theology, the military, the government, and so on.

Introduction

NO ONE KNOWS the name of the artist who portrayed her in the mosaics of the basilica of San Vitale in Ravenna [fig. 1], even though he was one of the leading craftsmen of the first Christian millennium. Each year, hundreds of thousands of people flock to this northern Italian city solely to admire the portrait of Empress Theodora and the image of female power and pomp that she projects—still a rarity in world art.

Her portrait exudes an authority that lingers like a seduction in the visitor's memory, and yet many of her admirers are hard-pressed to link her to an exact event, or even to situate her in the immense grid of space and time.

In this, she differs from the other famous women of classical and Judeo-Christian tradition, women such as Sappho, author of achingly beautiful love poems, or Delilah, who stood up to arbitrary law by cutting Samson's hair, or Judith, who beheaded Holofernes. Women such as Cleopatra, who dared to kill herself after having mastered the art of power and love, like Lucretia, the Roman virgin who put virtue before life, or like Perpetua, the early Christian martyr who chose faith over life.

But the famous—even notorious—Empress Theodora: What did she do?

One thing she undoubtedly did *not* do. Like most ancient women, she did not write her story; it was a man, Procopius, who wrote extensively about her. The scion of a distinguished family, he was proud of his

1. Mosaic of Theodora with her retinue, c. 545–50, basilica of San Vitale, Ravenna. Some scholars have identified Antonina and her daughter Joannina among the attendants to her left.

extensive studies in literature and law, although he was not very powerful in life.

Procopius was ten years older than Theodora, having been born in A.D. 490 in Caesarea, Palestine, at the time one of the many attractive "small capitals" of the Mediterranean Levant; it is now known only as the ruins of Qaisariayyah, south of Haifa. He was in a good position as an observer, for he had been an advisor to Belisarius, the most brilliant military leader of the time, and he spent many years in Belisarius's retinue. Procopius had been at Belisarius's side in Mesopotamia from 527 to 531; had followed him in 532 to Constantinople, the capital of the empire; and had accompanied him from 533 to 534 to Africa, where he had remained at his side until 536. Still later, he had rejoined his general in Sicily on the march to reclaim Italy from the "barbarians." In 540, Procopius had witnessed the storming of Ravenna, an event that seemed to mark the end of that conflict. In short, Procopius had witnessed firsthand the most promising expansionist period of the "Roman" empire of Constantinople in the

2. Mosaic of Justinian with his retinue, c. 545–50, basilica of San Vitale, Ravenna. Some scholars have identified Belisarius and Anastasius among the attendants to his right.

Mediterranean. The expansionist policy was conceived and pursued by Emperor Justinian, Theodora's husband, who is portrayed in the mosaic opposite hers in San Vitale [fig. 2].

Procopius, an eyewitness to historic events,[1] considered himself the person most suited to write the chronicles of his times, so that's what he did. He left us three different types of works, all written in Greek and each one a masterpiece of sixth-century literature; they are, however, fraught with unique problems of interpretation as part of world literature.

His major accomplishment is his eight-volume *History of the Wars*, the first seven volumes of which were composed within the years 550 and 551, and the eighth after 553. In the *Wars*, Procopius tries to imitate the painstaking approach of ancient historiographers, drawing inspiration from their lofty impartiality, so much so that he even includes hints of reproach for the imperial couple and their circle—Belisarius is implicated as well—and praise for their enemies, including the Goth Theodoric, the famous "barbarian" king of Italy. In his work *On the*

Buildings (c. 554), Procopius strikes a different note with an emphatic celebration, in the encomiastic genre, of Emperor Justinian's truly extraordinary activity as a builder of religious and secular edifices.

Though a marginal figure in the *Wars* and in *Buildings,* Empress Theodora appears in a positive light. But she and Justinian are portrayed negatively and in depth in Procopius's most controversial work, the *Secret History,*[2] a surprisingly scathing critique of the imperial couple's achievements. It has been suggested that this third work, begun in 550, was a sort of rough draft to be reviewed and completed before its official release, something that would have happened only after the death of Justinian. By delaying, Procopius would have given an account of the aspects—particularly the economic and administrative aspects—that he had intentionally neglected in his other writings: "It was not possible, as long as the actors were still alive, for these things to be recorded in the way they should have been. For neither was it possible . . . if detected to escape a most cruel death."[3] If that was indeed his plan, it failed, because Procopius died before Justinian.

It would be perhaps too simple to identify the voice of the *Secret History* as the authentic voice of Procopius, in contrast to the "rhetoric" or "convention" that supposedly informs his other writings. It would be tempting to include this work in the contemporary category of underground, anti-dictatorial opposition literature, but too many common threads run through all of Procopius's works, including conceptions of the divine, the supernatural, and the oneiric. The rhetorical tradition is especially strong in the *Secret History,* which may be classified as a caustic sort of critique, a genre that has enjoyed a long literary tradition.[4] Therefore, no "genuine" Procopius—devoid of rhetoric—exists: such a thing is not even conceivable.

Dissatisfied with the conditions of the Roman Empire around A.D. 550, perhaps disappointed because he had been left on the sidelines of power, or suffering from the typical syndrome of the veteran (who prides himself on having seen life's true face in war, and thus devalues all other kinds of experience), Procopius chose to express himself not only in celebrations of the imperial couple but also through the rhetoric of vilification. And so, in order to describe the "base deeds committed by . . . Theodora"[5] on the throne, he began slandering her from her earliest childhood history. While ancient biographers (Plutarch, for one) had lauded exemplary models of Greek virtue and Roman gravitas by presenting childhood signs that heralded the excellence of their heroes, Procopius identified and highlighted the earliest origins of what he calls her "abominations."

Fortunately for historical research, his condemnations are so detailed and rich in information that, caustic as they may be, the *Secret History* is still the best tool for researching the life of Theodora. At the same time, it also documents a misogynist mind-set uncomfortable with innovation and social confrontation.

As specific elements of Theodora's controversial personality, Procopius illustrates the typical traits of the environment in which she was raised, which was as lowly as it was uninhibited. He ascribes to the character and disposition of his imperial "victim"[6] what might actually have been the result of a (forced and painful) acceptance of a private situation. While it is true that Theodora was born into a family where the father worked as a bear keeper and the mother had to start her daughter on a career as mime actress while quite young, Procopius reduces everything to an exercise in prostitution—and he depicts it as voluntary, not forced, prostitution.

With his skillful rhetoric, in a section of the *Secret History* on Theodora's "nurture and education,"[7] he describes what he finds especially scandalous: the fact that a woman born and raised in such humble circumstances could ascend to the imperial throne and exercise absolute power. Procopius narrates Theodora's life by illustrating a progression of scenes that follow an elaborate narrative dynamic, much like the Biblical story cycles in early Christian murals—albeit, of course, with a different intent.

Just as the narratives in church frescoes were meant to illustrate the glorious sequence of sacred history, the unfolding of episodes and scenes in Procopius reveals an analogous intent of progressive exposition. He wanted to highlight his protagonist and characterize her within her environment. Preferring to focus on specific details rather than general descriptions, Procopius succeeds in separating Theodora from her context, and then lingers over her with ever-increasing detail, even focusing on the different parts of her body, including the most hidden and private, not to celebrate them as sacred, but to scorn and debase them as "unworthy." Procopius displays an attention to anatomical detail unparalleled in ancient historiography.[8] In modern terms, we might say that he "zooms in" obsessively for close-up shots.

Procopius claimed he was telling about the "nurture and education" of Theodora. In reality, he denigrates her by writing reductively about the sexual history of Theodora the woman. And yet by so doing, he confers substance and seductiveness on the stately apparition that gazes down at us from the mosaics of San Vitale in Ravenna, casting a spell on hundreds of thousands of visitors each year.

This paradox, this unique quality, is the key to the *Secret History*'s fame and that of its protagonist; that fame spread in 1623, when the first printed edition was published. Merely because a biased account of their private sexual life has survived, the characters of the *Secret History*, Theodora above all, have been ambiguously perceived as being "more modern" or "more interesting" than other characters from late antiquity or the Middle Ages.

Many controversial, mythical versions of Theodora's character have appeared in modern times. There have been sentimental, lascivious, and cruel Theodoras created in turn by Edward Gibbon (1737–1794), Donatien-Alphonse-François de Sade (1740–1814), Victorien Sardou (1831–1908), Charles Diehl (1859–1944), Gabriele D'Annunzio (1863–1938), and even Robert Graves (1895–1985). Whether ancient or modern, the literary fables spring to life when they are read in their historical context, especially the history of the political, legislative, military, social, religious, and cultural issues so important to Theodora and her contemporaries. For while they prayed for eternal Christian bliss, they also trusted that their accomplishments in those earthly fields would guarantee them future fame.

In order to present the life of Theodora against the background of her time and her world, therefore, we must analyze and interpret many often contradictory historical and literary sources (primarily the writings of Procopius), supplementing them with knowledge about monuments and physical sites studied by archaeologists and historians of art, architecture, and epigraphy. But the biographer's task is not simply to reconstruct a documentary file on Theodora (the reader will find a synopsis of such documents in the appendix to this volume); he must push forward, he must try to ask questions of Theodora herself, the source of all sources, as he glimpses her through the fabric of the events in her life.

Those events, with all their reversals, reveal a basic unity in Theodora's very own "culture,"[9] remote from the official canons of the time, a culture that she built all by herself and that marked her soul. She coined her unique, precious identity during her unusual, proud education, and in less than a decade (from about 518 to 527) it enabled her to embark on one of the most admired and controversial ascents in European history, in a career path that rose to the splendor of the imperial throne of "the second Rome."

And it was no fairy tale. Theodora knew how to draw strength from her cultural and moral roots, to *resist* in impossible situations, when "men no longer knew where to turn."[10] She found the model for her resistance in the archaic, mythical Hellas, the culture whose emotional depths had remained hidden for centuries beneath classical and Christian virtues, only to resurface in her, the daughter of a bear tamer. (Perhaps they still linger about, waiting to be evoked anew in the future.)

This book aims to evoke Theodora's character on the historical stage where she lived, searching as necessary in the gaps between documents and trying to provide a voice where the sources are silent.

Because of its author's fears (there was no way for him "if detected to escape a most cruel death"), the *Secret History* was not widely circulated in the Byzantine era and was largely unknown until the Renaissance. Thus the extraordinary Theodora did not join the roster of famous ancient women that men of letters suggested to painters seeking iconographic material. Thus Pietro Aretino never discussed Theodora, and Titian never painted her.

And there is some irony in the fact that the *Secret History* was

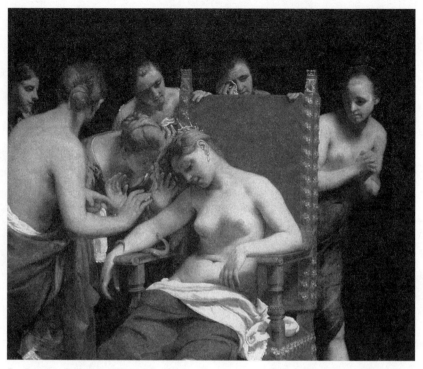

3. *Death of Cleopatra*, Guido Cagnacci, oil on canvas, 1657(?), Kunsthisto-
   risches Museum, Vienna.

published in 1663 as part of the collection of Byzantine historians promoted by Louis XIV for the Louvre library, the first systematic presentation of the history of the empire of Constantinople in the modern
West. In that same year, the painter who would have been the ideal
modern portraitist of Theodora died at the court of Vienna. He was
born in Sant'Archangelo di Romagna, not far from Ravenna, in 1601,
and his name was Guido Cagnacci [fig. 3]. Cagnacci was and remains
the portraitist of the most unforgettable Cleopatras, Lucretias, Judiths,
and other famous ancient women. Discarding all superfluous decoration, he lovingly portrayed them in an intense light that delightfully
exalts their bodies and their beautiful, delicate faces caught in unique
emotional moments. He explored their bodies not in order to belittle
their looks or character, as Procopius did in his *Secret History*, but to
restore them to artistic memory, and thus to life.

THEODORA

Empress *of* Byzantium

"Keeper of the Bears"

Constantinople, c. 503

FROM THE VERY FIRST, life for Theodora was a public event, a ceremony. She had no father to introduce her to life or to protect her. Her father was no more.

There was little decorum or privacy. The coffin was open. Everything took place under the open sky. The body of Acacius, Theodora's father, had been laid out in his garment as "keeper of the animals."[1] His face was exposed to the curious stares or merciful gazes of strangers; arms folded, he seemed lost in reverent slumber. The arms of other men carried his lifeless body to the cemetery near the city walls. The coffin was overflowing with cut flowers; next to the body, someone had placed Acacius's favorite tools, leather and metal objects fit for strong hands such as his had been: the whip he cracked to keep the wild animals at bay and the pitchfork he used to goad them into their cages.

Standing on their doorsteps, shopkeepers bowed their heads; passersby made the sign of the cross in answer to the gestures of the priests who escorted Acacius to his last Christian abode, blessing his soul's release from the body and its return to the Ancient Maker "in the high heavens." The chants of the priests were serene, as serene as the figurative art of the time: idyllic scenes of flocks of animals, doves, peacocks, and symbolic monograms.

Other individuals harboring different feelings also attended the funeral of Acacius the bear keeper. A choir of mourning women—plaintive reminders of an ancient Mediterranean custom, surely an irritant for the Christian priests—gave melodic form to the empty feelings of the survivors, Acacius's widow and his daughters in particular. From their repertory of funeral lamentations, the mourners sang dirges dedicated to young bridegrooms, not unlike those that still survive to this day in the Salento region of southern Italy:

> I had in my garden a fair pomegranate tree,
> But the wind came and uprooted it,
> Taking it with him.
> I had in my garden a carnation,
> Red and sweet-smelling.
> Come women neighbors, see how it's torn.
> My young groom, my darling,
> I call but you don't speak.
> The sun has set but your fair eyes
> No longer see the moon.
> Yesterday, today and every day I call you,
> And speak to you.
> A fire rages in my heart:
> For your fair eyes no longer see.[2]

As the funeral procession wound its way through orchards, gardens, and untilled overgrown land, leaving behind the network of city streets, it seemed even thinner. From time to time, isolated figures appeared on the horizon: women drawing water from wells, or wandering creatures chasing a dream, perhaps, of a life free of earthly obligations, "like the angels" of Paradise. Finally, the procession reached the grand complex of walls, towers, and moats protecting the city that was considered "impregnable" [fig. 4]. They could hear the blare of trumpets that signaled the changing of the guard. And so the majesty of the empire was projected onto the very first ceremony and the first grief of a little orphan girl of about three named Theodora. But no one in the procession that day could have felt very close to the immense power of the imperial throne.

On that particular day, at the funeral, public authority came in the guise of a man named Asterius. Acacius's widow—the mother of Theodora and her sisters—was careful not to stray too far from him.

4. "Theodosian" walls of Constantinople, 5th century.

She tried to smooth her hair, worn loose on her shoulders in mourning. They exchanged only a few words, *sotto voce*. Asterius seemed to nod his head in assent. Then the smell of incense grew more intense. The priests were escorting the corpse as it dropped into Mother Earth by drawing large crosses in the air with their censers, singing increasingly higher-pitched melodies as the grave diggers dug deeper. The soul of Acacius had left the body. The women had become separated from their Acacius. There was a widow. There were three orphan girls. Someone was needed to protect them.

But for now they protected themselves.

These events took place in Constantinople, present-day Istanbul in Turkey, which was at the time the European and Asiatic capital of an empire that still called itself Roman. It was shortly after the five hundredth year of the Christian era, perhaps around 503, though at the time the calendar ran differently. Based on holy scripture, it was generally agreed that God had begun the creation of the world on a Sunday in March. It was a matter of dispute, however, whether that day was March 19 or 25, and whether it happened in the year 5494, 5500, 5501, or 5508 before Jesus Christ's birth to the Virgin Mary in Bethlehem.

Whatever the correct year, that first Sunday in March marked the beginning of the "eons," immense time-measuring units. Each eon was to last one thousand years, and as there were seven days to Creation, so the "fair race of the millennia"[3] would be seven laps long. At the close of the seventh eon, therefore—seven thousand years after the world's creation—God would raise a tremendous spirit on the earth. The bones of the dead would be gathered in the Biblical valley of Jehoshaphat to reassemble themselves into bodies; the bones would be clothed in nerves and flesh; the dead would be resurrected for the Last Judgment. This is what seers and ascetics preached under the porticos and in the taverns of the city.

Judgment Day could be forecast with great accuracy, using the different chronologies: the event would occur in A.D. 1506, if 5494 B.C. was accepted as the year of the creation of the world; in 1500, if 5500 was the beginning of the calculation; and in 1499, supposing the world had begun in 5501. In the end, it was agreed that the world had begun in 5508, and in an attempt at consistency the year 1492 was projected as the last year of the seventh eon. After that, the eighth and last eon would begin, an eon that would have no end, a period that would raise the just to a state of perfect joy and keep sinners in an everlasting punishment.

Those who, like Theodora, were born about six thousand years after the creation of the world—around the year A.D. 500—were therefore born at the beginning of the seventh eon. Of course, mankind would have to wait another long thousand years for the fulfillment of the promise of joy and justice ushered in by the incarnation of "the Son of God, Our Savior Jesus Christ,"[4] but this final lap in the great race of time allowed some hope. Just as Sunday was the well-deserved day of rest after a week's toil, so the seventh eon glorified the new man, moving him closer to the Divinity who had found him worthy of His sacrifice. And while it was always a good thing to trust in Providence, it was especially good to do so in the seventh eon. There was a whole millennium to be filled with charity and good deeds. Never had the world hosted so many devout resolutions.

Those high hopes and good intentions had spread throughout the inhabitants of the lands around the Mediterranean, that sea once called a "frog pond"[5] by the ancient philosophers who were deemed to lack the enlightenment of divine grace but were still celebrated for their eloquence. According to modern demographers, approximately 50 million people lived around the Mediterranean basin. Of them, about 1 percent—half a million, or perhaps 600,000 people—believed themselves to be God's chosen. These were the inhabitants of Constantinople and included Acacius's widow—whose name isn't known—and her three daughters: Comito, the eldest, Theodora, and Anastasia, the youngest.

Constantinople had been founded in A.D. 324 and inaugurated six years later on the site of the ancient Byzantion, where Europe and Asia face each other, by Constantine the Great (emperor from A.D. 306 to 337), who had granted freedom of worship to Christians and had chosen to be baptized himself. The true cross had come to him in a dream, and when fighting under the sign of the cross he had won great battles. Buried in the church of the Holy Apostles as the "thirteenth apostle," his presence was still felt in the city that guarded the remains of his earthly body, a city filled with columns and great statues dedicated to him, where the people told and retold an endless number of stories and folk tales.

The city of Constantine was called the "new Jerusalem" because of its religious, Christian importance, and also the "second Rome" because it had inherited Rome's political primacy as well as its urban and administrative structure.[6] It was said that no tribe could ever vanquish it: had any opponent dared to attack the capital, they would have "smashed their heads" against the fortified walls in the attempt.[7] Only God could raise his hand against the city, but He would do so only on Judgment Day. The end of the city would signify the end of the Roman and Christian empire, and with that, the close of the seventh and last eon, and thus the end of time.

(In 1453 the Ottoman Turks stormed the city of Constantinople. Assuming that the Creation occurred in 5508 B.C., the year 1453 fell within the proper chronological period. But the world did not end in 1492, the last year of the seventh eon; on the contrary, with the discovery of the Americas, that year marked an upheaval and expansion of the world. One world, however—that particular Roman and Christian world—did indeed come to an end.)

In the evenings and nights, in the dim light of oil lamps, Acacius's widow would recount to her daughters the tales of the capital's fabled past; at other times, she would comfort them with predictions about their future in the city during the seventh eon. By day, she faced the hardships of daily life.[8] As a widow she was protected by the highest church authority in the capital, the Patriarchate, which was in charge of guiding the "widows' battalion."[9] So she probably turned to the Church's charity network, which operated as a sort of public welfare center distributing necessities such as dried or preserved food staples, fabrics, thread, and used clothing, and dispensing some form of medical care, all supplemented with spiritual exhortations to patience, forbearance, and trust in divine mercy.

Two popular solutions of the time were available to Acacius's widow: she could entrust her daughters to strangers who would adopt them, or consign them to a convent or a hospital in the hope that some high-placed benefactor might come along for them. As for her, she could retire from active life in the city and enter an almshouse for poor widows. Given her present hardships and the prospects for the future—she had no sons—these appeared to be reasonable solutions to her predicament.

These solutions seem particularly likely insofar as Acacius's family was thoroughly Christianized, judging from their names. Names such as Acacius, Comito, Theodora, and Anastasia, while unambiguously Hellenic (Greek was the language spoken at home), also signal a strong Christian element. And they offer us important circumstantial evidence.

The name *Acacius* is derived from the Greek privative *alpha* and from *kakos*, bad: it means "he who does no harm to others," or "he who knows no evil," similar to the Latin Innocentius (a name chosen by twelve popes). Saint Acacius, a Christian soldier who died a martyr in 303 or 305, was worshipped in the city. Also, from 472 to 489 an Acacius had been patriarch of Constantinople.

Because at the time people married extremely young and sought to have children as soon as possible, and because we suppose that Theodora was born around the year 500 and Comito was perhaps three years older (born around 497), it is reasonable to assume that Acacius was born during the tenure of Patriarch Acacius and had thus been baptized with the name of the patriarch. This would place his birth in or near Constantinople in the year 475 or shortly before. Acacius's family was probably linked to the patriarch by patron-client bonds or some other dependent relationship. When Acacius the bear keeper died in 503, he may have been thirty years old; life expectancy for a man at the time was barely forty years.

The Greek names of the three orphan girls are further evidence that the family held the Christian religion in high esteem. Theodora (*theou dôron* in Greek) means "gift of God": quite a different meaning from her modern myth as a toxic femme fatale. The name of Anastasia, the younger sister, evokes not only *Anastasis*, the resurrection of Christ—a fundamental tenet of Christian faith—but also Anastasius, the emperor at the time of her birth, who ruled from 491 to 518. No information has survived about Anastasia, but Comito, the eldest, has left historical traces. She married into an illustrious family and bore a daughter, Sophia ("wisdom"), who became the first woman after her aunt Theodora to ascend the "Roman" throne of Constantinople.

The name *Comito* echoes the Greek verb *komaô* and the noun *comet*: the name means "she of the bountiful locks," or the "long-haired one" (comets can be seen to have long "tresses"). Possibly Comito was born with an unusual shock of hair, and that was reflected in the name her parents gave her. Or perhaps they were thinking of a comet in the sky, and chose the name to invoke a happy destiny for their firstborn "star." Since there is no evidence that any real comets were racing through the skies at the time, it is most likely that her parents referred to the star that marked the birth of Jesus, the one the Eastern Magi followed to reach Bethlehem.

These, then, were the three daughters of Acacius the bear keeper and of a mother whose name and background we don't know, although a later (unreliable) legend claimed that she was the sister of a great general of the empire.[10] At most, we can guess her age: she might have been twenty-five years old when Anastasia was born, the last of these daughters to be baptized with such clearly Christian names. Possibly these female births did not satisfy the parents. They would have wanted sons who could soon contribute to the family income. Sons who could work at trades suitable to their social class: in the footsteps of Acacius, working with wild beasts or spurring chariot horses; or maybe going into military service, perhaps even at the emperor's palace, where they would wear splendid plumed helmets.

There must have been several failed pregnancies in an effort to bear a son, especially because spontaneous abortions, premature births, and stillbirths were common at the time, the infant mortality rate standing at about 50 percent. If that was the case, we might detect—in Theodora's name especially, meaning as it does "gift from God"—a hint of thanksgiving: if not for a male child, at least for a successful pregnancy.

It was a Christian family, but it was not the kind to withdraw from the world. As a matter of fact, Acacius's widow seemed especially unsuited for such a prospect. She had strong ties and alternative relationships that complemented the church-based network, and she made good use of them. As a result, when her husband died she was able to maintain her lifestyle as a mother of three young children and as a woman—not just as the heartbroken widow of Acacius or as a "bride of Christ," as her religion would have wanted. Soon, the little orphan girls had a new father, a stepfather "who . . . would later assist her in both the care of the household and in her first husband's occupation."[11] There is a slightly disparaging tone in the Greek words of the only primary source we have on this topic, Procopius's *Secret History*, and it is not clear whether the union was a common-law arrangement or an actual second marriage.

These changes happened thanks to Asterius, the highest public figure to attend Acacius's Christian funeral. He wielded power in a city that, while not exactly opposed to religion, stood at some distance from it, according to Saint John Chrysostom ("Golden Mouth"), who had been patriarch of Constantinople about a century earlier and had compared it to a Satanic temple.[12] This is harsh criticism, but it is true that around A.D. 500—at the onset of the seventh eon—Constantinople was poised not only between Europe and Asia, but also between antiquity and the Middle Ages. There was a thriving worship of holy relics such as fragments of the Golgotha Cross, the Nails of the Passion, the Crown of Thorns, the Virgin's Cloak, and other signs and mementos of Jesus and Mary, of saints, martyrs, and the elect. At the same time, ancient classical life lingered on.

For example, in spacious aristocratic mansions—of which there were hundreds—servants drew baths for their masters and mistresses and prepared and served meals for their comfort and pleasure; domestics and secretaries delivered polished epistles; and litter bearers carried the rich to their destinations in elegant sedans. The masters drew the curtains across the sedans' windows to block out the sight of beggars (heirs to a very Mediterranean patron-client tradition) who loitered about the famed porticos flanking the city's wide streets and majestic squares.

These lords, the potentates, would be carried to the imperial palace for a court function, or to the thermal baths that were as heavily patronized as the city churches. Or they might visit those "Satanic" theaters for lighthearted shows such as mime sketches, farces, and tableaux vivants, or sophisticated mute pantomimes that retraced the exploits of divinities that had been evicted from their "pagan" temples but were still dear to the public. Or the masters might visit other places, such as the Kynêgion (the amphitheater) or the Hippodrome (the racetrack): the show-business world of Acacius the bear keeper and of the powerful Asterius.

✛ ✛ ✛

The broken columns that now stand as sad mementos in the center of At Meydani Square in Istanbul were intact at the time, and majestic. Like other monumental works, they decorated the central track (*spina* in Latin) of Constantinople's Hippodrome. The chariots raced round and round, and the charioteer's skill was measured by his success in overtaking the other chariots around the curve at the end of the *spina* after racing down straight tracks about twelve hundred feet long. These

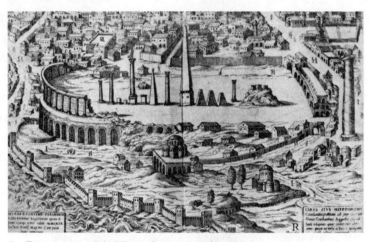

5. Constantinople's Hippodrome in a late-15th-century engraving. From Onofrio Panvino's *De ludis circensibus*, Venice, 1600.

shows were so popular that the public was known to watch as many as twenty-four races in one day.

According to ancient travelers' accounts (confirmed by modern archeological finds), the vast size of the Hippodrome was a spectacle in itself, a wonder of the civilized world. About fifteen hundred feet in length and more than six hundred feet wide, it could seat at least one hundred thousand spectators, or about one-fifth of the entire urban population [fig. 5]. In ancient imperial Rome, it was equaled only by the grand Circus Maximus beneath the Palatine Hill. The Hippodrome was an important hub of city life. It was central to the city's emotional life as well as its economy, traffic, and supply network. It attracted loafers, greedy bettors, and fans who rooted for the two rival teams or

"factions." These factions—the Blues (also called the "Venetians") and
the Greens (known as the "Prasini")—had inherited and simplified a
tradition of the first Rome, which had four different teams (Whites and
Reds as well as Blues and Greens).

The stands of the racetrack were off-limits to clerics, monks, and
ladies, but the games gained ceremonial dignity from the presence of
the emperor. In At Meydani Square we find traces of this custom in the

6. Bas-relief at the base of the column of Theodosius I,
c. 390–95, Hippodrome, Istanbul.

bas-relief [fig. 6] at the base of the column of Theodosius I (r. 379–95)
that depicts the emperor sitting in the famed gallery or loge (the
Kathisma) that connected the Hippodrome, where he saw and was
seen by everyone, to the Sacred Palace, where he was accessible only to
the circle of potentates who also appear around him in the sculpture:
ministers, military men, functionaries, superintendents, and dignitaries.

The Hippodrome spawned myriad interpretations and allegories. To
some it seemed a sort of microcosm, at once an imitation and a revelation of the mysteries of the universe. The arena symbolized the Earth,
the gates from which the chariot races started symbolized the twelve
months of the year or the twelve signs of the zodiac, and so on, in a
sophisticated game of correspondences that posited the Hippodrome

7. Front and back of the marble tablet used for playing
with marbles, c. 500. Staatliche Museen, Berlin.

as the navel of the Christian-Roman world, with the emperor as its or-
acle.

Other, simpler inhabitants of the city spent hours gathered around
elaborate marble tables carved with slightly sloping paths for marbles
bearing the colors of the teams [fig. 7]. The marbles always rolled down
randomly toward the holes at the bottom, so the game required no skill
and was ideal for anyone who enjoyed betting.

The amphitheater of the Kynêgion (comparable to Rome's Coliseum) was used for hunting games that involved the killing of wild
beasts such as stags—guilty only of being bigger than man—or lions,
or the bears that Acacius had kept. Constantinople's multifaceted ceremonial and entertainment industries had needed Acacius's strong
arms, as well as the arms of many tamers, veterinarians, physicians,
nurses, cleaning and security personnel, cooks, grooms, and black-
smiths.

Society's rigid division into ten different classes, designed for military purposes, placed the performers and the show-business laborers in
a single category—the lowest one—at the very margin of social life. But
this category was the highest in terms of fame: charioteers such as
Faustinus, Constantine, Uranus, and Julian were celebrated by poets.
Porphyrius, the greatest of charioteer heroes, had statues dedicated to
him, and epigrams such as the following:

This Porphyrius was born in Africa, but brought up in Constantinople.

Victory crowned him by turns, and he wore the highest tokens of
conquest on his head, from driving sometimes in one colour
and sometimes in another.

For often he changed factions and often horses.

Being sometimes first, sometimes last, and sometimes between
the two,

He overcame both all his partisans and all his adversaries.[13]

The games at the Hippodrome and the Kynêgion, theoretically regulated by consuls who for censturies had exercised only nominal
power, were a triumph of pomp, wealth, and liberality. Dances, tourna-
ments, hunting games (*venationes* in Latin), and generous donations
offered entertainment and sustenance to the whole capital, and many
jobs as well. The animals had to be groomed; the hunters (*venatores*)
who killed them in the arena were trained to be agile and powerful
marksmen; the choreographers planned dances; the charioteers practiced with their horses and chariots; and the city's craftsmen turned out
precious objects in ivory. Designed and carved in limited numbers, the
prized ivory diptychs—a respected art form—celebrated the glories of
the current consul for both the eyes of the power elite of the time and
the pleasure of future generations of museum visitors [fig. 8].

Like a snapshot straight from the past, one diptych shows the consul seated on a throne, dressed in magnificent garments that are in and
of themselves a statement of rank and power. In his right hand he
waves the prize cloth to start the games. Below him, the performers,
intentionally carved in a smaller scale, are shown in the usual postures
of their daily tasks. They are male dancers and ballerinas, actors and
actresses wearing theater masks, charioteers on their chariots, subju-
gated "barbarians," hunters with their ropes, straps, and irons aiming at
wild beasts. Do these figures represent the dream of a life that might
please the consul in power? Or do they represent the nightmare of clerics such as Saint John Chrysostom?

On this particular diptych a Latin inscription—for Latin was still the administrative language of the empire—praised the consul for his career and his moral virtues. As emphasis, images beside the throne and at the top (the area symbolizing goodness and Heaven) portray Christ and the Virgin Mary with angels in flight, together with winged victories and the effigy of the ruling imperial couple. All of this denoted the consul's role of guardian and protector, and it was no less religious or Christian for being set in the Hippodrome.

8. Ivory diptych of Anastasius, Constantinople, 517. Bibliothèque Nationale, Paris.

Those ceremonies, those dreams, and those nightmares required the brute strength of men like Acacius; they required wild beasts; and they required the athleticism and dexterity of dancing masters and set designers. They also required administrative and political skills, the skills practiced by men such as Asterius.

Like Theodora's father, Asterius worked for the Green team but held a much higher position. Technically, he was in charge of organizing shows, hiring personnel, and managing funds. His name, of Greek origin, recalled the stars and the heavenly bodies, and he was a guiding star in the destiny of Acacius's family. The new bear keeper of the Greens—who became the new man in the life of Theodora's mother— would have to report to him, as Acacius had done. Indeed, Asterius might have chosen and promoted the man who was to succeed Acacius both in the bear cages and in the home of the widow and her orphan girls. We don't know if Asterius received any compensation for this, and if he did, what kind. What we do know is that in Constantinople there were clear patron-client rules in the assignment of any job, and the case of Acacius's widow was no exception.

While it's not easy to distinguish between Asterius's personal or personalized attentions and his official duties, we can depend on historical sources regarding the Green and Blue factions, although these do present problems of historical interpretation. For a long time, historians believed that belonging to one faction or the other implied an identification with ethnic, religious, or political groups, but recent research has shown otherwise, and indeed the two factions had important similarities. They were simply associations, partially financed by the empire and by private patrons, that attracted an enthusiastic following at the Hippodrome races, where each team sported a different color. Because of the institutional and ceremonial nature of all the spectacles, the factions had been directly entrusted with management of the shows. This was true not only in the capital but in other cities of the empire as well, where both the Greens and the Blues had built solidarity networks to assist their own; these were the opportunities that Theodora's mother grasped. There were especially active organizations in leading metropolises such as Antioch, Alexandria, and—of course—the capital.

No information has survived about the man who took on the role of stepfather to the three orphan girls. He was less an individual than a function on the stage of history, his role being that of a replica, a "double," as if his only task was to maintain Acacius's position and income. So one could float many theories about his authority and status in a female household dominated by Acacius's widow, especially with regard to the education of daughters who were hers alone.

✛ ✛ ✛

Females were encouraged to stay within the sheltering walls of the women's quarters—the ancient gynoecium. The rare women seen on the street and in public had humble jobs such as innkeeper, washerwoman, or fryer, and were often the subject of unsavory rumors. But because of their age and, most of all, their low social level, little girls such as Acacius's daughters probably played outdoors and in the street. In particular, Comito and Theodora, who were older, were probably allowed to leave their home (most likely an apartment in a multistory building where lower-class families lived, sometimes in promiscuous arrangements) and walk to the Kynêgion, where first their father and then their stepfather would show them the animals and invite them to offer morsels though the bars of the cages.

Although it was too early for Comito and Theodora to learn the proper conjugation of Greek verbs according to the rules of grammar (it was a costly education and, anyway, it would have been premature before the age of about ten), they could learn some forms of nonverbal communication from the man who knew the art of taming ferocious and frightening beasts before large crowds. The children could discover what kind of voice was best to soothe animals; not just bears but also horses, dogs, and colorful parrots imported from the East. Possibly, the words were short, one- or two-syllable interjections, sometimes with onomatopoeic sounds, sometimes articulated clearly, sometimes repeated like a lullaby. We know Greek interjections such as *my*, *ppy*, *gry*: childish phonetics that might become a secret language for animals. Undoubtedly, their visits to the Kynêgion could be useful for Comito's and Theodora's lives in the theater, for there they probably learned about using a peremptory voice, a proper posture, a controlling gesture.

Historical sources agree that once she became empress, Theodora preferred to wield power in secret, remote, inaccessible places, a preference born perhaps in the caves of the Kynêgion, where she would visit the cages containing the bears sent to Constantinople from Italy, Thrace, or Illyria.

✛ ✛ ✛

Some sources and popular folklore maintain that Theodora and her family were not originally from Constantinople but from Paphlagonia, at the farthest southeastern corner of the Black Sea or Pontos Euxeinos, or from the island of Cyprus, or even from the vast Syrian-Mesopotamian East, which Constantinople's "Romans" were trying to wrest from Persia, their historical enemy. Close reading of these sources leads nowhere, so we must continue to consider that Theodora's ancestral land, her native habitat, her ideal site, was the capital, in the spectacular shows and ceremonies of the Hippodrome and the Kynêgion, where profane spectacle mixed with religious ritual, the cult of personality with the flattery of the masses, violence with games, imperial majesty with the homage of subjects.

It was a world indisputably linked to her family. This is the context in which her prodigious ascent was to take place.

"He Removed These Persons from That Office. . . . They Conferred This Position . . . upon Them"

Constantinople, c. 504

C LASSICAL CULTURE idealized rural life but it was nevertheless thoroughly urban. And even in the fifth and sixth centuries the prestige of cities lived on, in the ancient tradition, in the eastern Mediterranean. Alexandria in particular—the city of Alexander the Great and of the Ptolemies, the city of Cleopatra, Marc Antony, and Caesar, of the celebrated library and lighthouse—boasted almost a thousand years of history and a population as large as, if not larger than, Constantinople's. Yet the capital, the center of a multiethnic, highly structured empire, was still the ultimate city. Constantinople was like Babylon or Rome, Baghdad or Beijing, like Paris, London, or New York now. Constantinople was the last great city of the late ancient world, its quintessence. Its emperors, in their celebrated munificence, regularly distributed cash and food to thousands of households in the city.

People survived on this tangible largesse while waiting for the wonders of future eons; it made a difference, particularly in the countryside. Rural life was celebrated by poets but it was utterly dependent on the crop cycle, subject to famines and epidemics, and at the mercy of invasions such as that of a bellicose "barbarian" tribe that, in the late fourth century A.D., had almost reached the capital, stopping only four days' march away. In the ensuing battle the Roman emperor had been killed, despite his auspicious name of Valens ("valiant"). Everyone was shocked to see that the borders were not totally safe, though an army of over 200,000 soldiers defended them.

Furthermore, in this empire of most Christian rulers, taxes were wrung from the countryside as the rulers sought new revenues without consideration for differences in language and custom. Only Egypt was partly exempt, privileged because of its ancient history and its position as the breadbasket of the capital and of the whole empire. The harsh central bureaucracy and its army of tax collectors were increasingly in charge of collection in outlying regions, thus weakening the ancient (and not always efficient) town councils.[1] Part of the revenue, which increasingly consisted of payments in cash rather than in kind, flowed into the empire's treasury, and the rest went into the Crown's private coffers, where it was earmarked for specific uses.

The revenue collected in the countryside, more than the taxes on urban commerce, allowed the court to rival the splendor of the court of Persia, the other great "Eye of the Ecumene"[2] or pinnacle of the civilized world; it also allowed the empire to maintain a military force on three continents, from Carthage and Cyrene in North Africa to Asian Mesopotamia and the European water frontiers of the Danube River and the Adriatic Sea. And it perpetuated the bureaucratic and managerial class, which inherited—at least formally—the ancient Roman magistracies with all their stipends and privileges.

This second Rome, Constantinople, avoided the fate of the ancient, Italian Rome, which was humiliated by the sack of the Visigoths in A.D. 410. This terrible blow led Saint Augustine, "Roman citizen" and bishop of Hippo, to relinquish all hope in the earthly city, placing his trust solely in the City of God. But in the eastern Mediterranean, one could still have faith in the emperor's city, protected as it was by the thaumaturgic body of Constantine (the city's founder), by the venerated robe of the Mother of God, and by other sacred Christian relics; by walls, ramparts, and armies; and by cunning diplomacy that skillfully exacted peace from the "barbarians," even at the cost of paying for it in gold.

So chronicles of the time are full of stories of young men and even boys who left the fields and villages and set out with only a cloak on their shoulders and a few crackers in their sack. They would march for weeks down the ancient roads of the empire, drinking from wells, sleeping in caves or under the open sky, willing to face all kinds of danger on their way to the city. Nor were they the only itinerants in those remote rural landscapes. Other men scoured the land instead of heading for the city, but they were neither imperial tax inspectors nor land-register surveyors: these men sought only the poorest of young girls. To the girls and their barefoot families dressed in sackcloth, they offered garments and footwear, though not out of charity. They were interested in taking the girls to the city on the basis of vague contracts in which nothing was clearly defined except the services that the girls would be required to perform.

Infants and children needing more food than a family could expect to supply were often cast off in the hope that they might be found and delivered to a church or a convent; or that they might die quickly in the peace of the Lord. This was the fate of girl babies especially, just as it is today in some parts of Asia.

Immigrants descended upon the city from the West, from Thrace and Illyria in particular. They spoke their native dialects but little standard Latin and no Greek. Greek was the language not only of Theodora's family, but of the whole loquacious capital (an early father of the Church had written that "the populace argued furiously about impenetrable issues, and even the baker, when you asked him for the price of bread, replied that in the Trinity the Father is greater than the Son").[3]

Other immigrants came from the Asiatic East, which had been better protected from the fourth- and fifth-century "barbarian" migrations, and was more strongly woven into the ancient web of cities and commercial networks of the classical and Hellenistic tradition. They hailed from Anatolia, Cappadocia, Armenia, and Paphlagonia, but also from Mesopotamia, Syria, and Palestine. In addition to their native dialects they knew some rudimentary Greek—which they had heard in the more prestigious of the ancient cities, the *poleis*, but they also knew that the official establishment tongue was still Latin, and they were intimidated by it.

All these strands made up the urban mass of Constantinople. These newcomers didn't come for the ancient artistic wonders that the emperors had selectively pilfered to beautify the city's squares—the ancient Egyptian obelisks, or Leysippus's celebrated team of four bronze horses now crowning Saint Mark's basilica in Venice (the seafaring capital that owes so much to Constantinople). Nor were they interested in the city's precious manuscripts, their pages saturated with purple dye and embellished with decorative initials, miniatures of allegorical figures, and representations of exquisite classical and Christian virtues.

What they sought was a promise of future salvation granted by the Christian relics that abounded in the city. And, first and foremost, they sought work, because the young imperial capital needed hard manual labor: men to unload the goods in the wholesale markets that supplied the butchers and greengrocers and fishmongers, and workers for the iron smithies and the silversmith shops located in the Bosphorus and Golden Horn districts. It needed smelters for the imperial mint that manufactured the most famous of all coins, the pure gold imperial solidus. (The root of this term has survived in many European languages, from the Italian *soldo* to the French *sou*, the Castilian *sueldo*, and even the Welsh *swllt*.) Laborers and bricklayers were needed for the construction of public works, for building the roads that were the pride of the city and that celebrated imperial power, and the walls, basilicas, and churches. There were always openings among the policemen, firemen, nurses, and soldiers. Bodyguards were needed for the emperor,[4] who was both the leader of the Christian "new Israel"[5] and the "Augustus" ceremoniously applauded in the Hippodrome by "senate, army, and people"—the interpreter of the ancient Roman imperial role. His subjects loved him most when he handed out the wheat that came from Egypt, the "happy cargo" of the ships that sailed from Alexandria.

Bread and circuses were provided, but not kindergartens or public schools. Education was a private, domestic matter, especially when it came to girls. Wealthy and respectable families took good care of their little girls, who were considered "the apple of their eyes,"[6] and kept them at home, away from indiscreet eyes. The girls spent their days spinning thread and taking alphabet and grammar lessons in which Attic tragedies and Homeric epics were increasingly replaced with edifying passages from the holy scriptures (the *Psalms* in particular), which were often learned by heart.

The little girl left the family residence (the Latin *domus*) only briefly, always chaperoned by female servants. She went out only for hygienic purposes: to clean her body at the public baths or, even better, to edify her soul at places of worship or by visiting monks of exemplary holiness. No form of public entertainment was allowed. Frequenting the theater was unbecoming, let alone going to the Hippodrome. Even the most influential of adult matrons, curious about a successful show, had to arrange for a private performance. Her majordomo, a eunuch, would arrange for the programs and for the compensation of actors, dancers, and musicians.

This segregation of women was codified, reinforced, even exalted in late ancient and in later Byzantine texts. It did, however, allow for exceptions, especially at the bottom rung of the social ladder. Theodora and her sisters probably did not learn the basics of arithmetic or Greek reading and writing from private tutors. More likely, they attended group classes in one of the city's charitable institutions.

According to the literary account of a dramatic event that took place during Theodora's imperial tenure, her speech as an adult was full of erudite allusions; but that ancient source—with its rhetorical implications—probably over-refined Theodora's actual words. Theodora was not, nor could she have been, a refined exponent of late ancient cultural literacy, though she knew how to use words well. And it's likely that her skill was due to her mother's ambition.

In any case, the childhood years of Theodora and her sisters must have been spent mostly outdoors playing in the city's streets, squares, and orchards. We can easily imagine Comito, Theodora, and Anastasia absorbed in tag and other running games including the Four Doors game: then as now, it consisted of the children running from one door to another, with a penalty for the last child to reach the goal. Girls, and probably boys too, played the Devil in Chains game, where one player

9. Marble fragment
   showing children
   playing the Devil in
   Chains game, c. 500.
   Staatliche Museen, Berlin.

was tied down for each turn, as we can plainly see in a marble fragment conserved at the Berlin Museums [fig. 9]. Or they played the
Kingdoms Game,[7] in which the children drew lots for a deep red strip
of fabric symbolizing the purple robe permitted only to the emperor.
The child with the strip was the emperor, and his playmates would
gather around him as ministers, servants, and maids. The emperor
would threaten war, issue commands, demand homage. Maybe
Theodora wished the game would never end; maybe she preferred to
keep the red badge of power tucked inside her sleeve.

(During those same years, a man named Flavius Petrus Sabbatius—
later known as Justinian—had left his native Roman province of
Illyricum in the Balkans and moved to Constantinople at the invitation
of his uncle, Justin, a military man. He was about twenty at the time,
and he wasn't playing any street games: he needed to continue studying politics and administration. He was to become the most knowl-
edgeable expert on the power machine in the entire empire, and
someday he would share his imperial power with Theodora.)

The three sisters probably challenged one another in singing contests, as song was the primary pastime of ancient man, a constant in all premodern societies. They might have learned the melodies of the various trade guilds (necessary channels for the barter economy of the reigning city): the shoemakers' songs, or the songs of incense vendors, butchers, and the like. Separately or as a trio, perhaps, they went into shops to sing these songs, or to ask to learn others. Sometimes they might have gotten material items in exchange, such as pieces of string and fabric with which to make a doll's dress, or oil to keep their lamp lit at night as they shared the stories and legends that were then, as they are now, gymnasiums of the mind and the psyche, building blocks of what we call "identity."

Paul, that most Christian and highly educated of apostles, when asked who he was had replied simply that he was a "Roman citizen."[8] For Theodora and her sisters the streets and squares of the city—with their obelisks, their columns, and their statues—most likely inspired a complex sense of pride, for they were Constantinopolitans and Romans and Christians. The girls repeatedly heard about the exploits of the emperor Constantine, who had defeated the tyrant Maxentius in the name of the cross, or the tale of Saint Helena, Constantine's mother, who had found the true Golgotha Cross. These tales celebrated an empire that had existed continuously since the famous twins were suckled by the she-wolf; a lasting empire, changed but uninterrupted; an empire that would surely last another eon, because it so pleased God.

To the three sisters, Christianity must have seemed a happy mystery, for Jesus had promised that the last would be the first, as it had been in ancient Israel when David had defeated Goliath and Judith had beheaded Holofernes. They must have loved to hear the story of the three Jewish boys thrown into the raging furnace of Babylon: the fire had not touched the boys because they were singing lovely songs in praise of God. It was a good reason to keep on singing.

While the girls were busy with the crucial formation of their identities, their fruitful activity did not protect them from the uncertainties of fate. The calm period for Acacius's widow and daughters turned out to be only a temporary lull. Asterius, the Greens' chief organizer, suddenly overturned their lives: according to the *Secret History* he "removed these persons from that office."[9] It's interesting to note that Acacius's widow shared the official position: Asterius removed "these persons." Asterius himself must have enjoyed great latitude if he had such power.

The widow and her partner had done their job well and were beyond reproach. And yet Asterius "removed them from that office," perhaps for reasons that had nothing to do with [them], just as people are dismissed these days "because of corporate restructuring." Asterius received an outside offer he could not refuse: someone else's cash.[10] We mustn't simply deride this as corruption; the fact is that society in late antiquity was structured so that mobility and even overnight wealth resulted from bonds that were rarely formal or merit-based, but were dictated largely by family relationships, geography, or religion—in short, by a patronage system that was arbitrary and insecure.

Clearly, someone claimed to have better patrons and a greater right to the job of bear keeper for the Green team at the Kynêgion. He could certainly offer more, not only to Asterius, the administrator and operations manager, but also—most important—to the faction's treasury. It was natural, even advisable, for Asterius to yield, for this meant strengthening his position in a power clique, or maybe allowing one of the many cliques to solidify their strength in the Kynêgion and therefore in Constantinople's entertainment industry, which was both ceremonial and institutional. It was an arbitrary decision, no doubt, but codified nonetheless.

One can only speculate whether this change of personnel came on orders from the highest imperial circles, or because of seditious activity taking place on the radical fringes of the factions, where the city's tensions—fueled especially by immigration and growing demographic pressure—found a violent outlet. Perhaps "the militant group of the Greens"[11] influenced Asterius, claiming the position, and paying for it, on behalf of one of the group's members or protégés. If indeed heavy political pressures were at work, Acacius's widow had little or no chance of redressing the wrong: she could pay, she could pray, or she could find other ways.

✛ ✛ ✛

Theodora's mother was not a woman who gave up easily; she was even less likely to suffer in silence when she was wronged. And so she claimed what she believed was her due, and she did so in an unexpected way, with a spectacular act of daring. Maybe the inspiration came to her as she saw her three girls singing or acting out a scene they had glimpsed in a square or on the street. Or perhaps it was a dream that drove her to act, for at the beginning of the seventh eon, Christian Constantinople, the "Beacon of the Ecumene," was still very close to the archaic Greece of Pythias and of the old myths.[12] Whatever the reason behind her decision—whether it came to her in a dream or in the long hours of a sleepless night—she did not hesitate; she put her plan together and she acted.

She summoned her daughters and told them that the time had come to stop pretending and to start doing. And so they studied rituals, funerals, and processions, and they rehearsed gestures feverishly, to learn how to suffuse their performance with the entire grammar of grief, to learn every nuance of affliction. They practiced in secret, without letting anyone know, linked by their female complicity. The mother may have gone out late in the evening, a torch in her hand, to "make the final arrangements." She would speak with the theater ushers and guards, and the following morning the girls would question her.

Finally, the fateful day arrived. It was a holiday, with flowers strewn everywhere, partly in homage to the city's secret name, "The Flourishing" (*anthousa* in Greek, *flora* in Latin). The girls too were adorned with flowers: in their hair were garlands similar to those worn by rulers and saints, and in their hands were flowers, held close to the breast against a white dress.

According to legend, one day the emperor Constantine the Great had gone into the arena and won a fight against a bear and a lion. Similarly, the girls were going into the arena to triumph over poverty and the abuse of power. They passed through the gates of the Kynêgion and walked along the vaulted corridors, dimly lit by torches, beneath the stands of the amphitheater. As they proceeded, the light at the far end of the corridor grew, and the roar of the audience, excited by a *venatio*,

10. Mosaic of a procession of Holy Virgins, c. 560, church of Sant'Apollinare Nuovo, Ravenna.

grew louder and more distinct. The girls stopped and rehearsed their gestures. Then the roar subsided and finally stopped.

The family started walking again, and they moved closer to the light. The mother exchanged a signal with a man draped in a green cloak, who motioned them forward and lifted his right hand to pull open a curtain. Acacius's widow and the little girls set foot in the Kynê-gion arena, where deer, bears, and lions had just been slaughtered. Theodora didn't know it, but she was stepping onto the very first of many public stages.

The times of the pagan emperors were long past: no wild beast would pounce on the women and tear them to pieces (as beasts once massacred the martyr Perpetua and her maid Felicita). In the empire's capital, the mother and daughters could walk into the arena safely, toward the section reserved for the Greens, their longtime patrons and interlocutors. With garlands in their hair and flowers in their arms, dressed in white, they might have recalled a sacred procession, like the one we can still admire in the mosaics of the church of Sant'Apollinare Nuovo in Ravenna [fig. 10] showing the holy virgins of Jewish and Christian history—the history of the elect—rejoicing in the reward "prepared for them by the Father"[13] in Heaven.

Not a reward but rather a right was what Theodora and her sisters sought that day. They stopped in front of the Greens. They threw flowers and garlands toward the seats, and the audience fell silent. The rules of communication of the time demanded that private issues be settled publicly, that appeals be turned into theater, that supplications be turned into verse: the vast audience sensed that it was going to witness the ceremonial expression of some sort of passionate claim. Now the voice of the supplicants' spokesman was heard in the arena, intoning a plea along these lines:

> Long life to you,
> Most Christian and glorious Greens!
> Life and victory to you!
> O glorious Greens
> We are oppressed
> And we ask for relief.
> Here we are, daughters of Acacius
> Who in this Kynêgion
> Was a fine keeper of wild beasts
> And whom we have lost too soon!

Then the supplicants knelt in a gesture of submission. The audience turned to look at Asterius, who stood up and extended his right arm in the usual gesture of the ancient orators rising to speak in the Forum: signaling respect for authority and requesting silence. And the audience did quiet down. Asterius turned slowly, running his eyes over the audience; then he looked down at the arena without uttering a word. His look sufficed: his wide eyes and his raised eyebrows signified scorn for supplicants engaging in such a shameless show of female insolence and childish delirium, so far beneath his dignity and everyone else's. (In retrospect, his judgment seems shortsighted.)

The supplicants on their knees, mute, Asterius standing and mute: their opposition created a theatrical scene in the arena of the Kynêgion. There was no explicit violence, but this did not make Asterius's behavior any less hostile. By refusing to speak, he indicated that the plea did not deserve a reply. However imprudent the little girls' gesture might have appeared, he was being deeply arrogant.[14] His behavior was the extreme opposite of that gentle kindness recommended to the powerful by the dialectics and politics of ancient culture. The Blue faction, opponents of the Greens, watched the contrast between the kneeling supplicants and the powerful, standing man as he punished them for their daring supplication by his similarly daring silence. When it became clear that Asterius was not going to reply—when he exhibited behavior unworthy of a potentate, behavior typical of an abusive tyrant—the Blues might have spoken thus:

> O evil, loathsome Greens,
> Oppressors of little girls!
> O Greens, who cannot even speak
> May you lose forever the power of speech!

If the inspiration had come to Acacius's widow in a dream, she now saw that the dream had been prescient. She instructed her daughters to get up, she arranged their garments and garlands, and they quickly walked to the other side of the arena, where they knelt. The organizer of the Blues, Asterius's counterpart (there's no trace of his name), rose to his feet. Since his faction happened to need a bear keeper, he could afford to make a humane, generous, charitable gesture, just as the emperor alone usually did. In this ceremonial role-playing, before opponents who scorned defenseless little girls, he saw that for one day he could be king of the Kynêgion. So he acted quickly.

Like Asterius, he extended his right arm, requesting silence. Unlike Asterius, he spoke. He noted that there were three supplicants, three like the trinity worshipped by the orthodox Blues; and that the white of their garments signified a welcome purity of heart. Therefore, the most glorious Blues were acceding to their request. The mother signaled the little girls, who stood up, and the Blues erupted in cheers and applause.

And so the companion of Acacius's widow was given a position, although it was not necessarily *his* position. ("They conferred this position . . . upon them," wrote Procopius.[15]) "Knock and the door will be opened to you," the Gospels exhort.[16] But the door that opens is not necessarily the one you knocked on.

The plea in the Kynêgion is one of the major events in Theodora's childhood, and it is recalled often by her modern biographers. Her relationship with the Blues before and after her ascent to power, and her bitter hostility to the Greens as empress, have been read as a life-long revenge for the humiliation she and her sisters suffered in the Kynêgion. It is undoubtedly an important episode in her life, and it sheds light on some traits of Theodora's personality that go beyond her future choice of sides.

As at the time of her father's funeral, Theodora had been thrust onto a public stage in a highly ritualized, theatrical context. But this new experience was not one of loneliness or loss. Her kneeling and pleading before the Greens was her first experience of confrontation between the weak and the strong, between the last against the first, following in the example of the Biblical David and Judith. It was also the struggle of the few against the masses and of woman—women—against a man, against men. Here the mother was teaching the girl and her sisters the virtue of resistance, of self-defense, of using all possible tools in the most adverse situations.

Theodora's experience continued and deepened with her sudden shift of allegiance to the Blues, and it is easy to infer that it was precisely here that Theodora learned from her mother how to turn an impossible situation to her advantage, in public. Perhaps the arena of the Kynêgion in late-ancient Constantinople had witnessed the revival of what the scholars of another form of public spectacle—the ancient Attic tragedies of Aeschylus and Sophocles—call reversal,[17] such as when, for example, Oedipus, once the happiest of men, is suddenly transformed into the unhappiest. But also when the raging Furies become the pious Eumenides.

The scene in the Kynêgion did not involve the expert, diplomatic, Byzantine art of mediation. It was also far from "all or nothing" radicalism. What it did display is an ancient, strong, clear familiarity with conflict, with the experience of an explosive conclusion that redefines and reorganizes everything. It was a lesson that Theodora was never to forget; nor would she forget how deeply humiliating a public display of silence could be, the silence used by Asterius to show that he despised her and her family.

As in all great stories, the story of Theodora begins with a loss, her father's death. As on the day of Acacius's funeral, the Kynêgion supplication brought her face-to-face with an experience of life as ceremony. Except that now life appeared to her—to the "metal of her heart," as Proust termed it in another context[18]—as conflict, clash, struggle. A hand-to-hand combat to be fought in public, without delay or mediation.

Procopius was not an eyewitness to this event, and he wrote about it in the *Secret History* some fifty years after it happened, but his account is rich in concrete details. In this scene, we catch a glimpse of Theodora for the first time. She is beginning to reveal herself. She is not seated on a triumphant throne amid gold and purple. Nor is she in the rarified environment of the Imperial Palace, as in the San Vitale mosaics in Ravenna. She is not surrounded by elements that bespeak her erudition, such as the great Lady Juliana Anicia (c. 461/3–527/9), who was depicted about the same time as the Kynêgion plea [fig. 11] seated amid triumphant virtues on the opening page of the marvelous Dioscorides manuscript that she commissioned at the turn of the sixth century A.D. Procopius's first presentation of Theodora in this light—kneeling, debased, dependent on others—is not the work of an objective chronicler (especially because he did not witness the scene): his presentation of her was a literary choice dictated by his rhetoric of blame. Similarly, other works (including texts by Procopius) were encomiums, with different rhetorical dictates.

In Procopius's narrative plot, which was meant to reproach

Theodora for "her nurture and education," her first appearance is in a public setting, and a promiscuous, indiscriminate one at that, with an undifferentiated mass audience in the background. More to the point, in that undifferentiated mass Theodora appears as part of a smaller subset, her family, where she counts as a number, not as a voice or an individual. According to the *Secret History*, the first scene of Theodora's story is one in which she kneels in supplication in an arena. But the last scene in the *Secret History* describes all the dignitaries, senators included, kneeling before her in homage, ready to declare themselves her "slaves." They would have been punished if they referred to her as less than "Mistress."[19] Thus, the most extraordinary and unexpected of reversals had occurred.

11. Portrait of Juliana Anicia, miniature on the introductory page of the Dioscorides manuscript, c. 512. Ms.Vindob. Med. Graec. 1, Oesterreichische Nationalbibliothek, Vienna.

It is fair to say that Theodora won in the arena of history. But that day, in the Kynêgion arena, it was her mother especially who deserved the victor's laurels. Her behavior matched the grand gestures of the great angry women of classical mythology, from Medea to Dido. Unlike them, however, she had not been born a queen. And unlike her daughter Theodora and her granddaughter Sophia, she did not become the "Augusta" and mistress of the Christian Roman Empire. She did, however, inspire those two descendants.

Compared to the historical data available for the family of Flavius Petrus Sabbatius—Emperor Justinian—there are no traces that might allow us to reconstruct the life of Theodora's mother. But if the emperor succeeded in keeping his power in impossible circumstances, and in strongly influencing the history of three continents at the watershed between two great historical epochs, it was partly because Theodora never forgot her mother's response to a dire situation and her ability to suddenly reverse it in public. The courage, the dignity, the astuteness of Acacius's widow have been sufficiently illustrated. It is only a historical irony that she is anonymous rather than famous.

THREE

"As Each One Seemed to Her to Be Ripe for This Calling"

Constantinople, c. 510–512

ROUND THE YEAR 500 of the Christian era, a transformation had already occurred in ancient culture—that exquisite intimacy with the loftiest thoughts and written words, from epic poetry to tragedy, from the philosopher's prose to the orator's speeches. Flowery speeches were still being produced, of course, but one tradition was long lost: the tradition of lively eloquence from the citizens during debates, in the forums and in the town councils, about the betterment of public life.[1]

The right of earthly citizenship that sanctioned status and property, and for which so much blood had been shed throughout the Ecumene, had been replaced by the promise of an otherworldly citizenship, perhaps in the City of God, as evoked in the title of Saint Augustine's masterpiece, written in 413–26 when he was bishop of Hippo in North Africa, a region of the western Roman Empire reeling from the barbarian invasions. In the eastern Mediterranean of Byzantium, however, the structure of the Roman Empire was still vigorous. But the very basis of its strength—its copious bureaucratic and administrative apparatus— had led to a progressive emptying of public places for meeting and debating: both the Forum, where individual claims and wrongs were settled, and the town councils that for centuries had been in charge of local government, including tax collection.

No longer the measure of a citizen's duty, eloquence was now a marker of social prestige. And so it served only to educate and burnish the self-importance of the upper echelons of the public bureaucracy;

beyond that it served as a field for technicians (for professional teachers in particular), or it dissolved into a purely private pleasure. As a matter of fact, it was in those years that reading, after centuries of being a public act performed out loud, became an individual, silent act. Even the word *philosopher* had lost its ancient meaning. It no longer referred to the men who debated and theorized in the public gardens or porticoes.[1] Now it referred to monks (literally, the "isolated ones") who lived outside the ancient city walls in solitary, almost wild dialogue with the mystery of the cosmos—perched atop columns, or on tree branches, surviving on plants, or even walled up in cells or in caves.

Culture had undergone a particularly severe transformation in Constantinople, the beacon of the Ecumene, a miracle in time and space, suspended as it was between antiquity and the Middle Ages and between the European continent and Asia. The last nostalgic followers of Hellenic learning took issue with the Christian monks, accusing them of neglecting philosophical thought with the "flower of their minds"[2]; they saw these Christians as regressing into violent brutes. These Hellenists had their own lay martyr in Hypatia, a rare example of a woman philosopher, who had been stoned and burned at the stake in Alexandria in 415 by Christian fanatics who were protected by highly placed clerics.

But the calmest and most clear-eyed among the followers of Christ despised all forms of degeneracy and revered exemplary figures such as Basil (c. 330–379), bishop of Caesarea in Cappadocia, now the Turkish city of Kayseri. He had encouraged his flock to collect and store every passage from pagan antiquity that benefited the soul, every precept of virtue, every example of expressive precision.

Meanwhile, several authors belonging to the final chapters of the history of Greek literature, but whose education ensured them illustrious careers in the ranks of the Christian Roman Empire, rediscovered the magic spell of ancient, pre-Christian mythological creatures in actresses, dancers, and lyre and flute players—women such as Rhodoclea, Helladia, and Libania—who performed in the baths and theaters and in the celebrations that enlivened everyday life in the Sovereign City. These were new muses who deserved to join the original nine muses;

they were sweet new companions to the Three Graces[3]—an earthly trinity easier to define than the heavenly one.

Theodora was destined for a different career, with different events and transformations, in a different empire, and by a different path. Antiquity—the mythical, miraculous antiquity—would be revealed to her not in papyrus rolls or parchment volumes but through tales, images, and visions. She was attentive and curious enough to grasp all of this. She developed her own, unique education, more visual than verbal, through what she saw even before what she heard, on the stages of the Hippodrome, the Kynêgion, and the theaters: her open, outdoor libraries. It was an unusual education because it happened in spaces that were meant for mass entertainment of plebians, not for the sensitivity of scholars or the power elite. It was atypical also because it was a woman's education, and thus it was free of any presumption that it had to serve a public function.

Under the protection of the Blue team, Theodora most probably had access to the Hippodrome, both during the performances and when the great urban entertainment machine was readying itself to receive its audience. Walking along the barrier of the *spina* that separated the two straight tracks of the arena, Theodora must have admired the ancient statues rising up toward the sky and reflected on their stories [fig. 5], maybe stopping before the Serpentine Column meant to support Apollo's tripod, which the Greeks had dedicated to Apollo when they defeated the Persians at Platea in 471 B.C. While the little girl may not have absorbed the historical details, she must have admired the bronze highlights of the tall column shining under the sun, its coiled, intertwined snakes ending in three heads, three sets of fangs open in a ferocious, challenging grimace [fig. 12]. In it she may have detected a message for herself and her sisters, who were also three heads but one single being: anyone

12. Bronze serpent's head from the Serpentine Column, 5th century B.C. (?), Archeological Museum, Istanbul.

who dared attack or offend one of them would have faced their poison.

A bronze statue in the Hippodrome represented Scylla, the Homeric twelve-footed monster with six faces and six mouths, each with three rows of teeth. Other children must have been terrorized by it, but not Theodora, familiar with animals since the time of her father, Acacius. Nor must she have felt any particular tenderness for Ulysses' comrades "of the strong, vigorous arms"[4] who were seized by the monster when they dared disobey their leader, Ulysses. The story of the hero who survived by his cunning through so many trials, who had defeated the Cyclops and the Suitors, probably revealed to her the potential of a world rich in transformations, metamorphoses, even miracles.

Cities, too, were undergoing miraculous transformations: Rome, the first and greatest, had lost its primacy after the foundation of Constantine's city and was now relegated to a minor, secondary role. The name of the king of Italy and of Rome, Theodoric, was often mentioned in the capital-on-the-Bosphorus. Theodora might have asked if his name was the Latin version of her own name, if he also was a "gift from God." It might have been explained to her that such was not the case, for Theodoric was a barbarian prince who could coin money carrying his profile in Italy only for as long as the great "Augustus," the emperor of the Romans with his seat in Constantinople, allowed it. One day, Italy and the first Rome would be brought back into the fold of the empire. It was widely believed that this also would come to pass in the seventh eon. No one could imagine that it would happen under Theodora.

Just like Ulysses, who pretended to be a beggar in order to regain his kingdom of Ithaca, or like a snake that sheds its skin, Theodora was changing: she was different now, she was becoming what she had not been before. No longer a child, she was not yet a woman. Even those who disparaged her acknowledged that she was "fair to look upon."[5] It was both her personal vocation and her family's fate that she was not to live life in the shadow, that she would see and be seen and admired.

Once more, the mother arranged events. She was benefiting from the new acquaintances she had made among the enthusiasts of the Blue team. If the three young girls showed some talent for acting, music, and dance, it was certainly because the mother had guided them firmly in that direction. Possibly, therefore, Theodora's mother was the first of many women with a direct experience of the theater who would meaningfully shape her destiny.

When Acacius's orphan girls reached adolescence, it was their mother who directed them to the stage, using their beauty and possibly also the tradition of inherited careers that was typical of ancient guilds. The girls' debuts must have taken place at different times, "as each one seemed to her to be ripe for this calling."[6] And of course only the mother knew best how to determine if each girl was mature enough for the task. Certain stages in a woman's growth and development had to be respected; in a society where custom required that a woman marry and become a mother around the age of fifteen or sixteen, a girl's introduction to the stage had to occur at about the same time.

The eldest daughter, Comito, was the first of the sisters to appear on the stage. She became quite successful in a short time. It was around the year 512, and Theodora was about twelve years old, not yet "mature" enough to embark on a life in the theater with all that it implied. And yet she already frequented the theater. As a matter of fact, she was part of Comito's crew, "clothed in a little sleeved frock suitable to a slave boy. . . . [Theodora] would follow her about, performing various services and in particular always carrying on her shoulders the stool on which her sister was accustomed to sit."[7]

Here we have a portrait of Comito, a rising star on the city's stages, a very young, beautiful actress (or courtesan, according to the terminology of the *Secret History*), accompanied by her younger sister, the not-quite-mature Theodora, who was just as beautiful, dressed and perhaps coiffed as a boy. It's a scene that recalls seventeenth-century genre paintings, both French and Italian, depicting the multicolored world of the commedia dell'arte. But it also recalls how theater was destiny for Theodora, much more than simply a family-imposed duty. It was a natural propensity, an individual drive that went hand in hand with her determination to be second to no one. Not even to her older sister.

On the other hand, theater—where Theodora and her family ended up—met with solid disapproval from official society, because of Christian moral principles, or because of ancient standards inherited from a class aristocracy, or from a melding of these two elements into a new morality.

Religious fundamentalism distrusted any collective activity that was somehow connected with the ancient traditions of city life, and thus it looked askance at the baths and the Hippodrome, but mostly at the theater, where it detected the seeds of vice and temptation. Any generous use of the body, or any generous act toward the body, seemed to conflict with the kind of love that is given to God and received from Him. The ancient morality founded on pagan beliefs, as we already noted, placed entertainers on the lowest rung of social life, regarding them as necessary only insofar as they represented the expression of an intrinsic pathos of collective life, its release valve. Apart from that function, actors were indefensible individuals, marked with "infamy." The grave and serious Roman Empire did not allow actors to enlist in the military, deeming them unworthy to serve the state. Given this context, it is not surprising that actresses were identified with prostitutes.

There were exceptions, of course. It was merely a private issue when more or less austere champions of Roman virtue or power took a fancy to an actor or an actress. But when the entertainment sector was defended and even celebrated in writing, the issue took on a different meaning. This was precisely the situation in late antiquity.

Flavius Magnus Aurelius Cassiodorus (485–580), author, statesman, and nearly centenarian monk of the noblest rank who had a resplendent career, wrote a beautiful text in Latin with an amazed and admiring description of the seductions of pantomime, praising it precisely because the performance is allusive: "it is spoken without speaking, and said without saying, and the fingers are the tongue."[8] And in Greek, Coricius of Gaza, a rhetorician also active in the sixth century, offered the theater much more than praise, seeing it as an opportunity for social redemption. For example, he did not accept the belief that the mimes were tainted with the same "vices" that they performed on stage: "The more common the suspicion that they lead a dissolute life, the more I feel duty-bound to come to their defense."[9]

In everyday life, young intellectuals who flocked to Constantinople from the provinces of the empire, armed with ambition and supported financially by their parents, often neglected their studies in law or philosophy in favor of the chariot races, fights, and pantomime of the Hippodrome and the variety shows of the theaters. Some would later write poetry and thus regale future readers with what they had experienced as a simple distraction from the regular routine of daily life.

In the *Greek Anthology* of epigrams (also known as the *Palatine Anthology* because of the manuscript copy discovered in the Palatine Library of Heidelberg) we find sixth-century Constantinopolitan poets praising the physical beauty of their actresses, courtesans, and other women with choice terms and noble verses, claiming that no words could describe their beauty and no music could reproduce the spell of their voices. The svelte dancers they sang about had "feet as swift as wind"; singing and playing sweetly, they touched the kithara "with skilled fingers."[10] Some images are indelible, such as the face of a beloved Lais, flooded with tears as she fears that her lover has broken the oath of love;[11] or a poet lingering affectionately over a wrinkle on the face of his beloved, because

> Your autumn excels another's spring,
> And your winter is warmer than another's summer.[12]

These texts restore a world of delights, of sensuality, of caring, that was still widespread. It was inseparable from the world of the stage and theater and was nourished by it, even as it was scorned by the dour Procopius and earlier by Saint John Chrysostom, patriarch of Constantinople from 398 to 403 and a father of the Eastern Church, who in a most unchristian spirit censured theater and racetrack performances, even blaming the actors for their humble origins: their "fathers are ropemakers, fishmongers, and slaves."[13] An unexpected criticism indeed from someone who valued and preached a Christian approach to life. It was a strong sign of the anti-theater mind-set of late antiquity when disparate, if not incompatible, attitudes combined to form an elite culture that was grounded in an ancient ideal of literary learning reduced, for the most part, to mere technique.

In the face of all this, the actress who became empress was not so much a paradox as a scandal in the perfect, evangelical sense of "a stone one stumbles over."

Procopius, the leading historian of the time, could not attend the first performances of Comito and Theodora, her boyish "little slave," in the city's theaters. Around 512 and 513 he was still in the Levant, busying himself with legal and literary studies. Thus the information and images that he supplies are valuable not so much for their historical reliability as for being part of the narrative process of his work. Procopius had framed his first close-up snapshot of Theodora in the grand setting of the Kynêgion, in the midst of her family and in the act of pleading; but now her character comes more sharply into focus. Her relationship with the older sister is stressed; he specifies that there is a hierarchy in which Theodora is subordinated to Comito for "various services" that she performed, and he specifies her "professional" role in her career in theatrical entertainment, which immediately gets a negative connotation, branded as prostitution.

Procopius's rhetoric of blame offers many unexpected, concrete details for a historical reconstruction of the period. Theodora's boyish "little slave" tunic is a precious clue for identifying the roles that she regularly played on the stage with her sister: maybe our Theodora was the boy servant to Comito, who played the mistress. We have examples of this type of play both in Attic comedy (from Aristophanes to Menander) and in the mime tradition that had seduced even the stern philosopher Plato.[14]

It is doubtful, however, that the two sisters performed artistic plays. More likely, they acted in variety sketches with very little dialogue and much physical posturing and gesturing, similar to modern vaudeville-style shows designed to please and entertain an undemanding audience. The sketches were chock-full of "intrigues, betrayals, poisonings, fisticuffs, magic spells, serenades, and forsaken women."[15] The mistress would accuse the servant of some wrongdoing and would try to slap him. The servant would flee, or would try to convince her that she was wrong—that it wasn't his fault. Or maybe the mistress unfurled lofty monologues about life, destiny, and fate, while the servant went about his domestic chores and, in a "parallel" dialogue, exaggerated his daily tasks in gestures and words. "How tiring are the nights, how tiring,"[16] as Aristophanes had written a thousand years earlier.

From a historical and biographical point of view, Comito's professional advancement, with the pay she brought in from her acting and any occasional supplemental income (as alluded to by Procopius), must have been financially important for a family that had lived through difficult times both just after Acacius's death and later during the emergency that had caused them to plead in the Kynêgion. We do not know whether Comito continued to live at home or whether her professional career required an impresario or a protector. In any case, the mother most likely continued to supervise her daughter's career to some degree. But what about Theodora? In an unexpected, brusque passage, the *Secret History* reports the following:

> Now for a time Theodora, being immature, was quite unable to sleep with a man or to have a woman's kind of intercourse with one, yet she did engage in intercourse of a masculine type of lewdness with the wretches, slaves though they were, who, following their masters to the theater, incidentally took advantage of the opportunity afforded to them to carry on this monstrous business, and she spent much time in the brothel in this unnatural traffic of the body.[17]

Theodora was still immature sexually (and therefore professionally), but Procopius does not hesitate to separate her from the family and follow her alone, in her relationships and behavior. He ascribes to her practices that were defined as "unnatural" and links her sexually to slaves, and therefore to men on social rungs below even hers. It's a scathing criticism, especially if we consider that during Theodora's years as empress (when she was at the apex of society) very strict laws were enacted against homosexuality and in particular against sodomy, an act that the *Secret History* claims was a professional specialty of the young girl, as if it were her personal inclination, her personal passion.

+ + +

As we follow the gradual unveiling of the character of Theodora in the successive scenes of the *Secret History*, we find that the unveiling and the baring are more than just etymological. We also encounter the author's eye, his intentions, his sophisticated rhetorical technique, his skill in setting up his materials. By studying the logic of that authorial gaze and the technique of that rhetoric and comparing it with other information pertinent to those years, we can reconstruct Theodora's story (and somehow sketch her body, which, as even Procopius acknowledges, was "most fair"): We see Theodora, wounded by that gaze and "victimized" by that rhetoric.[18]

According to Procopius, as we saw, Theodora was already sexually active at an extremely young age, and she engaged in perverted sex. The perversion was chiefly social, for while Comito, the actress-courtesan, shone among the powerful and could maybe take her stool to the notables and sit with them, Theodora stayed behind the scenes and mingled with the dregs of society, with "wretches and slaves." The masters liked Comito; perhaps she pleased them and satisfied them. Meanwhile, there was mingling between their respective slaves, both on the stage and in life (Theodora and the "wretched"). The criticism is even more scathing and cunning considering that as the imperial couple Justinian and Theodora later reinforced certain ceremonial aspects of their position, endowing imperial power with sacredness, to the point of reducing even the highest state offices to positions of "slavery" beholden to the emperor and empress.

Procopius's social reproach is pregnant with moral reproach, because Theodora's sexual activity was sodomitic. The writer claims that she engaged in these acts not only in theater basements but also in "brothels," though it is not clear if he meant the "immature" girl or, later, the woman who had reached full personal and sexual development. He did not consider that Theodora might have been in financial trouble. To him, it was simply a question of personal inclination, of her indulging in "a masculine type of lewdness . . . this monstrous business . . . this unnatural traffic of the body."

The link to Christian moral standards is extremely weak, since the

Church condemned all sexual practices not aimed at procreation, even if they were done within a church marriage. On the other hand, Christianity had introduced a different view of prostitutes, declaring that even loathsome harlots could precede proper Pharisees into the Kingdom of Heaven. As a matter of fact, the controversial Mary Magdalene had been the first to be certain of the Resurrection. Later, the Byzantine eastern Mediterranean was enthralled by the adventures of reformed women "sinners" such as Saint Aphra, Saint Pelagia, Saint Margaret-Marina, and even Saint Mary the Egyptian, whose biography was written in the seventh century, although the core narrative of her life occurs earlier. According to Christian doctrine, the gates of Heaven stood open and ready to welcome any whores who repented of their sins. In the meantime, late antiquity viewed the daily practice of their trade as an evil that was somehow necessary and tolerable. In effect, in the words of an early father of the Church, it kept lust away from the undefiled world and restricted it within the boundaries of institutionalized prostitution.[19]

Ancient pagan morality was much stricter, since its discriminating point was not divine grace or the Kingdom of Heaven that Jesus Christ the Galilean had opened to everyone—slaves included—but the primacy of the male. Roman cultural influence, in particular, determined that a woman, no matter what her social condition, ought not to get pleasure from sex, whether it was practiced "according to" or "against" nature. She merely had to give pleasure. And to give it especially and solely to free Roman men. Prostitution was acceptable so long as a prostitute was simply a sexual thing, the recipient of irrepressible male virility, men being the only part of the sexual equation that ought to be valued and satisfied.

When an adulterous relationship resulted in a lawsuit, it was the woman who suffered most. Still, there was no worse fate than that reserved for the *pathicus*, the passive partner in a male-to-male relationship, the one who was subjected to *pedicatio* (anal penetration) instead of imposing it, as a "true Roman male" should.[20] The Roman world had no concept of the subtleties of the ancient Athenian custom of homophile relationship between an adult male lover or pedagogue and a beloved boy who was to be initiated to sexual rituals, rituals that were understood chiefly as a necessary stage in a boy's growth into manhood.

In the Christian era, the compilers of the body of laws known as the *Codex Theodosianus* (Theodosian Code) of 438 did not extend any brotherly love to the *pathici*: they confirmed the strict ancient penalties for it, including burning at the stake. Thus writers such as Procopius could not have detected a worse infamy in Theodora. For not only had she, from a very young age, dared to seek pleasure for herself rather than for her sexual partners, but she had also distinguished herself in the loathsome specialty of the *pathici*, and then had dared to sit on the imperial throne. To the historian from Caesarea, she was indeed a living abomination.

The mind-set of the ancient historian or the Christian homilist (as we saw in Saint John Chrysostom's attitude about actors' low social extraction) is quite distant from our modern sensibility. Such a writer could not conceive of the question that springs immediately to the mind of a modern scholar: Were the sexual practices attributed to young Theodora "other-directed," dictated primarily by external situations and outside forces, by financial or social constraints?[21] When these factors are denied or omitted from consideration, it is easy to present sexual promiscuity as an avocation, deeply rooted, practiced early on, in vaguely identified brothels or even in the vaulted basements below a stage (the *fornices*, root of the word *fornication*). Our modern sensibility has a different interpretation of perversion: it considers contemptible not the child or minor who might himself need protection and care, but the knowing adult who lays hands on the child's body.

Soon, according to the *Secret History*, Theodora's sexual life ceased to be passive and she began to interact with her men, moving from sexual acts "against" nature to a more mature phase of sex "according to" nature, a transition that paralleled the rise in her social rank. But here too there was a reversal of sexual behavior: she took not a traditionally passive (female) role but an active, even sinister one.

"She Immediately Became Admired for This Sort of Thing"

Constantinople, c. 512–518

Within the macrocosm of Constantinople's Christian Roman Empire, the chronicles of 513 to 515 dealt primarily with a political, religious, and military struggle. Emperor Anastasius, a supporter of Monophysitism (the belief that Jesus Christ's divine nature prevailed over his human nature), was pitted against Vitalian, the military man who crusaded for the pro-papacy religious orthodoxy that Christ, the Incarnate Word, partook of two natures, divine and human. At the time, nothing was further from Theodora's microcosm than any sort of imperial destiny. During these years of adolescence she matured enough to establish her theatrical career. And so, writes Procopius, "she joined the women of the stage and straightway became a courtesan, of the sort whom men of ancient times used to call 'infantry.' For she was neither a flute-player nor a harpist, nay, she had not even acquired skill in the dance, but she sold her youthful beauty to those who chanced to come along, plying her trade with practically her whole body."[1]

Far from being not yet "ripe," Theodora had now matured; from an apprentice in the service of her sister Comito, she had become a full-fledged actress. Possibly she joined a women's professional association similar to the guilds of the male mime actors; her mother might have recommended her to the director of one of these guilds.

At first glance, Theodora's career seemed to follow a different path from Comito's. She seemed to have poor acting skills. While her sister "had already scored a brilliant success among the harlots of her age,"[2] Theodora was described as a failed actress. The *Secret History* blamed her because she could neither play a musical instrument nor dance, an implicit comparison with perfect courtesans such as the famous Aspasia must have been: Aspasia was Pericles' mistress in fifth-century B.C. Athens, more than a thousand years before Theodora's time. But this temporal gap was of no consequence in the millennial Greek literary discourse, and Procopius's readers might have caught a refined echo of distant days in his disparaging labeling of Theodora as an "infantry" or "troop" courtesan, the antithesis of the courtesan known as a "knight"— a highly prized, high-level courtesan (these terms were already used in ancient Attic comedy).[3]

Theodora seemed limited to being a group dancer, just another body in the corps de ballet. Of course she was on the stage now, no longer in the wings. But the stage merely revealed—even highlighted— her weakness as an artist. Instead of redefining her through her talent, it underscored Theodora's identity as a pure sexual object, on account of her great physical beauty. And now she offered her entire body, as she had not done before. She now belonged to everyone, to "those who chanced to come along." While Theodora the person seemed to conquer the stage, she was in fact losing it, passing it on, as it were, to her body. To her beauty.

Like a skilled director in the theater that he so detested, Procopius— the only source we have on Theodora's youth—turns off all the stage lights, leaving only one spotlight focused on the young girl. She appears in all her physical splendor, but it's a short-lived effect. When called upon to sing and dance she reveals her inadequacy, he reports, and this serves the purpose of the *Secret History* though there is no concrete evidence to support Procopius's claim of acting mediocrity. In fact, Theodora's theater background that he condemns must have at least given her some experience with ruses, with the art of deception. Possibly Theodora was too young to land leading roles in which she could display whatever skills she had. And so she built up her experience in secondary roles, in the background. Procopius reproaches her for failing to do what in any case she *could not* do.

We must assume that in her early acting days Theodora, like Comito, had her mother's protection, fueled as it might have been by self-interest. In choosing and scheduling her daughters' progressive appearances on the stage, she must have also filtered the progressive stages of Theodora's sexual and artistic coming of age. In all likelihood, she discreetly paraded her daughter's beauty on the stage before offering her young, beautiful body. And not, clearly, to "those who chanced to come along" but to reliable, financially stable men of high rank. Possibly the connection with the Blue team helped here too. Probably Comito and her mother prepared Theodora for her first encounter and those that followed.

In her sexual training there may have been someone who, with a delicacy uncommon for the times, taught her both how to pleasure a man and how to find pleasure herself; but more probably, she had to figure out on her own how to live with the "service" that was being requested of her.

Emma Hamilton (1761–1815), last great love of the heroic Admiral Nelson, had a life not unlike Theodora's, at least in the early years. She leaped up the ladder of society in London and in Naples (the liveliest Mediterranean city of her time, as Constantinople had once been) with the support of the mother who had introduced her to artistic circles and to a courtesan's career, even though Emma had never displayed any specific penchant or desire for this. And yet, the two women tactfully compared their satisfying erotic experiences, without envying or begrudging each other; and these experiences in turn did not weaken their faith in a just and providential God.

While Theodora might have appeared artistically weak in the early part of her stage career—her "infantry" period—the reason might be that her mother, in particular, needed to protect her at the outset. Combining the career of actress with that of courtesan meant not only being sexually available, but being subject to the primitive remedies against the possible effects of an active sexual life. It was risky for young Theodora, and not only for her; life at the time was harsh for all women. Most girls at her age, sixteen, were already married or close to it. Many had already given birth to their first child. Theodora was no exception: she became a mother around 515 or 516. We do not know the name of her daughter, but the girl was to play a significant role in history.

It is difficult to connect Theodora's motherhood to other events in her life. What we do know is that at some point Theodora suddenly reappeared in public, with the self-assurance and inevitability that always marks the young and talented. Around 517 or 518, when she must have been seventeen or eighteen years old, Theodora joined a mime troupe possibly connected with the Blue team. At that point, she was able to land roles in which "she immediately became admired" in the theaters of Constantinople's suburbs, far from the monumental and intellectual center of the great Christian Roman capital. Perhaps one of the theaters was in Sykae (today's Galata), beyond the Golden Horn, and another in the northern district of the city outside the walls, in Blachernae. Now Theodora's qualities were recognized even by the first of her detractors, Procopius, who writes:

> Later on she was associated with the actors in all the work of the theater, and she shared their performances with them, playing up to their buffoonish acts intended to raise a laugh. For she was unusually clever and full of gibes, and she immediately became admired for this sort of thing. For the girl had not a particle of modesty, nor did any man ever see her embarrassed, but she undertook shameless services without the least hesitation, and she was the sort of a person who, for instance, when being flogged or beaten over the head, would crack a joke over it and burst into a loud laugh; and she would undress and exhibit to any who chanced along both her front and her rear naked, parts which rightly should be unseen by men and hidden from them.[4]

The mimes were allowed to stage this type of show, and the productions were financially lucrative, so clearly the public did not spend all its time fretting over political issues and theological disputes, as gloomy official histories, chronicles, and scholarly tracts would have us believe. People were interested in things other than culture, solemnity, and virtue.

The low esteem in which theater actors were held in the Roman era and in late antiquity, banished as they were to the margins of cultural life and to the bottom of the social ladder, is reflected in the lack of historical sources about this light entertainment. Except for Sophron, Eronda, and Theocritus (who all preceded Theodora by eight to ten centuries), mime theater pieces were not elaborately collected, transcribed, and studied, as were classical works. Therefore, the scripts were written only for the internal use of the acting crews, who, like Theodora, did know how to read.

Those who claimed to defend proper "values" had a further reason to denigrate the mime. According to these moralists, the mime drew his expressivity not from the strength of a fine voice reverberating behind a stage mask, but from the deforming of a face exposed to the public, in imitation of everyday attitudes and behavior. (The root of *imitate*, *mimêsis*, is linked to *mime*.) Instead of the stock, draped costumes used for the mythical characters of ancient theater, the mimes used everyday clothes, and the actresses (the mime was the first theater genre open to women) were scantily clad in particularly see-through attire—when they wore anything at all. For in the show's grand finale the actresses stripped off their clothes and paraded around.

The stage where Theodora was now a protagonist did not require speeches. When picturing what the theater was like then, one should imagine neither Theodora's voice nor anyone else's, but only noises. Instead of noble poses, there was a flurry of frenetic gestures. Laughter alternated with crying, and there were chases and running, shuffling about, loud slaps on cheeks, the dull thump of a punch, someone being tripped, the perfect arc of a somersault. The actors bugged out their eyes and rolled them wildly; they clapped their hands over their ears to block out the ruckus on stage; they crossed their arms or rested them on their hips to signify authority or demand respect; they raised a finger to point or scold. And all the movements were underscored by the jingle of *sistra* and cymbals.

Sometimes, the scripts expanded the duets that young Theodora had performed with Comito. For these plays, more actors and richer settings were required. In those years, mimes were referred to as "biological," meaning that they mimed *bios*, "daily life." Caricatures and sketches were not unlike those of our silent movies: there was the quarrel between the scrooge and the spendthrift; the inheritance being swindled from an old uncle or a senile grandfather; the contrast between city sophisticate and country bumpkin; the soldier returning home to discover his wife in someone else's arms. This "lowbrow" repertory proved popular, and it has endured: it is comparable to our genre comedies or romance magazines, or the publications that made Eva Perón famous[5] with the proviso that these days, we don't infer an actor's tastes from the characters that he or she plays from a script. Today, playing the role of a wife who is caught in the act means only playing a role, but in Theodora's time, it wasn't seen that way.

The young actress attracted an audience: she was a source of income, both for herself and for her acting company. Dressed in see-through clothes when she wasn't practically undressed, Theodora generously put her young body on display, but she was never totally naked: she always wore at least a loincloth. She had a talent for humor, for she was as "clever and full of gibes" as she was beautiful, something that even her detractors admitted. And although mimes were not the embodiment of highbrow culture, no one could deny their sense of rhythm. Perfect timing was essential for creating the befuddled excitement that marks good mimework even today, and guarantees its continued popularity. The young Theodora, in addition to a strong will and great ambition, deserves recognition for her personal and professional gifts such as irony, memory, and a sense of timing. Without these, she could not have achieved success in her field. Maybe these gifts were inborn, but undoubtedly she refined and practiced them daily on the stage. These were qualities that she strengthened in later years, together with a sort of joker's farcical attitude that never failed her, even on the greatest of stages, the imperial throne.

Was Theodora's talent similar to that of a modern, popular comic actress? Yes. Her specialty was defusing dramatic situations and violent conflicts, reversing them with ironic ruses ("when being flogged or

beaten over the head, [she] would crack a joke over it"). They are unexpected traits for the solemn female figure depicted in the mosaics of
San Vitale, but they're not surprising: in her childhood in the Kynêgion
arena, Theodora had learned that her prayers could be answered only if
she knew how to turn the whole situation on its head.

Had Theodora revealed her brilliant miming talents early on, and had
she then vaulted directly to the throne of the greatest empire of her age,
hers would still be an extraordinary, unique story: a Cinderella-like
fairy tale. The German Romantics or an Anatole France would have
turned her life into a rosy myth. Instead, the European literature of the
nineteenth and twentieth centuries re-created a Theodora painted in
dark, sexy, violent colors, from Victorien Sardou's *Théodora* (1884),
interpreted by Sarah Bernhardt [fig. 13] to Gabriele D'Annunzio's *La
nave* (The Ship; 1908), in which Basiliola, a character inspired by
Theodora,

> knew all forms
> Of incest and beastly couplings,
> All sorts of animal-sounding lust.[6]

So it was not her skill or her persona as an actress that cemented
her in modern mythology as the most celebrated of Constantinople's
empresses, but rather her verve and her lust as a lover. She even inspired colorful biographies written for the vast public that is presumably drawn to books with subtitles like *The Empress with a Shady Past*.
This shadiness and these contradictions are all traceable to Procopius's
Secret History, the work that so powerfully marked her legend, always
identifying the actress with the courtesan and emphasizing over and
over again the parallel between her career as a theater actress, her
social ascent, and her sexual life.

> And as she wantoned with her lovers, she always kept bantering
> them, and by toying with new devices in intercourse, she always
> succeeded in winning the hearts of the licentious to her; for she
> did not even expect that the approach should be made by the

man she was with, but on the contrary she herself, with wanton
jests and with clownish posturing with her hips, would tempt all
who came along, especially if they were beardless youths. Indeed
there was never anyone such a slave to pleasure in all forms; for
many a time she would go to a community dinner with ten
youths or even more, all of exceptional bodily vigour who had
made a business of fornication, and she would lie with all her
banquet companions the whole night long, and when they all
were too exhausted to go on, she would go to their attendants,
thirty perhaps in number, and pair off with each one of them; yet
even so she could not get enough of this wantonness.[7]

This scathing portrayal of Theodora, not necessarily true as to fact but
consistent with his literary strategy, displays Procopius's rhetorical bent
and emphasizes several elements. First of all, "time": *always* new sexual
techniques; she *always* won the men's hearts; sex *all* night long. Then
"number": she provoked *all* who came along, a slave to pleasure in *all*
forms; *ten* youths or *even more*; they *all* were too exhausted to go on;
thirty attendants; she would pair off with *each one* of them. Finally,
"social context": in addition to adult men, Theodora also enticed boys
and *passed* from free men to servants.

Oddly, there are no allusions here to Theodora's voracity for food
being equal to her sexual gluttony (it was, after all, a "dinner" in the
spirit of Casanova, lover and gourmand), but the *Secret History* implied
that in a typical night Theodora "exhausted" at least ten dinner companions of proven sexual strength. Such potent men might be expected
to rise for at least four or five unions in the course of the night (for
example, infamous Renaissance murderer and lover Cesare Borgia
claimed six couplings on his wedding night[8]), which adds up to a minimum total of approximately forty couplings, plus another thirty for the
servants. So the report is that Theodora engaged in about seventy couplings *per night*.

These are the sort of impressive numbers found in literature (comparable to the boasted debauchery of the Marquis de Sade's libertine

13. Sarah Bernhardt performing Victorien Sardou's *Théodora* (publ. 1884).

Madame de Saint-Ange), but they are not consistent with objective data gathered by authoritative organizations at the turn of the twenty-first century: sociological statistics about prostitution rates, and clinical statistics collected by organizations that treat fashion and show-business stars and others afflicted with "sexual disorders."

Aside from quantity, another constant theme of Procopius's

account of Theodora's sexuality is a literary emphasis on perverted or degrading sex. Now it is no longer just a question of couplings "according to" or "against" nature. The issue is more subtle, since Theodora's dinners and nights, according to Procopius, inverted the traditional relationship between men and women in classical antiquity. In them, the woman is no longer subjected to the pleasure and the power of the man; on the contrary, it is the man in the fullness of his strength who kneels before her, enslaved by her sexual charge. From being the prey of male pleasure, woman has become the huntress. But there is more: the huntress is enslaved in turn, subjected as she is to "pleasure in all forms." Her lust is never sated, no matter how frequent the couplings or how varied the positions. The woman, traditionally submitted to male pleasure, is now self-directed and dominates men, all men. At the same time, she is enslaved by a superior, outside force.

In anthropological terms, her status is no longer human but "demonic." With her autonomous sexual charge, Theodora's demonic elements are not of the Christian kind. She has nothing in common with the whores who, instigated by what was believed to be a diabolical force, appeared to the hermits of the Syrian and Egyptian deserts, disturbing their spiritual exercises and offering the pleasures of sexual gratification. Theodora is different. She shows the signs of what the ancient Greeks called hubris—that is, arrogance, almost a subversion of natural and social values and laws.

Her social background had situated her below what was considered proper to human society. Her career then began to move her elsewhere, outside society. While at first she was notorious or unworthy, now she became an alien. Nor was she her own mistress: she was pulled around by irrational, uncontrollable drives beyond any intelligible logic, following her "demon"[9] into the abyss of degradation. And so she was destined to meet, in the depths of vice and at the apex of power, the man whom Procopius's *Secret History* literally presents as "the Lord of Demons,"[10] Justinian.

It would be simplistic and incorrect to reduce the life of young Theodora to what is defined as prostitution. She was the one who chose, who requested, who demanded. The young star of Constantinople's mime theater "forever" won the affection of the inevitable influential protectors, not by collecting fees but by accepting gifts of clothing, jewels, servants, apartments. It is difficult to believe that at this point she still lived at home with her mother and her younger sister, Anastasia; but she likely often asked the advice of her older sister, Comito. They must have regularly exchanged information about acting companies, performances, or scripts. Maybe they reciprocally introduced one another to their worthiest admirers, or naughtily stole them from each other. The men probably insisted on coming around to prove the intensity of their attraction, reinforcing their words with gifts and actions that might encourage the girls to grant favors of a different kind, to the extent that it might please them—that it might please Theodora in particular.

In all likelihood, high-ranking dignitaries and wealthy traders would set Theodora up in apartments or villas that they owned, equipped with maids and eunuch servants, so that they could easily visit her: provided, however, that she led a discreet life and kept herself available. Some delightful residences outside the city, along the verdant banks of the Propontis (today's Sea of Marmara) were the favored locales for this. They were the precursors of the Ottomans' waterside residences (*yali*) that so enchanted European travelers and Turkish potentates long after the seventh eon, when Constantinople had already become Istanbul. The young actress was no doubt seduced by the Asiatic shore of the Propontis, just as she was drawn to it even after she became empress. There she may have found moments of rest and quiet, her leisure time. Interrupting her refreshing naps and her beauty treatments to welcome her lover of the moment, she might have been reminded of what enchanted her most in that arrangement: crossing the strait in a felucca (a small open boat), with eunuchs and maids holding a canopy to shield her face from the strong rays of the sun, the wind filling her skirts, the dolphins leaping, the schools of tuna knifing though the water, and finally, the skyline of the city seen from the east. It was a skyline that she herself would change one day.

When her lover was kept in the city by urgent business and she was seized by a sudden need for company, she would probably dispatch a servant to the city before evening with invitations for friends or colleagues to join her at the villa. Jealous admonitions from her lover were to be expected, but she could probably bring his smile back easily, just as she turned quarrels into laughter on the stage. As her beauty was greater than any eloquence, Theodora did not need many words. Her lover, on the other hand, might carry on promising her many things, dazzled by her face and her body. Theodora knew the art of listening. For her, it was closely tied to the art of obtaining.

Lacking affectation and never ill at ease, she most likely found it amusing to be the only woman in the company of men—mime colleagues and the sort of people who are always drawn to the world of entertainment, in every era, all over the world. Priests and monks were excluded, of course, and very rarely did conversations touch on the single or double nature of the Incarnated Christ (these were issues best left to the Monophysites and the Dyophysites) or the political and military situation at the Persian front. Frequent subjects of conversation were the exploits of the Green or Blue teams and their enthusiasts, the whimsical enthusiasms of Emperor Anastasius, or the rumors from the entertainment capital of late antiquity, the city of Antioch (then part of Syria, now in modern Turkey). The wealth of dignitaries and foreigners took on legendary qualities: one had to get introduced to them and introduce them in turn to others, and try to organize expensive plays and parties in each unique, incomparable mansion.

When the conversation turned to other women, or when other women joined in, Theodora might have knit her brow. Her unfailing denigrator writes that she was poisonous and ruthless toward female colleagues, to the point of being "very envious and spiteful"[11] of them. More probably, she reacted with early diffidence that could turn into hostility. Because she could benefit from men through her wiles, she saw other women as alternative Theodoras, rivals who could not and should not be given any room to maneuver. She also had the perennial complex of the prima donna, combined with that ever-present, sometimes forced competitiveness among "stars" that has always permeated the world of sports, the circus, music, and the theater—environments

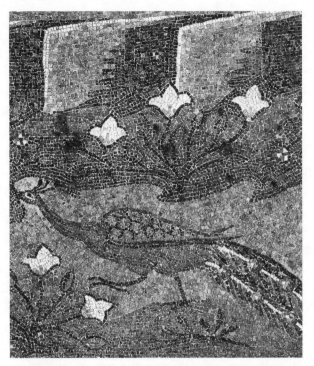

14. Mosaic peacock, c. 545–50, basilica of San Vitale, Ravenna.

always marked by informal relationships and lifestyles, implicitly founded upon a casual approach in sexual customs, among other areas of life.

Theodora performed not only in the public theaters before easy-to-please audiences but also in other, more prestigious locales, such as the private homes of illustrious dignitaries and upright Christian matrons. In public, their calm looks and sophisticated ears did not betray an appreciation for the mime's coarse humor, but in the privacy of their homes they would turn that same commonness into an exclusive attraction, for their own entertainment and that of selected guests. Our young star and her theater company might have been cautiously approached by a eunuch majordomo charged with arranging a date and compensation for their performance in a great city residence. Decorated with rich floral arrangements and ancient polychrome statues of gods and heroes, those mansions had sumptuous furnishings, and enchanting floor mosaics whose elaborate scenes danced in the flickering light of torches.

Theodora must have admired the mosaic tesserae, the tiny chips of marble, terra cotta, and glass paste that formed idyllic scenes from the Golden Age or the Garden of Eden, with peacocks, flamingoes, fish, and plants of the great river Nile, and crocodiles hiding among the rushes [fig. 14], or the allegories of the Virtues cherished by the pagan world and later embraced by the common culture of Christianity—Temperance, Generosity, Mercy: all words that Theodora knew well.

While she readied herself for the performance, Theodora might have seen the lady of the house stroll around her peristyle or cloistered garden amid ponds, delightful fountains, and rose bushes studded with buds as abundant as the jewels that adorned the lady herself. The lady of the house would show the fine decorations to her important guests, easily alternating between Latin and Greek, her mastery of the languages reflecting her perfect control of the situation.

These occasions allowed the young actress to fully grasp the meaning of what the Greeks called *kyria* and the Romans *domina*: "mistress," "lady." A lady never needed to chase after things, or to struggle to keep what she had.

Theodora was due to perform at any second. She waited. She could still only vaguely glimpse real life, the life of the men and women who count and who are in charge, who decide whether and when to speak. She had come a long way from the day she and her family pleaded in the Kynêgion, stepping out of the barrel-vaulted passageways under the arena. Now she was standing behind an embroidered velum, the curtain that separated one room from another, which can be seen in so many mosaics and frescoes [figs. 1, 15] of antiquity and late antiquity. Theodora might have glimpsed the guests reclining on precious triclinia, the Roman dining couches. She might have listened to the mingling of Greek and Latin, which meant that important dignitaries and military officers were present. She might have glimpsed the vaulted dining room recess, where servants prepared dishes that pleased the guests' eyes even before they began to eat. Thracian game was garnished

15. Mosaic depicting a palace with vela (curtains), early 6th century, church of Sant'Apollinare Nuovo, Ravenna.

in elaborate shapes, bowls of water perfumed with oils were offered to the diners to clean their fingers, and shining goblets were filled with Cypriot wine.

For the daughter of the bear keeper, it was at once a vision and a challenge. She was filled with sadness, nostalgia, and energy all at once. She could not contain the passion surging through her; the ancient Greeks had called that passion *thymos*.[12]

And now the musicians beat their *sistra*; Theodora made her entrance into the large dining room, running through her show from the very slow opening to the excited finale, in a late-ancient version of the Mediterranean belly dance or in a foreshadowing of the bolero. Seized with passion, she gave an outstanding performance that people remembered and spoke about for years, though in the *Secret History* we find only a pale, generic echo of the event: "On one occasion she entered the house of one of the notables during the drinking, and they say that in the sight of all the banqueters she mounted to the projecting part of the banqueting couch where their feet lay, and there drew up her clothing in a shameless way, not hesitating to display her licentiousness."[13] According to Procopius, it was an impromptu performance, the drunken exhibition of a Bacchante; but in truth she and her mime troupe were the attraction of the evening (and of many evenings like this).

Theodora was sought out, admired, and applauded by the same high society that publicly feigned indifference. But it happened in private, at banquets in the great city mansions or in the secluded and exclusive seashore villas where the rich and powerful enjoyed their leisure hours on the Bosphorus outside the city. While touching the relics of a saint or a holy man benefited the soul, being grazed by Theodora's garment in the street, maybe along the Mesê (Constantinople's main artery for traffic and trade that ran west from the Hippodrome to the Golden Gate, and north to the church of the Holy Apostles), was considered a contamination, for she was, after all, an actress and thus taken for a whore.[14] What is more, any exchange of words, any form of public recognition connecting the world of that disreputable woman with the world of respectable people, would be an unbearable scandal. It was for this very reason that Asterius had not uttered a word in answer to the plea of Acacius's widow and children on that distant but unforgotten day in the Kynêgion.

In such a context of denial and perversion, it was easy to say and write of her that she seemed to have "her privates not where Nature had placed them in other women, but in her face!"[15] Procopius's conclusion seemed to follow logically, but only if we believe that Theodora's body was ruled by lust, reacting to lust like a perfectly tempered mechanism.

FIVE

"Contriver of Shameless Deeds Above All Others"

Constantinople, c. 518

MANY CENTURIES after Theodora, thousands of miles from Constantinople, a twenty-year-old actress left Sweden for the United States. Greta Lovisa Gustafsson soon became a movie star under the name of Greta Garbo, but for many years her admirers could not hear her voice. When talking pictures were invented, the 1930 posters advertising her starring role in *Anna Christie* proclaimed: "Garbo talks." The first words of her sound debut were carefully chosen: "Give me a whiskey, ginger ale on the side; and don't be stingy, baby."[1] These few words made her low, throaty voice unforgettable. Central to the plot of the film, the words also marked her from the start as a feminine ideal: an emancipated woman with a take-charge attitude, precise and on her own. This was the "Garbo style."

Procopius's *Secret History* allows us to reconstruct a similar episode from the Mediterranean of late antiquity, when Theodora was a star. Up to this point we have overheard only the noisy clatter of her performances in the theaters of Constantinople: the slaps and laughter accompanying the winks and gestures. We sensed the turmoil that her body aroused, the magic spell of her beauty. All this, before she could even utter a word. And then, suddenly, Theodora also talked, and her first words confirmed her legendary status: a sexual and literary legend. The first time she speaks in Procopius's account she chastises Nature: "And though she made use of three openings, she used to take Nature to task, complaining that it had not pierced her breasts with larger holes so that it might be possible for her to contrive another method of copulation there."[2] Under the yoke of her "utter wantonness," Procopius's Theodora is no longer part of the kingdom of nature, but outside it. She has left civilized human society for a private, alien, non-human realm, the realm of hubris. She addresses Nature, claiming that it is robbing her of pleasure—sexual pleasure. Robbing her, a woman!

Did Theodora truly speak those words, and if so, to whom? Did she say them to one or more of her tireless lovers, who could never sate their erotic frenzy? Did she whisper them to another actress? We have no way of knowing. Here, as in other instances—such as the night (or nights) of the seventy couplings—the primary sources are missing. All we have (once again) is a literary version, and it is stated in prose that richly echoes Greek literary tradition; the echoes were easily grasped by Procopius's natural readers, sensitive as they were to literary nuances.

"Four openings": the protagonist of the *Secret History* speaks for the first time, and her words stand as the high point of her narrative. They are also the high point of a literary theme, for early Greek authors had attacked some women by criticizing their sexual customs. For example, in the Attic oratory of the fourth century B.C., Lysias had criticized Anthiopa, a courtesan, for "using immorally" two orifices. Later, with exaggeration common in ancient rhetoric,[3] the author known as Pseudo-Demosthenes had accused the courtesan Neaira of "abusing" three parts of her body. Procopius, familiar as he was with these authors, exaggerated the number of orifices even further, bringing it to four.[4]

But quantity did not suffice to feed this denigrator's elegant rage. To quantity he added quality. What Anthiopa and Neaira had merely proffered or performed, and what Lysias and Pseudo-Demosthenes had criticized as an abuse, Procopius's Theodora *longed* for. She wanted pleasure. She desired, for her pleasure, more of what had been previously characterized as an abuse.

If the words of Procopius's Theodora—contemptuous as they are of natural law and human custom alike—do bespeak hubris, then she is not unlike the mythical Prometheus who stole fire from the gods, or the modern Don Juan who made fun of piety for the dead. Indeed, in clamoring for sexual pleasure—to the point of taking Nature to task—Theodora asserts herself as a literary creature, apart from declaring her personal sexual appetites. And while Procopius succeeds as a writer in his own genre, paradoxically he fails in his attempt to humiliate Theodora, for never has such a resentful work bestowed so much fame on its target.

In *The Decline and Fall of the Roman Empire*, Edward Gibbon (1737–1794), the great Enlightenment historian, paraphrased the passage about the "four openings"; he wrote that Theodora "wished for a *fourth* altar, on which she might pour libations to the god of love."[5] The use of a sacred, ritual vocabulary to write about sex is typical of the contemptuous libertine style as used, for example, by the Marquis de Sade. Cesare Baronio (1538–1607), a cardinal and church historian, brought a different, more malicious attitude to the matter. In his *Ecclesiastical Annals*, he noted that Theodora "surpassed all other women in wickedness. She deserved the names given to the Furies in Hell."[6] Although Cardinal Baronio could identify what was different, his judgment was faulty.

Thus Theodora's irritated reproach to Nature is an instance of a literary device that both preceded the *Secret History* and followed it; it may also hint at her physical traits, just as a fossil hints at an ancient life-form. Perhaps Theodora's breasts were seen to offer little material for erotic play; her beautiful body was probably boyish rather than buxom and matronly.

What were the "true" features of that young face and body that could "win the hearts"[7] of so many men and kindle so many different passions? From the mosaic of the San Vitale basilica in Ravenna [fig. 1] we know how she looked as a mature woman, about thirty years after this period. Even if we assume that the artist or the mosaic installer had access to the palace and saw Theodora, still the majestic, stately portrait reveals little of the mime actress whose career had caused so much scandal. In the *Secret History*, even his hatred doesn't blind the author to her beauty. As a matter of fact, he describes her almost impartially.

She "was fair of face and in general attractive in appearance, but short of stature and lacking in colour, being, however, not altogether pale but rather sallow, and her glance was always intense and made with contracted brows."[8]

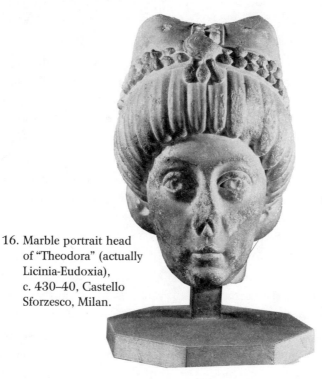

16. Marble portrait head of "Theodora" (actually Licinia-Eudoxia), c. 430–40, Castello Sforzesco, Milan.

The literary source (Procopius) and the visual source (Ravenna), date to almost the same time, but they are far apart geographically and opposite in meaning and intent, and they do not agree about Theodora's height. (In the mosaic, she is the tallest figure, possibly as a mark of hierarchical respect.) But they do agree on Theodora's expression, for in the mosaic her dark eyes appear particularly deep. Focused attention seems to be Theodora's dominant trait: she seems to scour her surroundings, scrutinizing them for dangers, glimpsing opportunities. She is not lost in gentle or transcendental contemplation like an icon, nor does she wear an expression of detached serenity, like the marble bust of an emperor or a philosopher. Her beauty is diaphanous, well proportioned, restless, and expressive. It is a beauty that could easily qualify as "modern."

In pursuit of that seductive beauty, some scholars have identified as Theodora an exquisite marble sculpture of a head, discovered in the course of demolition in the center of Milan, Italy, and now housed at the Sforza castle there [fig. 16]. The statue's oval face resembles the Ravenna mosaic: it shares a delightful restlessness in the lips, an intent expression, and a haughty impatience that recall Theodora. But recent research on the artifact's form and style leads scholars to attribute it not to the infamous mime actress but to Licinia-Eudoxia (daughter and heir to Theodosius II, Emperor of the East, and his scholarly wife Athenais-Eudocia), who in 437 married Valentinian III, Emperor of the West, and was acclaimed Savior of the East and Joy of the West.[9]

Undoubtedly, a face such as that of the Milan sculpture could "win the hearts" of men. And though it may not be Theodora's face, we could legitimately infer that it resembles her. Maybe one day, with the help of computer graphics, we will be able to turn Ravenna's imperial mosaic into a 3-D reconstruction of young Theodora's face.

Soon Theodora began to care for her face and body, in order to preserve and enhance her beauty and maybe to perfect it. In the years spent in the theater and at the palace, she did not let a day go by without looking after her beauty. Thermal baths, massages, face masks, and skin treatments were daily activities. During her stage career she would frequent the cosmetic shops annexed to the bathing establishments of the city. The baths were probably an ideal place for making new acquaintances (to fuel her lusts and passions, according to her critics); later, as her career progressed, she would follow her beauty regime in the privacy of home.

Her lifelong familiarity with bath establishments and makeup, and her habit of caring for her body daily, explain why an imperial statue to her was erected near the Arcadian baths of Constantinople, and why the baths of Carthage were called "Theodorian." These habits emphasize the fact that she was among the last to hold an ancient attitude toward the body, at a time when the world was turning toward medieval customs. (But as we shall see later, she herself contributed in no small way, as empress, to that evolution toward the medieval.)

Both when she was young and when she was at the palace, sleep was a necessary complement to her beauty treatments. Sleep revived her soul as well as the muscles of her face, which got such a lot of exercise in her work as a mime. And sleep took her to the oneiric dimension that was so meaningful in that epoch, especially to those who, like the girl of the Hippodrome and the Kynêgion, might have been familiar with unorthodox, even esoteric disciplines such as astrology or the interpretation of dreams. Baths and rest were also important to her because they offered moments for reflection about herself and those around her. She did not even like to receive visits in the morning, and she was not bothered by the fact that some criticized her morning extravagance. She knew only too well that a woman such as she, whether an actress or an empress, could show herself in public only if she looked perfect.

She was criticized for lacking self-discipline also when it came to food: apparently, she willingly "partook of all manner of food and drink,"[10] a reproach informed by coarse ideas about people of humble birth who finally had more than a subsistence diet. Furthermore, archaic taboos about food survived: taboos, for example, about women drinking wine. Some extreme conservatives could have objected that in drinking wine a woman took into her body an unacceptable vital principle other than that socially acceptable vital principle, her legitimate husband's seed. But it might have been that Theodora simply had a petite, high-energy body that quickly burned all the calories she took in. Her culinary whims led her to quality rather than quantity. She did not like fowl or condiments, but seemed to enjoy small, sugary, high-calorie treats such as sweets made of figs and roses, dates, nuts, grapes, cookies, and "Persian-style" sorbets.

Often, women procurers who hoped to introduce lusty new admirers to Theodora would contact the masseuses and makeup women who pampered her face and body. But Theodora enjoyed total protection, and the reply was always the same: They admire her?—let them come to the theater and pay to admire her over and over again. And there was a lot to admire, as the *Secret History* reports in a passage about her performances in about 518.

> And often even in the theatre, before the eyes of the whole peo-
> ple, she stripped off her clothing and moved about naked through
> their midst, having only a girdle about her private parts and her
> groin, not, however, that she was ashamed to display these to the
> populace, but because no person is permitted to enter there en-
> tirely naked, but must have at least a girdle about the groin.
> Clothed in this manner, she sprawled out and lay on her back on
> the ground. And some slaves, whose duty this was, sprinkled
> grains of barley over her private parts, and geese, which happened
> to have been provided for this very purpose, picked them off with
> their beaks, one by one, and ate them. And when she got up, she
> not only did not blush, but even acted as if she took pride in this
> strange performance. For she was not merely shameless herself,
> but also a contriver of shameless deeds above all others. And it
> was a common thing for her to undress and stand in the midst of
> the actors on the stage, now straining her body backwards and
> now trying to [offer her] hinder parts both [to] those who had
> consorted with her and those who had not yet done so, running
> through with pride the exercises of the only wrestling school to
> which she was accustomed.[11]

It seems an artless performance; even stern historians smile over the relative innocence of these infamous "pornographic" scenes. But one should distinguish between the two episodes described in the *Secret History*. The second one, where she performed "in the midst of the actors," leaves little to the imagination: Theodora "strained her body backwards" and pushed her (seminaked) belly forward, emphatically shaking her pelvis, throwing her head back, and shaking her hands toward the audience. This traditional move is documented as far back as early Attic comedy, perfected a thousand years before Theodora and still alive in today's burlesque. When she offered "her hinder parts," we extrapolate from the Greek text that it was an abrupt movement, "like that of a wasp or scorpion."[12] This sounds just like the bump-and-grind of the hips, the burlesque move appreciated even by the proper middle class in modern Paris. (On the other hand, Procopius seems to have some kind of obsession, insisting again on Theodora's "hinder parts," her buttocks, her customary "wrestling school." Her buttocks may be the one part of Theodora's body that he scrutinizes most closely.)

The first episode, with the geese, is part of a more sophisticated kind of pantomime or tableau vivant in which players reenacted ancient mythological scenes. The theme of Theodora's performance was derived from the legendary union of the god Zeus with Leda, the wife of Tindareus, king of Sparta. From this union came Helen, whom the ancients called the most beautiful woman on earth. To enjoy Leda's beauty, the god transformed himself into a swan; his miraculous embrace was rendered on the stage by trained geese who picked grains of barley from Theodora's mons veneris, the object of desire, the true "navel" of the theater world at the time. Replacing swans with geese indicates that this was a parody, maybe even a veiled critique of the myth; in any case it proves the latitude of expression permitted in the capital of the great Christian empire.

Theodora, whom we saw "frowning" or "with contracted brows," finally appeared "proud" of her performance. To Procopius, her relaxed smile was one more sign of her shamelessness. It's likely, though, that the smile reflected not the actress's feelings but the requirements of the show: the smile was a dutiful reaction to the audience's applause. Furthermore, Theodora followed the rules of the form, which called for each actor to play various roles. So she played Leda—she lay with the god, simulating the coupling of the two lovers by lifting her pelvis and trembling, and then she acted out the labor of childbirth—and afterward she became the fruit of that coupling: Helen, sweet smiling Helen, the most beautiful of all women.

This episode is more than evidence of Theodora's successful career. The surprising and engaging aspect is the young woman unperturbed by the birds pecking at her groin. It indicates the contempt for danger that characterizes circus life but, even more important, it confirms that

Theodora had become accustomed to a remote, alien, even wild world. She had been raised, after all, in arenas and city streets, observing animals and people and statues—creatures of many different worlds—switching roles and swapping identities. This truly had been her education.

Nor were the stage geese the only danger Theodora faced. Sexual promiscuity, which went hand in hand with her success as an actress, posed drawbacks to her career, her beauty, even her health. And so, after reproaching Nature for not having endowed her with a better body, Theodora now criticized what was, after all, the law of nature. That "woman . . . had not only encompassed herself round about with every other rank and refinement, but had also practiced infanticide time and again by voluntary abortions," and "though she was pregnant many times, yet practically always she was able to contrive to bring about an abortion immediately."[13] But she did not always succeed. A long passage from the *Secret History* tells the story of Theodora's secret child:

> Now she had chanced to conceive a child by one of her lovers while she was still on the stage and being late about discovering her misfortune she did everything to accomplish, in her usual way, an abortion, but she was unsuccessful, by all the means employed, in killing the untimely infant, for by now it lacked but little of its human shape. Consequently, since she met with no success, she gave up trying and was compelled to bear the child. And when the father of the new-born child saw that she was distressed and displeased, because after becoming a mother she would no longer be able to go on using her body as she had done, since he rightly suspected that she would destroy the child, he acknowledged the infant by lifting it up in his arms, and, naming it John, since it was a male, he went on his way to Arabia, whither he was bound.[14]

On his deathbed, the father told John, by then a grown boy, the truth about his mother. John then traveled from Arabia to Constantinople to meet his mother, and Theodora, "fearing that the matter would become known to her husband,"[15] entrusted him to one of her domestics. And that was the last that was heard of John.

Is this an outright literary invention created to heap more scorn on Theodora? (Note the fairy-tale motifs: exotic Arabia; the innocent country bumpkin in the palace.) Or is it proof of imperial wickedness? There is no historical evidence about this John. And it is unlikely that the father could so easily recognize the child as his own, if indeed Theodora was as promiscuous as was claimed. Therefore, the prevailing opinion holds that this is one more literary device.

On the other hand, the historical sources about Theodora's daughter, mentioned earlier, are quite different. In particular, we know that this daughter had a son (Theodora's grandson), Anastasius, who was at least sixteen years of age in around 547 or 548. So he was born around 530 or 531 to a woman who, by simple subtraction, must herself have been born around 515 or 516, in the early days of Theodora's "scandalous" acting career. The actress thus became a mother when, according to modern law, she was still a minor; by the time she was thirty she was already a grandmother.

The bonds of family solidarity, of faction loyalty (among the Blues), and possibly even ecclesiastical charity allowed Theodora to keep in touch with her daughter without compromising her professional and social ascent. Besides, maternity did not seem to seriously affect Theodora's career or her behavior. Herself the daughter of an unusual woman, she was not cut out to be an anxious mother. Instead of focusing on the baby's whimpers or first words, she was concerned with expanding her horizons, leaving the confines of her social milieu and her profession. She had to quickly establish a relationship, perhaps even a respectable marriage, that would allow her, too, to become a "lady," a *kyria*.

Pregnancy's physical and psychic effects on her lovely, petite, elastic body made it a plague to be avoided, not only for Theodora but for all women in her situation. Her need for personal growth—in today's parlance—her need to achieve social and professional status (or to satisfy her lust, her enemies claimed), meant that she had to have contact and even sexual encounters with the powerful and the important. On the other hand, she found it difficult, if not impossible, to formally enter their world as the full-fledged wife of an influential man. There were legal handicaps, of course, but the chief obstacles were the customs and social conventions of her time.

Theodora had to stubbornly seek out the relationship that she needed. Her mother's experience with Acacius first and with her stepfather later, the memory of their supplication in the Kynêgion, her marginal position with respect to the world of the "ladies"—all of this reminded her that she was in a precarious position, which only deteriorated with the passing of time. In Constantinople in the second decade of the sixth century A.D., a twenty-year-old girl was no longer young: she was not simply on the threshold of life, but already at midlife. It was so uncommon for an eighteen-year-old girl to be unmarried that people would comment: "She is still unwed."[16] One hagiography stressed the anomaly of a woman saint who was still unmarried at the age of twenty-four.[17] Theodora could not wait that long. Hence, she was obliged to go on stage and to have sexual relations. This might lead to undesired pregnancies, but it was the only avenue leading out of her state of slavery.

Consequently, Theodora was well versed in the contraceptive and abortive practices of her age ("she practiced infanticide time and again by voluntary abortions"). After the third month of pregnancy, when the fetus took on a human shape, abortion was no longer viable. It was censured by Procopius, a layman, as "repeated infanticide"; the Church treated it as a full-fledged homicide; and it was punished by both civil and canon law. The guilty woman was subject to exile, whipping, or excommunication. Even her accomplices were liable to be punished: the wizards and witches at the Hippodrome, for example, who might give Theodora and her coworkers not only generic astrological advice (she was curious about it) but also herb potions or other concoctions. Some women brought on abortions by placing a stone or heavy weight on their abdomens; others resorted to gory and horribly infectious archaic surgery.

Abortion was the dramatic, risky finale of a defense strategy wrapped up in superstition and witchcraft; it was common practice for women to consult the stars and horoscopes for contraceptive purposes. There were amulets to be worn on the left ankle in a tiny ivory tube, consisting, for example, of strips of a female cat's liver or fragments of a lioness's uterus. (One scholar notes dryly that, whether or not it was effective, the latter material was so scarce that it was surely the most difficult contraceptive.[18]) Among the popular contrivances that were thought to effectively block the sperm's journey toward the egg were herbs, pomades, suppositories, and, in particular, vaginal pessaries made of wool soaked in honey, olive oil, resin, alum, white lead, or other substances. Unlike modern contraceptives, so synthetic and aseptic, the contraceptives of Theodora's time had a primal, almost feral relationship with the elements.

We should not take Procopius's words literally when he writes that she was often pregnant and underwent repeated abortions; and we need not resort to modern sociology or demographics to recognize that Theodora was subjected to psychological and physical dangers. While not a prostitute in the technical sense of the word, she was exposed to all the risks of prostitution, and if she died before reaching fifty there may have been a link between her difficult early life and her untimely death. (She died early in comparison to the other women who preceded or followed her on the Roman throne of Constantinople: Ariadne, wife of Zeno and later of Anastasius, who died at the age of sixty-five; Lupicina-Euphemia, the wife of Justin I, who died at a ripe old age; and Sophia, Theodora's niece, who lived past seventy.)

Theodora's iron will, which allowed her to reach impossible goals, was housed in a body that needed fastidious care. So there must have been days when, if she blamed Mother Nature at all, it was certainly not because she wasn't endowed with larger breasts, but because she wasn't born a man.

"She Was at a Loss for the Necessities of Life"

Constantinople, Cyrenaica, the Levant, c. 518–21

> This is the period of life in which such moments of which I have
> spoken are likely to come. What moments? Why, the moments of
> boredom, of weariness, of dissatisfaction. Rash moments. I mean
> moments when the still young are inclined to commit rash actions,
> such as getting married suddenly.

T HESE WORDS are not Procopius's: they are the words of Joseph
Conrad (1857–1924).[1] The sailor without a ship in his novel
The Shadow Line (1902) is a very different character from our
brilliant and resolute mime actress of the second decade of the sixth
century A.D. And yet young Theodora also was aware that it was time
to transform herself again, leaving behind a place that weighed on her,
even though she lived in the greatest metropolis of late antiquity.

At the age of eighteen, life was no longer just a blank, like a tidy
ivory tablet ready to be engraved. Especially not for a mime actress.

Theodora's future depended on her talent, but it was not a question
of sheer survival. In this way she saw that her life was quite different
from that of her father, Acacius, or her mother. But just as her mother
had succeeded in overturning events with the Kynêgion supplication,
so too Theodora's lifeboat needed a firm hand to guide it into a safe
haven, a secure spot like the ones that respectable families had already
negotiated for their daughters of Theodora's age, for the virginal creatures beloved by conservatives. Where was her haven?

At this point, one figure emerged from the amorphous crowd of lovers and admirers. Until then, Procopius had described them generically, passing judgment on their morals (they were either perverted or "licentious"), their physique ("they were of exceptional bodily vigour"), or their number (they were "many," "all," "so many," they were all "who chanced to come along"), but now he moves on from these generic descriptions to an identification of the first—actually the only one—of Theodora's lovers of whom we have proof. In a passage invaluable for its concreteness, the *Secret History* reports: "Later she was following in the train of Hecebolus, a Tyrian, who had taken over the administration of Pentapolis, serving him in the most shameful capacity; but she gave some offense to the man and was driven thence with all speed; consequently it came about that she was at a loss for the necessities of life."[2]

Most historians agree that by 518 Theodora had gone to the northern coast of the African continent as part of Hecebolus's entourage. Biographers tend to see this journey as an exotic, sentimental interlude: a languid sea voyage under the stars, almost a hedonistic cruise. But they neglect other elements of the couple's relationship, which was the actress and courtesan Theodora's first major known union with a powerful man. And so it behooves us to look deeper into her affair with Hecebolus, not least because she used the lessons of that experience in her triumphant later union with the man who was to become the most powerful of the powerful, Justinian.

Hecebolus hailed from the great Mediterranean Levant, the ancient "Phoenician" city of Tyre (now Sur, Lebanon), which was at the time the capital and the ecclesiastical seat of the Roman province of Phoenice Maritima. For centuries, it had been the leading manufacturing center for the royal purple dye and purple garments that, against all expectations, Theodora would wear someday on the imperial throne. But the manufacture of high-quality goods was not Tyre's sole contribution to civilization: it was also famous for its entertainment. The most ancient fables were said to come from Tyre, and its inhabitants were reputed to be spellbinding—though not always reliable—storytellers. The city was known for its Hippodrome with Green and Blue teams, its amphitheaters, the excellence of its actors, and its numerous pleasure houses.

If the expression "quality of life" had existed then, Tyre would have been called one of the great quality-of-life cities; and Hecebolus most probably embodied its spirit.

Those who claim Syrian origins for Theodora interpret her relationship with Hecebolus the "Phoenician" as proof of an ethnic link. Some theorize that the couple spoke a sort of Aramaic language that was widely used in the Mediterranean Levant (spoken by about ten million people as a popular alternative to the official Latin and Greek). But the two met in Constantinople, where Greek was the predominant language, and they must have spoken Greek together; *Hecebolus* is a Greek term, an ancient appellation of the gods Apollo and Artemis.[3]

Ethnicity was not a factor in Hecebolus and Theodora becoming a couple. But the environment in which they met was certainly a factor; another was the set of goals that they shared; and the most important factor was Theodora's strong will. She had her reasons for choosing Hecebolus from among all her admirers and for stepping across her "shadow line" with him. They were united by different but complementary quests for advancement and promotion. Certainly, the young Theodora knew how to choose as she rose to power, just as her man, who aspired to rule a province of the empire, was careful about the circles he moved in—even though he might have had a taste for actresses and the variety shows that were major attractions in his hometown of Tyre. It is not unlikely that the two met through the Blue faction.

It has often been suggested that Hecebolus was a trader, but this is only one of many possibilities. Perhaps in Tyre he had a supervisory role in the imperial works that produced purple-dyed cloth, or other textile products, or glassware. Given the importance of Tyre as a port, he could also have been a local shipowner with strong ties to the capital: the Greek Mediterranean has always had shipping magnates, and they have always had splendid female companions (even in modern times). Or perhaps he came from high-ranking Hellenized circles in the provinces that had long been the backbone of society in the eastern part of the empire. In this case, he would probably have studied at the prestigious law school of Berytus (today's Beirut), a few miles north of Tyre, the same university that educated Procopius (whose hometown,

Caesarea, lay slightly south of Tyre along the coast). Later, Hecebolus would have traveled to Constantinople in search of powerful contacts that would help in his swift ascent to lofty positions and a successful government career.

Whatever his background, Hecebolus noticed Theodora: perhaps it happened at a dinner, or at the theater, or in both places. He must have sent tangible proof of his devotion, and she must have finally accepted it; they met; Hecebolus must have considered her unique, since he decided to take her with him to Pentapolis (or accepted her proposal to join him). His appointment as governor of the province probably came in exchange for a substantial bribe, in accordance with the customary practice of buying and selling public offices, part and parcel of the patronage system of the imperial administration.

At his side, Theodora could be no more than his concubine. She was probably officially introduced as an "escort," maybe even a "maid" in his retinue. This was the meaning of the "most shameful" services mentioned in the *Secret History*. Of course, in the capital an imperial governor could not marry a mime actress, no matter how widely she was celebrated as a new Helen of the civilized Christian world, and no matter how much others envied his sharing his free time and his bed with such a jewel.

It's not hard to understand how Theodora "won the heart" of Hecebolus, for everyone came under her spell. The opposite is what is important in this story: understanding why she chose to attach herself to him. The theater star of the capital left Constantinople, "Beacon of the Ecumene," for a remote province, in an ambiguous position, because she invested in Hecebolus with determination and resolve: she chose *him* over everyone else. And presumably it was not because he told funny stories about Tyre. Evidently Hecebolus looked like he could give her what she needed most, a safe haven for her ship.

Theodora's choice and her departure are important not just from the point of view of chronology or psychology. They must be seen anthropologically, insofar as they involve a radical change in the perspective of a woman who had already moved up from being a "troop" courtesan to being a selective "knight." Just as she had glimpsed a light at the end of the underground passageways of the Kynêgion, Theodora saw a light shining ahead in her life's corridor: the possibility of becoming a "lady." This is why she gave up all other certainties or attractive possibilities and followed Hecebolus.

Eager to succeed, she agreed to become a secondary figure in his retinue, but not because of an infatuation: she was quite lucid when she made her decision. By leaving the stage, by devoting herself to Hecebolus, and through his support, she believed that she would surely become wealthy, and then become his wife. Years later, she would be able to come back to the city purged of the labels of infamy and indignity, identified with other, more appropriate qualifications. She would definitely be a lady, the consort of a man who by that time would be important. To respect all the ancient laws and to keep up appearances, he could and would have to marry her before being allowed to reap the highest honors.

It must have seemed to her a masterpiece of cunning, a transformation worthy of Ulysses: to conquer the heart of the capital by traveling through the outermost edge of the provinces. Her shadow line went through Pentapolis.

As soft and enticing as her body was, and as flexible as her behavior was, her character was just as unyielding. She knew that her roots put her too far below the powerful people who counted in the city, where her reputation had been compromised. Therefore, the man who suited her plan could not be someone from Constantinople, although he also could not be a stranger to the city. Hecebolus was the perfect man for the job. Thanks to the bribe he had paid and the connections he had built, he was appointed governor of a province that was sufficiently rich (in wheat, olives, and fish) that he could expect to become even wealthier through a careful policy of tax collection and political networking. At the same time, Pentapolis was sufficiently distant from the capital for any of his abuses not to reach attentive ears too soon or too loudly. As for Theodora, she would accept a few years in the provinces as long as she could become a lady.

✛ ✛ ✛

The two lovers were not welcomed by the applause of a theater audience or by dinner guests reclining on triclinia. They were received only by the sands of the northern shores of Africa (today's eastern Libya). The province of Pentapolis had been carved from the vast former province of Cyrenaica, named for the ancient and illustrious city of Cyrene. It was the homeland of the Biblical Simon, who had shared the weight of the cross with Jesus, and later of Sinesius (c. 370–415), a neo-Platonist poet and authoritative Christian bishop who denied absolution to imperial authorities who abused civilians "in the name of the empire." For Hecebolus and Theodora, that act was an invitation to consider that the exercise of power is a grave matter.

Pentapolis was composed of "five cities" (*pente poleis*): Teuchira, Barka, Ptolemais, Boreium, and Apollonia. Apollonia, the capital, was about twenty days' journey from Alexandria, the only city that could compete with Constantinople as a cultural and ethnic melting pot of the Mediterranean, and the most efficient patriarchate of the Christian ecclesiastical organization. Alexandria was also the vital port that, each September, sent transport ships loaded with wheat—"the happy cargo"—toward Constantinople to bring food to the urban masses.

So while Pentapolis may not have been an actual place of exile, it was at least a frontier: it separated the urban fabric of the empire of the thousand cities[4] from the desolate desert, dividing the civilized Mediterranean basin of wheat fields, vineyards, and olive orchards from the barbarian wilds of the hinterland, source of frequent armed raids by troglodytic tribes such as the "Mauri." What's more, Pentapolis was close to the kingdom of the Arian Vandals who, after sacking Rome in 455, used the most formidable fleet in the Mediterranean to conquer all of northwest Africa.

Around the year 518, when Hecebolus and Theodora were in Pentapolis, the empire's provinces were administered by separate civilian and military authorities. The highest local military chief[5] was charged in particular with providing safe operating planning and a regular supply of food and weapons to the troops strung along the increasingly fortified defenses built to repel raids by the hinterland nomads. Governor Hecebolus, on the other hand, was the chief civilian administrator in charge of justice and tax collection, aided by a large corps of assistants and technicians. It was an office in which he could potentially rake in a lot of local wealth, provided he did not cross paths with any new Sinesius—any churchman who defended the weak. Luckily for Hecebolus, the proximity to the patriarchal see of Alexandria meant that the local clergy was pro-Monophysite—they recognized only one, divine nature for Christ. And the most Monophysite emperor of all time was Anastasius, who must have approved Hecebolus's appointment as provincial governor. The appointee had probably paid personal homage to the ruler before taking office. On that occasion, the emperor, who had a policy of moderation, might have advised him to avoid extreme behavior. Perhaps Hecebolus, in recounting the meeting to Theodora, further embellished the already extraordinary seductions of the court. It was no accident if he was a master storyteller—after all, he had been born in Tyre.

It's unlikely that Theodora found Apollonia, the capital of Pentapolis, particularly seductive. It was hardly the destination of an ideal journey, such as the rare excursions made in late antiquity by noblewomen such as Athenais-Eudocia (c. 400–460), the learned wife of Emperor Theodosius II, or Egeria (Etheria), author of an enchanting *Itinerarium* (Travels). Protected by their names and their prestige, they had gone to the illustrious Christian sites of the Holy Land and brought even greater dignity to their souls by following the very footprints of the Savior in Bethlehem, Nazareth, and Jerusalem. Theodora, however, daughter of the Hippodrome and the Kynêgion, had left the city for the homeland of the Cyrenian, not of the Savior. And if Hecebolus was a savior for her, he was so only on a very private—not universal—level. He brought not the Gospel of love, but earthly authority over the subjects of his province.

Recent archaeological excavations in Apollonia, in particular of the mansion known as the Palace of the Dux or leader[6] (a dwelling somewhat similar to the Arab-Mediterranean houses known as *dar*), give us some clue as to what might have been the home of Hecebolus and his concubine, Theodora. It was a stone structure built to offer shelter from the scorching summer sun, with diminutive windows overlooking the street and rooms carved out of stone like small caves. The rooms ran directly into one another without any concessions to our modern notion of privacy: no passageways skirted around the chambers. Clearly very few rooms in the palace afforded any privacy: perhaps there was a chapel for Christian worship, or a room with erotic frescoes (such as those in Pompeii) used by Hecebolus and Theodora when they wanted to be alone. One important attraction of the house was undoubtedly the large peristyle with dancing fountains and small cages holding animals such as turtles, peacocks, or migrating cranes captured in the winter as they came to the marshes of Pentapolis. Perhaps Theodora, sitting in the garden, likened herself to the migrating cranes.

She must have listened closely when Hecebolus spoke. She knew that some men enjoyed listing their numerous weighty tasks with their attendant duties and problems. She also knew how to steer these men toward different pleasures than the contemplation of their success. But this was not just any passing fellow: she gave Hecebolus her very special attention as he talked. He probably told her about his plans for becoming wealthy. Told her his ideas for speculating on the tax money collected in the province, and the actual amount he would deposit in the imperial treasury. Told her about how he settled trials. Told her his tactics for cautiously drawing in, and then paying off, the most influential local landowners, whose consent and assistance he needed in order to control the territory. Told her about his approaching the upper clergy (which was linked to the large landowners by close family or business ties), for the marriage that was to crown their journey to Pentapolis could happen only with proper support and assistance. Only then could they return to the capital, transformed and richer than before.

In the meantime, they were going to enjoy their privileges.

But events took a different turn. Reductionist readers of Theodora's life have theorized that in Pentapolis she suffered from sexual boredom or frustration. Her exclusive relationship with Hecebolus might have had unexpected or unpleasant consequences for her. But maybe the problem wasn't sexual. She had attached herself to him like one of the suppliants or refugees who, clinging to church altars, had the right to asylum and could be removed neither by canon nor by civil law. But she discovered that in Pentapolis the powerful Hecebolus alone had rights. He had rights over property, over time, over people—even over her. And as time went by, it was becoming more and more difficult to get him to make good on his promises.

Soon, Theodora found her confinement in Apollonia weighing on her. She had not forgotten what she had left behind in the city. Hecebolus demanded that she be isolated as "proper" women were, and she had neither the rich cultural resources nor a network of acquaintances with which she might transform her semiexile into a scintillating extended vacation filled with reading or with intense epistolary exchanges. She missed the world of the theater. She would have endured all of this, however, if only Hecebolus had respected the commitment he had made to her. But he was delaying and finding various pretexts for postponing.

She must have found the idea and the reality of being totally dependent on this man unacceptable. She, like the cranes in her peristyle, was in a cage. She probably used her body to sway him, alternately seducing and rebuffing him. Then she may have started to think and speak more frankly, first with gibes and then with increasingly blunt and harsh judgments. Most likely, she finally began to mock him openly. She reproached him for being indecisive about taking the one step that he owed to her alone, though he did not hesitate to abuse an entire population in the collection of taxes or the settlement of trials. Maybe she derided him in the privacy of their frescoed room, simulating the type of farces that she used to play before city audiences, the same shows that Hecebolus had enjoyed so much in the early days of their affair. Perhaps she threatened to perform them before their friends and the powerful people he cared about so much, or in front of priests, from whom he kept her hidden in the seclusion of their home.

An actress without a stage in Apollonia, she claimed the daring "freedom of speech before the powerful" that the ancient Greeks had granted to philosophers alone,[7] (men such as Diogenes the Cynic, who asked the great Alexander of Macedonia to move aside because he was shading him). Christianity had extended the same right to monks, who had recently evolved from philosophers, but not to a woman, and never—of course—to an actress. And yet this infamous woman took liberties with a powerful man, a high magistrate—liberties that not even a lady was allowed.

It was easy for Hecebolus, once "offended," to put his dignity as a mighty official before the body, the face, the lips of Theodora. He summoned up his full honor as Roman citizen against his defenseless concubine, and he drove her away. Soon the name Theodora would elicit no more curiosity in Apollonia: Theodora who?

It was, for Theodora, the most unexpected of situations, the most impossible of developments. And yet the archaic logic of reversal would reward her courage, just as it had rewarded her suppliant mother in the Kynêgion. From her failure in Pentapolis, from the failure of a relationship in which she had placed so much faith—just as her mother had placed her hopes in the Green faction—she set off on the path that would lead her to a metamorphosis even more momentous than the one she had originally set out to achieve. In effect, this was the beginning of the unpredictable chain of events that in less than a decade would bring her to the throne.

The young woman was cast out on the northern shores of an unfamiliar continent that was not her home. And yet her unlikely destiny stretched invisibly before her: a return home to an imperial future.

Theodora and Hecebolus would probably not appear in the annals of history had their relationship continued, had she been willing to accept the situation, had Eros prevailed over Hecebolus's smugness about his office and his career. After a few years of farsighted decisions in distant Pentapolis, the couple would have returned as husband and wife—laden with gold, older and heavier, maybe even with children—and taken up residence in an attractive mansion in Constantinople, ready for new imperial appointments. They would have enjoyed their wealth and, by their success, confirmed that imperial functionaries in the provinces deserved the poor reputation that they had. They would have merited a footnote, perhaps, or maybe nothing at all.

Africa. Pentapolis. Apollonia. The governor's palace. Theodora is cast out. The *Secret History* reports that Hecebolus left her "at a loss for the necessities of life," though in another passage of the same text is an apparent contradiction: Theodora, returning from Africa, "was very distressed and vexed . . . because she had lost some money on that journey."[8] Hecebolus probably offered no financial help when he banished Theodora, so as she set off she could count only on her own strength and on that part of her assets that she had brought with her.

Theodora's financial autonomy was stronger than her legal standing. She did own property, and she controlled the money, clothes, and jewels that had not already been sold or transferred to maintain the child left behind in the city. She never expected that she would need that money in Pentapolis, but money was not what she was most sure of in this unexpected new beginning. The one thing she must have known beyond any doubt was that she had to return to the city. Her mother, too, after Acacius's death, had not thought of retiring, but had plodded on. She would do the same. Back to Constantinople. Back, alone.

She probably did not reproach herself for the free spirit and the free words that had caused her banishment. Her unwise calculation had come at the beginning of the affair. Her plan had been reckless because there was no legal parity between her status and his, and because she was in a foreign land. She would not let this happen again.

Therefore, it was imperative that she return to her own land, to her friendly city. She knew that she was not a Homeric hero returning home with the honors of a victorious war.[9] And yet her journey back to Constantinople was just as slow as Ulysses': it might have taken her about three years, with major pauses and setbacks. Theodora traveled thousands of miles, crossing all of the eastern Mediterranean: Africa, Egypt, Palestine, Syria, the whole of Anatolia. She finally reached the capital after having seen much, like Ulysses, and heard much in Greek and Latin and in Coptic and Aramaic, the dialects of Egypt and the Levant.

The sophisticated Greek language of the people considered cultivated and well bred must have seemed to her delightful but fragile and superficial. It was a language eminently suited to the ancient, illustrious cities, connected as they were by a network of imperial roads, with their marble palaces lining wide boulevards, while under shadowed porticoes merchants displayed wares that came from territories both civilized and barbaric. But around the cities was a vast, archaic world where everyday life was not refined, a world that appeared to her naked and defenseless. These were the villages of the imperial Levant, built of stone or clay, unprotected by city walls (the result of people's worldly experience and skill). Their only protection was a church promising Christian redemption in the next world. In this arid world below, the only tangible blessing was a stream, a pond, or a well. So she saw more of the empire than any other woman of her time, even more than most eminent men. She saw its people, their homes and their workplaces, their pastimes, their daily lives, their hopes for immortality. Hundreds of years had elapsed since those unforgettable emperors who were famous partly for their talent as travelers. Trajan, Hadrian, and Marcus Aurelius visited the cities of their empire and were welcomed joyfully with elaborate processions and ceremonies. But for more than a century now the emperors of Constantinople had lived like recluses in the palace, their city within the city, a sacred enclosure of almost twenty-five acres running down a gentle slope on the city's European shore. From that faraway seat, like a modern command center, they followed the events of their empire.

Proud and perhaps dismayed by the difference between her current life and the path traced by most other men and women, the repudiated actress headed back to her roots. She was open to what she saw: she was not trying to confirm any preconceptions, unlike the merchant Cosmas, a contemporary traveler who was celebrated in literature.[10] He traveled by ship, perhaps even as far as the Indies, and wrote about his interpretation of the world as an image of the Biblical Ark of the Covenant between God and Israel. In his remarkable imaginary geography, the Earth was a perfect rectangle with enormous winches on each side. Cosmas believed that the winches were used to support the double heaven that arched over the Earth, like the chest (or perhaps the cosmic roof) of the Holy Ark.

Theodora was less like her contemporary, Cosmas, and closer to the founder of Greek historical thought, Herodotus of Halicarnassus, even though he had lived a thousand years before her and she most probably did not know his name. Theodora was a traveler in the great ancient Mediterranean tradition of *autopsia*, the "seeing for oneself" that Herodotus had first identified.[11] (This was supplanted by the medieval tradition of *auctoritas*, where instead of actually seeing for yourself, you surrendered your judgment to an established "higher" voice.) Both now and later, on her throne, Theodora needed to see something only once with her intent gaze: seeing was knowing.[12]

How *did* Theodora complete her journey and get back to Constantinople? There is something miraculous in the fact that she returned at all, instead of vanishing. It was a journey of thousands of miles that required substantial assets and extremely good health. In Procopius's contemptuous view, it was simple:

> she proceeded to provide in her usual way, putting her body to work at its unlawful traffic. She first went to Alexandria; later, after making the round of the whole East, she made her way back to Byzantium, plying her trade in each city (a trade which men could not call by name, I think, without forfeiting forever the compassion of God), as if the devil could not bear that any spot should be unacquainted with the wantonness of Theodora.[13]

The reference to God, and especially to the devil, is a rhetorical intensifier, a repetition of the "demonic" element that, according to Procopius, Justinian shared with Theodora. But although the corrosive historian made short work of her journey, here at the end of his section on Theodora's "nurture and education" he leaves historians with many unanswered questions, because the journey back to the capital thoroughly transformed her.

SEVEN

"The Pious . . . the Saintly . . . the Devout"

Alexandria, the Levant, Constantinople, c. 518–521

STUNNED BY THEODORA'S epic return to Constantinople, most biographers reach for simplistic stereotypes. Her miraculous journey drove historians toward outlandish fantasies that seem to be influenced by modern fairy tales. What these biographers have neglected, however, is the context: the actual chronology, to start with, and even the evidence of written sources. The "sources" are plural now, for at this point in Theodora's life Procopius's critical *Secret History* no longer stands alone: now it is complemented by other reports, some with a different orientation, in texts that have a different origin and purpose from the *Secret History* and that were written in languages other than Greek.

These texts are chronicles and religious histories written by authors who, although they shared some of Procopius's classical cultural heritage, and although they were subjects of the same Roman and Christian empire, chose to write in Syriac rather than in the Greek used in the *Secret History* and other choice literary works of the period. More often than not, Syriac translations were the only surviving versions of many texts originally written in Greek and later lost.

The so-called Syrian authors had attended similar schools, had similar careers, and might even have been collaborators or interlocutors of Procopius and of the other "pundits" of the time. They shared one belief that, crucially, kept their works from being passed down by medieval scholars, the Orthodox-Catholic Byzantines who worked in the Greek language. These authors shared a belief in Monophysitism, the doctrine about the nature of Christ that had been banned as a heresy at the Fourth Ecumenical Council of Chalcedon, held in 451. Monophysitism was still the great unresolved religious and political issue on the Mediterranean stage, especially in the eastern part that was so vital to the Christian Roman Empire of Constantinople for both economic and military reasons.

In terms of political weight and influence both theological and cultural, Monophysitism was even more relevant than the Arian creed denying that Jesus was fully divine, which was embraced by the rulers of the Mediterranean West, the "barbarian" Roman kings (only some of whom were considered legitimate by the empire of the second Rome). The Monophysite dispute persisted from the middle of the fifth century through the middle of the seventh century in various forms, with a number of reversals, negotiations, victories, and defeats for each side, until new issues arose with the emergence of Islam (which the Christian theologians initially interpreted not as a new creed but as a heresy).

Not coincidentally, the Arab-Islamic expansion into the empire was particularly successful in those areas where Christian Monophysitism prevailed, such as Egypt and Syria. In fact, belief in that doctrine—in defiance of imperial and Roman orthodoxy, and even directly opposed to it—was a powerful feature of "national" as well as religious identity in the region, a response to the Roman empire that sought unity and uniformity above all else. Once Islam replaced Christianity as the ruling local belief, one could practice Monophysitism almost undisturbed in the melting pot regulated by the *pax islamica*.

Thus, while Procopius vilified the former actress in Greek, Syriac texts produced by Monophysite authors[1]—either translated from the Greek or written originally in Syriac—present a spiritual world in which Theodora is celebrated as the "pious," the "saintly," the "devout" empress. Her piety, saintliness, and devotion—her Christian example— were linked both to her influence on the development of Monophysitism and to her journey throughout the Mediterranean, that very same journey that the *Secret History* interpreted as an unbridled exhibition of diabolical lust stretching from Alexandria to Constantinople. Are these contradictory sources irreconcilable? Perhaps not.

✛ ✛ ✛

Banished by Hecebolus in foreign Apollonia, thrown to the bottom of the social hierarchy, without any legal protection, Theodora could count only on her youth and on some of her possessions. She was a total outcast, without nearby family or compatriots, in a time when patronage based on familial or regional roots was all-powerful. (In those same years, in the imperial palace, a certain cultivated John achieved great success. A native of Philadelphia in Anatolian Lydia, he would not have had such a brilliant career without help from the prefect Zoticus, to whom a relative had introduced him. United by ambition and by merit, the three of them were bound especially by their common roots in Anatolia.)

For Theodora, aid and solidarity came from a different source, primarily from the "public-welfare ministry" run by the Church, perhaps in Apollonia, the seat of an important basilica, or maybe in nearby Cyrene. Theodora might have heard Hecebolus mention the name of the bishop or of other prelates or clerics. She might have turned to them, maybe pleading for the right of asylum at the altar, as a suppliant. Any supplication had to be considered seriously, although there might have been some understandable embarrassment about her appeal. The Church elites were close to the political elites, personified here by Hecebolus, the highest local authority, who had driven Theodora out. And Theodora's past surely did not match the paradigms of moral— specifically Christian—virtue that prevailed in late antiquity. Therefore, she was probably asked for exact words and concrete proofs of repentance and reform before her supplication could be taken into consideration. On the other hand, Theodora's request was probably a simple one: she needed support and protection so that she could at least reach Alexandria, about three weeks' journey away. There in the great Egyptian metropolis, she would try to connect with the city's Blue faction, relying on the intercity network of factional solidarity.

Theodora seems to have passed the test of repentance that might have been required of her, and we have no reason to believe that her performance was only opportunistic play-acting. Although her life in the world of show business and the Hippodrome had introduced her to astrological and magical doctrines, these were only superficial notions that had never become an alternative belief system contrary to her faith in Jesus Christ. She had grown up in that faith, as her very name testified. When she needed help, she turned to the Church.

Evidently, the prelate who had the responsibility of verifying her sincerity found nothing "pagan" in her. She was neither a "Jew" nor a "Manichean." He must have accepted her profession of faith in the tri-une Christian God of Father, Son, and Holy Spirit: one God in three persons, equal and distinct, in accordance with the dogmas of the early ecumenical councils of the Church that had rejected the Arian doctrine. Theodora furthermore accepted the orthodoxy (literally, "correct faith" in Greek) that the Virgin Mary be called Theotokos, "Mother of God," and not Christotokos, "Mother of Christ." (Nestorius, an Antioch theologian of the fifth century and later patriarch of Constantinople, had favored "Mother of Christ" and was condemned by the fathers of the Holy Church at the Third Ecumenical Council held in Ephesus in 431.)

Maybe the prelate asked for more. Maybe he specifically questioned her about Christ, who had been resurrected to declare the New Covenant, and therefore was truly God. At the same time, He had died on the cross as a man and so He was truly a man. And yet He was worshipped in the Trinity as one person only. How many natures could one person have? One, or more than one?

It is possible that Theodora did not reply right away. She had probably heard arguments on the subject in Constantinople. She probably intuited that the question might be difficult for her, and she probably solved the dilemma by asking her interlocutor for enlightenment. He must have introduced her to the subject of the dual nature of Christ, which had been the object of the Fourth Ecumenical Council, held in 451 in Chalcedon, on the Asiatic shores of the Bosphorus. The council had condemned the doctrine of the monk Euthyches, the first to launch the theory of Monophysitism (from the Greek *mone*, "one," and *physis*, "nature").

For Euthyches and his followers, Christ had only one nature: He was divine. He had appeared on Earth as a man, had died on the cross, and had been resurrected for humanity, but he was not consubstantial with humanity. He had a divine nature, with unique attributes, which had absorbed whatever seemed human about Him. The prelate must have acknowledged that Euthyches had radical ideas. It might seem as if he was denying the true humanity of Christ, just as Arius (founder of the Arian creed) and then Nestorius had denied or at least minimized His divinity. But what about the Council of Chalcedon's position? Perhaps the council had bent too easily before the bishop of Rome, proclaiming that Christ—*one* person in the Trinity—had *two* natures at once, human and divine, each distinct from the other, and yet each perfect as well as indivisible. That, according to the prelate, was Dyophysitism (from the Greek *dyo*, "two," and *physis*, "nature").

Defending these tenets seemed difficult, especially for those who relied on the ancient patriarchal cathedral of Alexandria where the revered patriarch Cyril had declared, "There is only one nature, from two, in God, the Incarnated Logos."[2] He did not subtract any of Christ's humanity, but he allowed for no separations within that nature.

The prelate must have recalled that Mark the Evangelist, one of Christ's apostles, had brought the Gospel to Alexandria. It was scandalous that the Second Ecumenical Council of 381 had demoted such an ancient apostolic see to being the subject of Constantinople, the new imperial capital and the birthplace of the suppliant who stood before him. He also found it abhorrent that Dyophysitism had prevailed in Chalcedon, for it posed a danger to Church unity and consensus among the patriarchates. He may have added that believers such as Theodora worshipped Christ because He was divine and resurrected, certainly not because He was human and crucified. This is why many regarded the see of Alexandria as the highest ecclesiastical authority, the stronghold of faith. (This was especially true in Egypt, among those faithful who knew little Greek or none at all.)

The broad spread of Dyophysitism was linked to the (possibly hopeless) dream of a perfect alignment between the second Rome of Constantinople and the first Rome of Italy. But the bishops of Rome were subject both to the kings of Italy, who were Arian heretics, and to the emperors of Constantinople. And yet the patriarch of Alexandria, direct heir of Mark the Evangelist, could rightfully be called "pope," just like the Roman heir sitting in Peter's chair. In addition, the see of Alexandria spoke to its faithful not only in Greek but also in Coptic, the local Egyptian tongue. This brought Alexandria honor, but it brought dishonor to the Church, for the Church's truth is to be found in unity, the prelate might have continued. "Let not man put asunder,"[3] he might have admonished, citing the Gospel.

His speech had by now become a monologue. He recalled the "pious" departed emperors in Constantinople, such as Zeno and Anastasius. Zeno had published the *Edict of the Union* in 482, wherein he accepted the Trinity as defined by the first three ecumenical councils, and confirmed the condemnation of Nestorius. He had declared that Christ was perfectly human and perfectly divine, without mentioning the Council of Chalcedon and the subject of the two "natures." And yet he had not won out. On the contrary, the Church had been torn asunder. The current situation and the prospects for the future were all in God's hands. It behooved them, the prelate said, to offer God their suffering and their witness.

Theodora must have followed the arguments, asking questions, asking to know more. Her mind, once used to the rapid-fire conflicts and plot reversals of the theater, might have lost its suppleness during the dreamy time spent with Hecebolus. She was probably now awakening to a wholly theological exercise. The prelate might have told her that in order to deepen her ideas and turn them into knowledge, she needed to go to Alexandria, the see of the patriarchate, and consult with learned men who could enlighten her. But he might have concluded with a reminder that Christianity was always a matter of faith and of charity above all, not only or not chiefly a matter of dogma.

While as a child in Constantinople Theodora had received a generic water baptism into the Christian faith, this meeting abroad, during her early maturity, marked her verbal baptism in theology. Throughout her life theology would comfort and encourage her.

The suppliant was thus most likely sent, duly covered in a black habit and wimple, with a group of prelates who were going to a synod in Alexandria. Her worldly apparel and jewels were hidden in a bag. The cart must have followed an ancient route along the North African coast, protected from the threatening inland Berber tribes. They must have stopped at church buildings and military garrisons, for it was unbecoming for prelates to sleep at inns. During this journey, Theodora's behavior was no doubt exemplary. She must have slept or listened quietly, or even tried to join the choir of prelates who were singing the *Trisagion*, the "thrice holy" hymn:

> Holy is God
> Holy and strong
> Holy and immortal
> God crucified for us

She might not have known the fourth line before this journey, proof, she was perhaps told, of her youth and the fact that she had always given little thought to religion. The fourth line—a recent Monophysite addition made during the reign of Anastasius, one of the "pious departed emperors"—had been opposed by the Dyophysite monks of the capital around the year 512. In due time, she would understand why. In the meantime, the epithet "departed" confirmed her suspicion that the emperor was no longer alive. Increasingly attentive, Theodora most likely attended every religious function, trying to grasp the meaning of formulas that she had once known only by rote, and memorizing other formulas for the first time. She might have carried with her a letter of introduction to a convent in Alexandria, asking the nuns to welcome her and give her assistance.

In the caustic prose of the *Secret History*, Alexandria was only one of the many stops along Theodora's wanton and inflammatory journey through the Levant. We know, however, that it was *the* all-important stop. We do not know how long she stayed in that city, but we do know that it had a lasting effect on her life and, in the longer term, on the development of Christianity on three continents.

Instead of hurrying to sail from the Egyptian metropolis on the first ship heading for the capital, Theodora chose to deepen the experience that the city offered her. Through the Church and other religious channels she was able to approach the two highest Monophysite authorities who lived in Alexandria, the theologian Severus and the patriarch Timothy.

Severus had been born in the city of Pisidia, now in southern Turkey, to a leading Christian family; he was a vastly learned scholar and a monk of exceptional character. In 512, when he was almost fifty, the pro-Monophysite emperor Anastasius had appointed him patriarch of the third metropolis of the empire, Antioch. It was a very lofty position in the Christian hierarchy.

In Antioch, Severus was very active theologically, doing work heavy with political implications. He dogmatically defended the doctrine of the *Edict of the Union,* considering it a tool for the possible reconciliation of Christians. On the one hand he derided Nestorius's position minimizing the divinity of Christ, but he also attacked the writings of Euthyches, the historical leader of radical Monophysitism. He used his talent as a brilliant polemicist—he was skilled with classical rhetorical forms—to argue with the positions of practicing pro-Chalcedonians. He stripped Monophysitism of the extremist positions that might have troubled the unity of the Church that he sought (provided it was on *his* terms).

He also attacked a fellow Monophysite, Julian, bishop of Halicarnassus (now Bodrum in Turkey). Severus had called him and his followers "phantasiastae" (visionaries) because they did not attribute a real human body to the Incarnated Christ, claiming instead that Christ's body was specifically divine and that it succumbed to human passion, weakness, and suffering only as a result of an ongoing miracle. This position seemed particularly weak to Severus's stringent mind, for it denied Christ's humanity. To him, this error was the diametric opposite of the equally wrong ideas of Nestorius and Arius, who were fundamentally opposed to Christ's divinity.

Severus the Monophysite fully accepted the humanity of Christ, the topic that aroused so many disputes. He accepted it as long as that humanity was not reduced to one, specifically human, nature. His sophisticated philosophical studies made him unable to accept that a *person* and a divine one at that, could have more than one *nature*. To preach that Christ had two natures—as had Leo the Great, the Roman pope from 440 to 461, and the Council of Chalcedon—would mean embracing the abhorred Nestorian heresy. Therefore, the Dyophysites, from the Roman see and the pope on down, were all heretics and were anathema.

Severus was a virtuoso of theology who used all his great learning in Greek philosophy, but his Eastern followers did not think at his level of elegance. One of the leading clerics under him was the bishop of Bambyx, a city strategically located along the road between Antioch and Mesopotamia in northern Syria. This bishop was sometimes known by a Greek name, Philoxenos, but he claimed not to know Greek even though he held such a powerful position in the empire.

Subject to these ecclesiastical authorities were even less cultivated monks who represented and defended Christianity in the lands between Antioch and the Euphrates. They tended to radicalize every complex theological issue in terms that sound strangely familiar to our modern ears: theirs was the true faith, against the diabolical heresy of others— especially in Rome but also in Constantinople, since both the patriarch and the emperor were moving toward Dyophysitism. Clearly, the situation was ripe for a "nationalistic" turn of events, similar to what was happening in Egypt.

A rapprochement between Monophysites and Dyophysites seemed politically unlikely, even impossible, but Severus, with his full faith in the humanity of Christ, could have been the man to lay the theoretical and cultural foundations for it. (Indeed, scholars stress that he had many substantial points in common with Roman orthodoxy: they refer to his Monophysitism as being merely "verbal.") And yet the slightest verbal or theoretical nuance was enough to spark relentless civilian conflicts, such as the one in 513–15 that brought General Vitalian right up to the gates of Emperor Anastasius's capital.

One stormy night in July 518, a few years after Anastasius repulsed Vitalian, the emperor died. The new emperor, Justin, was a military man from Illyricum, a Roman province in the Balkans, and was there- fore a subject of the papal Church of Rome. After thirty-five years of schism, he immediately sought a reconciliation with Rome, to the detriment of Monophysites such as Severus. Vitalian asked Justin for the head of Severus, and the theologian was deposed in September 518. Under the benevolent protection of Timothy, who had been patriarch of Alexandria since 517, Severus settled in a suburb of that city, which he chose partly because he had studied there as a young man and partly because it was the historical cradle of Monophysitism. Any imperial move against him would have led to riots, maybe even endangered Constantinople's vital annual shipment of wheat from Alexandria. The capital needed the grain, as did the new emperor. Even as he lost the patriarchal throne, Severus kept his theological head and continued to write (for scholars and for the learned clergy) and give lectures interpreting the scriptures or—drawing even larger crowds—confuting his theological opponents. He lectured in lavish mansions that served as cultural centers, or at convents and monasteries. The lectures were always attended by women, and Theodora, who had once been a theatrical star, might have now become an audience member, absorbing and approving of the theology. It is easy to picture Severus's audience; they must have shared the alert and solemn look of the touching faces that still gaze at us from the vibrant Fayyum funerary portraits.

Thus the traveling former actress and the great deposed theologian crossed paths in Alexandria. But Severus was not the only star that shone for Theodora. Her other lodestar, as noted before, was Timothy, patriarch of Alexandria since 517, practically a local pope. Although he reported hierarchically to Rome and Constantinople, he was already the highest religious authority in the region, with a large following in Egypt among the Copts,[4] who had split from the assembly of Christians because they believed that Christ had only one nature. (The split might also have been based partly on the ancient idea that Egyptians were "different," though the difference was not clearly defined.) Timothy's position was most delicate, and he was the most appropriate person to fill it.

He may not have had Severus's theological subtlety (or he may not have had the leisure to develop it), but he had great pastoral qualities and an innate authority over his difficult, unruly flock. Although he remained a Monophysite and widened his "national"—specifically Copt—grassroots support, he was enough of a politician to maintain contact with the other Latin- and Greek-language patriarchs in Rome, Constantinople, Antioch, and Jerusalem. He was also an exceptional administrator who could manage the era's most complex structure of urban welfare: an army of thousands of men and women devoted to caring for the sick and assisting the needy. But Timothy did not wish to be seen as a Christianized version of a public health secretary. In his dialogues with Severus, he dealt with the fine points of deep dogmatic mysteries. And he also had other interests, outside of the city.

He paid frequent visits to the Egyptian desert beyond the Valley of the Nile, which in the third century A.D. gave birth to Anchoritism, one of the most extraordinary of Christian phenomena. The anchorites (from the Greek *anachôrêsis*, literally "flight from society") were hermits, all originally Egyptian; the first of them, Antony (250–356), had believed that Christianity was incompatible with civil life. After him, "a lonely multitude" had opted for a life eating berries and roots in the desert, hiding in tombs, or even buried in the sand, offering themselves up in a direct, almost savage way to the fire of divine love. The text of the life of Antony is attributed to the Alexandrite patriarch of the time, Saint Athanasius, which indicates the link between such radical asceticism and the structured, institutional Church of Alexandria; indeed, the two enjoyed a long tradition of complicity and solidarity, a counterpoint to the power of the Roman state that was perceived as oppressive, greedy, arrogant, and distant.

Timothy and his circle visited the hermits, prayed with them, and gave them the Sacrament. Although they were "laymen"—or perhaps precisely because they were laymen: they were the humblest of the humble, without even the pride that a priestly habit encourages—the monks were believed to be the most perfect mediators between man and God. Their visions, their prophecies, and their words were law. And though they neglected what we call hygiene, the old texts say that they always gave off the sweet scent of Paradise.

✛ ✛ ✛

For Theodora, Severus and Timothy made Alexandria into a city where anything was possible. Saint Mary the Egyptian had lived there: after working as a prostitute for seventeen years, she had spent the same number of years in total solitude in the desert, in a state of indomitable ascetic ardor. As she was dying, a lion had meekly left his lair to offer her an eternal resting place. Alexandria really was a transformative place.

In this city of over half a million inhabitants, the immense daily work of the patriarchate ranged from cultural activities to concrete assistance to the needy, under the protective shield of the faith-healing monks of the desert. This effort had to be maintained and defended, not only against Rome or against the new Dyophysite throne of Constantinople, but against self-inflicted deterioration as well. While Severus admonished the "phantasiastae" strictly, a new kind of Monophysites, the Agnoetes, arose. They believed that Christ's having been human meant that he had also experienced ignorance (*agnoia* in Greek) about many things, including the future. Timothy's task was to reestablish the truth.

Theodora was neither a theologian nor a philosopher. She was not a new Hypatia, the laywoman martyred by Christian fanatics, and maybe she could not fully grasp the subtle disquisitions of the two theological luminaries of Alexandria. But Monophysitism had a special meaning for her, for she owed a lot to her body. She could not be unaffected by the theological perspective of a body (Christ's) completely redeemed by Monophysitism as divine, without abstract distinctions that might limit or undermine the experience of the faithful. She was profoundly moved by the gravity of figures such as Severus and Timothy, especially in juxtaposition to her memory of Hecebolus. How could the new emperor of Constantinople persecute or banish them?

These elements—some conceptual in nature, most of them personal—figure into what some have interpreted as Theodora's religious "conversion" in Alexandria, which was primarily an inner revelation, a personal experience even more than a conviction or the acceptance of a dogma. She was seeking salvation for herself and, at the same time, she felt loyal to these admirable men. Nor did she change her view once she ascended the imperial throne. She always believed that Timothy was her own spiritual father, the one who knew how to touch her heart, and that Severus was the light of theology, the beacon flashing into the darkness of ignorance.

There was nothing scandalous about the former actress frequenting and maybe even getting close to these religious luminaries. We should not see her interior revelation as insincere, nor imagine that her presence made these men act intemperately. On the contrary, the strength of the early Church was shown especially by such unexpected encounters, such apparent contradictions, such impossible bets on an ecumenical scale—such as the beginning of the seventh eon demanded.

(Theodora had a conversion, a revelation, and even an initiation into an illustrious group. Although the cultural, multiethnic crucible of Alexandria was not the Egypt of the deep hinterland, thanks to Alexandria and the champions of Monophysitism Theodora joined the list of those who, in legend or in fact, were transformed by Egypt, the land they recognized as the mother lode of wisdom: Homer, Pythagoras, Herodotus, Alexander the Great, even Julius Caesar, and now Theodora, a woman, who took the final spot, at the end of antiquity.)

Theodora was forever grateful to Alexandria, but she did not settle there. She did not take the monastic veil, nor did she retire to the arid desert, which, like an ocean bursting with blessings, beckoned to so many men and women. Among them there may have been a Caesaria, a woman from Emperor Anastasius's family; it has been conjectured that Theodora met her here, and that their encounters were later useful to Theodora in Constantinople.

Like her widowed mother, who had been presented with similar opportunities to flee from society, Theodora remained faithful to her nature and chose not to retire. Eventually, she began to arrange to return to her native city. Because the new emperor in Constantinople had eliminated the Monophysite structure in the other patriarchal sees and bishoprics, it was difficult for Timothy and Severus and their circle to help Theodora with any more than a blessing and a little money. In practical and logistical terms, Alexandria and Egypt had become Monophysite islands in a Dyophysite sea.

Besides, in Alexandria Theodora had been able to renew her connections with the Blue faction. They had saved her once, long ago, in the Kynêgion of Constantinople. They had supported her career as an actress in that city. And they were also active in Alexandria, where they organized theater shows and performances and kept in touch with their correspondents in the other cities of the Levant that were rife with public baths, hippodromes, and circuses (the signs of Roman colonial power, sites offering entertainment to anyone worn out by exhausting theological debates). One particular stronghold of the Blues was the pleasure-loving city of Antioch, the magnet of the entertainment industry of late antiquity.

The *Secret History* offers us a glimpse of this reality in a passage that describes Theodora's meeting with a dancer named Macedonia, who had gained "great influence"[5] with the Blues of Antioch. She had become a privileged informer for the palace. The fact that Macedonia went to "greet Theodora as she came from Egypt"[6] confirms that the faction had built intercity assistance and support networks. The fact that Theodora kept up her contacts with the Blues hints at a different, perhaps more correct, interpretation of Procopius's words about the "trade" that Theodora plied during her "infamous" return trip. She must have worked as an actress, and this was again interpreted caustically by our denigrator, who identified actresses with courtesans. But the time spent in Alexandria had changed Theodora's soul; she had become more sober and measured in her "otherness," though Procopius failed to mention it.

It was possibly in 520 or 521 that Theodora arrived in Constantinople again, thanks to her connections with the Blues of the Levant, and she saw for herself once again; again, seeing was knowing.

Nothing matched her original plan, and she too was no longer the same person. While remaining true to herself, she had once again been transformed and redefined in an unexpected way, sweeping away all the clichés that were used (and have been used ever since) to label her neatly. Procopius labeled her, as did the Church historians who called her "the second Eve, the new Delilah, the other Herodias who thirsts after holy men,"[7] and even the Monophysites who built a new stereotype image for her: body hidden under a chaste tunic of rough linen, two hands holding a candle, or arms extended and hands open in prayer, the pose so often found on the tombs and baptismal fonts of Coptic Egypt [fig. 17].

But Theodora could never be contained by these stereotypical portraits.

17. Limestone funerary stele with praying figure,
6th century, Coptic Museum, Cairo.

EIGHT

"I, Consul"

Antioch, Constantinople, c. 521–22

THE PALACE OF CONSTANTINOPLE, focal point of the whole civilized world, had first touched Theodora's humble life when Hecebolus was appointed governor of Pentapolis. That had looked like a positive development, but the affair ended in failure. Then in 518 the palace launched an offensive against the Monophysites, which continued through Theodora's stay in Alexandria. That might have looked like a negative development, but it was actually fundamental to her life's next turn, to the fate of the empire, and even to the history of Christianity, which is so strangely linked to the life of this young actress.

Of course Theodora had no inkling, as she made her way back to Constantinople around 521, of the changes that were to come; but Procopius knew it all when he was writing the *Secret History*, around the year 550. He knew, but he mentions none of it in his account, because he wants to show Theodora as being in the grip of the Devil during her whole return trip. And so he colored the historical and cultural perception of Theodora for centuries to come, laying the groundwork for her decadent legend as a *vamp* (a "she-vampire"). He thus set the tone for her meeting with her future imperial spouse, Justinian, whom he introduces as "the Lord of the Demons."

The prelude to this diabolical theme had already been sounded at the time of Theodora's debut on the stage (and in the back rooms) of Constantinople, for her unnamed lovers had supposedly reported that "some sort of demon descended upon them at night and drove them from the room in which they were spending the night with her."[1] Here we see the archaic tradition of the succubus—a mysterious female monster who was believed to have sexual relations with unsuspecting men during the night—revived, with its gender switched. But Procopius's insidious "creature" is chiefly a foreshadowing of Justinian, not only because, according to rumors, he practiced satanic sex,[2] but because throughout the *Secret History* Flavius Petrus Sabbatius Justinianus is a demonic figure, not a man: "And they say that Justinian's mother stated to some of her intimates that he was not the son of her husband Sabbatius, nor of any man. For when she was about to conceive him, a demon visited her; he was invisible but affected her with a certain impression that he was there with her as a man having intercourse with a woman and then disappeared as in a dream."[3]

Other great historical figures have had nonhuman parents attributed to them in propaganda or literature. It was said that Alexander the Great was the son of the god Ammon and that Scipio was the son of Jove; even Octavian Caesar styled himself *divi filius,* son of god. But while these figures were all linked to Olympus, the *Secret History*'s Justinian is the polar opposite of a "valiant prince" of the Roman empire. He was a son of darkness, a chthonic creature, "a demon"—the "prince" of demons—and as such, he was an anti-Christ who had come to signal the end of time, maybe even to upset the course of the eons with a plethora of natural disasters such as earthquakes, famines, and plagues.

It might seem surprising that Procopius resorted to so many superstitious and apocalyptic elements here, while his other works are masterpieces of classical culture. But he was a product of his time, which was rife with messianic, visionary elements, both Christian and pagan. We easily accept that the lives of the Christian saints could be filled with thaumaturgic and teratological elements, but in those years even commentaries on Plato invoked the stars or astrological themes, throwing ancient dialectical wisdom to the wind. It is also true that Procopius's rhetoric of blame demanded that the strong emotional overtones of his narrative spread to characters beyond Theodora herself.

So Procopius attacks the man who would become the most famous emperor of late antiquity, the man who has even been dubbed, aptly, "the last Roman Emperor on the throne"[4] of Constantinople. To do so, Procopius deploys every possible literary effect, setting himself squarely in an ancient tradition that considered historiography part of the fiction writer's trade. He uses anecdotes from many sources, and some that he clearly invented. He writes of a virtuous monk who was admitted to Justinian's presence and who immediately "recoiled and stepped back . . . [for] he had seen the Lord of the Demons in the Palace, sitting on the throne."[5] Other reliable "men whose souls were pure," he reports, were working with Justinian late at night when the emperor suddenly disappeared, and the men saw a headless ghost walking up and down the halls of the palace like an automaton. Then again, Justinian "was never accustomed to remaining seated for long,"[6] unlike the immobile, statuelike potentates of yore.

Other witnesses whom Procopius considered credible saw the face of Justinian transformed into "featureless flesh,"[7] as in a modern horror movie. Perhaps this image was lifted from the *Testament of Solomon*, an Eastern apocalyptic text from around the third century A.D. that featured a headless demon claiming to be "homicidal."[8] Procopius also accuses Justinian—literally beheaded in the account above—and Theodora of being homicidal: he calls them "a twin bane of mortals."[9]

In the *Secret History*, the closing lines of the chapter on the "nurture and education" of Theodora are demoniacal, and the remainder of the book maintains that theme ("when Justinian either, if he is a man, departs this life or, as being the Lord of the evil spirits, lays his life aside"[10]). More to the point, Procopius describes the meeting of Justinian and Theodora, the prelude to their career together, as happening under the sign of the Devil.

The city of Antioch played a pivotal role in the life of Justinian and Theodora. In the early 520s, this Syrian metropolis on the river Orontes was still considered the third greatest city after Constantinople and Alexandria (which retain their historical and strategic importance even today). Antioch was the most hedonistic town of the Mediterranean basin. The Hippodrome races, the mime shows, and the theaters afforded its more than 300,000 inhabitants the chance to release pent-up passions, and the tradition was even older there than in Constantinople. The shows satisfied a large upper class grown wealthy from trade, very different from the urban immigrant masses prevalent in Constantinople. The shows were also an antidote to the religious disputes that flared up after Emperor Justin (and Justinian, his nephew) deposed Severus, the city patriarch. And as the city aligned itself theologically with the Dyophysitist Roman papacy, in the milieu of show business the Blues were coming back into favor in Antioch as in the capital and other major cities.

The excitable nature of the citizens—the fact that they "care[d] for nothing else than fêtes and luxurious living, and their constant rivalries with each other in the theaters"[11]—might have been linked to the chronic instability of the earth beneath their feet. Violent earthquakes periodically shook the monumental buildings of the city center and the elegant villas of the suburbs, disasters that were taken as repeated invitations to enjoy the present. Another powerful stimulus to pleasure was the proximity of the Persian empire of the Sassanides, the other great Eye of the Ecumene, the Romans' only worthy adversary in terms of magnitude, civilization, and military strength. This proximity had led some emperors to choose Antioch as an imperial residence in the fourth century.

As we noted, there was a prominent dancer named Macedonia among the Blues of prosperous Antioch. She was very powerful: "For by writing letters to Justinian while he was still administering the Empire for Justinus, she without difficulty kept destroying whomsoever she wished among the notable men of the East and causing their property to be confiscated to the Treasury."[12] Macedonia, a discreet and dedicated informant, operated outside the official political administration that left Justinian dissatisfied, perhaps because he had not yet appointed his own trusted agents to it. He wanted control, and to have control he *had to know*. Show-business connections suited this purpose perfectly. Macedonia could report people who might deserve a hearing or could be persuaded to collaborate. She could also report on possibly dangerous types: independent thinkers (in religious matters, for example), people who failed to fulfill their obligations to the palace, or even outright rebellious or insubordinate characters.

The Blue faction, at least in cities like Alexandria or Antioch, had such a well-developed grassroots network that it could do more than simply report to the upper echelons of the palace. It could even assist its members; this is why Macedonia met Theodora as she passed through on her journey from Alexandria to the capital. The traveler was "despondent [and] discouraged"[13] by the high-handed treatment she had received from Hecebolus and by the expenses of her journey. This indicates that Theodora preferred to travel alone as much as possible, avoiding any escorts who might have ulterior motives. It was an expensive way to travel, and she could afford it only if she had well-paid theater engagements or difficult-to-obtain loans.

Macedonia offered encouragement and comfort to Theodora, assuring her that "Fortune was quite capable of becoming once again a purveyor of great wealth for her."[14] These may seem like empty, conventional words, but in fact they hint at the specifics of the situation. "Once again" confirms that Theodora was already used to having ready money. "Quite capable" suggests that Macedonia could recommend her to the faction leaders, whose political ties reached all the way up to Justinian. In the course of her conversation with Macedonia, Theodora must have described in detail what the other woman had generically referred to as "Fortune." Procopius says that she revealed her feelings to Macedonia, telling her that "a dream had come to her during the night just past and had bidden her to lay aside all anxiety as far as wealth was concerned. For as soon as she should come to Byzantium, she should lie with the Lord of the Demons, and would quite certainly live with him as his married wife, and he would cause her to be mistress of money without limit."[15]

Did Theodora really have such a dream? If so, her dejection seems unjustified. What's more, her spontaneous revelation of the dream is uncharacteristic of her: she rarely made psychological confessions. And finally, when we consider that the source of this conversation was a rumor (according to the *Secret History*), we must conclude that this episode is merely literary embroidery on a real event: what happened was that Theodora received concrete support in Antioch from Macedonia and the Blues, and that they referred her to Justinian. Therefore, while "Theodora talks" once again in Procopius, what she says is mostly literary fantasy, heavy on the visions, the oneiric elements, and the nocturnal. Theodora may really have had a revelation in Alexandria that gave her new reverence for religious figures, but the *Secret History* did all it could to erase it or debase it.

It is likely that Macedonia recommended Theodora to Justinian; possibly the message was written on a papyrus roll.[16] Sealed with wax bearing the imprint of Macedonia's ring, the roll addressed to the Illustrious Consul Flavius Petrus Sabbatius Justinianus was most probably given to the actress herself, not entrusted to the imperial mail service. Macedonia's words must have given Theodora hope that she could be introduced directly to the addressee; the Antioch dancer must have praised him for his attentiveness, his calm, and his receptivity to petitioners, which he followed up with quick action on their behalf. Such qualities were rare in people in prestigious posts such as Justinian's: he was a consul and an advisor to Emperor Justin, his blood uncle, who had gone so far as to adopt him. She probably avoided drawing any sort of comparison between this powerful man and Hecebolus.

Macedonia's letter was the magical key that was to let our heroine into the heart of the palace. This was one more reversal . . . and all the less predictable because it brought Theodora before the man who was making life hard for the Monophysites, the only persons she had genuinely admired up to that point. Yet the letter opened the door to a new relationship with a potentate, and her affair with Hecebolus had left her wiser and more skillful in presenting herself.

Theodora hurried now. She played the minimum number of theater performances that the Blues might have offered her along the way from Antioch to Constantinople. She hastened through the ancient cities of Asia Minor—Tarsus, Seleucia, Attalia, Miletus, Ephesus, and Smyrna—that had once represented ancient Hellenic culture and later become vital centers of Christendom. We do not know whether, before reaching Antioch, she visited Palestine, the preferred destination for Christian travelers at the time. She may have done so: sources allude to some sort of aid that she might have received from a "Samaritan" native of Palestine by the name of Arsenius.[17]

Finally she saw the Bosphorus again, lapping at its Asian and European shores. After years away, she watched a boat approach to ferry her to the city. It was the most ordinary and yet the freshest of sights, and it conjured up promising scenarios.

Flavius Petrus Sabbatius Justinianus was a very busy man, perhaps the busiest of men. It was said that he did not even have time to sleep. He ate only raw vegetables, lightly dressed, and drank only fresh water, to conserve all the energy of his robust frame for intellectual labor. Even his harshest enemies acknowledged that he always had "a ruddy complexion."[18] If the porphyry sculpture of a head now in Saint Mark's basilica in Venice [fig. 18] does indeed portray him in his early maturity, he was a handsome man with a lively expression. A reassuring figure.

18. Porphyry portrait head of an emperor ("Justinian"), c. 520, Saint Mark's basilica, Venice.

With his very busy schedule, Flavius Petrus Sabbatius Justinianus was clearly not waiting for a "gift of god," a *theou dôron*, a "Theodora," to fall from the sky. Now about forty years old, he was still unmarried, and the best aristocratic families of the empire competed to draw his attention to the charms of their accomplished virgin daughters equipped with fabulous dowries of gold and land. There were no rumors of women visiting him regularly in his legendary home overlooking the water of the Propontis. (It was called the palace of Hormisdas, after a Persian prince who had been exiled to Constantinople in the fourth century A.D. A short, invigorating stroll amid enchanting gardens and buildings brought him from home to the imperial palace.)

Justinian was born in a town called Tauresium near Naissus (now Nis, Serbia); his uncle Justin was his connection to Constantinople. Like so many others, uncle Justin had left the extreme poverty of his native hamlet, Vederiana (near today's Skopje, Macedonia), and trudged hundreds of miles, sleeping under the stars, to seek his fortune in the capital. A man of great vigor, strong "like an oak," he had enrolled as a palace guard[19] around the year 470, when he was twenty years old. Decade after decade, promotion after promotion, he had advanced in the military until in 515 he became commander of the palace guard.

A semiliterate man, Justin was serious about his duties. Sometimes he was derided, for example on account of his woman companion, Lupicina, whose name recalled the Roman term for brothel, *lupanare*. But he kept to his own path. Around the year 500 he summoned his nephew, Flavius Petrus Sabbatius, born around 482, so that he could provide the boy with an adequate education (the eternal dream of the underprivileged). His plan succeeded, and his nephew became a man of deep learning. In the end, Justin adopted him, and the nephew took the name of "he who comes from Justin": Justinian.

Only once did the faithful Justin disobey orders, while he served in a military campaign in Asia Minor. He was condemned to die, but General John the Hunchback, who was in charge of the execution, could not follow through with it. Three times the general dreamed of an immense figure, each time more threatening than the last, who commanded him to release Justin. The vision declared that in the future it would "have need of this man and of his family."[20] The apparition was nocturnal, oneiric, even demonic, because this is Procopius's version of the story, and anyone related to Justinian was obliged to conform to the stereotype.

But no visions ever came to Emperor Anastasius, who died when he was nearly ninety without appointing a successor. The Great Electors of the empire were arguing over the succession when Justin suddenly became the most popular candidate. It seemed like a spell or a miracle: crowds in the Hippodrome began cheering him with *Tu vincas* (Victory to you!). One day his human wreath—the guards he commanded—parted to reveal him standing tall in the imperial robe and the purple mantle. It seemed clear that God was with him: the succession was decided, and the patriarch of Constantinople crowned him with the imperial diadem.

Justin spoke and his words were taken down. His appeal to divine Providence and his emphasis on the emperor's love for his subjects were not original. But the people appreciated and remembered his promise of immediate, generous gifts of money.[21]

Justinian, who was thirty-six in 518, was the one who had secretly paved the way for his uncle's coronation. He was immediately rewarded with an appointment in the new government: he joined the daily meetings of the Ruler's Council, where public affairs were discussed and laws and policies were made. He was the engine of the entire imperial machine, in charge of day-to-day situations and future planning. His life was not ruled by the ancient rhythms that alternated business with leisure, work with play. Because of this, his schedule seemed chaotic to his detractors: they failed to grasp his working rhythm or his larger plan.

Justinian was already developing the agenda for his own future government. Using all kinds of means (including Antioch's female dancers), he scrutinized men who might be suited to work for him; he studied and commissioned research on every single public office and magistracy to determine which ones were outdated and which might still be useful; he read theological tracts about the mysteries of God, and bureaucratic reports about the customs of the peoples at the farthest reaches of the empire.

His education was intense and demanding (and he was largely self-taught). Although both his uncle and his demanding career forced him to spend some time in positions of military command, he was still "the least military of men."[22] He liked the military life less than he liked books, in Greek or particularly in Latin, about the glories of ancient Rome, which was geographically, linguistically, and religiously so close to his native Illyria. He wanted to resurrect Rome in the city of Constantinople, which would soon—he thought—be his.

In the meantime he stretched and strengthened his mind with historical texts, collections of imperial writings, and the immense legislative and judicial library of centuries of Roman power. He was perhaps the last man of his time for whom scholarship was a vehicle for arriving at a mature sense of authority, not the authority of one citizen talking to another, as in antiquity, but the authority of an autocrat speaking to his subjects. Absolute devotion and absolute power. He was absolutely devoted to absolute power.

Soon Justinian became "the most dreaded man in the world."[23] He and his uncle were quick to eliminate the notables who had been especially close to Anastasius. Then, beginning in the second half of 520, uncle and nephew put to death even those who had been enemies of the old power establishment. They started with Vitalian, the general who had rebelled against Anastasius, whose orthodox, pro-papal position should have brought him close to the new emperor and his nephew. In the name of their identical religious views, Justinian "[had] previously given him a pledge for his safety by sharing with him the Christian sacraments. But a little later, when he was suspected of having given him offence, he executed him in the palace together with his followers for no just cause, by no means consenting to honor his pledges, terrible as they were."[24] Justinian had detected or suspected Vitalian of the crime of high treason against him or his uncle. Whether or not his suspicion was well founded, Justinian broke his pledge and showed his propensity for murder—in the words of Procopius, "he used to proceed with the lightest of hearts to the unjust murder of men."[25] Just like a "Lord of Demons."

✛ ✛ ✛

The energy Justinian poured into his studies had allowed him to devise a plan so vast and precisely detailed that he was far ahead of any other hypothetical competitor for the throne. The fundamental concept of his vision was clear, and it could be summed up in a single word, *restitutio*, which means something like "restoration."

Justinian's analysis of the problems of the empire led him to conclusions different from—even contrary to—those of the earlier great reformers. Diocletian, emperor from A.D. 284 to 305, had transformed the institutional structure of the Roman polity by subdividing it into eastern and western empires, each with its own Augustus and its own Caesar, and reorganizing each unit into administrative, territorial, and fiscal structures. Constantine, emperor from 306 to 337, discerned that Christianity, formerly a source of discord, could build community among the various peoples of an empire whose center of gravity had shifted, by then, to the Orient. Constantine considered even Theodoric, the Goth king of Italy (and thus formally a subject of the emperor of Constantinople), a reformer because he had aimed to synthesize Roman and Germanic elements under the aegis of "reconciliation."

Such an idea seemed vague, relativistic, and utterly unacceptable to Justinian. He demanded standardization and unification because his policy was based on the ancient philosophical concept that the highest good lay in the *One*. So he sought to stretch his empire across all the Mediterranean lands that had once been Roman, "from one to the other boundary of the ocean."[26] He did this by waging war on the many recent "barbaric" kingdoms (the Vandals in Africa, the Visigoths in Spain, the Ostrogoths in Italy) ruling the traditionally Latin countries that he felt closest to because of his own upbringing. Besides, the invaders were Arian heretics who had strayed from the one true faith.

He felt it was his duty to improve the lives of his subjects on Earth, so that living in the empire would be a sure passport to Paradise; but this could only happen if the empire was in a state of serene religious unity. This was another reason why Monophysites such as Severus had been deposed, and why a long period of discord ended, in March 519, in a harmonic rapprochement between the empire and the papacy. Support from the bishop of Rome was crucial to Justinian's renewed conquest of the West.

The early Roman rulers of Christian faith were already legendary, and their empire was the model for the "restoration" that the new strongman from Illyricum yearned for. While his religious absolutism followed the policies of Theodosius I (r. 379–395), who had demoted non-Orthodox Catholics to second-class subjects, his plan for territorial restoration meant expanding the empire to the size it was when Constantine the Great was the sole emperor (324–337).

But Justinian did not simply wish to erase two centuries of history. His restoration would bring new power dynamics. For him, the throne would not act simply as the supreme moderator among the empire's various movements and power groups; it had to launch new initiatives and steer the entire political and social body. To this end, he would have to strengthen his grip on all the tools needed for the job, starting with direct access to and control of fiscal revenues. So the provincial elite were to feel the effects of his policy: he found them unreliable, self-interested, and focused on local matters, not engaged in working for the glory of the empire that Justinian felt would soon be his.

In 521, Justinian at nearly forty was inaugurating his first consulship: it was an office that, since its establishment more than a thousand years earlier in the first Rome, had become largely honorific. He was replacing Vitalian, one of his victims, and he needed to make people forget his predecessor.

Justinian ordered that feasts and banquets be held; in addition to horses and chariots with splendid trappings, his arena shows included lions, leopards, and other wild beasts. The animals came from the most remote provinces of the empire, or were purchased from merchants and ambassadors to exotic kingdoms that were friendly to the new Rome, such as the Ethiopian kingdom of Axum, whose major Red Sea port, Adulis, enjoyed mercantile and ecclesiastical relations with Constantinople.

Justinian ingratiated himself with his city's populace by dispensing gifts, surprises, and games, but he used other means to prove his mettle to the power elite. It was said that he spent 288,000 golden solidi in consular celebrations. Assuming that this is a reliable figure, and that Procopius elsewhere reports reliably on the empire's gold reserves at the end of Anastasius's reign (23,040,000 solidi), Justinian's celebrations burned up 1.25 percent of the gold reserves accumulated in almost thirty years of administration. Such a figure would make a cautious imperial administrator pale—but not the self-confident Justinian.

19. Ivory diptych celebrating Justinian, 521,
Castello Sforzesco, Milan.

He showed similar self-confidence, even arrogance, in the ivory diptych that celebrated his consulship [fig. 19]. The piece gives a unique twist to the visual conventions and the content traditionally seen in these self-promotional displays. Unexpectedly, his portrait does not appear on the ivory, but only his name and his majestic series of titles: "Flavius Petrus Sabbatius Justinianus, Illustrious, Count, Master of Cavalry and of Rapid-Response Infantry, Regular Consul." An elegiac couplet is inscribed in the radiant discs that decorate the diptych:

> *Munera parva quidem pretio sed honoribus alma*
> *Patribus ista meis offero consul ego*
>
> I, Consul, offer to my elders these gifts
> that carry a small price but great honor.

With the arrogance of the powerful, Justinian downplayed the monetary value of the diptych, while stressing the honor and prestige that he offered the senators (the "elders"). In the final analysis, everything— from the value judgment to the offering itself—revolves around him. So sure is he about the quality of his offer that he doesn't even feel the need or the duty to have his portrait on the diptych. He has become a mere voice, an *authority*: this is a foreshadowing of medieval custom, appearing in the context of the most classical of Roman institutions.

The word *ego,* "I," the last word on the inscription, emphasizes his gesture, his will, his concession. He gets the last word, and it is the key to interpreting the entire text. This artifact and its inscription make it quite clear that Justinian thought highly of himself as a man and a politician. Eight centuries later, Dante Alighieri expressed it concisely in his famous line in the *Paradiso*, "Caesar I was, and am Justinian."[27]

Long before rising to Dante's Paradise, Justinian met Theodora on the Earth—but when? She must have spent considerable time with Severus, Timothy, and their circles, long enough that her Monophysite beliefs sank in quite deep, and long enough for her to consider Timothy her "spiritual father." Then came her journey across a great distance and her important sojourn in Antioch. These factors are crucial in trying to pinpoint a date for the meeting between the actress (or former actress) and the most powerful man in Constantinople. It must have occurred in the year 521 or 522.

In the absence of solid data, literary myths have flourished: Syrian Monophysite legends, the various Western medieval versions, and that of Robert Graves in his *Count Belisarius* (1938). In the Byzantine Middle Ages there were numerous folk tales about a "house of Empress Theodora" in Constantinople.[28] In that house, people said, the reformed actress spent her days "spinning wool." It's an evocative and edifying image, but the house belonged to another Empress Theodora, who lived in the ninth century.[29]

Having finally set foot in Constantinople, Theodora awaited an audience with Justinian, whose power was visible all around her. She must have led a secluded life, renewing relations with her family (starting with her sister Comito) and with the city's Blues. At the same time, she tried to exchange letters regularly with Antioch and with her spiritual teachers in Alexandria.

If any former theater colleagues had suggested that she ask the stars about her future, they would probably have found that Theodora was less than enthusiastic. Her soul had changed during her journey, just as her complexion had probably darkened: she had become more introspective and serious. She must have been twenty-one or twenty-two years old, and she left other young women to chase after the old flattery: cheering audiences, the lust of powerful men, proof of one's own powers of seduction. She had no idea whether she had come back as a "lady," as a *kyria* with dominion over something; she was mistress only of herself.

She may have viewed the chance to meet the powerful Justinian as a secret interpretation or transformation of her very name. That meeting was God's gift. She would not fail to honor it.

The day came when she was invited to the palace of Hormisdas. Comito probably wanted to supervise her sister's makeup and her choice of garments; she must have made sure that no fewer than eight slaves carried her litter [fig. 20]. Even though Theodora was unwilling to return to her former life, both sisters knew that such an occasion was also a theatrical event. In a vestibule of the palace of Hormisdas, we can picture Theodora waiting, thinking about the "lord" hard at work behind a velum [fig. 15]. Perhaps she too examined her position:

20. Lady Danelis going to the palace in her litter, miniature from Ms. Matrit. Gr., Vitr. 26-2, second half of the 12th century, Biblioteca Nacional, Madrid.

once more she was outside, in the hallway, the waiter and the pursuer. And the pursued? He was probably busy studying a map or reviewing the draft of a law.

When Theodora was finally admitted into his presence, he must have thought that he was seeing for the first time. Before him stood the actress he had heard something about, who had belonged to the Blues by destiny and by vocation since her earliest childhood. But he saw more: he saw in her the new Helen of the Ecumene. Theodora must have appeared to him to be truly a "gift of God."

To her, Justinian must have appeared a fully accomplished man. His regular features bespoke health and a full and active life. He had no markings or affectations. He asked precise questions, and listened thoughtfully to the answers.

The lord preferred to speak Latin but probably graciously shifted to Greek, with which his guest was more familiar. In Greek, he most likely expressed himself in archaic, twisted sentences that she found belabored but amusing. With Macedonia's letter in his hand, perhaps he pretended to need help from Theodora (who was young enough to be his daughter) in deciphering the Greek that he "did not possess fully, while you," he might have said, "possess it innately."

"I wasn't able to study as much as I would have liked," said Theodora.

"I said that you are mistress of it [*kyria*] innately," he replied.

In that palace, the powerful man used the word *kyria* for her. It was a sign, a gift.

In its long history human language has evolved from the simplicity of an exclamation to the complexity of a subordinate clause; but in that first meeting Theodora and Justinian traveled the other way. The elaborate expressions, the hypothetical, conditional, and subjunctive verbs, the sophisticated Greek optatives were streamlined into a linear, indicative style. The present tense became the only tense. There was a pause, then an imperative. Sentences crumbled and shrank to single words, then to monosyllables. Conjunctions between sentences fell away from their conversation while buckles and pins fell away from their garments. Then only sighs were left.

Justinian's hands, which were accustomed to handling papers and unrolling maps, now slid over Theodora's smooth body as it lay there pulsing with life. She didn't curl up into herself like an inanimate parchment roll or, as the sacred texts write, like the heavens will roll up on the day of reckoning (when all lives will end, at the end of time and of eons).[30] Justinian stretched himself out beside her and embraced her youthful form.

And Justinian asked her, the "infamous" one, to embrace *his* body, the body of a "lord," of the man who wielded the highest political power. He must have wondered how he had survived, in his former life as Flavius Petrus Sabbatius and later as Justinian, without this embrace.

Perhaps he asked to hear her story. He must have been pleased to hear about the Blues and how they had saved her in the Kynêgion. He might have been disturbed to hear about her life in the theater and her adventure in Pentapolis, and surprised to hear about her experience in Alexandria. And he must have admired her for her journey, the cities and the lands that she had seen.

Probably Justinian told her little about himself, not only because the powerful rarely confide in others, but also because of manly habits common in the ancient and then the Byzantine world. He probably told her more about himself in later encounters, not directly but by referring to his readings, whose echoes enriched his conversation. He must have told her over and over again that she was "as desirable as the treasures of Solomon" and much, much more. Justinian longed to emulate Solomon, the king of ancient Israel and builder of extraordinary buildings; he had been a man of exemplary justice and author of wonderful works. Above all, he had written the passionate *Song of Songs*.

> Let him kiss me with the kisses of his mouth
> for thy love is better than wine.
> . . . .
> The king hath brought me into his chambers.
> We will be glad and rejoice in thee.[31]

Justinian must have whispered this to her, and then explained it. He must have laid out the Orthodox interpretation, whereby the *Song of Songs* celebrated the union of the Church with Jesus Christ, or of the individual soul with the Incarnate Word. He probably did not gloss over another interpretation that was suspected of heresy, the literal interpretation: that the poem described the physical union of King Solomon with the daughter of the king of Egypt, the fair Shulamit, his legendary bride.

We do not know what language the two lovers spoke together. Theodora probably listened most of the time. Then, one day, she must have discreetly reminded him that she too came from Egypt, even though she was not a king's daughter. And that she had finally "entered *her* king's chambers" where there was so much "rejoicing and exultation"[32] together. She hoped she was not uttering heretical words. But if it was a diabolical heresy, which was guilty—the body or the mind? It was her king's privilege to illustrate that point if he wanted another embrace, where their two different "persons" (if not their two "natures") would be joined.

NINE

"They Received Imperial Power"

Constantinople, 522–27

T HE YOUNG MIME ACTRESS who had returned from the Levant driven by an ardent—if not erudite—passion for theology was now settled in the palace of Hormisdas with Justinian; one could easily imagine the "playful and pleasing conversations"[1] (both verbal and physical) he was having with her.

The mighty Justinian could perhaps be criticized for his passion, which has been called an "overpowering love," an "extraordinary love."[2] He did not follow the etiquette of proper behavior at court; he was practically sick with love—mad for love. This was all the more scandalous because he was not a young man and he was famously not hotheaded. People wondered why. Some mentioned the ever "new devices in intercourse"[3] that they heard Theodora had used, years earlier, to keep her lovers. Others recalled hearing that the daughter of the Hippodrome was an expert in witchcraft, spells, in love potions and poisons. And others mentioned the low-class background of the former consul: "Birds of a feather flock together,"[4] they would say, seeing unhappy omens in their relationship.

The critics could not accept the fact that Theodora might represent for him all the diversity and wonder of life. That, with her defenselessness and proud dignity, she and her family deserved help. The critics also failed to consider that the empirical logic she had developed in the theater, and refined in Alexandria, might help him to see his political problems in a different perspective, from a nonofficial point of view.

Nor did they consider that she had full experience of the life of the period, both in Constantinople and elsewhere.

But nothing escaped Justinian. Because of his broad studies and his position, he might have been impatient with all the customary ways of doing things. He had everything, and there was nothing that a sixteen-year-old virgin daughter of an illustrious family could offer him. His relation with Theodora, though—that little female Ulysses—made him more completely and more deeply a man. He felt that she provided some of what he needed to become a kind of Solomon who would also be a perfect Roman man.

But what about Theodora, who sparked an "erotic fire" in Justinian as soon as she set foot in the palace of Hormisdas, and kept it smoldering until the end of her life? No one—not even Procopius, who packed his narrative with so many denigratory rumors—openly accused her of having failed Justinian during the long union that lasted more than half her life, until her death in 548. Although he cast so many aspersions on her "nurture and education," not even Procopius dared to attribute any explicit affairs to her after she entered the palace (unlike Sardou in his play), or any licentiousness at all (as Sade suggested in his work).

Historians have asked whether her behavior was motivated by fear, opportunism, or simple gratitude. But—and this speaks volumes about the depth of her critics' prejudice—no one has considered the idea that she might have harbored deeper feelings. Such feelings might have been difficult to acknowledge and hard to mention for a woman who, like her, had been born in society's gutter. But her feeling was so deep that it led her ultimately to resist Justinian in order to defend what was, in her eyes, loftiest and most unique about him, something that she perceived so clearly because she had always lacked it: power.

Observers in Constantinople had to resign themselves quickly and acknowledge that this affair did not have the lighthearted quality of a passing fancy. It was a grave imperial issue. Unable to think small, Justinian began to move resources toward Theodora and her family. People in the palace muttered that public funds "became fuel for this love,"[5] and the capital's leading families gradually lost the hope of forging marital alliances with the crown.

Theodora was promoted to a high position at court: she became a "patrician." By around 523, therefore, she held the same rank as Justinian, who everyone expected to be the next emperor. The couple lived together openly in the palace of Hormisdas. During ceremonies in churches and basilicas, Theodora shone more brilliantly than the candles in the women's gallery: the Christian temples were the new stage for displaying her beauty. The learned statesman used these occasions to mount fresh challenges to the old conventions.

Theodora was becoming a lady, the mistress of riches, mansions, lands, handmaids, eunuchs. She took a splendid retinue along when she visited almshouses or places of worship to display her Christian sharing of suffering. And, all the while, other people tended to the constant growth of her assets, to ensure her dignity and well-being and that of her family.

As in any court, the newcomer was subjected to minute scrutiny and endless comments on her beauty and her career. Merciless comparisons were made between Theodora and Empress Lupicina-Euphemia, the aged and much-derided woman on the throne. Mischievous comparisons were drawn with a great lady of the time, Juliana Anicia, who had commissioned elegant manuscripts and lavish basilicas. Like her, Theodora was a "patrician," but much younger and low-born: she came not from an illustrious family but from the Hippodrome and the Kynêgion. Some whispered that there really was no respect anymore for age or noble blood.

They must have scrutinized her face, her "intent, frowning" expression, and commented that although she appeared beautiful, she lacked the measured serenity that softens the features and clears the eye. It was considered imperative for people with great power to present a serene, impassive countenance. Any startled or impatient gesture got noticed; observers must have found it odd that this actress did not maintain a smooth, affectless mask.

Some probably recalled the example of Marcus Aurelius, Roman emperor from A.D. 161 to 180. The embodiment of stoicism on the throne, he always appeared calm, resigned, as if the "sphere of his soul was lit by true light."[6] He once called Herodes Atticus to answer charges of serious abuse of authority, and the defendant, who was mourning a loved one, departed from his customary polished language, speaking gracelessly and even insulting the emperor. And yet Marcus Aurelius "never knit his eyebrow nor changed expression."[7] His philosophical mind gave him self-control: he was emperor of himself.

Some busybodies also recalled the Roman journey (in A.D. 357) of Emperor Constans I, the son of Constantine the Great, who was also a master of self-control: "He always looked straight ahead, neither turning his face to the left nor to the right, almost like a statue; and though the coach moved to and fro, no one saw him gesture, or spit, or clean or wipe his mouth or nose, or move his hands."[8] It was best to carry oneself like a statue, but Theodora's expressiveness and her intent frown seemed to flout this custom. Justinian was criticized too for flouting customs: he paced through the palace in the dead of night. Given the prevailing ideals of sovereignty, some critics even doubted that these lovers deserved to have their features sculpted in marble, or that their features should be "more lasting than bronze."[9] Others observed that such infractions were evidence of the demise of ancient ideals.

The actress who had been let into the palace may have looked around with "intent and frowning" eyes because she too was scrutinizing others: courtiers and functionaries, prelates and military officers. Whatever reservations these people had were spoken under their breath; publicly, they bowed to Theodora's unexpected ascent and good fortune, "for that which appears unaccountable is wont to have the name of Fortune applied to it."[10]

She carefully observed every single gesture or word and memorized it forever. Then she told Justinian, or asked him for an explanation. She knew that she represented his position of power, that she was living proof of the effectiveness of that power. She was like a symbol, his badge: anything done to her was indirectly done to him, because he was the one who held the power. And if she demanded respect and homage it was not for herself but for him, she told him. An oversight or an impolite gesture toward her might imply a possible threat against him.

If he disregarded protocol because he was busy reading, Theodora might have reminded him that it was not his studies that guaranteed his position. She confided in no one. She kept her guard up. She collected rumors, secrets, information. Even about her "new Solomon." And she surprised the scholarly Justinian by reminding him that he had ordered Vitalian's abrupt end.

The legal and institutional gap between her and Justinian was far more vast than the gap that had separated her from Hecebolus, and the setting was no longer the provinces but the very heart of the empire. Theodora too had changed. She deemed her position with Justinian to be so strong that she could afford *not* to ask him for anything. She understood that the more impossible a challenge, the more he was attracted to it. It was impossible, for instance, for a man of senatorial rank to marry an actress, albeit a patrician such as herself: it was "a thing forbidden from the beginning by the most ancient laws."[11] But Justinian saw this as one more reason to change those laws immediately. The fact that Theodora had a daughter—who must have been around eight years old in 523—was no obstacle for him. As a matter of fact, it was a guarantee that Theodora could bear children. For Justinian had decided by then to make her his wife, the mother of his future progeny.

But Theodora's daughter, and her whole past, were not mere details for Lupicina, the slave that Emperor Justin had bought and made his concubine, then his wife and empress, with the new name of Euphemia [fig. 21]. The former slave hoped for a very different bride for the man they had adopted and raised with such solicitous devotion. She opposed the union. The learned forty-year-old Justinian argued with his uneducated adoptive mother: if Theodora had maintained so many qualities despite all her misadventures, it was a sign of divine favor and grace. And her recent exemplary behavior revealed her true character. But Lupicina stubbornly resisted the wedding. Procopius, the product of a very different culture, wrote that Justinian might have taken his choice of the whole Roman Empire and have married that woman who, of all the women in the world, was in the highest degree both well-born and blessed with a nurture sheltered from the public eye, a woman who had not been unpracticed in modesty, and had dwelt in chastity, who was not only surpassingly beautiful but also still a maiden and, as the expression runs, erect of breast; but he did not disdain to make the common abomination of all the world his own.[12]

Had Lupicina survived to read (and been able to read) these words, she would have agreed with Procopius completely.

21. Bronze portrait head of an empress ("Lupicina-Euphemia"), c. 520, Narodni Muzej, Nis (Serbia).

While waiting for Justin's wife to change her mind about the marriage, Theodora and Justinian enjoyed the unshakeable certainty typical of any satisfying new love affair.[13]

Theodora must have rejoiced in her body more now than at any other time. Early on, her body had been inseparable from her theater career and her need to survive and rise socially. Later, an heir to the throne would be demanded of it. But right now was the time for pleasure. Standing on the roof terraces or the balustrades of the palace of Hormisdas, we can imagine that she often gazed at the sea, which calmed her. Then a herald—the blast of a trumpet—a roll of the drums—would signal that her lord had arrived, and she would quiver. If public protocol at court required that she stand like a statue, she was ready to be sculpted by her Pygmalion. But when it was just the two of them, she knew better than he the private protocol of their bodies.

It was not only the couple in the palace of Hormisdas who felt entirely secure; at the Hippodrome, the Blue faction also felt secure. Both Justinian and Theodora had been "members of the Blue Faction from of old."[14] Justinian guaranteed impunity for the radical fringes of the faction, who could be useful in destabilizing the capital, thus helping him to prove that the elderly imperial couple was no longer capable of ruling the empire, that a strong man like him was needed at the helm. The Blues' abuse and their provocative acts were unusual: "barbaric," ethnic, and untraditional. The Blue radicals broke away from the conservative image of the Roman citizen:

> for they did not touch the moustache or the beard at all, but they wished always to have the hair of these grow out very long, as the Persians do. But the hair of their heads they cut off in front back to the temples, leaving the part behind to hang down to a very great length in a senseless fashion . . . indeed for this reason they used to call this the "Hunnic" fashion. . . . Also their cloaks and their drawers and especially their shoes as regards both name and fashion, were classed as "Hunnic."[15]

We modern observers can easily relate to this mode of protest. Urban violence was also part of it: "They carried weapons."[16] Robbery and murder went unpunished, and among the young extremists "men who had previously never taken an interest in these affairs . . . were now drawn to it."[17] The magistrates refused to investigate. They knew that in the end they would have to face the protector of these extremist fringes—powerful, fearsome Justinian—and so they adopted an attitude of indifference. Justinian wasted no pity on the Blues' victims—especially if the Blues involved were from senatorial families and might be crucial in his ascent to the throne. Even in the ivory diptych that celebrated his consulship in 521, he had only one word—*ego*, "I"—when addressing the "elders" of the Senate.

Lupicina-Euphemia died in 523 or 524. After the proper display of grief and compunction, Justinian brought Emperor Justin the draft of a law that he had prepared earlier, and the emperor approved it (perhaps under duress). Explicitly designed to meet the needs of the two lovers, the law ("On Marriage," *Justinian Code* V 4, 23) covered any "reformed" actress who led an "honorable" life. Such a woman was granted leave to appeal to the emperor to marry a man of high rank, and even without an appeal marriage was permitted if the "repentant" actress had been previously awarded an honorific title. In addition, children born to actresses before their "repentance" could also marry freely.

Since Theodora was the first actress to be awarded the honorific title "patrician" (not as a public recognition of her acting talents, but because of a private sentimental relationship), Justinian could marry her without appealing to the emperor. Maybe the passage of the law was a reward for the patience with which she had endured Lupicina-Euphemia's hostility; undoubtedly, it was a pledge for the future. It was important not only personally but anthropologically. For with it Theodora was finally approved, ratified, and accepted. The promulgation of the law marked her consecration, her transformation from unworthy to worthy, from infamous to illustrious. Finally she could step out from the hallways and stairwells, the antechambers, the vestibules, the backstage shadows. She achieved full freedom of movement on a new stage: not the theater stage, but the power stage; this was her *own* "gift from God." In 524, Theodora was reaching the midpoint of her life—which was to be a short one, by modern standards—and she began the second half sturdily protected both personally and legally by Justinian's specific design.

The law "On Marriage" had a larger significance: it reflected the social mobility of the empire in late antiquity, when the throne and the imperial purple were accessible to certain illiterate farmers, slaves, and former actresses. While the emancipation was initially conceived only for Theodora, it liberated other actresses, promoting social dynamism. Of course, Christian repentance was essential: the acting profession continued to be considered evil, and therefore in need of redemption. But without the real case of Theodora on the one hand, and Christian influence on the other, the established powers would never have extended these rights.

Ten centuries before the law "On Marriage," the *Lex Canuleia* (Canuleia Law) had permitted marriages between patricians and plebeians, launching a lively period for the first Rome. But the emancipation and social dynamism promoted by "On Marriage" is more of a historical irony; the radical transformation of actresses' status happened, paradoxically, just as antiquity was drawing to an end.

As the Middle Ages approached, the culture was growing more distrustful of the body, of bathing, of entertainment. Soon, public works such as the baths and the theater were seen as "creations of the devil" just like pagan temples, and they began to serve as quarries for construction material for other buildings: not urban, secular structures but churches and religious strongholds—spiritual and material fortresses for a transformed world.

So because of "On Marriage," Theodora and a few women in her circle were practically the only ones able to combine a theater career and even sexual promiscuity with Christian reformation and social dynamism. Theodora's daughter, born of the kind of relationship the law defined as "a mother's mistake," was given in marriage—opportunistically, not exactly "freely"—to a scion of a leading Constantinople family. Theodora's older sister, the actress Comito, married one of Justinian's closest collaborators, General Sittas, in 528 or 529. Since she was not a "patrician" at the time, she may have filed an appeal with the Serene Imperial Highnesses: by that time Justinian and Theodora were already on the throne and were busy strengthening their circles with good marriages.

Theodora's former colleagues also benefited. We know that one woman named Indaro and two women both named Chrysomallo, former dancers and actresses, were admitted to the palace, where they

dealt with politics "instead of the phallus and the life in the theater."[18]
The daughter of one Chrysomallo married a young dignitary, though
she caused a scandal among the conformists. We will examine her case
later, and look at Theodora's "right arm," the controversial Antonina.

Although "On Marriage" freed a class of marginalized and segre-
gated women, the innovation was short-lived. It foreshadowed a historical paradox of society under Justinian and Theodora: it was supposed
to be a restoration—epic, dynamic, totalizing—but it was only an "un-
stable synthesis." The precariousness undermining the society was also
visible in the military conquests and even in the pictorial style of the
age. Indeed, the art of the time has been described as merging two very
different styles[19]: it drew on classical naturalistic ideals and yet it had
abstract, early-medieval elements.

Meanwhile, Theodora had achieved her goal. The law guaranteed her
legal and institutional security. Now her life took on a different narrative tempo. The *fortissimo* orchestral passages were now balanced by
pauses and *pianissimo* moments. The tempo was no longer an urgent
presto but a majestic *andante.* She was absorbed but not overwhelmed
by life at court. Her private time gave way to the general, public time of
the palace, and a time for court ceremony definitively supplanted the
time for theatrical spectacle. Before, walls might have seemed constrict-
ing to her: she had lived under the open sky in the amphitheaters, on
the stone seats of the Hippodrome, in the infinite spaces of the Levant.
Now she was surrounded by frescoed walls and coffered ceilings. Her
feet glided across mosaic floors and polychrome marbles. The palace of
Hormisdas protected her like an oyster protects its pearl. Finally, she
too was "sheltered from the public eye."

Theodora had gained recognition—she had earned a new beginning. It was another one of her transformations, and her body was also
transformed. Whereas she could once show herself to "everyone,"
naked on the stage, now she showed herself—only after her regular
beauty sessions, when her body was carefully draped in clothing—to
just the few men and women she had chosen to be part of her
entourage.

Her marvelous robes were adorned with embellishments: the *tablion* (a rectangular decoration embroidered in gold on her garments) and the buckles decorated with pearls and precious stones that fastened the *stola* over her right shoulder. Her dressing required time and attention from assistants, handmaids, pages. When she spoke to them, we can presume that she slowed down her speech and her gestures and her commands. As time went on, everything became more concentrated, more intense. As the days passed, the young mistress of reversal was learning to embody a spirit of continuity.

The lovers were making arrangements for their wedding. The priests of the church of the Holy Wisdom (Hagia Sophia), perhaps even the patriarch himself, were teaching them the catechism, based on the precepts of Christian faith consolidated over the centuries. They did not discuss whether the nature of Jesus Christ was single or double, although Theodora (Justinian already knew) was likely eager to discuss this topic. The priests most likely did remind her of the basics of Christian and imperial motherhood. Theodora was sensitive to the subject: she wanted to—she knew that she had to—give Justinian an heir, but there had not yet been a pregnancy, despite the lovers' passion, the physicians' checkups, and the prayers of the devout. And there had been one troubling event.

In about 524, Justinian had fallen ill. Many have conjectured that he was weakened by orchitis, an inflammation of the testicles. With time, and maybe also with the help of a legendary healer, Saint Samson,[20] he recovered his famous energy, but even the doctors of the time knew that sterility often follows orchitis contracted in adulthood. Justinian was already past forty.

The two lovers understood that only a miracle could give them an heir. They were challenging destiny, but not for the first time. Theodora, once an expert in contraceptives, now discreetly ordered a search for fertility-inducing amulets and concoctions: blood from a rabbit, goose fat, even turpentine. People in the imperial entourage whispered suggestions. Others consulted stars and horoscopes. Still others shook their heads, convinced that it was God's punishment for Justinian's erotic and legislative hubris, his excessive lust for innovation.

Justinian recovered his health and then his anger, raging about the authorities having punished his favorite radical fringe of Blues while he was ill. (Perhaps old Justin had had a last gasp of pride.) Justinian went after the city's director of public safety, who was forced to seek ecclesiastical sanctuary.

But if Justinian had intended to make the instability work for him, he failed. There was now even greater friction between the new centralized power that he personified—which leaned ever more toward absolute individualism—and the long-established magistracies that had their roots in ancient Rome. Justinian was trying to eliminate this with his network of informers. In the meantime, a small anti-Justinian opposition group had formed, gaining some influence over his imperial uncle. Theodora noted it and brought it to Justinian's attention.

That group did not prevent the two patricians, Justinian and Theodora, from finally crowning their spectacular—and, to some, scandalous—affair with their wedding. It probably happened in 525; the month and day are unknown, as is the location of the ceremony. Was it in the ancient church of the Holy Wisdom, which was smaller than it is today? Or in a sumptuous hall of the palace? Did Patriarch Epiphanios officiate? The scanty documentation indicates that it was an understated ceremony, kept deliberately discreet to avoid opposition from more traditional quarters, or to avoid irritating Justin, who in his old age was becoming increasingly isolated and jealous of Justinian's power. The splendors of Justinian's consulship in 521 were not repeated; but this ceremony had a deeper meaning and it affected people far beyond the couple and their guests.

Theodora wore a veil on her head; rings were exchanged; blessings were spoken; wine was drunk from a single chalice; a reciprocal pledge was made (fig. 22). But all of this perhaps did not suffice for a couple with such lofty feelings. They must have also pledged beyond themselves: the entire world was the pledge with which they entered into their covenant. The formula that sanctioned their union also pledged the entire world that they would change together: from the desert villages of the Euphrates River to the vineyards of Cyprus; from the ports of North Africa to the pine forests sloping down to the Adriatic near Durrës; eastward to the first Rome, and farther east to the Pillars of Hercules (today's Strait of Gibraltar) and the great wide ocean.

22. LEFT: Gold marriage ring, 6th century.
23. RIGHT: Gold marriage belt, late 6th to 7th century.
Both Dumbarton Oaks, Byzantine Collection,
Washington, D.C.

The wedding ritual was a magic spell that they cast across the entire world, the object of their feelings both as potentates and as Christians. Its whole population—the furnace worker melting metal for imperial coins, the fisherman on the windy Propontis Sea, the stylite hermit watching the world from atop a pillar in Syria, the soldier standing watch in his fortress near the border with Persia—would be affected by the marriage of Justinian and Theodora.

The marriage was celebrated by court prelates who were probably Dyophysites, as a mark of religious reconciliation between Constantinople and Rome. Justinian's beliefs on the matter were further bolstered at the end of the same year, when John I, the Roman pope, visited Rome-on-the-Bosphorus. He probably wanted to welcome and give his Latin blessing to the wife of a man who was so learned in theology and so busy on behalf of the empire.

While Theodora might well have begun her career "backstage with slaves," now she was probably the only person in all of Christendom to have been blessed both by the "pope" of Alexandria (her favorite Monophysite, Timothy) and by the Roman pope, as well as by the patriarch of Constantinople. An imperial crown awaited her; meanwhile she wore a crown of blessings. And around her waist there shone, perhaps, a precious belt of gold coins [fig. 23], an exquisite wedding present gracing the belly that still had not given Justinian the heir he expected from her.

The nephew kept putting pressure on his uncle the emperor. In 526, Justinian became a *nobilissimus*: this was the highest rank, created specifically for him. Although he wielded great power, his coronation kept being postponed. Justin felt threatened by the biological nephew he had raised as a son, and he clung to life as a person does when his life is ending. He would shake his purple mantle and say that it was not meant for young men (although at the time the *nobilissimus* was almost forty-five).

The emperor was also hesitating because his more traditional advisors were pushing another nephew of his during Justinian's illness. Germanus, the other nephew, had always chosen the broader horizons of military life over the narrow confines of libraries or the palace archives. He had a serene attitude toward command and a sober, analytical mind. He always set aside time for leisure for himself and his retinue. Instead of tumbling into matrimony with former actresses, he had married into an aristocratic family. He was therefore a serious candidate deserving of Justin's attention, and choosing him would still keep the power in the family.

Nevertheless, Germanus did not act like an alternative to Justinian: he never opposed him; he always recognized his cousin's primacy. But whether he meant to or not, he became the first cloud in the horizon after Theodora's marriage. She immediately warned her husband about it. She exhorted him to move cautiously but act resolutely.

Thus we see the first signs of a mechanism that appeared throughout their marriage. It has been written that "they did nothing whatever separately in the course of their life together."[21] It is doubtful that Justinian consulted Theodora about the technical aspects of legislative and military matters, but she undoubtedly advised him with respect to his collaborators and his entourage, the people who represented him. With her keen eye and her experience, Theodora assessed people and situations, just as Justinian assessed books and documents. It was important to her that he assert his *person*, his power, even more than his *program*. And so she observed people and their movements and decided what was needed to ensure continuity for her husband's precious, irreplaceable power.

"They did nothing whatever separately in the course of their life together," we are told, and yet there is no evidence that Theodora accepted the theory or the ideology of Justinian's grandiose restoration program. It is unlikely she did, for Justinian's Western, nostalgically Roman leanings contrasted with her personal experience in the East, where she had had a different set of religious and linguistic experiences.[22]

Justinian had a formidable education and he was terrible in his anger; yet he was rendered unusually hesitant and indecisive by Uncle Justin's procrastination and the possible threat from Germanus. It was Theodora who drove him to action, to finally grab the imperial power. She reminded him that he had actually been holding the reins of power for years. That sometimes he even left their bed at night to attend to pressing government issues. And that only by possessing all the power would he succeed in fulfilling his plans and the promises they had made to one another. It was time for him to assert himself, either directly or through pressure from other quarters.

When his uncle finally died, the least uncertainty about succession would be disastrous for them. Something similar had happened to the candidates officially favored to succeed Anastasius in July 518, when no one considered Justin a candidate; history might repeat itself. The anti-Blue measures promulgated during Justinian's illness had been a warning. And if a son was born, it would be all the more necessary to lock in the institutional dynasty. Now Justinian grasped Theodora's working vocabulary: tactics, practice, experience, seeing for himself.

Emergencies struck the eastern provinces of the empire in 526, and it was imperative that the palace respond with a strong signal. Ephesus, the city where Mary the Virgin had passed to Heaven in her sleep, was flooded; Palestine was in the throes of an unbearable drought; Antioch was hit by a devastating earthquake that killed hundreds of thousands of people in and around the city. This avalanche of disasters made such an impression that the elderly Justin appeared in the church of the Holy Wisdom in dark robes without his imperial mantle or his crown.

All the disasters appeared to be signs of divine displeasure. According to the Monophysites in Egypt and the provinces, with whom Theodora must have kept in touch, God wanted to punish the Dyophysite persecutors who were sitting on the throne. The devout faithful of the Orient pleaded for Theodora to intercede with the man who had all the power.

Finally Justin relented; he was nearly eighty and had a gangrened leg from the illness that would kill him. He agreed to let Justinian ascend to the throne during Holy Week of the year 527. It turned out to be about a hundred days before the death of the old soldier from Vederiana: Justin died on August 1, his timing as perfect as in a theater performance.

Holy Thursday of the year 527, April 1, in the Sacred Palace of Constantinople: in the Triclinium of the Nineteen Couches, the vast hall where the emperor gave gala dinners, the members of the Senate and the Council, the empire's "government," were standing in dress uniform. Before the triclinium, in the Delphax Court, the emperor's palace honor guard and military escort were lined up. They shouted their ritual Latin cheer: "Tu vincas!" ("Victory to you!"). They shouted "Hooray!" three times in Greek. And the golden imperial crown was placed on the head of Justinian. The coronation was done either by Uncle Justin or by Patriarch Epiphanios, who recited prayers of blessing and good omens.

Dressed in the purple imperial chlamys, Justinian must have kept a waking vigil from Holy Thursday to Easter Sunday. He most likely took part in religious functions, asked for edifying readings, and fasted. It was a deliberate effort, an offering to the Passion of Christ, an earthly sacrifice marking the achievement of his life's goal, of what was to be a "passage" (in the wording used for the Easter celebration) to a new era for him and the people he felt were his. When he finally appeared in the gallery of the Hippodrome—the Kathisma—for public acclamation, his face was perhaps rested and fresh, as if he were himself renewed.

Justinian had reached the summit of power at the age of forty-five, in the second half of what was to be his long life. He came to it later than most: the illustrious ancient rulers such as Alexander the Great or Octavian Augustus started young. Only Julius Caesar had been older, and he was always Justinian's favorite; Justinian once wrote: "Caesar, our dearest, who gave a good beginning to our monarchy."[23]

Just before Easter, the emperor's encounters with Theodora must have been rare, brief, and chaste, not only because of a ceremonial duty or precept, but from a shared inner need for self-examination. She probably reminded him of the vast studies in which he had absorbed the great heritage of the past, a long and elaborate history that had become more complex than it once was. He was the worthiest of all. The strongest. With him, the world could rest easy in the long seventh eon. Their eon.

We do not know whether she was counseled in the days before Easter by the same spiritual fathers who advised Justinian. Perhaps they were not seeking the same advisors in their shared honor. The Monophysites that she preferred spoke more intimately and contemplatively, but were officially banished from the capital. Maybe from Alexandria she received a letter with blessings, joy, and wishes for a radiant future. She probably lived the days marking Christ's Passion without much rigorous fasting or vigils. If she received any visits, it must have been for concrete reasons: fittings for her robes; discussions of whether it would be more suitable to move immediately into the imperial apartments or to await Justin's passing; consideration of the meals to be prepared by the court chefs, or the order of precedence in her retinue.

Sunday, April 4, 527: Easter. Historians and Theodora's biographers have called this day "the best performance of her entire career,"[24] comparing politics to the stage yet again. They have imagined spectacular patriarchal coronations, processions from the ancient church of the Holy Wisdom to the Hippodrome, the applause for the two sovereigns who jointly greeted the celebrating crowds, the glance of complicity exchanged by the new rulers, and the excitement in Theodora's soul: she who had once probably danced or stood naked in the same arena, now dressed in a ruler's ceremonial robes of rich gold and brocade. But those who have carefully read the sources conclude that "we have no information about it."[25]

Probably the ceremony took place in a hall of the palace (perhaps the Augustaeum) before dignitaries, the patriarch, and Theodora's chamber retinue. Prayers were recited by the light of torches or candles. Petite, majestic Theodora made her entrance covered in a veil, which was then removed so that she too might wear the purple chlamys, the traditional regal mantle. Then the patriarch blessed a second crown and offered it to Justinian to place on his spouse's head. We can imagine that there were no shouts, no cheers; only an immense silence. The masses in the outdoor theaters had once applauded in a different way, but today, a select audience paid respectful homage to the woman who was becoming empress, an Augusta.

As the purple chlamys settled heavily on her shoulders, we might picture the images that flashed through her mind, snapshots from the bewildering mystery of her life. The purple fabric was from Tyre, as Hecebolus had been. The bright scrap of cloth she might have treasured as a child in the Kingdoms Game had magically become the completely real mantle she now wore. The colors of her troubled past—purple, green, blue—had given way to her imperial purple, which was hers to wear until she died. The chlamys flowed around her shoulders, its hue as deep and intense as blood.

Now her pace as she walked through the palace was slower, because of the weight of the robes that only they, the Augusti, had the right to wear, symbolizing that the whole world was with them and upon them. But the couple was also lighter and taller than everyone around them. Having "received imperial power"[26] together, they could consider themselves closer to God than anyone else. When he appeared before the people in the Kathisma gallery of the Hippodrome, the first thing Justinian did was make the sign of the cross. It was no casual coincidence that this took place on the happy day of Easter. God had spoken through men to elect him emperor, and the emperor had chosen God's day to appear before his subjects, who were, therefore, the chosen people.

Now Theodora was more than a lady: she was an Augusta, something that had been by no means inevitable. In the two centuries since the founding of the empire of Constantinople, from 324 to 527, there had been twenty-six emperors and a total of thirty wives. Only nine of these wives had been made Augustae, and not one of them from the very start like Theodora. (Three or four other women became Augustae because they were mothers or sisters of emperors.) Why had fate been so kind to her? The answer lay in her personal qualities, in the obstacles she had surmounted, and in her ties with the Orient, at least as much as it lay in Justinian's soul and his immense ego.

"Harmonious Movement"

Constantinople, 527–31

THEODORA TOOK UP RESIDENCE in the imperial apartments of the sacred palace of the second Rome and filled it with her spirit. It was a triumph marking the complete reversal of her fortunes: how far she had come since Governor Hecebolus cast her out of *his* palace in Pentapolis!

Here at the farthest tip of Europe, the peninsula of Constantinople where her imperial palace once stood and where the sultans of Istanbul later built the Topkapi palace, the chief ritual today is the procession of tourists. But in Theodora's time there were other gatherings, other festivities. Every ecclesiastical feast, every secular holiday, every audience—meetings with imperial dignitaries or with legates from remote, "barbarian" populations—was codified according to a sophisticated system.

It would be a mistake to imagine that this was just formal etiquette or an antiquated, conservative set of customs, for the system at the palace did not look backward: it looked ahead and upward. Its purpose was to abolish time and space and to create a direct relationship with the unchanging eternal. As the emperor was an intermediary between Christendom and the higher power above, his palace was invested with all sorts of symbolism. Weren't the chariot races in the Hippodrome a perfect microcosm? All the more reason, then, that the well-ordered workings of the palace and of the imperial ceremonies took on a symbolic, metaphysical, even religious nature.

It was not what we would recognize as modern efficiency, or

national "order" enforced by repressive police or judicial mechanisms, or by technical or technological innovations. In Constantinople, it was believed that "imperial sovereignty, exercised in an orderly and measured fashion, reproduced the harmonious movement conferred by the Creator on the entire Universe"[1] for the greater majesty, pleasure, and glory of the empire itself. The palace held a mirror up to the harmony of the world for the glory of the empire and the happiness of its subjects, and for their hopes for the afterlife.

In the view of some contemporaries of Justinian who looked longingly to the past, Justinian's survival and his victory—even more than Theodora's arrival—had destroyed the balance of that order: "For everything was thrown into confusion in every part and nothing thereafter remained fixed, but both the laws and the orderly form of the government were completely overturned by the confusion that ensued."[2]

Only a few months had passed since the decisive Easter of 527, but one notable already confided to his intimate friends that he had had a disturbing dream:

> it seemed to him that he was standing somewhere in Byzantium on the shore of the sea which is opposite Chalcedon, and that he saw this man [Justinian] standing in the middle of the strait there. And first he drank up all the water of the sea; so that he had the impression thereafter that the man was standing on dry land, since the water no longer filled the strait at this point, but afterwards other water appeared there that was saturated with much filth and rubbish and welled up from the sewer outlets which are on either side of the strait, and the man immediately drank even this too and again laid the tract of the strait bare.[3]

Was this a false vision, or a foreshadowing of future events? The dream seems to allude to Justinian's economic policy and its costs. The pure water could be the revenues accumulated in the state treasury by "frugal" Anastasius, and the wastewater the monies siphoned off—

arbitrarily?—in the years of Justin and Justinian's joint rule, from 518 to 527. The strait was dry: evidently it was perceived that the new regime lacked the financial and moral resources needed to bring off its ambitious political program.

This was a radical criticism; more nuanced opinions came from officials who planned and conceived new programs or actually organized their implementation. For example, the author of the *Dialogue on Political Science* (a work whose authorship and exact date during Justinian's reign are still in dispute) painted a picture of the sovereign and an idea of power as an "imitation of God," identifying God-given imperial authority with political philosophy. The divine imitation described in the *Dialogue* included generous gifts to one's subjects, a sure sign of an emperor's superior munificence and liberality. So this text seemed indirectly to approve of Justinian's characteristic spending; and yet it declared that an ideal emperor would be chosen from the nobility—whereas our emperor was merely a provincial who had been educated thanks to his uncle, the illiterate emperor before him. Was this author perhaps contesting the *person* in power?

Agapetus, an author and deacon in the early years of Justinian's reign, took a different tack. He wrote history's most famous mirror of princes (a late-Roman type of moral and political treatise that continued to be produced in the Byzantine and then the Slavic cultures) that may have been commissioned by Justinian. The seventy-two chapters of Agapetus's *Exposition* specifically addressed to Justinian did not stress the body politic as such—that is, the benefits subjects got from imperial imitation of the divine—but focused on the sovereign's moral figure as the bearer of absolute, unequivocal values, the channel for a divine philanthropy. It was not very different from a theocracy.

The Justinian restoration project has often been interpreted in a primarily geopolitical, legislative, and administrative sense. But no expansion could take place without roots, and Justinian found those roots in Christianity. Particularly in a united Christendom, which he considered the highest good, within the Catholic Church and the Holy Orthodox faith, under the protection of an emperor who was "equal to the Apostles." He perceived any discord within that faith as a threat to the unity of the empire.

Was this Catholic orthodoxy simply a tool for power, based on what has been called Justinian's "Caesaro-papism?"[4] To define it that way underestimates Justinian's real theological passion, his concrete, personal, almost existential commitment to the search for an ideal formulation of faith that might resolve the problems—so typical of late antiquity—caused by applying ancient philosophical categories to the Christian Gospel.

Certainly since the beginning of Uncle Justin's rule the throne had been reconciling itself to the authority of the Roman Catholic see. Moreover, starting from that fateful Easter of the year 527, Justinian was rigorous with heretics and Christian schismatics both, starting with those who denied the centrality of the Resurrection in the great design of universal history: the Manicheans, the Samaritans, the Jews, the pagan "Hellenes." These groups were targeted in the first legislative provision ascribed to the new emperor, which was launched in the months between his coronation and Justin's death (between early April and the end of July 527).[5] It was both an affirmation of orthodoxy and a return to older imperial traditions—for the most *anti*-Christian of all emperors, Diocletian, had (more than two centuries earlier) issued a directive against Manichaeism.[6] The Manichean devaluation of earthly life was intolerable to the empire even then, and the movement— actually a philosophy rather than a religion—remained a crime against the polity, subject to capital punishment, right into Justinian's reign.

Worshippers of other kinds were barred from holding office, from the army, and from the liberal professions. Their meetings were forbidden, their places of worship shut down, their property confiscated. They were even denied civil rights: they were unable to sue orthodox Christians for private or public debts, and could not testify against them in a lawsuit. By this time, full Roman citizenship was being equated with Christian orthodoxy; those who did not profess it survived only by the grace of the emperor, in the expectation that they would change their ways.

These basic elements of any fundamentalist government crop up in different forms in different times and places depending on the government's targets, but the result is always the same: "many were being destroyed by the soldiers and many even made away with themselves, thinking in their folly that they were doing a most righteous thing, and . . . the majority of them, leaving their homelands, went into exile."[7] Many fled to the Persian empire—traditional enemy of the "Romans." This violent outcome was quite the opposite of the unity that Justinian sought. Even the last remaining followers of Montanus, a rigorous second-century apocalyptic, were persecuted. They were awaiting the imminent end of the world, when Heavenly Jerusalem would suddenly descend from above. To escape the persecution, they shut "themselves up in their own sanctuaries, [and they] immediately set their churches on fire, so that they were destroyed with the buildings."[8] The Arians were treated less harshly: they were able to maintain a following in the "barbarian" enemy kingdoms of the Mediterranean West (the "persecutors of souls and bodies"[9]) and especially amid the rank and file of the "Roman" army that was so necessary to the emperor.

The Jews' worship was restricted, as was the worship of the Samaritans, who in 529–30 rebelled violently in the countryside of Palestine. The subsequent repression was so harsh that, according to Procopius, "it is said that 100,000 men perished in this struggle, and the land, which is the finest in the world, became in consequence destitute of farmers"[10] with serious repercussions on the local economy and the population count.

Paganism was another religious option, but it was limited to a fringe of nostalgic intellectuals and backward native populations. The two groups shared a proclivity for irrationality, witchcraft, and prophecy; the dialectical refinements of Socratic origin had been lost, and paganism was no longer linked to ideas of glorious virtue, either Hellenic or early-Republican Roman.

Over time, the imperial troops stamped out the worship of Ammon in Pentapolis and destroyed the temples from the age of Diocletian that had been erected at Philae on the Nile in the hinterland near Nubia. The deities of the Greek Olympus had been worshipped there, as were Isis, Osiris, and Priapus, and human sacrifices were still performed.

The year 529 has long been seen as the death date of ancient paganism: in that year Justinian ordered an end to the nearly thousand-year-old Academy of Plato in Athens. But although Justinian forbade pagans from holding teaching positions, and although those who refused baptism lost their property and were exiled, recent studies show that the wealthy academy's property was not completely confiscated even as late as 560, thirty years after Justinian's order.

So the imperial hand often wore a velvet glove when dealing with thinkers. Justinian knew that he ran the risk of glorifying his opponents. The result was that the last students of Plato, Plotinus, and Proclus turned their attention to the measured, modest words of Epictetus (A.D. 55–135), whom they appreciated as a model of moral philosophy suited to their period of tyranny and crisis. And even Olympiodorus, a totally pagan author, worked undisturbed in Alexandria beyond 565— well after the death of the Most Christian Justinian.[11]

The laws of 527 refrained from targeting the Monophysites, who had been persecuted in 518–19. Certainly the empress had direct influence on her husband here. She probably reminded Justinian that despite their virulent written polemics and the rise of nationalism in Syria and Egypt, the Monophysites were still the Christians closest to Catholic doctrine and—at least for figures such as the theologian Severus and Timothy the Patriarch—the most sensitive to the great idea of unity among Christians.

It did not escape Theodora, or Justinian, that Monophysite Alexandria and Egypt were very valuable economically, or that Monophysite Syria was very valuable strategically and politically in the face of Persia's military threat. Whatever the two decided, they had to avoid turning those places into opponents; they had to gather deeper knowledge of the situation, to verify, and to mediate—and in the meantime the Monophysite situation was stalled. Under the protection of the empress, some Monophysite monks and preachers discreetly came to Constantinople.

Ten years after the death of Anastasius and the new union with

Rome, a dialogue started up again, thanks solely to Theodora. The dialogue was particularly necessary from a historical point of view insofar as—as some historical sources have noted—it ultimately and ironically revolved around a single consonant of the Greek language, *en* or *ek*.[12] The Word incarnated "in" (*en*) two natures, or the Word incarnated "from" (*ek*) two natures: never before had the mystery of God seemed to come down to such a tiny detail.

In pursuit of unity, Justinian forged some new policies but gave priority to reformulating the existing body of laws, aiming to make them as clear and uniform as possible. Under the guidance of his trusted jurist Tribonian, a great legislative opus was launched. The *Corpus Juris Civilis* (Body of Civil Law) named the emperor alone as the source of *all* laws; this was the most important work of Justinian's absolutist ideology, and lasted as a monument for centuries to come.

Such a vast project required time and attention, but more urgent matters took precedence more often than Justinian would have liked. Foreign policy was one example, but the events that needed attention were not the ones that Justinian hoped for, such as the recapture of the West or the resurrection of Rome's glory. Instead he heard the din of weapons clashing along the eastern side of the empire's long borders. The One-Hundred-Year Peace made in 422 between the Roman Empire and the Persian kingdom had already been breached during the reign of Anastasius, and hostilities continued under Justinian. Instead of deploying his best young generals to recapture the West, as he longed to do, Justinian was forced to dispatch them to the Asian border to protect the empire. His new era was slow to begin, and history seemed to repeat itself.

Nisibis, Callinicum, Zenobia, Palmyra, and Edessa were among the legendary cities and strongholds that were forever being conquered, defended, and lost along caravan routes running through the heart of the Middle Eastern deserts as far as the banks of the Euphrates, the watershed between the two empires. In those distant regions, the only intelligible Latin words were the officers' clipped orders to the "Roman" soldiers. What language here could possibly express the universalistic, hegemonic claim of the Catholic Church and the Holy Orthodox faith, the alliance between the empire and the clergy?

What is more, every pronouncement was sure to bring a myriad of protests, a real Levantine sandstorm of options, alternatives, and exceptions exploding from combative theological schools, from the infinite stratifications of the Christian religious idea. Given a choice between their idea of Christ and a "Roman" empire trying to make them worship a different Christ, locals would choose the former, even under the Persian king if necessary. Doing so would take resources, men, and property away from the Romans. In the end, the restoration project might self-destruct.

Theodora had had a "direct vision," she had seen for herself: she knew those places and the character of their peoples, while Justinian knew only what he had read of them. Sensing that it was possible to avoid a clash of faiths over the nature of Christ, the Incarnate Word, she pointed out that he needed to search for common roots. Insistence on theological opposition could turn the age-old enemy, Persia, into a haven; the Roman subjects might become Persian taxpayers. This would be unacceptable, especially because Justinian's program created a heavy fiscal burden.

In this context, Theodora seems not unlike Anastasius, the Monophysite ruler who had given lip service to the lofty demands of Rome's "venerable Church" but maintained a down-to-earth understanding that many papal demands unfortunately could be met only "with much shedding of human blood."[13] But her attempt to "reconcile" the options on Christ makes her seem also like the western "barbarian" ruler, Theodoric (her near-homonym), the Italian Ostrogoth king who tried to reconcile local ethnic groups with the Germanic tribes before he died in 526.[14]

Just as a great and successful artist is rarely an isolated genius, any great political figure owes much of his fortune to a circle of collaborators. Early on, Justinian realized that he could rely on Theodora's advice and her life experience, and the empress in turn understood that within the palace, the courtiers who revolved around her had to be

❦

shaped to suit her needs. Her needs were clear: to guarantee continuity of power for Justinian and therefore for herself. While Justinian tended toward expansionism, Theodora's realism was primarily defensive. Her court had to obey and protect her.

She soon had the opportunity to test the loyalty and discretion of those who were at her service, in an episode that took place around the time her daughter was married. The child she bore before meeting Justinian was fifteen or sixteen years old in 530 and 531 and was, therefore, of age to marry according to the customs of the time. The sources refer vaguely to a high-ranking groom for her, someone from the family of the deceased emperor Anastasius—maybe a son of the emperor's nephew, Probus, a well-known Monophysite sympathizer (just like Caesaria, that other relative of Anastasius whom Theodora presumably met during her years in Alexandria). Theodora's daughter was spared the need for safety that had driven her mother to Pentapolis, and she married well. Soon the empress was a grandmother, the most admired grandmother in the civilized world; but she still hoped to be a mother again, providing sons for Justinian. In the meantime, her first grandson was, significantly, named Anastasius.

Theodora had ladies in waiting, chamberlain eunuchs, noneunuch dignitaries such as messengers, and high-ranking ushers who were charged with keeping and maintaining silence in the presence of the Augusti. Behind the chamber doors or vela (curtains), her entourage maintained a sacred confidentiality about the empress's famous meetings, audiences that unexpectedly made the women's quarters into a parallel court. (The empress was careful that this parallel court never cause conflict with the emperor.)

Once in a while, she allowed her servants some lighthearted moments. Her training as empress had not erased the part of Theodora's character that was famously "clever and full of gibes."

One day she graciously granted an audience to an older patrician. He prostrated himself in homage to the empress and made his case in refined terms, the product of many years at the service of the empire and of a proven expertise in matters of protocol. He had lent substantial sums of money to an attendant in Her Majesty's service, but the borrower was not returning the loan. And so he had run into liquidity problems that might be understandable for others but, he noted, were not appropriate for someone in such a lofty position. "Mistress, it is a grievous thing for a man of patrician rank to be in need of money." Hence his appeal, his supplication, his prayer, that she might intervene with this debtor in her service who—he added, with an obsequious allusion—was decidedly "not a patrician."

Theodora's eunuchs were ranged in a circle around the dignitary. After a brief moment of silence, the empress spoke. But instead of a speech, she practically chanted: "Oh Patrician," and spoke his name (which the *Secret History* did not reveal, "so as not to perpetuate the offense"). Even before the suppliant could exclaim in surprise, the eunuchs continued the song with, "It's a large hernia you have!" playing on the phonetic assonance between the Greek words *kêlê* (hernia) and *koilê* (hole), and even prompting another double entendre: "How great is your hole!" (in your finances, and perhaps not only there). The patrician persisted, repeating his speech, and received the same refrain in response. There was nothing for him to do but kneel again before his singing Majesty and take his leave, humiliated both personally and financially. He never collected on the debt. But the actress had unexpectedly surfaced again, on the palace stage.[15]

Theodora sought reference points among those who knew her well, starting with her family. While we have no information about her younger sister, the empress undoubtedly turned to the older sister, Comito, who had been her teacher onstage. We already noted that in 528–29 Comito had married Sittas, "a capable warrior, and a general second to none."[16] So we see that the families of the imperial couple— the emperor's provincial and military family and the empress's urban and show-business family—immediately started working to strengthen one another and build a new ruling elite bound closely to the throne. Years later, a similar arrangement would bind Comito's daughter Sophia in marriage to Justin, son of one of Justinian's sisters. The wedding was arranged and approved by Theodora before she died.

There is no evidence that Theodora used Comito for political affairs. The elder sister might have started the younger on the stage, but the younger one did not introduce the elder to the inner chambers of power. Theodora mostly used her as a confidante, as a representative, and in moments of pomp. More than cold politics, it was the warmth of life that united them.

General Sittas's marriage to Theodora's sister put him in the circle of "friendly" military. The situation was different for Germanus, Justinian's brilliant cousin. His wife, one of those elect souls beloved by conservatives, was not happy to march behind the former actress in processions. Her antipathy (or, at best, indifference) was probably reciprocated.

A third military officer just emerging at the time was to become essential not only to the outcome of Justinian's restoration program and to Theodora's personal life, but to sixth-century history on three different continents. More than most other characters appropriated by literary fantasists, Belisarius has become a legend remodeled to suit various times and places. Belisarius has been called Roman or Slavic (could his name come from *beli tsar*, the "white prince"?), or even Germanic.[17] The literature has described him in a variety of ways: as flawless or irresolute or even—in a late-Byzantine poem—ruined and disgraced. He was about the same age as Theodora: he was born around the year 500 to a family of landowners and he grew into an accomplished and vigorous knight. He began his career as an officer with an important victory against the Persians, enabling the Romans to dominate Mesopotamia for the first time in decades. The populace of the capital, and beyond, began to rally around Belisarius. Such success pleased Theodora, but it also alarmed her. Belisarius, like Germanus, could pose a threat to Justinian and, therefore, to herself. She needed to control him, and the tool she selected for this was a woman, Antonina. We might even conjecture that Theodora and Justinian "arranged" Antonina's marriage to Belisarius, so that they could be privy to every aspect of this skillful general's life.

Certainly Antonina was not the bride one would expect for Belisarius. She was at least ten years his senior and she was a widow (her husband may have been an Antioch merchant) with children, both legitimate and illegitimate. The *Secret History* reports that her father was "a charioteer who had given exhibitions of his skill" in the Hippodrome, and her mother was "one of the prostitutes attached to the theater"[18] (drawing the usual connection between prostitute and actress). It was a background uncannily similar to Theodora's: the two women had probably known each other for a long time. These details add more weight to the theory that the imperial couple (especially the empress) had a hand in this marriage, especially because the wedding took place around the year 530, when the empress's court was starting to acquire its own identity.

It is possible that Theodora suggested Antonina to Justinian, who had the authority to suggest that Belisarius marry her. Justinian must have declared that the woman was a good choice for the general: older, but experienced and still attractive, and especially careful in managing the wealth that the general would probably acquire in the service of the emperor and of his own ambitions.

Antonina is an extraordinary character in the *Secret History*, where she is subjected to biting criticism. Procopius spent many long years in the service of Belisarius, so he was in a unique position to observe the wife: he knew her far better than he knew the empress. His description of Antonina's exploits (especially her erotic exploits) are so graphically detailed and precise that they seem reliable. At the same time, Antonina must have been expert in the magic art of "love potions"; according to Procopius, she had "consorted much with the cheap sorcerers who surrounded her parents . . . having thus acquired the knowledge of what she needed to know"[19] to deceive Belisarius. On one occasion, he discovered her in a basement with a lover who had "loosened . . . the belt which supported [his] drawers . . . [that] covered his private parts,"[20] and yet Belisarius believed his wife when she told him that she was conducting a delicate financial audit.

Moreover, Theodora kept her eye on Antonina: the empress did not allow any extramarital liaisons that might disturb her universe. This made Antonina often restless, because "she dreaded the punishment the empress might inflict. For Theodora was all too prone both to storm at her and to show her teeth in anger."[21]

Anger on the throne? More than anything, this report shows the bond between the two women, a relationship that evolved with time into a very useful political alliance. On several occasions Theodora used Antonina as her right arm to eliminate prominent adversaries, while Belisarius remained in the background. The general had a direct bond with Justinian, and through Antonina he was subject to Theodora.

The military officers who executed plans for Justinian, the "least military of men," could become dangerous, so Theodora kept their wives close by. But she did not surround herself only with women: she depended on her eunuchs, particularly one named Narses. While his castration made him ineligible for the throne, he still had power and prestige. Besides, he was approximately the same age as Justinian and was therefore an ideal interlocutor for the young Augusta. He offered her all kinds of confidential information. Narses had immediately understood that Theodora's arrival would not harm his position as chief of the legendary eunuch "chamberlains with the sword" and might even improve it.

Narses came from Persarmenia in Asia Minor, the historical birthplace of the Roman Empire's eunuchs. He shared Theodora's Levantine aura, her cunning, her attention to detail, and her almost crude realism stripped of any archaic, mythological illusions. He had had an extraordinary career, fighting on the battlefield and participating in ambushes and massacres. He was as comfortable with palace intrigues as he was in the open country, at home in the city and in the woods. He saw everything, and he saw more of what happened than anyone else in Justinian and Theodora's era, because he outlived everyone. He was nearly one hundred when he died in Italy, a land he had helped to "liberate"—at great cost—from the "barbaric" Goths, as the emperor desired.

Narses was probably the coordinator of a whole network of friends (or spies?) of the empress who relayed important intelligence or at least the news that she wanted to hear; they supplemented the official channels of imperial functionaries and the information system supplied by her favorites, the Blues. Thus the women's quarters in the palace nurtured another branch of power that had no ideology or government program. Out of personal fealty to the empress, it operated for her satisfaction and for the continuity of her rule. Only a few years earlier, Theodora had been happy to finally see for herself. Now, like Justinian, she also felt the need to control.

During this early period John the Cappadocian was introduced to the palace. He was an expert accountant and tax advisor who was to become Justinian's favorite and Theodora's one great political enemy, as we shall see. But the empress always looked kindly on a certain cultivated Peter, "an Illyrian by birth, but a citizen of Thessalonica,"[22] who was a teacher of rhetoric in Constantinople; she liked him partly because of his innate deference. Instead of showing off his humanistic learning, he cultivated the art of homage: indeed, he dedicated his learning to paying homage to the imperial couple. He made light of his studies, as if they were no more than a private hobby, and this particularly endeared him to the omnipotent rulers.

Peter was reliable, an ideal envoy for diplomatic tasks and government business: he was entrusted with palace ceremonies as well as domestic and foreign duties. And he was erudite enough to help with the antiquarian aspects of the restoration: he was appointed to research and write historical works on imperial protocol. In later years, he was granted the rank of patrician.

Theodora understood that Peter's humility hid a "hope of great rewards,"[23] and she made use of him. One anecdote names her as the instigator and Peter as the orchestrator of the base murder of the Gothic queen Amalasuntha (discussed in a later chapter), insinuating that Theodora was "suspicious of her magnificent bearing . . . and at the same time [feared] the fickleness of her husband Justinian."[24] This episode is much disputed, but it documents Theodora's strong bond with Peter, who did get protection, favors, and wealth from her. The other courtiers looked at him askance, but he remained one the favorites of the throne.

✛ ✛ ✛

Peter was probably the person appointed by the two Augusti to review the court ceremonies and introduce an important change, which allowed them to express their autocratic and theocratic ideal in both gestures and words. The imperial ceremonials already reproduced a "heavenly image," and they became more exalted: they became a form of worship as they were in the enemy kingdom of Persia. And indeed, why should the Persian king receive greater homage than that paid to Justinian, when only Justinian was emperor by the will of the One True God, the God of the Christians?

Until this time, people admitted to the emperor's presence had been required merely to bow to him. Patricians could incline their heads in the direction of the breast of the Augustus and receive his kiss; the other senators genuflected on their right knee. Now that the empire had such vast political goals and such lofty religious and moral dicta, all the ancient formal customs and deep-rooted meanings were being changed.

Senators and patricians ceased to address the rulers with the technical, essentially neutral terms of "emperor" and "empress." They were to address them now as "lord" and "lady," if not "master" and "mistress." In other words, the technical appellation was supplanted by an admission of personal subjection; high-ranking dignitaries became "servants" if not "slaves" of the rulers. With this momentous change, the public affairs of the old Roman Empire became private affairs, the personal domain of the emperors.

The same potentates who had once avoided brushing against the garments of the "impure" former actress were now compelled to express their devotion to her with their body and even their lips. They had to prostrate themselves not only before the emperor but also before Theodora, their hands and feet stretched out on the floor, and kiss the foot of both Augusti before they could rise. Conservatives were scandalized by this innovation: they saw it as an unwise concession to external, "barbarian" or even Persian influences; but for the empress it soothed the memory of ancient rejections, of offenses suffered and suspicions endured.[25]

The emperor's power was believed to come directly from God, and he bestowed it on his wife as well. At his side, she gained more authority and influence: this empress received more homage than any *emperor* had gotten before.

The ceremonial protocol was designed to reflect the harmonious movement of the universe, and it inevitably had some anomalies, just as the sky has anomalous eclipses or speeding comets.

The obligations imposed on dignitaries and functionaries (not to mention commoners) were diametrically opposed to the freedoms granted by the Christian Roman Empire to those who rejected or left secular society in favor of a solitary relationship with the divine. These were the radical monks who lived in isolation, exemplars of an ascetic ideal interpreted in manifold ways by the many versions of Christianity. The anchorites were seen as variations or metamorphoses of the ancient role of "philosopher," and their unique status brought them complete freedom of speech and action (*parrhêsia*) with respect to the emperors, freedoms that were not permitted to others. They did not worship the Augusti but were worshipped by them. Magistrates prostrated themselves before emperors, but emperors knelt before ascetics.

In 531, Saint Sabas, a ninety-year-old monk who was a tireless organizer of monasteries in the deserts south of Jerusalem and around the Dead Sea, left his arid, thirsty Palestine to travel to the "Babel" of the capital. He brought with him a number of petitions for the emperor, who welcomed him with all honors: rising from the throne, bowing before him, and kissing him on the head. The emperor was in turn blessed by the holy man. Justinian listened to his requests and, as he withdrew to deliberate, invited the saint to visit Theodora in her apartments and to bless her.

The empress prostrated herself before Saint Sabas. Although Sabas's Palestine was a Dyophysite island between the Monophysite lands of Syria and Egypt, she acknowledged that his authority went beyond any dogmatic differences. Just as the holy man had petitioned the emperor, the empress now took a turn petitioning the monk. She spoke to Sabas as if to a "father," asking him to pray for her, "that God might grant her the Grace of bearing a child." It was the year 531, and Theodora was about thirty years old; she still believed that she could bear a child. Justinian also believed it, although he was almost fifty years old and had been sick around 524. To Theodora's plea, Sabas replied only: "God, the ruler and lord of all things, shall watch over your empire." Theodora repeated her prayer of intercession for mother-hood, and the Saint replied: "The Lord shall watch your empire in glory and in victory."[26]

Sabas's reply was *not* really a reply. Once again, the suppliant was weak. Like the widow and her daughters kneeling before the Green faction in the Kynêgion, like the patrician who had appealed to the empress to settle his debt, the empress found herself in a weak position right in her own palace, before someone who was considered an exem-plar of sainthood. In their dialogue, the power went to the one who claimed the right not to speak directly.

The monk then explained his behavior. He said that he could not pray on behalf of a heretical woman who would have given birth to a Monophysite child. Theodora had up until then given only slight hints of her theological views, but Saint Sabas had figured her out—the asce-tic was not blinded by the splendor of the palace.

(But not even this ascetic thought that he should blame Theodora or deny her anything on account of her theatrical past. For him—as well as for Timothy, Severus, and even Justinian—that past no longer counted. Theodora had once and for all resolved her earlier, controver-sial identity as an actress and remade her identity as purely *Christian*.)

A similar episode in Theodora's later life, possibly even more telling, has implications not only for the story of Theodora and Justinian, but also for the relationship between sovereignty and "holy madness." This kind of folly proved to be an enduring historical and cultural theme: Byzantine influence in the Slavic world brought the idea of holy fool-ishness as far as the courts of the czars in Moscow—a city that consid-ered itself a modern third Rome.

Mār the Solitary, a Monophysite ascetic monk who had come to the capital under the protection of Theodora, was welcomed by both rulers together, but he did not do homage to them or even give them any respect. He didn't even change out of his usual ragged tunic for the

occasion: its repulsive smell was proof of his devotion and his celebrated mortification. Mār the Solitary was not as old as Sabas: he was
a vigorous man, an imposing figure, "an athlete of God" with tremendous physical strength. One of his biographers wrote that he was
stronger "than ten criminals."[27]

The Solitary did not come to the palace to bless or admire anyone,
but to chastise. He reproached the rulers for their religious policy,
which he believed was hostile to the Monophysites, despite Theodora's
position. And he did not just blame them: he insulted them, wounding
them so deeply that the biographer's quill hesitated to specify how.
Protocol, the crown, and the purple mantle meant nothing to this
anchorite, accustomed as he was to the emptiness of his lonely retreat
in the desert.

His *parrhêsia* was met with surprising calm and majesty, like that
of the ancient emperors—like Marcus Aurelius's calm with Herodes
Atticus. The rulers were not disturbed. They said: "This man is truly a
spiritual philosopher," just as the Roman centurion at Golgotha had
said of Jesus, "Truly, this was the Son of God!"[28] Theodora had the
eunuch treasurer offer a remarkable quantity of gold to Mār the Solitary,
but the visitor refused it, throwing the gift back at Theodora. "May your
gift be damned just as you are!" he said, and fled. The rulers sent
ambassadors after him to explain that the offer of money was not meant
to buy his benevolence, but simply to aid in founding a monastery near
the capital.

This frank monk, who lived "outside the world," was the only person to whom the emperor and empress, "lords of the world," ever felt
the need to justify their actions.

ELEVEN

"Royalty Is a Good Burial-Shroud"

Constantinople, 532

All Nature, O Queen, ever sings thy might
For that thou didst destroy the ranks of the enemy,
For that after the evil broils thou didst kindle a light for prudent men
And didst scatter the civil troubles of the strife that loosed the horses.

NOT LONG AFTER January 532, a poetic courtier recited these verses (now found in the *Greek Anthology*, XVI 44), before Empress Theodora and her intimates. Was it a spontaneous inspiration, or had the poem been commissioned—and if so, by whom? Perhaps by Justinian, who wished to please his empress?

While the author is unknown, the meaning is clear. The empress is celebrated as the absolute mistress: her power is universal, acknowledged and acclaimed, worshipped just as the image of Christ *Pantokratôr*, the "Universal Master," was worshipped.

Theodora's power was no dogmatic invention: it was born from real circumstances. It was the result of a victory over enemies ("thou didst destroy . . . didst scatter") inside the empire: for there had been "civil troubles" ("the strife") right in the Hippodrome, a pivotal place in the fabric of Constantinople's life, and of Theodora's life in particular. And while ceremonial protocol forbade the Augusta from officially attending the games, still the poet saw Theodora's shadow hanging over the arena like a symbolic icon.

And indeed it was Theodora who determined the outcome of the

Nika insurrection, the most violent and momentous urban riots ever to occur in antiquity or late antiquity. More than thirty thousand, perhaps even fifty thousand, people died in the riots: in the most important metropolis of the Christian world, a tenth or a twentieth of the population perished. Some say that these deaths were the cruel sacrifice paid to the new idol of the Christian world, Theodora.

Like every great story, the events of the Nika rebellion have been told an infinite number of times; each retelling prompts new interpretations and debates. Like every story, it needs a beginning, and some later observers erroneously imagined that it began with a general desire to revive "virtuous" civil liberties, or with an elitist longing for bygone excellence during the decline caused by imperial absolutism (as in Victorien Sardou's *Théodora*). The Nika rebellion actually sprung from the grass roots of society, and it was prompted not by nostalgia for the past but by present needs; as was always the case in Constantinople, the truth was a complex mosaic of elements.

Some dignitaries of the empire had already likened Justinian to a sea monster that sucked up water and money. Others criticized his policies regarding the many nomadic tribes that moved along the dangerous borders of the empire from the Danube to Arabia: he had purchased their nonbelligerence at too high a price, they said.[1] Even Khosrow I, the new king of Persia, demanded gold before he would consider the possibility of peace along the eastern frontier. In addition, the emperor's imitation of God did not seem to be particularly welcome "in the high heavens." The tragic Antioch earthquake of 526 was followed by a second one in 528. In 530, yet another earthquake had shaken Antioch's historical rival, Laodikeia, one of the best ports of the Levant and the capital of the new province of Theodorias (recently established in honor of Theodora Augusta).

The two sovereigns had dug deep into the imperial coffers to help with post-earthquake reconstruction, displaying dedication and generosity, but their actions had not served to dispel concerns and suspicions aroused by the behavior of some of their closest collaborators. It was rumored, for example, that the jurist Tribonian, who supervised the great project of rewriting the body of laws and was quaestor of the sacred palace (a sort of minister of justice), "was always ready to sell justice for gain."[2] The perception of judicial disarray enraged the masses, who were already bitter about John the Cappadocian's fiscal policies. Capping a swift series of promotions, John had become praetorian prefect of the East,[3] the most influential of ministers. Justinian relied heavily on his skills, and for ten years, from 531 to 541, John exerted great power throughout the empire.

John the Cappadocian did not have a classical education, but he knew accounting very well. Justinian expected him to generate the income, or the savings, which he needed to pursue his "Great Idea" of renewal and restoration, and John met his expectations. He made sure that fiscal laws were obeyed. He supervised the landowners, the merchants, and the shopkeepers. Revenues were routed directly to him by his inspectors, instead of passing through the provincial élites, the curiae, as they once had. John the Cappadocian was pivotal in the process of centralization required by Justinian's plan. A manager with a sharp eye for cutting costs, John reduced and even eliminated part of the postal service, which is the essential glue of any polity.[4] The post had been among the empire's traditional glories—one of the services that set the Roman civilized world "of the thousand cities" apart from the "barbarian" no-man's-lands.

"The events taking place in each region, being reported with difficulty and too late to give an opportunity for action, and by then overtaken by the course of events, cannot be dealt with at all."[5] The public post not only guaranteed speedy communications, but also affected the supply of all kinds of raw materials and staples. The results of its elimination were disastrous for rural industry, a productive base that contributed food and tax revenue to the empire. The owners of large estates, who had been accustomed to "sell[ing] their excess crops," now saw "their crops rotting on their hands and going to waste."[6] The small landowners bore the brunt of the new situation, since they supplied the city markets. Unable to afford the cost of private transportation, the farmers (both men and women) trudged along the roads of the empire carrying their crops on their backs in the "Asiatic mode of production" (as economists call it today). Overcome by fatigue, many lay down and died on the road. Others abandoned their crops and moved to the city, trusting in some form of Providence, whether divine or imperial.

When the food supply is irregular, life gets harder in a capital over-crowded with mouths to feed. Besides, hungry people talk, and Constantinople always offered fertile terrain for all kinds of vicious gossip, both in late antiquity and in the Middle Ages. And so before long John the Cappadocian was being blamed on moral and Christian grounds, instead of being judged simply by bureaucratic or political criteria. It was rumored that he was an evil man who kept Roman citizens[7] in secret chambers, forcing them to pay taxes he claimed were overdue by threatening them with the same humiliating torture inflicted on slaves or highway robbers. All this, to channel money into Justinian's coffers. Or was it for personal gain?—some swore that John embezzled most of the taxes that the citizens believed they were contributing to the welfare of the empire.

The slanderous rumors intensified: John was getting rich; John was a drunk; John had an infamous retinue of jesters and prostitutes both male and female; he was a heathen who pretended to say Christian prayers while actually reciting magical pagan formulas. The rumors and accusations were not so different from those that once circulated about Theodora. In time, John and the empress would grow to be enemies, but they were both victims (for different reasons) of hostile preconceptions among those who considered themselves decent and upright citizens.

Because the factions were so active in the Hippodrome, that place became a natural sounding board for economic and political tensions. After the violent urban riots of 523–24, after Justinian's arbitrary protection of the Blue radical fringe, the Greens had even chanted:

Would that Sabbatius [Justinian's father] had never been born!
That he might not have a murderer [Justinian] for a son![8]

The disturbances continued for years, like a chronic "disease of the soul"[9] fed and nourished by a self-destructive instinct: "[the seditious factions] fight against their opponents . . . knowing well that, even if they overcome their enemy in the fight, the conclusion of the matter for them will be to be carried off straightway to the prison, and finally, after suffering extreme torture, to be destroyed . . . [all this] without a cause."[10] The factions were not acquainted with ancient philosophy, but an educated observer might have noted that their riotous behavior seemed to undermine Aristotle's authoritative description of man: "by nature a political animal . . . endowed with reason."[11] But Aristotle's Ideal City contained perhaps thirty thousand inhabitants, whereas the imperial city on the Bosphorus had a population at least twenty times greater.

The year 532 began with new trouble between the Blues and the Greens. Now focused on military issues in the west, Justinian ordered that the situation be brought under control with the same measures he had used in 524 against *his* Blues; such measures were now to be applied impartially to the extremists of both factions. Eudaemon, the city prefect, ordered the militia to arrest anyone engaged in violence, no matter what faction they belonged to. The Greens saw this as a continuation of the unjustified persecution of their group, while the Blues felt betrayed by their longtime patron, especially when they heard that the investigations and arrests were culminating in death sentences for members of *both* factions. Four rebel leaders, both Green and Blue, were sentenced to be hanged.

The scaffold where the sentences were carried out was in Sykae (Galata), beyond the Golden Horn, in a square near one of the many monasteries where religious men tried to merge heavenly and earthly life through prayer and exercise, without meddling in politics. Tensions were running high, and the hangman's hand was unsteady: two of the prisoners, one Blue and one Green, survived the first attempt. The noose was wound more tightly, but the two men fell from the scaffold still alive. Shouting, the public proclaimed it a miracle, a sign of God's favor.

With the help of the nearby monks, the two prisoners were ferried over to the city and brought to a church that had the right of asylum. Eudaemon stationed a circle of militiamen around the edifice, while the crowd demanded freedom for the two men who had been saved by the hand of God. It was Saturday, January 10, 532.

A few days later, Tuesday, January 13, was a day for the emperor to preside over chariot races at the Hippodrome. Both factions took the floor: the spokesman for the Greens talked with devout respect, but the Blues' spokesman had a more colloquial tone. They both asked for pardons, but Justinian rejected their pleas with the customary arrogance of the potentate who receives a supplication. He may have wanted to show how firm he was, but his stubbornness seemed unjustified and arrogant more than authoritative.

After twenty-two chariot races, the short winter day was coming to a close. It was then that an unheard-of, new shout rose from the Hippodrome crowd:

Long live the benevolent Greens and Blues!

It was shocking to hear the two names pronounced together: never before had one faction recognized the other's "benevolence" or humanity (*philanthropia*). Indeed, this virtue had always been considered a uniquely imperial prerogative. So here was a brand-new situation: the established power no longer appeared to be completely sacred.

For their part, the emperors of the past had always set the factions against each other so as to avoid potentially threatening coalitions. They simply applied the divide-and-conquer strategy learned from that ancient Roman culture whose glory Justinian sought to renew. But now events were conspiring against him. His great vision of the Mediterranean scenario had neglected some essential elements of the urban scene right under his nose. Meanwhile, the Greens and Blues were setting aside their reciprocal hostility and turning jointly against the palace. Maybe it was good medicine for healing the "disease of the soul" that affected them.

Justinian's ears ("donkey ears,"[12] according to his critics) heard the acclamation that was being shouted over and over, louder and louder. It rose like thunder, shouted by tens of thousands of voices. The emperor, the "Chosen One," could not bear it. He left the Kathisma and retreated to the sacred palace, the glorious public institution that was also his personal haven.

Now a new shout was heard in the Hippodrome, terrifying in its brevity:

Nika! Nika! Nika!

"May you win! May you win! May you win!" *Nika* was the Greek version of the Latin *Tu vincas*, the cheer from the crowds that usually greeted the Augustu*s* in his role as military chief. The crowd's change of language signaled a change in meaning. The phrase no longer exhorted the emperor to prevail over an enemy; now one faction was exhorting the other, one citizen wishing another, "may *you* be victorious!" Thus, the emperor was no longer "benevolent" and "humane" or "victorious." Strengthened by its size and its everyday language, the crowd had seized those prerogatives for itself, without any partisan distinctions. Being able to speak out meant being able to act.

The emperor did not lower himself to a verbal confrontation, for it would have meant recognizing the opposing party. Just as Asterius gave no answer when the little girls pleaded with him in the Kynêgion years before, the prefect Eudaemon, who was in charge of public order, gave no answer to the crowds that flocked to his palace to hear the fate of the two men who had survived the hanging. His refusal was the legendary straw that broke the camel's back. The crowd went on a rampage: it killed soldiers and officers, set fire to the prefecture, and threw open the jail doors. The factions joined against one common enemy, one oppressor: Eudaemon. (Ironically, the Greek root of his name refers to happiness.)

Then the crowd attacked the doors of the sacred palace. The elegant and decorative guards were not warriors: they put up no opposition. The crowd set fire to the palace vestibule (the Chalkê), to the senate building, and to the basilica of the Holy Wisdom (Hagia Sophia). These were some of the most distinctive buildings of Constantine's city: the palatial symbol of power; the home of the senate that had raised up the second Rome to equal the first; and the church that kept the city under God's protection were all lost in a single night of fire.

At court the next day, Wednesday, January 14, people were confident that the riots would die out with the fires. The chariot races were ordered to resume as if the city weren't enveloped in acrid smoke. But instead of returning to the Hippodrome, the crowd now moved toward the baths of Zeuxippus, another symbolic site near the palace. They weren't there to wash or to admire the collection of ancient sculptures that invited visitors to return to traditional virtues. The rebels set fire to the baths, then proceeded to the Hippodrome. And they didn't come there to watch the races. The protest was turning into a political statement. The heads of the two factions had met in secret all night long and they were no longer simply asking that the two condemned men be set free; now they wanted political changes: they wanted resignations.

The crowd asked for the dismissal of Eudaemon and his enforcement tactics, of Tribonian and his laws, and of John and his taxes. They demanded all this from Emperor Justinian: there was no direct threat yet to the emperor's power. He acceded to the crowd's demands and sacrificed his illustrious collaborators. He spent no time defending them: he expected to simply hire them back again after having entrusted the city, for a short time, to skilled technicians who could remedy the situation. The men that he removed from office were kept in the palace to protect them from possible violence and to reassure them of his high regard.

Some complained that a simple reshuffling of the government was not enough. This was especially true in conservative circles that were hostile to Justinian and his group and had criticized him in the past. Rumors circulated about a possible new political solution to the riots. People were looking especially to Anastasius's family: people said the family descended from Pompey the Great and thus represented the true glory of Rome. They were neither rough soldiers nor Illyrian shepherds, as Justin and Justinian were. (Besides, even Theodora had recently looked to Anastasius's family when seeking a safe marital haven for the daughter she had born during her performing days.)

Emperor Anastasius had left no children: his only heirs were his sisters' sons and daughters. Two of them, Pompeius and Hypatius, were out of reach, under siege at the palace along with the emperor and other notables. The rebels hoped that a third nephew, Probus, was in the city. They walked to his mansion, but found it empty; he had already left the capital. Perhaps he had been forewarned (maybe because of his tie to Theodora's daughter); perhaps he was following the Epicurean advice to "live in hiding";[13] perhaps he was avoiding trouble, giving an early example ideal of meek fidelity to power that became a rule in the Byzantine age. The rebels destroyed his house, making Probus the first victim of the rebellion he had almost been selected to lead. This signal could be interpreted in many different ways, and by Thursday, January 15, a debate about how to react was raging in the palace and across the whole city.

In such situations, the established power customarily resorts to the army, and Justinian was no exception; it helped that two excellent generals, Belisarius and Mundus, were at the palace, each with troops devoted to their leaders and their paychecks. Perhaps two thousand strong, the soldiers tried making a sortie outside, assuming that with their training they would easily prevail over the more numerous but less disciplined rebels. But once again some churchmen intervened unexpectedly, just as the Sykae monks had the past Saturday. Some ecclesiastics from the basilica of the Holy Wisdom appeared in the street: they were carrying the relics they had saved from the recent fire. They wanted to separate the crowd from the soldiers and save some lives, but Belisarius's troops saw them as an impediment, and trampled them on the pretext that they were obstructing military action.

Now the emperor looked really bad: he seemed to be heathen and inhuman, pitting his soldiers against devout and defenseless priests, against "benevolent," albeit incendiary, factions. The incident made such a powerful impression that even the women of Constantinople left their quarters and poured into the streets to exhort the men to fight.

✦ ✦ ✦

In January 532, Constantinople was the very image of a world turned upside down. The emperor, lord of the Ecumene, was holed up in his palace like a prisoner. Former prisoners walked the streets freely. Women were also in the streets, which was uncommon and exciting. Disorder and anarchy reigned in the city just as it was trying to codify new laws that were to stand gloriously through the centuries. The night sky was lit up by fires. Hospitals and churches were destroyed, and those with wounded bodies and spirits were left homeless. Even the house of the rebels' favorite candidate had been set on fire. In a perverse switch, the city once considered the center of triumphant civilization was suddenly home to every possible barbarity.

There were signs of disturbance even within the palace, which was believed to reflect the harmonious movement of the stars. Standing at the heart of the whole ceremonial system, the emperor detected anomalies in the movement of his planets: he suspected the dignitaries and functionaries around him of disloyalty and secret conspiracies. He ordered everyone to leave the palace. Only his closest council of advisors remained: John the Cappadocian, Narses, Belisarius, Mundus, Tribonian, and a few others. Anastasius's two nephews—Pompeius and Hypatius—asked to stay; perhaps they had heard that Probus's house had been set on fire. But their request only increased the ruler's suspicion. He ordered them, too, out of the palace. In essence, he provided candidates for the rebels who were seeking a leader. It was the evening of Saturday, January 17, 532.

"I know whom I have to face. But I will be the first one to speak." Justinian wanted to reassert his authority, and Theodora was listening. She still had not taken a position.

On Sunday, January 18, the emperor made an appearance in the imperial box at the Hippodrome. In his hands he reportedly carried the Gospel, and in his mind must have been two political, personal precedents. The first was from the time of the civilian uprising against Anastasius. In response to his critics, Anastasius had provocatively appeared in public without the imperial crown and invited the arena to choose a new monarch. Taken by surprise, the crowd did nothing but reconfirm his position and their trust in him. The second precedent was from Easter 527, when for the first time Justinian had blessed the crowd as the Augustus.

As he had done on that occasion, he now assumed a priestly role. Then he made himself into a sacrificial lamb, saying, "I forgive you the offense you have committed against me. I shall order no arrests as long as calm returns. You are not to blame for what happened. I am, for my sins." With this, Justinian drew attention to both his personal and his official selves, as he had done in the ivory diptych of 521. But in 521 it looked like arrogant self-confidence before a selected audience; now it was a pathetic plea before the crowd in the Hippodrome. And the Christian reference to his sins backfired, for the crowd grasped his weakness. They began to shout, blaming him for his lies, starting with the long-ago (and presumably long-forgotten) betrayal of Vitalian. Making a play on words between the assonance of the Greek Ioustini*anos* ("Justinian") and *onos* ("donkey"), someone even accused him of dense stubbornness. The jeering grew, and the emperor began descending the stairs of the Kathisma. The doors closed behind him, hiding him again in the protective shell of his palace. Instead of a possible arbiter and moderator in the dispute between ministers and factions, he had become an enemy, the greatest enemy.

In the burning city, the crowd found the leaders they were seeking: the two nephews of Anastasius who had been dismissed from the palace. The crowd was joined by groups of anti-Justinian potentates, but their union was quite ephemeral—it was never a political program. Still, they joined forces and chose Hypatius as their leader. He had once been an important, though not invincible, general. Now he was primarily a husband. His wife, Maria, wracked with dark omens, wept and reached out to him, trying to prevent him from accepting a fake imperial coronation. But the scene was not quite as moving as the ancient scene of the mythical, prophetic Andromache, who tried to hold back her Hector, her stolen hero, her noble, losing warrior. Hypatius was not the type of man who "wanted to do great deeds, leave something of himself to men yet to be born."[14] He was trembling, weakly saying "no, no."

Finally, the rebels succeeded in decorating him with a symbolic torques, the sovereign's neckchain. He knew many of the illustrious aristocrats among those cheering him as emperor, shouting "Long live Hypatius." And so Hypatius took heart. They reached the Hippodrome, and he was raised to the imperial loge, the Kathisma, the same box where Justinian had appeared shortly before—but he came directly from the arena, not through the palace. Behind him, palace guards stood watch at the single door separating him from the center of power. It was a modest physical barrier, but an enormous mental one.

Inside the palace, it seemed sacrilegious that Hypatius was so close. Belisarius wanted to do away with the usurper, and he tried to force the guards blocking access to the loge to carry out his command. But they resisted, because they were not sure whose side God was on. They were waiting for events to unfold before deciding whether Hypatius was a meteor that would disappear in a flash, or a true Augustus worthy of their support. One sign would suffice; it was still an era of revelations.

The right gesture might be taken as a sign, so Justinian's secret council considered all kinds of possible actions. A "true Roman male" in ancient times—even someone as abominable as Nero—would have killed himself to save his honor, but suicide was an unsuitable choice for a Christian. Flight seemed to be the only option left. The southern coast of the Black Sea (or Pontos Euxeinos) offered a safe haven, with lands and palaces still faithful to the crown. This would be a good temporary solution, a fine place from which to later recapture the city. But Justinian knew his ancient history, and he knew that such a solution was rarely successful.

Like a great ship, the *restitutio* seemed to have run aground even before setting sail; the restoration seemed to be sunk, and it looked as if the Augusti would never reach their glorious destination. But a real boat was at the palace quay, waiting to take the sovereigns on a far shorter crossing, to safety.

At this point—according to Procopius, who probably got an eyewitness account from Belisarius—Theodora stepped in. Her speech to the emperor's secret council is the longest one of hers ever recorded, and while her biographer may have polished it and added erudite allusions to suit his rhetorical purpose, it remains unique. It may not reflect the actual form of her speech, but it testifies to Theodora's intentions and her logical argument. She took the floor before the highest dignitaries of the empire and said:

> As to the belief that a woman ought not to be daring among men or to assert herself boldly among those who are holding back from fear, I consider that the present crisis most certainly does not permit us to discuss whether the matter should be regarded in this or in some other way.
>
> For in the case of those whose interests have come into the greatest danger nothing else seems best except to settle the issue immediately before them in the best possible way.
>
> My opinion then is that the present time, above all others, is inopportune for flight, even though it bring safety.
>
> For while it is impossible for a man who has seen the light not also to die, for one who has been an emperor it is unendurable to be a fugitive. May I never be separated from this purple, and may I not live that day on which those who meet me shall not address me as mistress.
>
> If, now, it is your wish to save yourself, O Emperor, there is no difficulty. For we have much money, and there is the sea, here the boats. However, consider whether it will not come about after you have been saved that you would gladly exchange that safety for death.
>
> For as for myself, I approve a certain ancient saying that royalty is a good burial-shroud.[15]

At that point, a hush fell over the council. (There was nothing ceremonial about this gesture of respect, even though the technical name for those meetings—*silentia*, "silences"—reflected the rule that only the emperor had the right to speak.) After Theodora spoke, the council thought it best to remain silent.

She gave no justification for her actions in her opening remarks, until she reached the words "assert herself boldly." Her perspective was practical, focused on action. She acknowledged that they faced a dangerous situation: they had reached the ultimate evil ("settle the issue . . . in the best possible way"). Courtly euphemisms or circumlocutions were totally foreign to her.

After analyzing the situation, she offered her conclusion: the impending danger was absolute and extreme, and she absolutely rejected the idea of fleeing. The empress continued with a logical syllogism: death inevitably accompanies life, but exile has no place alongside imperial dignity.

The pendulum swung from the absolute to the individual ("I consider," "my opinion," "may I never," "as for myself") and it swung again in the next passage: life is not life (the absolute)—or, better: *my* life (the individual) is not a life unless I can wear the purple, unless I am addressed as "mistress." (From this we can guess that the palace had already started to use the new ceremonial appellation and veneration of the rulers, the innovations that so irritated Procopius and other conservatives.)

Theodora's speech could have ended here, with the idea that life wasn't worth living if she wasn't wearing the purple. Some in Justinian's inner circle might have smirked, thinking it was certainly true that Theodora would be nobody without the purple, that she would once again be the woman—*that kind* of woman—that Constantinople knew so well. But right here her irrepressible actress's spirit flared up. After all her unexpected reversals—after venerated old laws were altered for her, after she took the throne against all expectations—her new scenario, impossible as it seemed, was the most unexpected reversal of all.

She was not speaking in abstractions, in general statements for the whole group; she spoke to Justinian, her preferred interlocutor. She looked only into the eyes of God's "Chosen One." The other characters had suddenly fallen to the back of the stage; they were mere extras, and the close-up was now on the two rulers.

They were separated from the group, and Theodora—in a move worthy of an Attic tragedy—separated her destiny from that of the emperor. The emperor could save himself if he chose: there was no dearth of money, the sea was open, the ships were ready to welcome whoever wanted to flee. But Theodora saw flight not as salvation but as a "second death," in the words of the Gospel[16]—a fate even worse than death.

She was accustomed to defying the world's customs and conventions: she would not run. Should Justinian choose to retreat, she would not share his fate; he would prove himself unworthy of the throne. In spite of his ego, his studies of antiquity, even his concept of messianic power, he might choose to flee, doing something that no Roman emperor had ever considered suitable or possible. *She* would remain faithful to her purple. She would carry on the traditions of antiquity, in the present, in her deeds—not just in words, not just in plans for the future. She would do so by resisting, even dying, because there was no life without the purple cloak of power. To avoid being separated from her purple, Theodora was saying, she was even willing to lose Justinian and marry death instead, to choose the purple over the man who had granted it to her.

While the legitimate ruler pondered the prospect of fleeing from the purple, Hypatius the usurper trembled at the possibility of wearing it. Things really were completely backward: suddenly the women were the only people in the city talking in a tough, "manly" way. A multitude of unknown women came out from their gynoecia and poured through the city streets, urging their men to fight, and on the other side, in the palace, the famous empress was challenging the emperor and his circle to resist.

Though she was a woman, she spoke like a man, like an emperor. She gazed at the *res severa* (the "solemn matter") of life and power with clear eyes, focusing on holding on to and perpetuating her power. She did not mention Christianity in her speech. The solemn, haughty spirit of ancient Rome spoke for the last time in history, through her. That spirit had one final metamorphosis—as a woman, as a former actress—and then it died like the prophetic voice of a vanishing sybil.

After this time, the concept of the true Roman man would be subsumed into the idea of the faithful Christian. Man would evolve just as the laws were evolving: whatever was *Roman* about a man (or a law) would survive only insofar as it was also *Christian*.

Even in those times of change, the old sayings still held, such as the adage that "royalty is a good burial-shroud": these words come from Isocrates, an orator who lived a thousand years before Theodora in the "democratic" Athens of the fifth and fourth centuries B.C.[17] Theodora had not necessarily read his writings; she might have read excerpts in some collection of famous quotations, or heard the words from the erudite Peter, for example, or even from Justinian—in which case she was throwing them back in his face during the crisis. It's not important for us to know her sources right now; what matters is how Theodora used them in her speech, her marvelous *coup-de-scène*, her reversal, her spectacle.

The reversal is particularly clear when we compare the measured beginning of the speech with its stinging conclusion. The ending, in ancient style, wraps up the whole argument just like a shroud wraps a lifeless body. A masterpiece of expositive progression, it is one of the gifts that Procopius, with his classical writing skills, gives the empress. Earlier, Procopius's reworking of his first controversial "quote" from Theodora (her lament about the "four openings") reaches back to an ancient tradition of literary disapproval; similarly, his version of the defiant Nika speech skillfully uses rhetorical progression to embrace references to the present, declarations about absolute values, citations and allusions that clearly reveal Procopius's literary intent. They are particularly inspired. The Nika speech was written by a man who clearly—at least as far as this episode is concerned—admired his empress.

(Again, Theodora probably did not utter these very words; but she did speak before the emperor's privy council, proof of her increased political and public role. And her speech certainly had an extraordinary effect on her audience: it became the stuff of legend. When the first book of Procopius's *Wars* was published, probably around 551, readers were already expecting a written confirmation of that oral legend, and they were not disappointed.)

The tangled developments that followed the speech were also necessarily theatrical. Backstage, none of the men in the imperial council dared look Theodora in the eye, for this woman with her "bold" advice seemed to be the only manly presence left. But the idea of fleeing had been discarded, and the men debated strategies for intervention and resistance.

Meanwhile, "onstage" at the Hippodrome, Hypatius seemed afraid of his audience; the tens of thousands of cheering people must have suddenly seemed to him like alien apparitions. He had an unexpected change of heart, and he scribbled a message to Justinian saying that he was pretending—just playing a role. For him, too, the rebellion was theater. Although he was wearing an imperial chain and sitting in the Kathisma, Hypatius swore his loyalty to the legitimate ruler. He wrote that he was keeping the crowd inside the Hippodrome so that it might more easily be routed by the imperial troops. He sent the message with one of his men; the messenger was admitted to the palace, met a dignitary, and requested an audience with the emperor. Impossible, came the reply: the rulers have already fled. Was this just misinformation, or had the dignitary been told to lie deliberately? We do not know. But when the rebels heard of Justinian's "flight," Hypatius and the others changed their minds again and began to feel more confident. They were beginning to believe that God was with them—but it was too late.

After Theodora's speech, the discussion in the palace must have shifted to the subject of colors. The word *purple* was repeated and, as usual, the color purple went with Blue and Green: the council considered how to approach the factions. In an attempt to regain the Blues's goodwill, Narses's eunuchs were sent into the Hippodrome crowd with cash from the palace coffers. They handed out the coins with ambiguous words: "Careful—you're allied with the Greens now, but Hypatius will favor them over you. . . . Remember what your situation was like before Justinian."

Meanwhile, another sortie was launched with another kind of metal: swords instead of coins. Belisarius and Mundus took their troops (Goths and German Herulians), and they slipped out; they were quiet and disciplined, and no one noticed them. Luckily for them, they did not meet any ecclesiastics from the Holy Wisdom church this time. It was an ironic twist of destiny: they were heading for a rout in the Hippodrome, just as Hypatius had suggested in the message that never reached Justinian.

Belisarius entered the Hippodrome from the western gate, which had direct access to the Blues's section; Mundus and his men used the entrance ominously called the "Deadman's Gate." The large crowd assembled in the huge arena was armed with only primitive weapons, and it could not resist the two select corps of military professionals. A ferocious slaughter ensued; this was perhaps the bloodiest Sunday of the first Christian millennium.

The palace guard, which had been hesitating between the rebels and the legitimate ruler, opened the doors of the imperial gallery and easily captured the frightened Hypatius and his followers, including his brother Pompeius. There was no resistance.

The uprising was defined as a crime of high treason, which was punished by beheading. The rebels were immediately led before the emperor. Hypatius told Justinian that he had given him proof in writing of his fealty.

"Your message never reached us," was the answer.

He added that he had been forced to act under duress.

"But you did not have to wait such a long time to show your loyalty to the emperor."

At this point Hypatius began begging for his life.

Since the two men knew each other well, the emperor was inclined to spare Hypatius in a generous act of clemency. Justinian may have thought about all the Christian blood had already been shed that day; he may have considered the lofty concept of "benevolence" that the rebels had wanted to grab away from the emperor. And, of course, he may have recalled the recent blame over his treatment of Vitalian. He was not eager to hear the same accusations again in the future.

Just as in the previous council, when debating between resistance and flight, the emperor's thinking was worlds away from the blunt realism of the daughter of the Hippodrome. She knew the arena habitat all too well. Theodora knew that a wounded beast has to be killed immediately.

Letting the two brothers live would be seen as proof of weakness, she argued; it would undermine the continuity of power, dim the splendor of the emperor's majesty, and rekindle the conspiracies. A few hours earlier, the emperor had appeared before the rebels with the Gospels in his hand—and what had been the result? Theodora insisted that the law be applied. She disregarded her family ties to Hypatius and Pompeius (through her daughter, who had married into the house of Anastasius). Theodora put aside her private life and reacted to public events. And in one stroke she implicitly shifted Justinian's personal, private position: from that moment on, he had to acknowledge that *he* owed his purple to *her.*

Monday, January 19, 532, the new character in town—the rebel fire—was joined onstage by one of the city's familiar old characters: the water of the strait. The water would be needed not to carry the emperor's ships away to a safe exile, but to put out the last of the smoldering fires. A mute witness, the water reflected the execution of Hypatius and Pompeius (which took place on the shore), and then—since they were denied a cemetery burial—the water received their lifeless bodies.

The two brothers' property was confiscated, as was the property of other notables who had joined the rebellion and then been exiled. After a suitable period—perhaps on the first anniversary of the riots—Justinian considered the lofty moral role ascribed to the emperor and pardoned the conspirators. The children of Hypatius and Pompeius reacquired their parents' titles. Other notables got back their property, their titles, and their wealth, or at least the share that Justinian "had not [already] happened to bestow upon his friends":[18] those who had lifted their swords for him (Belisarius, Mundus, Narses), and especially the woman who with her words had "destroyed the ranks of the enemy."

Hypatius's end and the tragic outcome of the Nika rebellion were Theodora's triumph, the universal "song of her might"; they have sparked a number of interpretations, some of them controversial.

That mercenary "technicians" in the service of money defeated the "virtuous" populace when it rose up may be disappointing to some advocates of civic virtues, or to the scholars of the "decline" and "decadence" of civilizations who follow in the footsteps of Machiavelli, Gibbon, or Montesquieu.

People who love symbolism may want to compare the cruel, victori-

ous Theodora—a woman who could be so virile and royally command-
ing in emergencies—to the strong, royal, androgynous warrior-queens
of so many myths, Eastern and Western, from ancient India on.

Scholars of cultural anthropology may try to read the Nika events
as a late ancient version of the archaic, widespread "King for a Day"
tale. (In this tale, the fictitious ruler is crowned, then becomes a scape-
goat, is expelled from the community, and suffers ritual revenge: instead of being buried, his body is torn to pieces and the community is
reborn, practically from the scattered fragments of his body.)

Undeniably, after the Nika uprising, the empire found the impetus
and the energy it needed to achieve the restoration it had postponed
for so long. So maybe the Nika slaughter was a propitiatory rite—and
perhaps Theodora was its idol, or its high priestess.

Some time after that bloody Sunday in January 532, a body washed
up from the Bosphorus and finally received a proper burial: it was
believed to be the body of Pompeius. Hypatius did not reappear, but
he was not forgotten. He had had a cultural bond with Julian, prefect
of Egypt, a high imperial dignitary and functionary and the author of
several epigrams collected in the *Greek Anthology*. Julian, who had perhaps been active in the Nika events, remembers his friend by writing
about an empty tomb and a commemorative cenotaph:

> I am the tomb of Hypatius and I do not say that I contain
> in this little space the remains of the great Roman general.
> For the earth, ashamed of burying so great a man in so small
>   a tomb,
> preferred to give him to the sea to keep.[19]

He even suggests that Justinian might have commissioned the
building of the monument.

> The emperor himself was wrath with the roaring sea
> for covering the body of Hypatius; for now he was dead
> he wished the last honours to be paid to him,

and the sea hid him from the favour of his magnanimity.
Hence, a great proof of the mildness of his heart, he honoured
the distinguished dead with this cenotaph.[20]

In a masterpiece of courtly reticence, the "ruler" described as kind and generous seems to have nothing to do with Hypatius's death. One wonders whether Justinian commissioned the epigrams—as he may have commissioned the poem to Theodora ("Nature . . . ever sings thy might"). Or maybe Julian offered the epigrams to the emperor in his anxiety to erase his support for the rebellion, and to remind the ruler of their earlier bond: Julian had also been praetorian prefect.

The speech that Theodora gave on January 18 was certainly a major moment in the history of *parrhêsia*,[21] that "freedom of speech" that she had used with Hecebolus long before, in Libya. Radical ascetics had also used it against her. But even though her speech had led to the death of tens of thousands of Christians on a "Holy Sunday," no strong criticism was voiced.

This was quite diffferent from the response to Theodosius I—the most wrathful of all Christian emperors—who in the year 390 had ordered the slaughter of seven thousand people in the Hippodrome of Thessalonika (present-day Salonika). He wanted to show an "exemplary punishment" to a city guilty of murdering the highest military officer of Illyricum, the German Botheric, the province's master of soldiers.[22] The revered Saint Ambrose, then bishop of Milan, dared to exclude Theodosius from the Sacraments and vowed not to readmit him until he had repented, which Theodosius eventually did. But Theodora suffered nothing like that in the second Rome; the temporal, imperial power in Constantinople didn't submit to the power of the Church as did the western rulers.

Theodora's great, bloodstained power did not attract any adverse reactions; as a matter of fact it was celebrated as "a light . . . kindled . . . for prudent men." The writer does not specify whether their prudence was born of moral virtue or mere opportunism.

TWELVE

"The Victories That Heaven Has Granted Us"

Constantinople, Bithynia, North Africa, 532–34

T HE VICTORY OVER the rebels was a grand statement from the couple in power, but it also isolated them terribly. Probably they consulted with their closest military and civilian advisors, and with their spiritual fathers both Orthodox and Monophysite, who urged them to pray. For despite the silence and deference that surrounded them, they knew that they were responsible for the violent deaths of tens of thousands of their Christian brethren. They wondered if unknown enemies still wished them dead. And they might have tried to discover when they themselves would die. How many years did they have left to accomplish the task (both divine mimesis and everyday governance) for which only the groundwork had been laid? Justinian was fifty years old, Theodora a little over thirty. And so they must have decided to consult not just military, civilian, and religious advisors but also the astrologers and magicians that their laws had failed to drive away.

It was an age when people believed that only a saint could foretell the day and hour of his death.[1] Such illumination was denied to other living creatures, whether they were peasants or emperors; so these people turned to astrology, which was strongly censored and yet still widely practiced.

Thus on some moonless night, or perhaps by the pale light of a silvery full moon, the rulers might have appeared in disguise on the seashore or riverbank. Perhaps they asked about themselves and their destiny, using roundabout allusions to avoid revealing their identities.

The astrologers might have told the emperor an allegory of a palm tree that rises in the desert and draws water from the deepest springs. He might have deduced that his glory would extend far and wide. He might have been pleased, without stopping to think about the desert evoked in the image. The astrologers might have told the empress an allegory about a diamond, treasure of the East, star of the night, whose adamantine power triumphs over everything. Theodora might have heard these words as a reflection of her role in the Nika events, and a sign of her invincibility as a lady and mistress. She might not have considered that the brilliance of the diamond remains hidden in a jewel case unless it is set in gold. When it stands alone, it is static.

In 532, Theodora stepped into the final, intense third of her life, her last sixteen years. Only now did she see the hidden, nocturnal face of the power that she had longed for "from the depth of her heart,"[2] which had once gleamed up ahead. The purple robe, which turned out *not* to be a burial shroud during the rebellion, lay securely on her shoulders but represented the heavy burden of maintaining the continuity of Roman power throughout the civilized world.

New and momentous challenges kept arising, knotty problems requiring wise answers that could only come from deep reflection—but the answers were needed immediately. Everything moved slowly across the vast expanses separating the thousand cities of the empire. By the time an imperial decision arrived at its destination, the situation had already changed and the problems no longer matched the solution that had been found. A far-flung imperial functionary, now considered the ruler's "slave," had to look past the letter of the emperor's message and grasp its deep underlying meaning; otherwise the message could become no more than an enigma or a mirage. (This is what happens in "A Message from the Emperor," a short story by Franz Kafka, the writer who has best explored the mysteries of powerful centralized empires.)

The modern historian looks at separate themes—finance, religion, law, the military, and so on—and treats each one independently, but at the time they were all inextricably intermingled. The tangle of issues was magnified by the expansion of time and space to produce an anomalous, almost hallucinatory effect. Neither a deforming mirror nor an out-of-focus image, it was an unsynchronized vision. Things that had appeared stable now trembled and shook. Things that had seemed indefinite now took on sharp outlines. Looking at the overall picture was like looking at a mosaic portrait by candlelight. Every passing breeze makes the flame flicker, revealing new details in the mosaic: unexpected shadows and bright spots, wrinkles in the face and in the fabric. It's impossible to be sure about the lines of the drawing or the exact nuances of color.

Justinian was built for analysis more than contemplation. He read every functionary's report and granted audiences to everyone. But he failed to foresee the Nika uprising gathering right in front of him. He suffered from intellectual farsightedness: he could spot major objectives off in the distance, but couldn't see the area right around him.

Theodora, on the other hand, was a concise thinker. She was convinced that the experience she had acquired outside of the palace—what she had seen with her own eyes—was increasingly necessary to Justinian, to herself, even to the empire. She had to defend, safeguard, and advise the emperor she had saved. She had given him back the purple that—against all obstacles and expectation—he had originally given to her. Now they were equals.

Theodora no longer needed to win; she had already won. Nor did she have to ask for anything; she simply took. The authority that she had showed at the moment of deep crisis was her greatest insurance. It was no longer a question of her right to the throne: now she had to resolve high-profile issues *from* the throne.

Procopius wrote that Justinian and Theodora "did nothing by themselves, or without each other": the observation is particularly true for their life after the Nika, when they worked by dividing and conquering. They simulated "conflicting behavior and intentions," knowing that if they had discordant views, "their subjects could not unanimously rebel."[3] A more likely explanation, though, is that they each took on separate aspects of government and then presented their achievements to the other in order to provoke a response, as if governing the empire were a card game or a game of wits. In short, they played with power:

power became the child they never had. They shaped it and grew it and groomed it, and exhibited it for one another's admiration, just like proud parents.

Justinian's favorite child was the legislative work famous today as the *Corpus Juris Civilis* (Body of Civil Law), a monument to a unique absolutist, imperial, and legislative ideology. To celebrate the second anniversary of the Easter coronation, in April 529 the *Codex Justinianus* (*Justinian Code*) was published; it was a collection of imperial ordinances or "constitutions" from Hadrian to Justinian. In December 533 came the *Digesta* (*Digest*), a compilation of jurisprudence that— thanks to the extraordinary organizational skills of Tribonian— condensed 3 million lines of text into 150,000 lines (a 95 percent reduction). And one month before, the *Institutiones* (*Institutions*), a legal-studies manual containing a summary of the *Code* and the *Digest*, had also been published. (The final draft of the *Digest* had been completed the previous May.) The legislative office was so busy that on November 16, 534, a second, augmented version of the *Code* was published. And the *Code* was followed by installments of the *Novellae* (*Novels*), the new laws that Justinian developed over the years in response to new situations.

In some of the *Novels* we can see Theodora's influence. Although she lacked specific juridical competence, she could and did recognize the need for laws on issues that were dear to her. What is more, she shared the fundamental goal of the project, which was to give a univocal certainty to law, basing it on Christian principles, stressing its authority, and regulating the life of the subjects during their brief earthly transit toward their longed-for Christian paradise.

In the complex military operations aimed at the restoration in the West—Justinian's pet project—Theodora's role was especially noticeable wherever military action might affect the religious cause of the Monophysites. Otherwise, for Theodora the Promised Land was in the East, in the land of diamonds: here one could buy peace with gold rather than risk battles, and conquer new lands by using personal ties or by sharing the faith in the same Incarnate Word.

This outlook was quite different from Justinian's militarism, which did lead to a vast territorial expansion for the empire—"from one end of the ocean to the other"—but which caused millions of deaths. By the time Justinian died in 565, the lands bordering the Mediterranean had almost been turned into a desert: much of the "empire of a thousand cities" was reduced to a "wilderness"[4] under the imperial flag—just like a palm tree in the desert.

While she must have been pleased with Justinian's victories, Theodora bore no direct responsibility for field operations, orders to attack, or the shedding of even one drop of blood on the battlefield. She knew little of the indistinct, nameless masses battling to conquer distant lands for the glory of the empire. The shining armor and the clashing swords were like ephemeral and childish fairy tales to her; they were no more real than the old-fashioned, cloying image of a winged Victory that she always saw stamped on coins and imperial medallions.

Theodora's primary goal was to strengthen her power. Others may have felt that "there is no survival without victory";[5] for her there was no life without purple. And so she was prudent, conservative, and defensive. In calculating all possible reactions to each one of her actions, she also drew on her experience in the Nika events. She sensed that there was strength in continuity, not in initiative or risk.

The woman who chose power and the purple mantle as her burial shroud loved to have wealth and honors bestowed on her, her family, and her loyal followers. She was proud of the fact that provinces and cities in Asia were now called Theodorias, such as the ancient Syrian city of Anasartha, now Khanazir, at the time near the Persian border. She was pleased to see her name joined with the emperor's in dedications and in monograms atop the columns of wonderful new churches. (Many churches were going up, some replacing the burnt ones in Constantinople, others in the eastern provinces, most of them built to a central-cross plan and filled with light.) And yet, however keen she was to safeguard her power, she also developed policies going beyond the purely personal; she worked for others, too.

She sought freedom of worship for the Monophysites. She would have liked to see them united with the Orthodox Catholics in one single

Church under the emperor of Constantinople, who would lead the Church to flower in the supreme seventh eon. She wanted women to have new status within the family, in harmony with Christian principles that would rule and discipline daily life. She supported curbs on abuses of power in the provinces, where Justinian's eye could not reach: she remembered the many local Heceboluses out there.

Justinian's goals were born in sleepless nights spent poring over books; Theodora's were the result of turning her life experiences into concrete action. There was nothing abstract about it: she shaped her goals to specific situations and individuals, and those individuals were rewarded if they contributed to her cause, or removed precisely, almost surgically, if they created obstacles. Her authority did not depend on any particular ministry; it was a personal quality that was innate to Theodora.

The tools of her power—or of her cruelty as a "bane of mortals," according to one unfavorable male critic—were discreet. There were rumors of bolts locking the doors "in some secret . . . dark, unknown, inaccessible . . . rooms of the palace."[6] Many military officers were imprisoned at length, and they suffered lashes "on their shoulders and back," a veritable "slave torture,"[7] despite their high position in the imperial hierarchy.

Others were gagged. Quite a few notables were forbidden to speak or protest, and were barely able to breathe. One such notable was Priscus, former personal secretary to Justinian, who seemed so arrogant and even downright hostile to Theodora that he was shipped off to a distant exile. He had been at the center of power; now he was forced to become a monk on some parched Aegean island. (Many centuries were to pass before the island would be seen as beautiful and tourists began to flock to it.)

Still others—including those who gave testimony that did not please her—were tortured with whips made of ox sinews. We know of at least one case of torture with a knife: a certain Basianus, a supporter of the Greens, "insulted her"[8] in Constantinople. "Without a trial,"[9] Theodora ordered him castrated, and he died as a result.

Sometimes, words alone sufficed. Antonina, Belisarius's wife, used webs of crafty words to serve Theodora, destroying the careers of ministers and even Roman popes who countered the empress's will. These men were sent into exile and left there to contemplate the ruin of their ambitions.

24. Reproduction of gold medal of Justinian reading "SALUS ET GLORIA ROMANORUM," Constantinople, 534(?).

Sometimes, words were written instead of spoken. Imperial officials filled parchment or papyrus rolls with deeds of confiscation or of donation—voluntary, forced, or forged. These ruses brought the enemy's houses, land, gold, gems, and coins to the public coffers of the empire, or sometimes into Theodora's personal treasury (several sources have mentioned a private treasury of hers, complete with its own managers[10]). According to the critics who saw the emperor and empress as demons of destruction, these were signs of ruthless cruelty, of a diabolical, savage nature. Other, more indulgent observers see them as proof of the great financial demands of an empire bent on the difficult project of restoration. Still others see them as the mark of a sinister, empty culture that gave legal cover to naked extortion.

Just as her power was never codified into law, so Theodora's face never appeared on the coins issued by Constantinople's legendary mint. The coins read simply IUSTINIANUS, or sometimes IUSTINIANUS, SALUS ET GLORIA ROMANORUM (Justinian, Salvation and Glory of Romans; [fig. 24]). And yet the emperor and the empress were as close to each other as two faces of the same coin, the coin of power.

After the Nika rebellion, the power of these two was the product of reciprocal favors and efforts. And a superior joint tolerance was called for. If in the course of Theodora's correspondence with foreign

ambassadors—something that no previous empress had ever done—
she wrote that Justinian "does nothing without my advice,"[11] only the
exotic foreign courts were scandalized. In Justinian's view, these details
did not diminish his *ego*. As a matter of fact, he felt supported by authoritative sources of religious wisdom, for in a Christian marriage
"everything between man and woman must be shared" and the woman
must "respect God first of all, then her husband," to whom "she can offer
advice" as he makes the final decision.[12] Thus Justinian and Theodora
must have seen themselves as a model couple for the seventh eon, the
Christian eon.

In the text of one law, Justinian spoke of Theodora as "given by
God," alluding to the etymology *theou dôron*, "gift of God." The auspicious name that Acacius chose for his daughter had become a reality,
sanctioned by imperial words. By mentioning Theodora, or simply
referring to her as an inspiration, Justinian gave individuality and speci-
ficity to his general, even abstract political vision. He made exceptions
for her alone, while armies and subjects continued to be no more to
him than abstract masses and numbers, tiny tiles in a mosaic that he
was continuously rearranging.

Theodora acted differently from him. Each of her activities had a
precise personal and psychological reference point: someone who was
beholden to her, who was loyal to her, some strategic figure that she
used to achieve her goals. Never openly stated, her goals nevertheless
were, and still are, recognizable in her many achievements throughout
the years and on many continents. She was shrewdly silent about her
objectives, allowing each one of her devotees to believe that his mission was the most important.

The former actress was a master of timing and she knew how to judge
an audience's reaction; she had not lost those skills even after ten or
more years away from the stage. She understood that after the Nika
rebellion certain signals were required, both in the fire-blackened city
and elsewhere. It was crucial to display the splendor and initiative
of that imperial majesty for which Hypatius and Pompeius—and the

Hippodrome crowd—had been sacrificed. Spectacular, theatrical pro-ductions were needed. And so she proceeded to create them.

She put her mark on the city, quite literally, with statues of herself. One was erected near the baths of Zeuxippus, which were rebuilt after the 532 fires; another rose atop a porphyry column at the Arcadianae, a thermal bath complex that was the most enchanting leisure spot in the capital, with gentle breezes and dappled light reflecting off the water. So attractive was the place that it was written that "those who stroll there can even converse with people sailing by." But most attractive of all was the statue: "The statue is indeed beautiful, but still inferior to the beauty of the empress; for to express her loveliness in words or to portray it in a statue would be, for a mere human being, altogether impossible."[13] The site is unrecognizable now, and the statue is long gone, just like Theodora's beauty itself. We can only imagine the har-monious effect of the dark porphyry against the white marble and the blue-green of the sea.

Even more theatrical, perhaps, was Theodora's legendary voyage to Bithynia, which took place possibly in the spring of 533. On light boats, she and her retinue crossed her beloved Bosphorus toward the pine forests that cast their reflections in the water on the Asian side. Once across, she went to the thermal baths of Pythium in Bithynia (near modern-day Yalova, Turkey). It may be that a court physician had sent her to the pleasant bathing resort, which was famous for its cura-tive natural hot springs. Perhaps she hoped the waters would help her to conceive an heir; it would have been a welcome sign of divine favor in the wake of Saint Sabas's refusal to pray for her (531) and the bloodshed of the Nika massacre (532).

For the empress, the journey was an occasion to display imperial pomp. Justinian had surprised the crowds with his lavish consular games in 521; now his consort celebrated *her* victory in the Nika by traveling with a retinue of at least four thousand and endless furnish-ings.[14]

Everything that the empress might want, she took with her: jewels, precious garments, and gold cups studded with diamonds. Costly litters carried her noble body, and embroidered curtains protected her from all discomfort. She even brought along giraffes and elephants: her journey was an itinerant show, a palace-away-from-home. John the Cappadocian (restored to the office of prefect of the praetorian guard in the autumn after the Nika revolt) was in no position to criticize the expense, since he owed his life to Theodora.

Her litter was a far cry from the carts on which she must have traveled through the Levant years before, but, even so, she saw how bad the roads were, perhaps because of the Cappadocian's underinvestment. She wished to meet her subjects, and as they knelt before her she promised them better roads. She had new palaces and other structures built near the baths, as well as an aqueduct. She exhorted everyone to have faith in and hope for the good of the empire.

She even visited the monasteries of Mount Olympus beyond Prusa (present-day Ulu Dã, beyond Bursa). Later in the Byzantine era the monasteries became a favorite retreat for intellectuals who could not stand life at court. When Theodora visited them, the simple monks and hermits spoke words of Christian wisdom and experience. But this was not the only religious aspect of her journey.

It wasn't enough to dazzle everyone along her route: Theodora also worked for the Monophysite cause that she cared so deeply about. Monophysitism was the first card that she played in her power game with Justinian.

In fact, some believe that a religious operative, the Monophysite John, bishop of Tella, was part of her huge entourage in Bithynia. Born in 483 in Tella (Constantina, Syria; now Vitansehir, in eastern Turkey) he was a tireless Monophysite supporter who had come to the capital under the empress's tutelage. In Bithynia, he preached his version of Christianity and was very popular: he got thousands and thousands of converts, which was particularly meaningful since Bithynia, historically tied to Constantinople, had none of the nationalistic elements that helped Monophysitism spread in Syria and in Egypt.

This was Theodora Augusta's first journey outside the city in the ten years or so since she had entered the palace of Hormisdas as Justinian's concubine. Although she might have seemed to be an exterminating angel in the Hippodrome, she was now billing herself as the Angel of Goodness, who cared about her subjects. After the destructive Nika events, the masterful staging of this spectacle restored majesty, dignity, and philanthropy as imperial prerogatives.

The renewed sacrality and majestic power she projected gave fresh impetus to the Monophysite issue. When she got home to the palace, Theodora and Justinian may have spent just as much time discussing theological issues and ecumenical policy as testing the reproductive efficacy of her cure at Pythium. Maybe even more time, because the journey to Bithynia was only one piece in a preexisting strategy that Theodora set in motion after January 532.

In the summer of 532, nearly fifteen years after the reconciliation between the Roman papacy and the empire of Constantinople, a knotty, unresolved issue was officially reintroduced. A meeting was arranged in the capital between six Orthodox and six Monophysite luminaries to address the issue of the nature or natures of Jesus Christ, the Incarnate Word.

The Monophysite leaders were invited to the imperial palace and admitted to the emperor's presence. The Augusta positioned herself as the perfect hostess rather than as an interested party. They held long sessions on theological matters, some attended by the emperor. Justinian engaged in learned disquisitions with the Monophysites and came away convinced that any discrepancy was a problem of terminology more than substance. Neither side doubted the human element of Christ; the only disagreement—the theological split that ended up as a geopolitical division—was about the number of His natures.

At the end of the sessions, Justinian promulgated an edict to defuse the problems. It was March 15, 533. First, he avoided the customary references to past ecumenical councils (including the Fourth Chalcedonian Council, which the Monophysites vigorously opposed). The edict affirmed the condemnation of Nestorius on the one hand, while on the other it attacked extreme Monophysitism, which denied "the consubstantiality of Jesus Christ and the Father in the Godhead, and of Jesus and us in humanhood."[15] At the time, Justinian could not do or give any more than this. The positions he established, however, were conducive to opening a dialogue with Monophysite luminaries such as Severus, Theodora's theological beacon, who had been deposed as patriarch of Antioch in 518 (when Justinian had come to power) for professing similar theories.

So a dialogue began and persecutions ended. The colony of Monophysites in the capital was growing so much that a Monophysite monastery (known as the "Monastery of the Syrians") was soon founded in the suburb of Sykae, beyond the Golden Horn. Theodora was repaying her debt to the Levantine "saints." And the emperor, who had been raised with pro-Roman, Dyophysite beliefs, seemed paradoxically to be acting according to the *Edict of the Union*, the pro-Monophysite tract of 482 that had launched the long schism with the Roman papacy (from 484 to 519).

Giving in to Theodora's political pressure and perhaps her emotional appeal, he conceded everything he could concede without breaking with Rome. The reconciliation with Rome was essential not only because of his religious beliefs, but also because of the Church of Rome's support for his military plan to recapture the West, starting with the "barbaric" Vandal kingdom.

The Vandals (who held North Africa from the Pillars of Hercules at Gibraltar to the Syrtes, adjacent to Hecebolus's Pentapolis) were Arians, so they denied the divine consubstantiality of Christ with the Father, which was a central tenet of faith for both Monophysites and Dyophysites. What is more, the Vandals had swooped down on the Mediterranean as invaders, not in answer to an imperial invitation. Instead of formally recognizing the primacy of Constantinople, they challenged it: their kings boldly wore purple. They considered themselves an autonomous, self-legitimated power, like the Persian empire, but without its ancient prestige. They did not work for reconciliation, as had Theodoric, the Ostrogoth king in Italy. On the contrary, they repressed the Roman and Orthodox Catholic elements in their kingdom.

Justinian refused to accept the Vandal kingdom as a concrete political force, and it certainly did not fit into his theoretical framework for the restoration. The empire of Constantinople needed safe transport for its men and supplies, but the Vandal fleet ruled the western Mediterranean. (In 455, those "barbarians" had used their fleet to come to Rome and sack it; the ancient Roman supremacy in the Mediterranean was now only a memory.) Might the Vandals try to attack "the happy cargo" on the unparalleled food-supply ships transporting grain from Alexandria to the second Rome? And once Italy was completely unified, how could it be safe if it was still under threat from Vandals in the Strait of Sicily or in the Tyrrhenian Sea?

Back in 530 Justinian had been given a pretext for going to war. But he was kept from attacking by domestic developments and conflicts, and by a turning point in the war on the Persian front, which culminated in the Endless Peace signed by the two great empires of the Ecumene in September 532. (Although the "endless" peace was to last less than a decade.) The costly peace in the East, though a drain on the imperial coffers, did now guarantee him freedom of movement on the western front. But John the Cappadocian strongly opposed the plan, and the military chiefs were skeptical.

Once more, a dream broke the stalemate. A bishop from the East (his name is now lost) came to Justinian claiming that God had visited him in a dream and ordered him to see the emperor and reproach him for his hesitation: "I will Myself join with him in waging war and make him Lord of Libya." These words, attributed to God, proved crucial.[16]

The military chiefs' concerns were understandable. It had been decades since the empire of Constantinople last engaged an enemy in a major naval war, and all of a sudden five hundred ships were needed, plus sixteen thousand soldiers and twenty thousand others to man the oars and the sails and provide other services. A whole city's worth of men was being sent out to sea, with all the attendant problems of logistics, supplies, hygiene, and discipline.

What's more, Belisarius was now commander-in-chief (because of his personal ties to Justinian and his successes in Persia and in the Nika rebellion); he was a brilliant young general of armies on land, but he was not an admiral. There was no predicting the outcome of a direct naval engagement. Sailing with him was an advisor who understood the predicament: the advisor was Procopius of Caesarea, whose writings would become the most influential and controversial historical source about Theodora and her times.

Justinian saw clearly the risks that the operation entailed. He did not forget that it took months for news coming overland from Carthage to reach Constantinople, and vice versa. Several seasons often passed before a person could get a reply to his letter. Sending a letter by sea took a little over a month, provided of course that the ship reached its destination instead of sinking (for the benefit of some future archaeology museum). Perhaps this was why the sailing of the fleet was accompanied by especially fervent prayers, votive offerings, and wild swinging of the smoky censers.

The North African expedition proved to be blessed, or just plain lucky; Belisarius turned out to be a wise and victorious commander even on the sea.

The Roman troops from Constantinople entered Carthage, capital of the Vandal kingdom, on September 15, 533. As early as mid-December there was a decisive battle, at Tricamarum, thirty miles west of Carthage. The Vandal army was routed and its soldiers scattered among the Berber tribes in the hinterland; some were even absorbed into the Roman cities. And so the Vandals were gone from the stage. They had made their grand entrance on the Mediterranean scene at the time of the death of Saint Augustine in Hippo, in 430; now their departure was marked by Belisarius's capture of Hippo.

While the treasures that the Vandals had stolen from the first Rome in 455 were recovered by the second Rome, the Vandal king Gelimer sought refuge high in the mountains of the Numidian interior. Tracked down and surrounded, he made a request to the imperial army. He asked for a lyre so he could accompany himself as he sang his poems; he asked for a sponge to wash his eyes; and he asked for bread, since the Berbers who gave him shelter—like the ancient Homeric Cyclops— did not eat wheat, the first mark of civilization.

In March 534, Gelimer surrendered. The Vandal kingdom was wiped out, and it no longer dominated the seas and the Balearic

Islands, the islands of Sardinia and Corsica, and the strongholds on the North African coast of the Mediterranean.

Alas, Belisarius's military and strategic foresight was counterbalanced by myopia in his private life. At the start of the war his wife, Antonina, had thoughtfully furnished his boat with wineskins full of pure water, and she accompanied him on his voyage. With them was her godson Theodosius, a "youth from Thrace."[17] She "fell extraordinarily in love with Theodosius [and] had intercourse with him, at first in secret, but finally even in the presence of servants of both sexes."[18] Belisarius, his eyes focused on a tidy vision of his victory, failed to see the disorder in his private life. (Just as Justinian, blinded by his grandiose vision of restoration, had not anticipated the public uprising of the Nika.)

Long before the Vandals succumbed, Justinian was taking the victory for granted. In 533, before the decisive battle, the dedication on the *Institutions* had described Justinian as follows: *Emperor Caesar Flavius Justinianus, conqueror of the Alamanni, the Goths, the Franks, the Germans, the Antes, the Alans, the Vandals, and the Africans, pious, happy, glorious conqueror and vanquisher, always August.*[19] The prologue to that work was far from modest: it referred to an Africa that had been "recovered to the Roman empire and added to our power, thanks to the victories that Heaven has granted us."[20] And the *Digest* noted that the Vandalic race had been "destroyed" and "all of Africa had been restored to the empire"[21]—this *during* the battle at Tricamarum in December, long before news of it could reach Constantinople. Such statements were typical of Justinian's sense of personal and institutional greatness.

Though "the least military of men," Justinian proclaimed himself "Africanus" just like Scipio in ancient Rome. At the same time, he devised a detailed administrative system for the conquered territories, creating a new structure, the African prefecture of the praetorium, alongside the Eastern prefecture (for Asia) and the Illyric prefecture (for Europe). The power structure was carefully mapped out, and there was also a celebratory element: the wealthy city of Hadrumetum (now Sousse, Tunisia) was renamed Justiniana. In Carthage, elegant baths were built and named Theodorianae. Ancient urban centers were rebaptized Theodorias (just as they had been in Asian lands already belonging to the empire), among them Vaga, an important mercantile town and crossroads in the Numidian interior (now Bajah, Tunisia), which was fortified with new city walls.

Even so, claims that "all of Africa" had been totally "restored to the empire" were pure propaganda. Pockets of resistance and intense guerrilla activity remained; then troublemakers were not Vandals but Berber tribes. Besides, Belisarius was not permitted to complete the conquest. He was recalled in the summer of 534: preparations had been made for him in Constantinople.

Belisarius was bringing a lot back with him: Gelimer the Vandal king and his retinue, other captive prisoners, and the Vandal treasure, including the spoils of the sack of Rome of 455. The second Rome had defeated Carthage just as the first Rome once had done. For Justinian, with his antiquarian spirit, this was an occasion to clear his name in the city's mind. Two years after the Nika rebellion, he would show them the true meaning of "victory."

The emperor decided to organize a triumph, apparently to honor his general. There hadn't been one since the time of Trajan's wars against the Dacii, early in the second century after Christ. And no Roman military chief had scored such a victory since Lucius Cornelius Balbus, under Octavian Augustus, had defeated the Garamantes of Africa in 19 B.C. The 553-year gap was enormous. For precisely this reason, a triumphal procession and a theatrical celebration of victory would give body and vitality to the idea of the restoration.

Belisarius marched through the city with his army. King Gelimer, dressed in a purple mantle that was even more "scandalous" for being neither imperial nor Roman, paraded along surrounded by his noblemen. He was followed by carts loaded with the treasure of Carthage, a profusion of silver and appealing trinkets from the elegant world of the North African elite, which could hardly be called "barbarian."

The only possible endpoint for the triumphal procession was the center of the imperial world, the Hippodrome. Justinian and the imperial grandees were watching the show from the Kathisma. We do not know whether Theodora was with them, but she certainly was watching from some vantage point. She knew every detail of the triumph; indeed, she may have had a hand in designing the event, since a triumph is nothing but a spectacle of supreme power, celebrating and exalting majesty with theatrical exaggeration.

Gelimer was stripped of the purple that he had usurped. He was ordered to prostrate himself before the imperial loge. The defeated king whispered the Biblical refrain "Vanity of vanities, all is vanity"[22] as he cast himself face down before Justinian, Lord of the World. Belisarius, the victorious general, made the same gesture of submission. All other would-be authorities had to bow down before the sovereign Augustus; so it only appeared that Belisarius was being honored. In reality, he was kneeling like a "slave" before his "master" in accordance with the new court ceremonial.

Some saw Belisarius's prostration as an arrogant abuse of power on the part of the emperor or—more probably—on the part of the empress, who had suggested it from behind the scenes. There was sympathy for the general: the humiliated conqueror, who had been seen as a butcher in the Hippodrome only two years before, was now a hero.

Gelimer's treasure included the great Menorah, the seven-branched candelabra from the Temple of Solomon in Jerusalem. The Roman emperor Titus had seized it from the Hebrews in A.D. 71; Genseric, the Vandal king, had plundered it during the sack of Rome of 455. Now the Vandals lost it to Justinian. Because the object had not brought luck to anyone who seized it, Justinian sent it and other objects from the Hebrew temple back to Jerusalem, their natural home, in the custody of the Christian community. But this gesture was not the only event with Biblical implications in the triumph.

The immense arena was crowded with cheering people, like extras on a movie set; Gelimer stood in sharp focus in the foreground. He had an inner vision, a revelation of the "evil plight [in which] he was."[23] As if in a trance, he repeated, "Vanity of vanities, all is vanity" from *Ecclesiastes*, which at the time was ascribed to King Solomon, the

Justinian model of an ideal ruler. And the admonition did not apply only to himself in this moment of humiliation and uncertainty about the future; with the typical ancient sensitivity to allusions, he was reciting the refrain for Justinian, too, for the conqueror, the emulator of Solomon.

For *Ecclesiastes* reminds us that "there is a time for winning and a time for losing,"[24] and Justinian, high in the gallery, truly evoked Solomon, "great and powerful, more than those who'd come before him,"[25] just as he had once dreamed. And yet, even for King Solomon "everything is vanity and useless anxiety."[26]

The heretic Vandal king warned that this day of imperial triumph was Gelimer's time for failure; some other day would prove to be Justinian's time for failure. When the *Wars* were published seventeen years later, Procopius's audience read the warning as a prophecy.[27]

Theodora was thinking along very different lines, and as usual her thinking was quite concrete. She was pleased about the events on the African continent. Justinian had achieved a real objective. The great parade through the city and the final scene in the Hippodrome affirmed his strength, his will, and the majesty of the crown on that most difficult and bloody of stages. She and the Augustus were avenging the sack of the first Rome in 455, setting themselves up as benefactors.

As always, she was taking the appropriate precautions. She was especially wary of Belisarius's growing popularity, and so she considered the general's kneeling before the emperor as a duty, rather than an arbitrary imposition. It was the ideal occasion to reiterate that the emperor was the one who truly deserved homage. She did allow that Belisarius and his men had been fundamental in crushing the Nika rebellion and that he had led thousands of his personal soldiers, at his own expense, to success in Africa. Still, as Theodora recalled, the general had also won enormous riches in the expedition. She had unmistakable proof of that from her private sources. So she had to be watchful. She could not allow Belisarius to use his wealth to buy favors and prepare himself a path to the throne.

His wife, Antonina, also had to be kept under watch, for the woman knew how to hide precious spoils of war even from Belisarius, in order to conceal them from the emperor. Besides, her naked "erotic rage"[28] for her godson Theodosius did not suit the feminine ideal that the Augusta championed. Theodora was willing to grant freedom, but would not tolerate open license.

The ruling couple agreed that Antonina and Belisarius (who was to be appointed consul in 535) would spend only a short time in the city. They planned to send him quickly to Italy, to recover the lands that had once belonged to the first Rome; the situation was just becoming ripe.

THIRTEEN

"Our Most Pious Consort Given Us by God"

Constantinople, Italy, 535–36

THEODORA'S "nature always led her to assist unfortunate women."[1] These approving words are not propaganda from Justinian's law texts; they are not inscriptions carved in the Eastern churches commissioned by the Augusti. They are from Procopius, the same author who had criticized Theodora so harshly in the *Secret History*. Their source is worth noting, but the words themselves are even more significant, for they give a new dimension to Theodora, describing something other than her expressions of pure power.

But perhaps it was more than "nature"; perhaps the Augusta was swayed by ceremony and by the protocol that required philanthropy, charity, and imperial mercy impregnated with the Christian ideals of late antiquity. Nor should we dismiss the importance of personal experience: Theodora, a child of the arenas, of the stage, and of the street, had a peculiarly feminine and ancient intimacy with sorrow; like Virgil's Dido, she could say, "An expert in grief, I learned to give succor to the wretched."[2] Whatever the reasons, the fact remains that Theodora was active on behalf of women. More than a philanthropist, we might say she was a "philogynist." Whereas she might have battled the other actresses, years before, when she was struggling to become a theatrical star, now that she was firmly seated on the throne, she was a resource for all the female subjects who needed her help.

The beginning of her relationship with Justinian had occasioned a legal provision regarding women, the law "On Marriage," which permitted a high-ranking man to wed a former actress if she was a "repentant"

Christian. Once she became the Augusta, Theodora developed her own political program for women, based particularly on her own youthful experience when she had traveled through the Levant from Pentapolis to the capital of the empire. She had learned then that women needed as much financial autonomy as possible. Her history justifies her social and political awareness of economic factors, which were not common in an empress of Constantinople.

Theodora had forgotten neither her widowed mother nor her own fatherless childhood; the provisions for inheritance in Justinian's laws were not random. Formerly only sons could inherit, but now the right was extended to daughters. Furthermore, the new laws allowed a widow to take possession of the dowry she had brought to the marriage. And the dowry now returned to the wife's family if she died (or if the marriage was dissolved).

Even beyond issues of dowry and inheritance, women's status was enhanced in these years. A woman became an autonomous economic entity, in charge of her own *parapherna*, the property (jewelry, garments, real estate, furnishing, and other items) outside of the dowry that she had got as a gift or an inheritance. A woman could buy and sell, lend and borrow—even to or from her own husband.

Justinian and Theodora sought to create a deeply Christian society based on marriage and the nuclear family. This meant that the new laws identified a woman as a wife, and marriage was endowed with deep meaning: Justinian's laws noted, "Marriage does not consist in sexual relations, but in conjugal affection."[3] This general intention underlay each legislative act on the topic; and the same intention is seen in the emperor's laws that expressed the love he felt for his wife, Theodora.

Theodora's sense of female solidarity was expressed spectacularly in 535, her great year. Theodora must have been about thirty-five, the age of perfect maturity for men in the classical tradition. She most certainly inspired the empire's decision that year to protect prostitutes, a group of women at risk. The "On Pimps" (*De lenonibus*) law (*Novel* No. 14) is known as an invitation to practice chastity. More specifically, it is a detailed analysis of the phenomenon of prostitution in the capital, whose population (as Theodora knew well) didn't slake all its appetites by simply worshipping Christian relics.

The law described the situation in the countryside, which was picked clean by official tax collectors and by pimps supplying Constantinople's brothels. Farmers impoverished by the tax collectors often delivered their daughters to the pimps, thus reducing the number of mouths they had to feed and also getting cash to pay their taxes. The illiterate young girls were taken to the city, where they signed contracts (inking a small Christian cross in place of a signature) in which they turned themselves over to brothel owners. And the owners would dispose of them when they were no longer useful.

Theodora found the situation unacceptable (even as an outside observer—even if she never worked as a prostitute, as some sources claim). And so the law forbade pimping and banished "pleasure houses" not only from the capital but also from the major cities of the empire.

It is common knowledge that many laws promulgated under Justinian and Theodora were not faithfully applied, and one of them was *Novel* No. 14. It never really took effect: it remained primarily an indicator of the emperor and empress's attention to this issue. It is meaningful that Theodora—who had climbed so high by means of the inhuman system of traditional sexism geared to the satisfaction of the male—would inspire laws opposed to that very system.

Because of the law, many former prostitutes were left to fend for themselves without the income they had once earned from their "profession." The well-meaning philanthropy may have unintentionally proved inhumane: Theodora may paradoxically have brought hardship to her protégées. To resolve this problem, the empress created a solution "among her other charities" and—possibly drawing from her private coffers (for perhaps John the Cappadocian objected to the use of public money for this purpose)—distributed one golden solidus to all prostitutes, allowing them some economic protection as they started new lives. But ten to twenty solidi a year was the bare minimum needed for survival at the time. And each pimp apparently received five solidi for every girl "that was returned to virtue."[4]

So the measures proved insufficient, and the ancient "vice of the flesh" continued to thrive. Theodora's next move was to house former prostitutes in a building on the Asian shore of the Bosphorus. It was called the Metanoia convent, the convent of Conversion or Repentance. Physicians, nuns, and devout women (especially widows) attended to the new arrivals there—maybe five hundred girls in all—and tried to reintegrate them into society with different jobs.[5]

The cloistered prostitutes clearly had less brilliant prospects than the "liberated" actresses of the law "On Marriage." The actresses had to make only a simple, individual choice, while the prostitutes were treated institutionally. In the Metanoia convent they spent their time in confession, prayer, and repentance, and at lessons in sewing, spinning, cooking, and nursing. These activities were all considered suitable for women freed from the old bondage and released into the "renewed" Christian society of the seventh eon.

Theodora's critics leapt at the opportunity to attack her for this initiative, and not simply because these measures proved ineffective in uprooting vice. Rumor had it that the Augusta wanted to force the prostitutes into a life they didn't want or understand. It was said that some girls hung ropes out their high windows and climbed down to escape their new destiny, and that others had even committed suicide, overwhelmed by the attention focused on them. Of course, it is possible that more than one "beneficiary" suffered attacks of depression in the Metanoia; even today, patients reject rehabilitation in therapeutic communities.

Again, Theodora's critics did not grasp the pressure or the outright compulsory element of the "profession." They were quick to reduce it to a personal inclination and even to ridicule it.

The redefinition of a woman's role in these and other legislative provisions was part of a general blueprint for a new society drawn along Christian principles, which Justinian and Theodora were developing for the entire Ecumene. The basic unit of this new society, the mononuclear family, answered to the complementary, all-encompassing power of the emperor and the Church. And the family had to be stable: a law in 542 abolished divorce on the grounds of "mutual consent," which had been acceptable in the Christian Roman empire for almost two centuries. As the mononuclear family was ratified, other social bonds were losing their centrality, including the centuries-old customs that had survived through Theodora's youth and had facilitated her miraculous imperial career. These were the associations centered around theaters, racetracks, and baths; after the Nika uprising, the factions were transformed and their roles redefined.

The redefinition of marriage was the most revolutionary aspect of this new perspective. It's no coincidence that the bride and groom from the most controversial marriage of late antiquity, Justinian and Theodora, insisted on the centrality of that institution. Marriage stood as the regulator and organizer of a Christianized society precisely because it introduced an individual and moral dimension, conjugal affection. It also leveled political, personal, or social expectations that the Augusti might have found unwelcome.

From the very start, Justinian and Theodora analyzed the marriages around them. The enemies who accused them of arranging marriages based on calculation failed to notice that before then, love had never been the only reason for getting married. Great aristocratic families had always ensured the continuity of their social position by shrewdly arranging unions with other excellent families carrying ancient, illustrious names. The very love that just a few years before had been criticized in Justinian as a personal "flaw" was now nostalgically considered to be something that the rulers had done away with, to society's loss.

The new Augusti from the lower ranks of society preferred to have an easy-to-govern mingling of the classes, in the shadow of their own power, which, in turn, they felt interpreted and reflected God's will.

In 535 and 536, all of Constantinople was gossiping about a famous marriage that had been "piloted" by the throne. The spouses were the son of a high-ranking dignitary and minister, and the daughter of Chrysomallo, the former actress and courtesan who had come to the palace under Theodora's protection. The young bridegroom, Saturninus, had been promised in marriage to a high-ranking girl, but Theodora tricked him into marrying her protégeé. Saturninus soon complained to his relatives that the bride Theodora had "forced on him" was not "untouched."[6] The rumor reached the empress, who took immediate action: she ordered some of her men to arrest Saturninus. As soon as they grabbed him, they threw him up in the air—a mocking, not a celebratory gesture at that time. Then they started to whip him, to teach him never to complain again.

It might seem that, by punishing Saturninus, Theodora was justifying sexual license for women. But she actually suppressed it, as proven by her continued opposition to Antonina's long affair with Theodosius and her treatment of two aristocratic sisters who were both young widows. The empress reproached the sisters in vain about their active sex lives; then she forced them to marry two men of modest social extraction. The two women even sought sanctuary in the Holy Wisdom church before the weddings, but the Augusta could not be swayed. Finally, the sisters relented. The sources say that after the weddings, the two men received all kinds of honors, and thus the sisters regained their dignity. Rather than "instigating adultery,"[7] Theodora seemed to want to mix the classes. She herself had inaugurated the mixing when, as a former actress who had lived outside the law, she married Justinian, who himself had become powerful and illustrious.

Theodora's attention to women has made some observers call her a feminist, although modern feminism has ideological elements that would have been quite foreign to the empress's spiritual concepts. Certainly Theodora was a feminist insofar as she focused on women and altered women's position in society. But she worked to strengthen women within the context of the mononuclear family—the basic cell of what was at the time an innovative blueprint for Christian society—whereas the explosive feminism of the twentieth century aimed to separate or "liberate" women from that nucleus.

It's off the mark to claim Theodora's accomplishments as protofeminist; if they must fit a modern standard, they can more justifiably be called historically progressive or even Marxist. But Marxist historical studies have so far overlooked the innovative aspects of Theodora's actions, blinded probably by a rigid interpretation of ancient societies. Marxism has never had much concern for women, especially women in what was considered the decadent period of late antiquity. In addition, Marxist ideology could not stretch to a historical and dialectical reevaluation of an empress who rose from the lowest lumpenproletariat dregs, from the Hippodrome. So Marxist historiography—which could have been more sympathetic—has only perpetuated Procopius's attitude.[8]

The fact remains that Theodora's conjugal relationship with Justinian, shaped by the Christian ideal of marriage, was different from the existing social arrangements, even among the ruling classes. And the two Augusti did not preach in vain: their example was followed by the couple who next sat on the throne of Constantinople, Justin II (Justinian's nephew) and Sophia (Theodora's niece)—particularly Sophia, who picked up where Theodora left off, and expanded the "feminist" part of her work.

But women's issues were not the emperor and empress's exclusive focus in the great year of 535. They also redefined the duties of provincial functionaries, rebalancing and "correcting" (to use a term that often appears in Justinian's laws) a situation that in Theodora's mind was doubtless personified by Hecebolus in Pentapolis. With her usual attention to economic implications, she must have exhorted Justinian to raise the officials' compensation and thus suppress their temptation to make money illicitly, especially their tendency to squeeze the most defenseless populations. If the officials got more satisfaction from serving the empire, they would be more efficient: the provision of law would thus reinforce the emperor's power, fulfilling Theodora's usual objective.

Raises in pay went hand in hand with a tighter bond of personal dependency on the Augusti. Anyone who served the emperor and the empress now had to take a solemn, demanding oath:

> I swear on the All-Powerful God, his only begotten son Jesus Christ our God, on the Holy Spirit, on Mary, the holy and glorious ever-virgin Mother of God, on the four Gospels I hold in my hands, on the holy archangels Michael and Gabriel, that I shall keep a pure conscience toward our most divine and pious rulers, Justinian and Theodora his consort in power; that I shall loyally

serve them in carrying out the office that their mercy has entrusted to me; and that I shall willingly bear any burden and trouble deriving from the office that they have entrusted to me on behalf of their suzerain Empire. I am in the communion of the Holy Catholic and Apostolic Church of God. In no way shall I at any time go against it, nor shall I allow anyone to do so, to the full extent of my powers.

I also swear that I did not give anything to anybody for the office to which I have been appointed, and shall not do so . . . but that I have been appointed to this office, so to speak, without any gratuity; and that therefore I can appear before the subjects of our most holy emperors satisfied of the treatment that the treasury has assigned to me . . . that should I fail at any time to act [with diligence, lack of self-interest, fairness, and justice], may I undergo, both here and in the afterlife, in keeping with the terrible judgment of our great Lord God and our Savior Jesus Christ, the fate of Judah, the leprosy of Gihezi, and the terror of Cain; may I suffer the penalties provided for by the law of their mercy.[9]

Was this a profession of Christian faith or a secular oath to a Roman emperor? By this time the secular and the religious, the Roman and the Christian, the Church and the empire, were indissolubly intertwined. The oath sends the message that would later be transmitted by the San Vitale mosaic in Ravenna depicting Justinian and his court [fig. 2]. In the mosaic, the Bibles and the thuribles of the clergy are visually and conceptually counterbalanced by the spears and shields of the soldiers. The empire and the Church were one.

Amid the profusion of Christian elements, the empress is mentioned; that is no surprise in an oath written just a few years after the Nika uprising. Evidently, a reminder of Theodora's reaction to the rebellion stood as an implied threat of punishment. But most significant is the mention of her name in the preamble to that law (*Novel* No. 8), which notes that the legal provisions were born from the vision shared by the sleepless Justinian, "always solicitous of the good of his subjects"[10] and Theodora, "our most pious consort given us by God"[11] (making the usual etymological allusion to her name).

Naming Theodora served two purposes: to threaten functionaries who did wrong, and to remind the minister who was in charge of enforcing the law—John the Cappadocian—about Theodora's authority. It was not a warning to be taken lightly.

The development of legislation on women's issues and the confirmation of the empress's power atop the hierarchy of imperial functionaries were basic elements of Theodora's inclusion in Justinian's great policy of restoration. But while the restoration aimed to embrace the whole civilized world, it couldn't quite contain Theodora's personality, which was so rich in idiosyncrasies and unmistakably personal moods. In fact, her autonomy and power were so great that she even had her own palace.

Justinian was fond of his native Illyrian town, Tauresium; he renamed it Justiniana Prima (Justiniana the First) and remade it as an "ideal city," center of the Illyricum prefecture and of the entire region between the capital and the natural border of the Danube River. But Theodora preferred the East, and she slowly acquired vast properties beyond the Bosphorus: in Bithynia, Pontus, Cappadocia, and Paphlagonia. She personally owned lands and mansions that were out of the reach of John the Cappadocian's tax collectors.

To oversee the management and eventual transfer of her personal property to her relatives and protégés, and to freely pursue her policies, Theodora established her own palace outside of Constantinople. Called the Hieron ("the sacred," and consequently "the imperial"), it stood in present-day Fenehrbace (a suburb of Istanbul), on the Asian shore of the Propontis. The Hieron was a true citadel: it had a port, thermal baths, squares, and porticoes. The establishment of a private realm by the emperor's wife became a tradition in the Mediterranean until the end of the nineteenth century when the Empress Elizabeth of Austria—the famous "Sissy," an empress so different from Theodora—commissioned her neoclassical villa Achilleion on Corfu, the island she loved.

In the summer the Augusta held court at the Hieron, but Justinian preferred to stay and work and spend his sleepless nights in his center of operations at the palace. The existence of two separate courts offered a splendid display of majesty: imperial boats went back and forth along the coastal coves until the early fall, when the two courts were reunited and the emperor and empress again shared the same roof in their palace.

With two centers of power operating simultaneously, daily life was full of surprises, but management and communications became more complex. Boats and messengers continually ran between the palace and the Hieron and back to the city; functionaries and courtiers went from one imperial seat to the other. Powerful breakwaters kept the waves at bay, so the moorings were safe; but the strait held treacherous currents as well as the Porphyry, a legendary whale that occasionally overturned and sank boats. Some malcontents spoke of the Biblical Leviathan, saying that the Porphyry was a calamity sent by the Heavens to punish the rulers in their seeming victories.

Surrounded by her court in her Hieron, Theodora was an unopposed mistress, far above the vile rumors of her long-ago past or her supposed present evils. Her life was packed with activity. She granted audiences to functionaries and courtiers; she received foreign ambassadors; she corresponded continuously with the provinces of the empire. Her foreign mail included simple petitions, concrete appeals for tangible aid and assistance (to monastic institutions or churches, for example), and even theological issues and discussions with her favorite Monophysite interlocutors.

She may have broken up her workday with poetic or musical interludes; certainly she was committed to the visual arts. Both Justinian's palace and Theodora's Hieron were full of architectural projects and plans for mosaics and other decorations aimed at increasing the prestige of Constantinople—which became a busy construction site after the damage caused by the Nika rebellion—and the other "thousand cities" of the empire. Before the great new basilica of the Holy Wisdom was finished, the most striking building was the brand-new church dedicated to the Eastern saints Sergius and Bacchus. Known as the "Little

25. Dome of the church of Saints Sergius and Bacchus, c. 535, Istanbul.

Holy Wisdom" [fig. 25], the church was next to the one-time home of the imperial couple, the palace of Hormisdas, which was now part of the Sacred Palace compound. Inside the church, a solemn inscription in beautiful Greek characters celebrated the "lordship of the sleepless emperor" and the "power of Theodora, crowned by God," her "illustrious merciful mind," and her "inexhaustible care of the poor."[12]

✦ ✦ ✦

Was every aspect of her life so official and aboveboard? Were there no personal distractions, none of the free-spirited behavior that had marked the life of the young actress (and even the life of the empress, according to Sade and Sardou)? A passage from the *Secret History* seems to indicate such a thing:

> And at one time a suspicion arose that Theodora was smitten with love for one of the domestics, Areobindus by name, a man of Barbarian lineage but withal handsome and young, whom she herself, had as a chance appointed to be steward; so she, wishing to combat the charge, though they said she did love him desperately, decided for the moment to torture him most cruelly for no cause, and afterwards we knew nothing about him any more, nor has anyone seen him to this day.[13]

Procopius describes a crazy passion, just as he did in the passages about Justinian's passion for Theodora or Antonina's passion for Theodosius.[14] But while it was indisputable that Belisarius's wife fell for the "Thracian youth," the empress's passion for the young "barbarian" (whose name suggests Gothic origins) was just gossip—"they said she did love him." Procopius suggested that the Hieron might have been the setting for a passing fancy of the empress's that did not, however, tarnish her public image; she still "shew[ed] her teeth in anger" to Antonina precisely because the latter could not separate her private pleasure from the public virtue demanded of the "ladies" of the empire.

Did it seem that the Augusta could rest easy, having achieved everything she cared about? No: the issue of Monophysitism, which was uppermost in her mind, had not yet been resolved.

The oath of the functionary speaks of the "communion of the Holy Catholic and Apostolic Church of God," therefore implying an overall agreement with the pope in Rome. But, unlike Rome, Justinian after the theological congress of 532–33 seemed inclined to co-opt the moderate Monophysites of Syria and Egypt. His eyes were focused on the larger landscape of imperial power: nothing but terminological minutiae still seemed to need resolution—for the population of the capital, traditionally pro-Dyophysite, was opening up to the preaching of the ascetics protected by Theodora.

Having created some consensus, Theodora's perfect sense of timing told her the moment was right to display her jewel: the theologian Severus, with whom she had been corresponding. Although he was already seventy years old, he accepted her invitation and left Egypt for Constantinople. His removal from the patriarchate of Antioch in 518 had been one of Justin and Justinian's first actions, and it was only because he had been deposed that Theodora had met him in Alexandria. Now that she was empress, she could offer him complete rehabilitation. Everything seemed to be part of a great design for her: she could finally bring together the two minds that she most admired, Severus and Justinian. She hoped they would resolve the Monophysite dispute in a way acceptable even to the West, and return her protégés to the peaceful fold of the Church.

Severus, though he was "anathema," made a strong impression on the pro-papacy Justinian, who admired the theologian's deep wisdom and great rationality. Rumors were already flying that Theodora had pulled off a diplomatic and theological masterpiece, but Severus was not convinced.[14] His intellectual prudence, or his old man's natural diffidence, or his prophetic power, made him doubt that reconciliation was possible.

Indeed, the rift between the Monophysites and the Orthodox went beyond the abstract issue of the nature of Christ. Pedestrian earthly elements also played a role: the character of the protagonists, geography, the slow pace of communications, and local traditions, especially in Syria and Egypt. But it would be wrong to dismiss the theological disputes as mere "superstructures" opposed to the real economic, social, or other material structures. As the historian Ferdinand Gregorovius (1821–1891) wrote about late antiquity, "theological disputes were the only form of spiritual development in the life of humankind, which was heading for a radical transformation."[15]

One very human element that had to be considered was the age of the protagonists. Death took the religious leaders of the three leading Christian centers—Alexandria, Rome, and Constantinople—between February and June of that year, 535. The empress grieved especially for her spiritual father, Timothy of Alexandria.[16] In his city, riots over the succession pitted two local Monophysite groups against each other: the moderates who followed Theodosius against the extremists who followed Gaianus. In just a few months, the assistance of the imperial troops proved decisive in Theodosius's victory; this was clear proof that the throne supported the followers of Severus, who was then a guest in the capital.

In Rome, meanwhile, the aristocrat Agapetus succeeded Pope John II, and in Constantinople Patriarch Epiphanius died: he had been a perfect example of a "political" patriarch, for he agreed with the throne's positions and was very close to Justinian and Theodora.

The empress's accomplishment in bringing Monophysitism back into favor meant that Constantinople could not have a new patriarch who strictly followed the Dyophysite creed. And yet the time was right for Justinian's Italian campaign, which had been bolstered by his most recent success over the Vandals; Rome would object, though, if a declared Monophysite were appointed. Finally, a bishop from distant Trebizond on the Black Sea (now Trabzon, Turkey) was chosen, a shadowy figure by the name of Anthimus. The Orthodox Dyophysites were initially relieved, but then perturbed: one of the first things Anthimus did in Constantinople was visit and pay homage to Severus the Monophysite.

So Constantinople's new Christian shepherd was open to moderate Monophysitism, which naturally pleased the imperial couple, especially Theodora. (Perhaps she and her husband had suggested him.) Monophysitism was now welcome in two prestigious sees—Alexandria, traditional stronghold of Monophysitism, and the capital—two of the great Mediterranean ecclesiastical seats, along with Rome, Antioch, and Jerusalem. The opposition Justinian feared was avoided, partly because Jerusalem remained basically neutral, and mostly because Justinian kept to his personal Dyophysite creed and acted as the supreme moderator of the two beliefs.

The equilibrium didn't last long: just long enough to begin the military expedition to Italy that had been delayed so many times. There was nothing inevitable or organic about the expedition. Since 476—when the last Western Roman emperor was deposed—no emperor from Constantinople had waged war in Italy. And for a long time after Justinian, no Byzantine ruler embarked on another military offensive on the Italian peninsula. This expedition was based on nothing more than the emperor's own will; it was part of his great plan, born from his ego as a man and an emperor.

In Justinian's vision, ideology informed his diplomacy just as religion informed his military strategy, and vice versa. The idea of a peaceful, unified empire under one emperor was part and parcel of his dream of restoring the golden age of Constantine and Theodosius I. But Justinian also felt that it was a strategic move to conquer Italy, or at least a part of the peninsula that could be easily controlled. The ancient Egnatia Road led from Constantinople to Dyrrachium (now Durrës, Albania), a favorite imperial Adriatic port. From there it's just a short hop to the heel of the Italian peninsula, where the Appian Way leads to Rome. This front had to be protected from all possible dangers.

These considerations did not particularly interest Theodora: for her, the East was the motherland and the cradle of the empire. Still, historical hindsight shows that protecting Italy's Adriatic and southern shores was indeed vital to Constantinople's security; Justinian's analysis held true even centuries later. But his program had high human and financial costs from the very beginning.

When Theodoricus, the great Goth king of Italy, died in 526, his daughter Amalasuntha [fig. 26] became queen regent for her young son, Athalaric. She worshipped ancient Rome as Justinian did, and she turned to him for protection. But in the spring of 535 the Gothic aristocracy, which supported different policies, rebelled, deposing and killing her. Then Peter, the rhetorician who had endeared himself to Constantinople's Augusti and become their expert on ceremony, arrived in Italy with new messages for the queen from Justinian. But he was too late. With the queen dead, he headed back to the palace in Constantinople, where her death was interpreted as an act of rebellion against the emperor himself, an act that called for retaliation. The Italian Goths were no longer seen as subjects or representatives of the empire of the new Rome: now they were its enemies. The Arian beliefs that they clung to were another reason for attack.

26. Marble portrait head of a queen ("Amalasuntha"), c. 530, Museo dei Conservatori, Rome.

The death of Amalasuntha meant that the Italian situation exploded at a bad time for Theodora. Severus was a guest at the palace and there was a chance for reconciliation, or at least rapprochement, between the Roman Dyophysites and the Monophysites in the East. Yet Procopius disregarded the logic of her point of view and accused her of orchestrating the murder of Amalasuntha. He wrote that the empress, "considering that the woman was of noble birth and a queen, and very comely to look on, and very quick at contriving ways and means for whatever she wanted, but feeling suspicious of her magnificent bearing and exceptional manner, and at the same time fearing the fickleness of her husband Justinian, expressed her jealousy in no trivial way, but schemed to lay a fatal trap for her."[17] According to Procopius, Theodora ordered Peter to do away with the queen, and later rewarded him generously for the deed. But even Procopius confesses that he did not know how Peter could have done it.

Undoubtedly, Theodora would not have been pleased to see Amalasuntha come to Constantinople to discourse in Latin directly with Justinian, debating issues of Western politics or evoking the glories of ancient Rome. If she had once been "venomous, spiteful, envious of her colleagues,"[18] there is no reason to believe that she was any different once she had ascended the throne. The hagiography of one saintly lady of the court even reported that the jealous Augusta had sent the lady Anastasia into exile in an ascetic convent in the Mediterranean just because Justinian seemed to like her.[19]

It is likely, therefore, that Theodora was personally hostile toward Amalasuntha; but she didn't have sufficient political motives for ordering her murder. And though Justinian might have been attracted to the Gothic queen because of her appreciation of the myth of Rome and her knowledge of Latin, all the other virtues that Procopius praised in her—especially her energy and her quick mind—could be found in Theodora, who was the same age as Amalasuntha and much more expert in seduction.

As soon as Belisarius began marching the imperial army, the new Goth king sent Pope Agapetus to Constantinople on a peace mission. But the pope did not come only to avert a war. The Western clergy was not controlled by the political authorities as was its Eastern counterpart: the pope started his series of meetings with Justinian by discussing not peace but doctrine. He pressed for true Orthodoxy, he insisted on the two natures of Christ, on the Council of Chalcedon, and on the communion of the Church. He refused to meet Anthimus, the new patriarch of Constantinople. Enraged, Justinian threatened to send the pope into exile, just like a lord threatening a servant. Noble Agapetus showed no fear; he burst out laughing. He called the emperor a "new Diocletian"—that is, a persecutor rather than "a most Christian"[20] emperor.

Theodora saw how dangerous it was that the bishop of Rome failed to tremble before the emperor's political power. She tried to win Agapetus over with a variety of promises, hinting at financial benefits, inviting him to personal meetings that might facilitate an agreement on substantive issues. And she planned to introduce him to the most valuable Monophysite in the city, Severus, who dedicated his days to meditation and self-discipline, but whom the pope considered anathema.

The clash between Agapetus and Justinian was not only a confrontation of two proud personalities, but also one of the first conflicts between two different Christian universalisms—papal Rome and the Constantinopolitan empire—each certain of their primacy and of their role as regents of Christ on Earth. They were disputing not only the single or double nature of Jesus Christ but also the possession of Rome and all Italy. There's a first move in every game. Fresh memories of the lucky North African expedition, and Belisarius's reputation for invincibility, ultimately prevailed over other considerations. Justinian hoped that the local population in Italy would welcome an invasion, but that could happen only under the Roman papacy, which was Dyophysite by definition. For the soldiers of Constantinople to be greeted as liberators from the ethnic and heretic yoke of the Goths, they had to appear, first of all, to share the same religion—to be Dyophysites.

And so the pope never did meet the new patriarch of Constantinople, Anthimus, or the historical exponent of the Monophysites, Severus. In March 536, Anthimus was deposed and replaced by another patriarch, a Dyophysite who had been consecrated by the pope. His name was Menas, and he came from the monastery of the Saint Samson who, according to legend, had healed Justinian around 524. Dyophysite blessings were said over the swords, spears, and arrows of the imperial troops, which could now conquer Italy under the sign of the restoration. Martial songs alternated with prayers recited in Latin.

The pope's behavior might be interpreted in light of the Gospel passage "Be as cunning as the snake and as simple as the dove":[21] he had promised Justinian a solid item, Italy—which was not his to give—in return for a concession about the controversial nature of Christ. Meanwhile, Constantinople still had to conquer all of Italy, mile by mile, battling an army that did not answer to Agapetus. And the Monophysites were left to either make amends or withdraw to the Levant, which they considered their true fatherland.

✤ ✤ ✤

These developments were so different from what Theodora had planned. She must have discussed them at length with Justinian in their private apartment at the palace. Finally, he must have convinced her to be patient. Strengthened by the pope's support and heartened by the quick military defeat of the Vandals, the emperor believed that he could take Italy with the same ease. He could not foresee that it would take years to win this war. He promised his empress that once the peninsula was conquered and the pope satisfied, he would review the situation. Meanwhile, he would create or maintain pockets of tolerance for the Monophysites, starting (paradoxically) in the imperial palace. Hundreds of Monophysites sought refuge there, most of them housed in the palace of Hormisdas ("a wonderful desert of solitary souls")[22] and in the church of saints Sergius and Bacchus. Other protected areas were in the suburbs of the capital and, as always, in Alexandria. Still, a few months later Anthimus and Severus and other Monophysite authorities were officially condemned for their beliefs (*Novel* No. 42; August 536). They were asked to leave the capital and the major cities and retire quietly to the desert. The writings of Severus were singled out for censure.

Meanwhile, instead of returning victoriously to Rome as planned, Pope Agapetus died in Constantinople in April 536, ending a very brief pontificate. He had not prevented the war in Italy (as the Gothic king had asked), and he had blocked the rapprochement in the eastern Mediterranean between Monophysites and Dyophysites, which had seemed within reach. In Constantinople his death was regarded as a divine punishment, especially by the Monophysite circles around the intransigent Zooras;[23] but Rome beatified Agapetus.

Less than two years later, in February 538, Severus died. With the empress's support he had repaired undisturbed to his beloved Egypt among the anchorites who had fled from secular life. His idea of faith had ultimately proved irreconcilable with the power of the Roman empire, confirming his most pessimistic predictions. In the meantime, the abuses of 518 were being replicated in persecutions in other provinces. John of Tella, who had probably accompanied Theodora during her memorable journey to Bithynia in 533, died in an Antioch prison just one day after Severus's death. The Monophysites worshiped him and still worship him now as a confessor who suffered for his faith.

Finally even Alexandria was brought into line. Timothy's successor there, Theodosius—the moderate Monophysite patriarch who had been forced upon the city by the emperor and empress's armies only a few months before—went into exile (a fairly pleasant one, under Theodora's protection). A Dyophysite patriarch was then appointed, but he did not take office.

In Alexandria (where the patriarchate claimed to be the seat of Mark the Evangelist, a direct disciple of Jesus Christ), and in the rest of Egypt, Christianity was setting off along two separate paths. In those vast lands were the Dyophysite Church now imposed by the throne of Constantinople (disparagingly called the "melkite" or "imperial" church), and another Church that worshiped Severus as a saint and that would eventually be identified with nationalism and the Coptic language. Although the authorities of this Church were in exile, the majority of the population supported it. And above all it was protected by the most powerful woman in the empire.

It might have seemed that Theodora was temporarily defeated, or at least brought down to size, but Pope Agapetus (or his ghost) had hardly triumphed. Justinian had hoped to unite the Church, and had therefore marched the imperial troops off to Italy, but the Church was in fact heading for a split. Meanwhile Anthimus, the patriarch that Pope Agapetus had insisted on removing, could not be found. Condemned in absentia, his shadow hovered over the city, and contradictory rumors flew about his fate.

At the palace, people wondered what would happen in Rome when news came of the pope's death. The projections were disturbing: Italy had yet to be conquered; now that Agapetus was dead, the Roman Church would be both inflexible about the nature of Jesus Christ and more conciliatory to the Goths; it might offer peace to Constantinople instead of victory. In her conversations with the emperor, Theodora might have shown unusual irritation. She might have reproached him for his mistake, for his infatuation with Rome, his bookish culture, his blindness about people's real intentions, and especially his negligence of the Christian East.

In Theodora's eyes, the situation was quite serious. The papacy was undoubtedly guilty of arrogance, and Justinian had been volatile and thoughtless. She might have recalled Tribonian paying homage to the emperor: the minister and jurist had said that he was "fearful that the emperor—so great was his mercy!—would not ascend immediately to Heaven."[24] Maybe that had been not reverence but veiled mockery. Instead of making her smile now, that sentence might have put her in a bad mood, for only she was allowed these sorts of liberties.

Now she had to act fast. Once again, Theodora dared what no one else would dare, trying to reverse a situation that looked unfixable. To save the Monophysites without losing Rome (which Justinian wanted so badly), she would have to gamble everything. She hatched the idea of putting a Monophysite on the papal throne—or if not a professed Monophysite, at least someone who could make peace with Mono-physitism. Justinian approved the plan, trusting in Theodora's judg-ment, especially because she believed she had a trustworthy person to carry out the initiative and take the papal scat.

The situation required a man who thought highly of himself and had protectors in high places. There was such a man in Constantinople, named Vigilius. He was papal nuncio at the imperial palace, but this was only his most recent distinction. The scion of an ancient Roman family of consuls and senators, he was used to vast horizons and great wealth. His family history made it easy for him to win popular sup-port, and gave credence to his promises and pledges. He had nearly been consecrated pope in 532; now he could, and should, get the position.

Vigilius was ambitious, but he had no deeply rooted ideals; and the discontented Augusta simply required a candidate. It looked like per-fect synergy could be orchestrated for Belisarius's army in Italy. After winning the papal throne that he so coveted, Vigilius could bring Monophysitism back into the womb and the communion of the Church. Bring back not only the individuals such as Anthimus (who had disappeared into thin air), but the ideas: he would revoke or tone down the pronouncements of the Council of Chalcedon. He wrote to the Augusta to commit himself.

Vigilius left for Italy with precise instructions for Belisarius, but it was too late. In June 536 a pope who pleased the Goths had been installed: his name was Silverius. Because of the war, Constantinople could not consider that its representatives had ratified the election, as had been the case for the popes enthroned in peacetime. The situation was further complicated and destabilized by the fact that the Goth king who had chosen Pope Silverius was soon deposed by the local aristocracy and died (not unlike Pope Agapetus, who had died right after completing his mission in Constantinople). On the stage of history, Justinian and Theodora kept finding themselves playing opposite new characters on the scene—no one had yet equaled their long run on stage and their focused strategy.

When a capable new Goth king, Witigis, ultimately started his long reign, Pope Silverius was left without protection while Belisarius's troops advanced up Italy, even conquering Naples, just a few days' march from Rome. Finally, Silverius agreed to support Belisarius. In December 536, he opened the doors of the Eternal City to the general.

This was a great military achievement for the *restitutio*; Justinian rejoiced that his empire was finally Roman in fact and not just in name. The first Rome and the Rome-on-the-Bosphorus were once again directly ruled by a single emperor, as had been the case under the Constantines and the Theodosiuses. It was the best possible augury for the full reconstitution of a unified empire.

But Theodora had a different view. In her palace on the Propontis she had planned not the conquest of the city of Rome, but the political correction of the papacy. So she immediately set out to test Silverius's character. She wrote to invite him to court and to exhort him to restore Anthimus to the patriarchal seat in Constantinople. The pope gave the lady Augusta a stern reply: "I shall never rehabilitate a heretic who has been sentenced for his wickedness." But the people around him heard him moan: "Now I know what shall be the cause of my death."[25]

"Inhuman Cruelty"

Italy, Constantinople, Mesopotamia, 537–41

THEODORA'S CLEAR SIGHT and the initiative she showed in the winter of 536–37 made Justinian more of a spectator than an actor. Constantinople's pressure on Rome and Italy was pushed by Theodora, the least Western and the least pro-Roman of rulers. Unable to tolerate Justinian's docility in the face of Agapetus's actions and Pope Silverius's later response, she took over. As long as Egypt and the Near East were in the hands of the Monophysites, it made sense to simply mark time and compromise with the papacy. But with Egypt and the Near East pledged to Dyophysitism—which was perceived as foreign if not outright hostile—action in the West could no longer be delayed.

Theodora wrote to Belisarius in Rome what no other woman—empress or not—had ever dared: she ordered the general to remove Pope Silverius. "Vigilius, our dearest, who has promised to reseat Patriarch Anthimus, is with you," she added. But the general hesitated. He was heard mumbling words such as "the Augusta shall be accountable for it to Jesus Christ."[1] A military man, Belisarius recognized that Silverius had, after all, kept his promise, throwing open the gates of Rome for him. But more than that, he was thinking about the impending arrival of the Gothic army: tens of thousands of soldiers under the direct command of Witigis, the new king. They were going to set siege to Rome, and he was expected to hold it with only five thousand men. Complications on the ecclesiastical front were not welcome.

In the meantime, there were rumors of secret pacts between the pope and the besieging Gothic soldiers. Antonina, Belisarius's wife, was particularly inclined to listen to such rumors; perhaps she even fomented them. She was being encouraged to act by the Augusta: they had a separate correspondence that was at cross-purposes with the direct official negotiations between Belisarius and the pope.

One day in March 537, Silverius went up the Pincio hill for one of his regular meetings with Belisarius, but this time something unusual happened: the pope was separated from his retinue and taken to a private chamber, where he saw a surprising yet domestic scene. Reclining on a triclinium was a woman, the patrician Antonina. Seated at her feet was the commander-in-chief of the imperial army in Italy, her husband, General Belisarius. Other people were also present. Antonina spoke first, saying, "Well, Mr. Pope Silverius, what have we done to you and all the Romans that you should be so anxious to hand us over to the Goths?"

Silverius's quill would have found the right words for replying to a letter from Theodora, but he may not have been able to answer Antonina. The meeting ended with Silverius stripped of his office and reduced to the status of a simple monk; the city was in shock when Vigilius was crowned pope. It was the most "female" installation of a pope in all of Christian history.[2]

Antonina, not Belisarius, turned out to be the one who "contrived the impossible"[3] in the name of the empress. Perhaps the general had wanted to show that he obeyed only Justinian, or that he recognized the honor of Silverius's rank; but Theodora must have been displeased when she heard about his comments and his behavior. Her latent suspicions about the general turned into open dissatisfaction that grew and sharpened in the following years.

Silverius's deposition looks in retrospect like an egregious abuse of power, just as it did at the time; but there might have been a precedent. Since the fifth century it had been customary for the election of the pope to be ratified by the imperial authority. Once the Western empire dissolved, it was Italy's "barbarian" king, acting as the representative of the sovereign of the new Rome-on-the-Bosphorus, who gave his consent. But, as we already noted, Silverius's election had been sponsored and approved by a Gothic king who was in a state of *war* with Constantinople and so, in the eyes of the emperor, the election was invalid. Vigilius was thus presented as the legitimate successor to Agapetus, not a replacement for Silverius.

It was still unclear whether this operation would, in the short term, help Belisarius's soldiers be welcomed into Italy, as everyone in Constantinople fervently hoped. In the long term the intervention might or might not be a concrete improvement for the Eastern Monophysites, for whose benefit it had been staged.

Silverius's removal was a weighty event. He was transferred—actually deported—to far-off Lycia in Asia Minor; then he was returned to Italy so his position could be reexamined. The official reaction at the palace alternated between displays of Christian virtue and feigned shock and ignorance about the events surrounding the deposition. Silverius was finally exiled, probably at Vigilius's and Theodora's behest, to the island of Pontia (now Ponza) in the Tyrrhenian Sea, where he died. He had shown the clairvoyance that the blessed were believed to possess: he had immediately understood that the first letter Theodora sent him had signified his doom. The Catholic Church worships him as a confessor of the faith; like the Monophysite John of Tella who died in an imperial prison in Syria, his victory was not of this world. (Nor was it for the same idea of Christ.)

As late as the summer of 536 a rehabilitation of Monophysitism seemed impossible; but now new things were changing. Apparently, Vigilius had secretly written to the Augusta that he did not believe that Jesus Christ had two natures. Rather, he interpreted Christ as being "one composite unit resulting from two natures,"[4] just as she would have wanted. But once again events took a different turn. Not, this time, because of any sudden deaths, as in the stormy period from February 535 to May 536, when the church leaders of Constantinople, Alexandria, and Rome had died (Rome actually lost two popes in that period). Instead, for the first time in her decade-long tenure, Theodora wondered if she had made a mistake with her point man in Rome.

It soon became clear that after becoming pope, Vigilius, the great

Western aristocrat, was running into personal obstacles. Among other things, he was being blamed for having gotten the papal seat in an irregular way; the seat had already been within his grasp in 532 and might have become his in any case. There were also theoretical and political snags because the Western, Roman world was solidly anti-Monophysite. Vigilius complained of the local pressures, and he procrastinated. He feared that any hurried actions favoring Anthimus and the Monophysites might ultimately ruin his chance of success and frustrate the promises he had made to Lady Augusta. But Theodora knew from past experience that a change in direction could succeed only if it was swift.

Despite all her work, Rome was once again a problem for the empress. Even though Justinian had rejoiced prematurely at the end of 536, he and his wife didn't really hold Rome firmly. Perhaps for the first time, she saw the stage of power as different from that of the theater, where the unexpected was codified and where misadventures were always resolved in a tidy disentangling of the fictional knots. In real life, the number of protagonists kept shifting and the pacing could not be controlled. The time never came when the audience could be dismissed and the players could leave the stage—events were just too big and lengthy and complicated.

From the Euphrates to the Danube, from Italy to North Africa—on all sides of the central city of Constantinople was a web of issues and events continuously evolving and affecting one another reciprocally: political and military issues, economic and legal questions, religious and social problems, public and personal matters. One example of this complexity was Vigilius's approach to the theological issue dividing Monophysites and Dyophysites. It was not possible to isolate and analyze each single phenomenon; the world that the restoration was expected to cure refused to sit still for an examination by and therapy from its two chosen physicians, the "sleepless" Justinian and the "merciful" Theodora.

Not even simple military issues were easy to settle. The generals who conducted the Italian campaign were split: some, like Belisarius, were "Justinianean," and some were apparently "Theodorean." (The latter may have been responsible for intelligence-gathering and espionage for the empress, who held latent, parallel power.) This led to operational conflicts and liaison gaps that were painfully evident, for example, when the imperial troops abandoned the city of Milan in 539 and the Goths retaliated, flattening the city walls and slaughtering the civilian population. The resulting depopulation of the area left room for Ticinum (now Pavia) to emerge as a regional power and later become the capital of the Longobards.

Milan had been the Roman capital of the West from 286 to 402 and had remained the leading city of northern Italy; among those killed there was the praetorian prefect for Italy, Reparatus, a brother of Pope Vigilius. The conquerors quartered his body, say the historians, and fed it to the dogs. We do not know whether the two Augusti in Constantinople wore mourning (as old Justin had done for the Antiochians after the earthquake of 526) or showed any Christian remorse for the residents of Milan, a city that had stood as "an outpost against the Germans and the other barbarians."[5]

No one could deny that the new Gothic king, Witigis, was a belligerent character, but he was also a skilled diplomat. He sought alliances among the northern populations—such as the Burgundians, the Franks, and the Longobards—and elsewhere. He boldly noted that the "emperor of the Romans had plainly never been able to make war upon the barbarians in the West before the time when the treaty had been made with the Persians,"[6] by which he meant the Endless Peace (of the fall of 532).

Witigis thought to stall the offensive in Italy by inducing the Persian king to take up arms again against Justinian. So he craftily sent messengers to the White Palace, the royal residence of Ctesiphon, Khosrow's beloved labyrinth city. The Byzantine court regarded Khosrow as the most greedy, hypocritical, and sardonic of men: he had even dared to ask Justinian for a share of the spoils seized in Africa, on the ground that "the emperor would never have been able to conquer in the war with the Vandals if the Persians had not been at peace with him."[7]

Culturally and historically, Khosrow was the anti-Justinian. While the emperor of Constantinople idolized a Rome that he didn't have, Khosrow considered himself a living idol in lands that were his and his alone. One was a scholar who carefully scrutinized data; the other was a hunter, a scoffing man who sought opportunities, who jumped at his main chance, who took liberties. One lived like a monk or a recluse in the palace; the other was a man of the great outdoors, of battlefields, of big-game hunting. Even their ideas about power differed. For Justinian it was a responsibility that kept him up at night; for Khosrow it was a license for fun. Khosrow scorned the exclusive tie that bound Justinian to Theodora; he also mocked their religion. The only thing the two men had in common was their enjoyment of splendor.

It is easy to understand that Khosrow was already bored by the Endless Peace of 532, even though his treasury benefited from it. As he was looking for a pretext to breach the pact, and as he had other designs on the eastern front, Khosrow responded eagerly to the message from the Gothic ambassadors. In the early spring of 540, when the ice on the Anatolian peaks was beginning to melt, the Persian king attacked Antioch, making the great Eastern metropolis suffer another great disaster. He set fire to it and razed it, but instead of killing thousands of imperial subjects like a barbarian would have done, he shrewdly chose to deport them and make them *his* taxpayers. Persian legends tell of the wonders of the city of Rumagan, known as "Khosrow's Antioch":[8] it was a splendid copy of Antioch built on the banks of the Tigris River in Persia by the original inhabitants of that city.

This is not what one expected from the other Great Eye of the Ecumene; nor did it correspond to the seductive promises of the seventh eon. The learned citizens of Constantinople asked themselves whether this new calamity was somehow related to the "swordfish" comet, also called "the bearded star,"[9] that had crossed the sky months earlier. Interpretations of the phenomenon differed, as they so often did at the time.

To conquer Italy, Justinian had chosen to sacrifice Monophysitism to a pope whose days turned out to be numbered. Faced with the new emergency on the eastern front, the emperor consulted with Theodora, who was all too ready to remind him of the several traps he had tumbled into as he reached for Rome: the traps of Agapetus, of Khosrow, and now of Witigis. Constantinople had once been considered very shrewd, but now that seemed no more than a distant memory. Finally, Justinian called Belisarius—the man who had proved the most successful and trustworthy of his generals—back from Italy, and put him in charge of operations in the East. Theodora, who had not forgotten Belisarius's conduct before Pope Silverius's removal, must have warned her husband to keep the general under tight rein.

Justinian most likely countered Theodora's arguments with facts: she could not deny that between 535 and 539 Belisarius had conquered or defended a large number of Italian cities. (This is proof that urban life continued substantially unchanged on the Italian peninsula, and that 476—the date that marks the end of the Western Roman empire—was not the dramatic break that the history books would have us believe.) On a map, Belisarius's series of victories look like the itinerary of some traveler on the Grand Tour, with the evocative name "Rome" set like a jewel among the names of delightful Italian cities big and small, such as Palermo, Naples, Cuma, Rimini, Urbino, and Fermo. These victories and other military operations that showed his energy, cunning, and caution earned him the respect of his soldiers, of the subject populations, and even of his enemies.

This was Belisarius's most valuable asset, even more important than the legendary riches Antonina managed. Antonina, by the way, continued her fling with Theodosius; meanwhile, the split deepened between Belisarius and the other generals, who were perhaps shrewder and more diplomatic in dealing with the Augusti. The Augusti, who had forced Belisarius to kneel to them even on the day of his triumph over the Vandals, were begrudging him reinforcements: they did not want to be outshined by him. Theodora and John the Cappadocian each had had their reasons for urging Justinian to let Belisarius handle the Italian question by himself.

Five years after the outbreak of hostilities in Italy, the developments on the Persian front caused the emperor and empress to decide that their geopolitical policy in the East should be a model for the Italian peninsula. In their plan, the Po River in northern Italy would act as the frontier and watershed, just as the Euphrates did in the Near East. Witigis would rule over the lands north of the Po, including the city of Milan, while the rest of Italy would go to Justinian, together with half of the Gothic king's treasure. These were the conditions listed in the official correspondence, conditions that Witigis and the Goths could accept, and which even historians have approved of in hindsight, as they understood the defensive implications of Justinian's militarism. What is more, even Theodora could accept this solution as the lesser of two evils, given her interest in having the center of the empire shift eastward.

But Belisarius objected to the plan, for he was sure that he could win the war on the battlefield "to the advantage of the emperor"[10] and bring Witigis back in chains to the capital, as he had done with Gelimer. The court feared that Belisarius would use the occasion to stir up the populace against Justinian in another urban uprising. Still others, however, recalled that Belisarius had sworn loyalty to the emperor, and concluded that he would never rebel.

The reaction of the Goths in Ravenna was quite different. Alarmed by Belisarius's firm strength (he had besieged their capital), they proposed an unexpected solution. They offered Belisarius sovereignty over all of Italy, Goths and indigenous Italic populations both, putting an end to the bloodshed and enthroning him like a new Theodoric or, better, a new monarch of the West.

To Belisarius it seemed a dream come true: the Gothic capital was surrendering to him, like an oyster opening to reveal a pearl. And because he had lost neither his military cunning nor his duplicity, he pretended to accept the offer; but as soon as he entered the city with his army, he put Witigis and the Gothic nobility under guard. He openly proclaimed that he acted only on behalf of Emperor Justinian. The generals and the ambassadors of Constantinople were rendered speechless by his stratagem. The Goths felt betrayed and bewildered: they could not understand why Belisarius preferred to be the slave of a faraway emperor instead of being their king.

Belisarius had conquered Ravenna for the second Rome without losing even one man, and the women of Ravenna, as they watched the imperial soldiers march through the city, "[A]ll spat upon the faces of their husbands, and pointing with their hands to the victors, reviled them for their cowardice."[11] The conquering army turned out not to be the forest of giants that people had feared. Procopius was there, and he wrote: "And while I watched the entry of the Roman army into Ravenna at that time, an idea came to me, to the effect that it is not at all by the wisdom of men or by any other sort of excellence on their part that events are brought to fulfillment, but that there is some divine power which is ever warping their purposes and shifting them in such a way that there will be nothing to hinder that which is being brought to pass."[12] He knew his general's weaknesses; he did not mythologize Belisarius, even though he had worked for the general.

Soon the victorious general left other officers in charge of the Italian lands beyond the Po River and returned to Constantinople with Witigis, king of the Goths, in chains. Witigis's wife was among the captives, as were local notables and soldiers and Matasuntha, who was Amalasuntha's daughter and thus a descendant of the great Theodoric. He also brought back another "barbarian" treasure. Belisarius was beloved in the capital because of his victory and his lack of arrogance. But the court thought a second triumph would be inappropriate. On the one hand, John the Cappadocian urged the court to limit its expenses; on the other, Theodora suggested that her husband not encourage the cult of Belisarius's personality, especially because the general's brilliant initiative in Ravenna was essentially an act of insubordination. Justinian agreed with her, and found a balanced solution.

The Gothic treasure was displayed, but inside the palace. There was no sequel to the triumphal procession of 534. The victories were celebrated, but only artistically: a mosaic representing the general returning from his victorious wars was commissioned for the ceiling of the Chalkê (the palace vestibule). His armies intact, he delivers treasure, spoils, and captives, including the kings of the Vandals and the Goths, to Justinian and Theodora, both depicted with "exultation on their very countenance."[13] It was a prestigious but atypical representation, for while it celebrated Belisarius it also confirmed his dependence on *both* of the Augusti. The couple was shown in the act of rejoicing, with facial expressions that would have been unthinkable for the solemn emperors of ancient times. But Justinian and Theodora were not ancient rulers. They quickly dispatched Belisarius to the Persian front to begin military operations in the spring of 541.

This time, Antonina did not follow him right away. She must have met repeatedly with Theodora. The empress continued to criticize her open liaison with Theodosius, but appreciated her efficiency in removing Pope Silverius from office. Theodora must have questioned Antonina about the possibility that a Gothic revival in Italy might disrupt the status quo, just as the frequent raids by Berber guerrillas disrupted the emperor's rule over the African lands he had captured from the Vandals. The Augusta must also have asked her how she interpreted Pope Vigilius's reticence and slowness.

Antonina probably replied as best she could. She feared that Theodora might secretly be planning to confiscate the wealth that Belisarius had accumulated in more than seven years spent away from Constantinople, which she managed together with her lover Theodosius. So perhaps she turned the conversation to other topics. She might have pointed out that Belisarius had never received sufficient money, supplies, or soldiers in the wars that he had fought. That he had written many letters to the Most Serene Augustus, but that John the Cappadocian had continued to skimp on resources. Antonina might have also reminded the empress of all the instances when she, a perfect Christian wife, had given concrete aid to her husband. John the Cappadocian, however, had supplied the troops sailing against the Vandals with spoiled, moldy food that was unfit to eat.[14] All because he wanted to contain costs—a weak excuse considering the enormous riches that he had accumulated.

"Weaver of deceit"[15] as she was, Antonina kept hammering away at John the Cappadocian, pointing him out as prey for what she recognized as Theodora's long-postponed hunger for recognition. But, most important, she diverted the Augusta's attention away from her wealth and that of Belisarius.

For years—ever since Justinian had yielded to Pope Agapetus—events and people had no longer followed their predictable course or obeyed Theodora's will. With Antonina at her side, she understood that she might be able to get rid of the Cappadocian. He owed her his life, at the very least, for in 532 the Nika rebels had been ready to slaughter him; yet in spite of that he did not give her the homage she was due. He disliked being obligated to her. He criticized Theodora in front of Justinian, accusing her of reducing the great policies of the empire to personal issues or, even worse, to intrigues among women or among priests. He accused her of being interested only in increasing her personal wealth, her *domus divina*.

John also found it intolerable that some of Justinian's laws that were addressed to him as praetorian prefect contained explicit, atypical references to the emperor's love for Theodora. They were warnings about the real balance of power, of course, but John did not see that, or he refused to heed them. The Cappadocian considered her a worthless woman, yet he feared that she might plot to have him killed, so he slept poorly at night (like Justinian, but for different reasons). Waking up one morning, John confided to someone that one day he would be the emperor. He had received a vague prediction.

In the city, the slanderous rumors about John kept growing, perhaps fomented by people close to Theodora. It's also possible that John's group disseminated many stories about the empress, some of which were reported in Procopius. Bitter rivals often have much in common, and so did the empress and the minister. They both had humble births. They loved power and money. They had free access to the emperor. They had both been disappointed by others (as is often the lot of people close to power and money). But the Cappadocian misjudged Justinian's feelings for Theodora, and the fascinating theological speculation in which she knew how to engage the emperor, satisfying a deep longing in his soul.

John was also envious and angry about Belisarius's victories in

Africa and Italy. He tried to undermine the general's position with the Augustus by accusing him of tax evasion in the form of embezzling and procedural irregularities. He insinuated that Belisarius was better suited to conquering capitals than winning wars, and he presented the emperor with accounts showing the cost of repressing Berber guerrilla warfare in North Africa, which Belisarius had failed to really subdue. He estimated that Justinian would probably have to spend similar sums to subdue Italy, which was far bigger and which the general had insisted on capturing, disobeying the emperor's instructions.

So Antonina had many good reasons for rechanneling Theodora's mounting irritation as anger at the Cappadocian. She had to push her affair with young Theodosius into the background, and she needed to divert attention from insinuations about her and Belisarius's conduct and wealth. For Antonina it was natural to "contrive the impossible"; this was the time to act. She prepared a detailed plan and got the Augusta's approval. For her plan, she used Belisarius just as she had when she removed Silverius from office. But this time he was at the Persian front, so she didn't use him in person, or his army: his name was enough.

During one of the Cappadocian's absences from Constantinople, Antonina, who was then perhaps fifty years old, approached Euphemia, the young, shy, beloved daughter of the prefect, "his little girl." She feigned interest and was able to gain the girl's trust and affection, as if she were her dearest friend. Then with insistent self-pity she lamented her fate and that of her husband, the man who had done so much to expand and enrich the empire and bring it glory. The couple had had nothing but ingratitude from the Augusti, she said. Euphemia, whom her father protected like "the apple of his eye," repeated to her "dearest friend"[16] what she must have heard at home: that the responsibility was all Antonina's and Belisarius's; they were the only ones who could have turned the situation around, but had failed to do so. Evidently women were not afraid to discuss political issues freely in the gynoecia of Constantinople.

Antonina seized the opportunity. She said that she and Belisarius needed support from inside the palace. They had been away for a long time. With her Eastern flair for drama, she drew a pathetic picture of the hardships she had endured, the dangers she had faced: the African drought, the winters in Rome, Belisarius's sorties out of besieged cities, the continual risks to his life. She had even had to personally outfit a fleet of ships in the shadow of Mount Vesuvius as the rumbling volcano prepared to erupt.[17] Euphemia shared her grief. She said that she would speak to her father, the very man who had begrudged all kinds of support to the general, and she did so when the prefect returned from a trip.

To John the Cappadocian, it seemed like a dream: his imperial prophecy was coming true. He enthusiastically requested a meeting with Antonina, but she postponed it until she was ready to leave for the East to join Belisarius. She suggested a seemingly casual meeting that could take place at the Rufinianae, a villa owned by Belisarius on the Asian coast of the Propontis. The official reason? John was to bring deferential greetings to Antonina and good wishes for the journey. Theodora approved the plan.

On the appointed day, after paying her respects to the empress, Antonina set out with her retinue for her journey to the East. The first stop was at the Rufinianae for the nighttime meeting with the praetorian prefect. As Antonina went, Theodora denounced the Cappadocian to Justinian, telling him that a plot was being hatched that would finally reveal John's long-standing imperial designs, his crime of high treason. Theodora depicted John as Justinian's deep and constant enemy, even more formidable than foreign or barbaric kings. She painted a dark picture, as if a second Nika were imminent. Once again, it looked like she was Justinian's savior.

Theodora's powerful pathos was equaled by her legendary speed. She dispatched Narses, the old eunuch, to the Rufinianae: over the years, he had been sharpening his military expertise. With him went the commander of the palace guards and an escort of armed men. They had clear orders from Theodora: to use the slightest pretext to eliminate John on the spot for the crime of high treason.

Theodora probably did not reveal this order to her husband. This is proof of both her violent determination and her fears. She might have thought back to the indulgence Justinian had shown to Hypatius in 532, or to his indecision over Pope Agapetus. She believed that in such predicaments action was the best course, and that it was proof of might and majesty.

In any case, Justinian learned of Theodora's orders. In spite of everything, he might have believed that John could still be useful to the empire. Even if he was personally offended and disappointed, his institutional persona might still have kept its balance. He sent a message to John, forbidding him to meet secretly with Antonina. Never had a potentate acted so solicitously toward someone who was plotting against him. Perhaps Justinian simply wanted to interrogate John personally, as he had done with Hypatius at the time of the Nika rebellion. In any case, although John received the message, he went ahead with the meeting.

It was night at the Rufinianae, and Antonina and the Cappadocian were working out the details of their completely realistic plan. Theodora's men lay in ambush nearby, behind a wall. The plotters' silk garments and adornments proclaimed their high institutional positions: one was the most powerful minister of the empire and the other was the wife of the leading Roman general. The patrician lady stressed the importance of Belisarius's army, but we shall never know what they decided about who would wear the purple after Justinian was eliminated, or what fate they planned for Theodora. We do know that Antonina was deceiving John, and that he was probably thinking of getting rid of Belisarius (and Antonina) once the general no longer served his purpose.

Meanwhile, the prefect was speaking freely and committing himself to the plot with the moral weight of those "most dread [Christian] oaths"[18] the law prescribed for the "service of the most divine and pious rulers, Justinian and Theodora." At that point, Theodora's men sprang into action, leaping toward John. But the cautious prefect had brought his own bodyguard. There was a scuffle, and John fled. He did not run to Justinian but sought refuge in a church, begging for the right of sanctuary, even though many literary sources have described him as a pagan.

It was an implicit admission of guilt. Theodora asked the emperor for John's head, but Justinian refused to sentence him to death, prefer-ring to exile him to the ancient city of Cyzicus (now Balkiz in Turkey), beyond the Propontis. John had dreamed of wearing the imperial man-tle; now he was forced to wear a monk's habit and be called "Brother Augustus." It was a bitterly ironic fulfillment of the prophecy that he would be Augustus.

His legendary riches didn't suffer such a bitter fate. They were quickly confiscated, but then a fair portion was returned to him; he had wisely hidden away other property for his beloved Euphemia. Soon it was rumored that he was living a carefree life, much better than when he was a powerful prefect. Theodora continued to detest him; her peo-ple hated him too. But for him the worst was yet to come.

In 542, the bishop of Cyzicus was murdered. Mutual animosity had developed between the exiled John and the murdered bishop, so the former prefect was immediately suspected of the foul deed (or suspi-cions were conveniently directed toward him). There was an inquest; John was jailed, interrogated, and beaten. While there was no conclu-sive proof of his guilt, still he was deprived of all his property. Dressed in rags, he was put on a ship and forced to beg for food at each port of call. He finally reached the remote place where he was to be interned, the city that the emperor Hadrian had dedicated to his lover Antinoos. The city, Antinoopolis (now Esh Sheikh' Abãdah, Egypt), on the banks of the Upper Nile, was about two hundred miles south of the urban opulence of Alexandria.

Still, John had not changed. Even in this faraway place, he oversaw tax matters that were no longer his responsibility, threatening to inform on people and reminding everyone of his prestige, and his former power. Theodora had also not changed: years later, she was still seek-ing evidence to nail him for the murder of the bishop of Cyzicus. She was implacable. She sought not victory for herself but complete defeat and humiliation for John. She failed to shed his blood, but she shed the blood of others: two men lost their right hands when they refused to testify in a trial against John, as she had asked them to. She was not punishing those who went against the law, but only those who did not bend to *her* law.

The history of Theodora and John the Cappadocian was not marked by the spirit of forgiveness that has often been professed as the essence of Christianity. The affair was a naked power struggle; Theodora's unrelenting fury might even give credence to those who denigrated her by attributing to her a sort of "inhuman cruelty" and "a mind fixed firmly and persistently upon cruelty."[19] Others might have defended her by recalling that before this affair she had never exercised power arbitrarily and that it was a one-time event, a personal reaction to the Cappadocian's provocations and accusations, not a case of wrath for "the destruction of men."[20] Many women, many poor people, and all the Monophysites could testify to Theodora's compassionate mercy.

From a historical perspective it's clear that the overall imperial project was subsumed to her personal hatred, and passion overcame reason. It was the first time that something of this sort had happened, and it showed her political irresponsibility, for there was no adequate successor at the praetorian prefecture. Only in 543 was the position filled, by Peter Barsymes, a protégé of Theodora's originally from Syria.

Public affairs were being managed like private affairs[21] because of technical problems, the debasement of offices and officeholders, the difficulty of communication in a multicontinental setting, and the interpenetration of the personal and the public. Private issues too easily became public; this is what happened between Belisarius and Antonina.

Antonina did much more than please Theodora and ruin John: she saved her wealth and that of her husband, as well as her relationship with her lover Theodosius. But beyond the Euphrates, in his camp on the Persian front, far from the wife who bewitched him "through her magic arts,"[22] Belisarius opened his eyes. Actually, someone opened them for him.

That someone was the general's stepson, a child of Antonina's first marriage. Photius was a high-ranking officer who helped his stepfather defend the empire from the Persians; but he feared his mother even more than he feared enemy archers. He was especially worried that Antonina might appoint Theodosius, her godson and lover, sole heir to the wealth that she and Belisarius had accumulated. Photius refused to accept a secondary role, and so he told Belisarius the whole truth about Antonina's behavior. It was a bitter revelation for the conqueror of Vandals and Goths. Threatened, he swore to act, and Photius swore with him, both of them using the kind of oaths "which are the most terrible among the Christians and are in fact so designated by them,"[23] but he did not intend to eliminate Antonina. "I love my wife exceedingly," Belisarius reportedly said; "I shall do her no harm . . . if it be granted me to take vengeance upon [Theodosius] the corrupter of my home."[24] To get his revenge, all he had to do was to exclude the younger man from the spoils of war.

After her triumph over the Cappadocian, Antonina was moving inland to join Belisarius with her retinue. The two winners should have had a happy reunion: her husband, in one of those military operations that made him "the best general of all times,"[25] had just stormed the enemy fortress of Sisauranon near Nisibis and the river Tigris at the eastern border of Mesopotamia. But his mind was not on military matters. As soon as he learned of his wife's arrival, he stopped battling for the empire's glory.

He did not push forward to attack the Persians, to advance into the heart of their territory and on to the undefended capital, Ctesiphon. In Ravenna the previous year, Belisarius had refused to become "a new Theodoric." Now he had the chance to become another Alexander the Great, and again he refused. He pulled back because he wanted to meet with Antonina.

He did not confront her explosively, or mete out harsh punishment. But did put her under strict surveillance that the patrician Antonina found humiliating. In focusing on her, Belisarius was "subordinating the most vital interests of the State to those of his own family"[26] without effectively resolving either. The result was total inaction on both fronts.

Photius had a different interpretation of the oath that he had sworn with Belisarius. He ordered Theodosius captured and he grabbed his riches; he hid the prisoner in southern Anatolia and transferred his loot to the capital. But his ugly display of manly loyalty and Christian observance was ill-considered, for through Theodosius he struck at Antonina, Theodora's untouchable assistant. He struck at the very heart of the empire.

Antonina and Theodosius's erotic escapades had already cost the lives of slaves and chamber servants. According to the *Secret History*, Antonina had their tongues cut out in order to guarantee their silence. Later, so the story goes, they were hacked to pieces, thrown into sacks, and tossed into the sea. Even assuming that our source was exaggerating, there is indisputable evidence that even a high-ranking officer had been put to death for having spoken out unwisely against Antonina.

Belisarius's wife had Theodora on her side, and since the Augusta owed her for having helped dispose of John the Cappadocian, Antonina could ask the throne for help against her husband and son. Theodora did help: the two women gave each other "unholy gifts."[27] The result was that many functionaries and army officers—the very backbone of the empire—were stripped of their rank simply for being friends of Belisarius and Photius. Some were exiled, others confined to the palace dungeons. Bound to a rack with ropes around their necks, they eventually died. Despite his position as consul, Photius was captured and held captive in the innermost recesses of Theodora's legendary quarters. Repeated floggings on his back and shoulders did not persuade him to reveal the hiding place of his mother's lover.

Finally, it all came to an end. With the help of a eunuch who had been the go-between for Antonina and Theodosius,[28] Theodora's agents were able to locate Theodosius. The *Secret History* describes how Antonina, who had come back to Constantinople with her husband, was called before the empress for a surprise reunion:

> [Theodora] summoned Theodosius to Byzantium, and upon his arrival, straightway concealed him in the palace; and the next day, calling Antonina to her, she said, "Oh dearest Patrician, yesterday a pearl fell into my hands, such as no man ever saw. If you wish, I should not begrudge you the sight of this, nay, I shall show it to you." And she, not comprehending what was going on, begged

her earnestly to show her the pearl. And she brought Theodosius out of the room of one of the eunuchs and showed him to her. And Antonina was so overjoyed that she at first remained speechless with pleasure, and then she acknowledged that Theodora had done her a great favor, calling her Savior and Benefactor and Mistress in very truth.[29]

Antonina clearly gave special emphasis to the term *despoina* (lady, mistress), which had come into use at the palace with Theodora of all people—an ex-actress. And the empress seemed to feel real affection for her, calling her "dearest Patrician" (whether or not the attitude was prompted by self-interest).

Great prospects were opening up for Theodosius, Antonina's lover and godson. People spoke of him as a future Roman general. Meanwhile, a true military man, Photius, was languishing in a dungeon. And Belisarius? The conqueror of the Western kingdom had already made his peace with Antonina. His concerns were ultimately overcome by his fear of the empress and his wish to live an untroubled life: his present position was good and he had the prospect of untold future riches. It was the winter of 541–42.

Photius tried to escape from his isolation several times, but Theodora's hardened soul doomed him. Once he fled to Constantinople's Blachernae temple dedicated to the Virgin Mary, and another time to the basilica of the Holy Wisdom. In both instances he was denied sanctuary: "the priests of the Christians, smitten with terror, stood aside and conceded everything" to the empress.[30] Only in 544–45, fortified by a "true dream," was he able to reach Jerusalem. The general became a monk, leaving behind the secular world and Theodora's vengefulness. This genuine general turned into a monk, and at the same time an aspiring general disappeared: Theodosius fell ill and died—it was "a sort of justice."[31]

While all this was going on, enemies had not been attacked. Resources had been lost, for the love of a woman. Private matters took priority over public emergencies. Ten years after the great wave of expansionism that had followed the Nika victory, the very structure of the empire seemed confused, devalued, obsolete. In early 542, Emperor Justinian was sixty years old, Antonina at least fifty, and the empress Theodora and Belisarius were a little over forty. No new leaders were emerging, and ancient institutions were fading away, including the thousand-year-old office of consul. The last man named consul was Flavius Anicius Faustus Albinus Basilius in 541; after him, the title became merely ceremonial.

In Italy there were homegrown uprisings; in the fall of 541, the stubborn Gothic resistance got a new leader. He was thirty-year-old Baduila, known as Totila, "the Immortal One," and he was to continue the war against the Romans of Constantinople. Hostilities against the great king of Persia, Khosrow (nicknamed "the Immortal Soul"), were to resume in the spring.

The Christmas festivities of 541 were celebrated by the Dyophysite patriarch Menas; meanwhile Pope Vigilius in Rome gave no signals that confirmed that Theodora had been right in insisting that he be pope. In fact, the empress had written to Pope Vigilius pressing him to make good on his promises and bring back Patriarch Anthimus, whom everyone believed was lost or had disappeared. Vigilius had replied to the Augusta: "Never. Anthimus is a heretic and an anathema. No matter how great my unworthiness, I am still successor to Agapetus and Silverius."[32]

Theodora had been deceived. She had placed a man on the papal throne in faraway Rome who turned out to be a true Dyophysite after all; and in her own city she had failed to defend Anthimus, who was a very moderate Monophysite. The time for action seemed to have turned into a time for waiting. It was unbearable for her to consider the mistakes she might have made or wrongs that had been done to her. Only venting her anger could lift Theodora from her deep feelings of discontent. And then even that changed.

FIFTEEN

"Solomon,
I Have Conquered You!"

Constantinople, Near East, Ravenna, 532–42

I N ANOTHER AGE, there would be an empire, the Holy Roman
Empire of Charles V, on which the sun never set; a thousand years
earlier, there was an emperor who never shut his eyes. He personally worshipped wisdom (*sophia* in Greek), which he prized because,
among other things, it was an attribute of his model sovereign (King
Solomon of the Bible). But his propaganda machine preferred to
emphasize his insomnia. That emperor, of course, was our Justinian.

Emperor Justinian's political vision was not always perfectly sharp:
he fell under the spell of the myth of Rome, for example, unlike
Theodora, the "most intelligent of all and of all times," in the words of
her contemporary John the Lydian.[1] But it wasn't in Justinian's nature
to retreat from anything. Justinian surveyed the big picture and also
focused on each of the goals he had set for himself, goals that satisfied
both the dignity of his imperial persona and the ambition of his individual ego.

Gazing ahead at his vision of the restoration, or just staring into
the dark during one of his late-night work sessions, Justinian was, paradoxically, almost like a groping blind man. He might really have
seemed blind to the people who died in his wars or were captured in
his many arrest dragnets; such things might have caused another king
(Witigis, for example) to literally review his plans. But his obdurate
blindness allowed him to press on. In the end, it meant continuity,
whatever the human or financial costs, across the whole Ecumene.

+ + +

The war being fought along the Persian border was not the only problem in the East. During a rebellion in Armenia in 538, Sittas, Comito's husband and Theodora's brother-in-law, had died, and the empire lost an excellent general. Meanwhile in Italy, as earlier in Africa, the management of the conquered territories was turning out to be a daunting challenge: it was a heavy price to pay for the prestige of victory. Some advisors suggested that the Italian peninsula, weakened by years of war, should not be expected to produce much tax revenue. But the emperor unleashed his ruthlessly efficient functionaries, who were able to extract money even from the generals on the battlefield by monitoring the use of their budgeted funds and requesting an account of expenditures to discover any possible waste.

Belisarius had earned such great prestige with his victories and he hadn't even been arrogant enough to usurp power when he conquered Ravenna; but the palace feared that other officers might do so. To avoid similar concentrations of power, the palace prudently installed multiple generals in Italy, each reporting separately to the emperor. Justinian and his councilors would lead the military operations from the palace in Constantinople, which was two seas (the Adriatic and the Aegean) away and several weeks distant from real-time events. It was a cumbersome solution, not a wise one. Meanwhile, Baduila, also called Totila, was starting to react: the new Gothic king was a valiant military leader and a true politician, and his influence was seeping down the peninsula.

Theodoric had envisioned an Italy with a peaceful multi-ethnic population, and Justinian nostalgically tried to create a restoration, but Totila thought primarily in social terms: historians have even called him "revolutionary." He worked to win the support, approval, and loyalty of the local population. Instead of working through the Church or the great landowners represented in the Senate, he instituted economic measures to protect the social strata most vulnerable to the emperor's restoration plan and to his tax collectors (small landowners and farmers, and the freed slaves who were prospective recruits for the Gothic army).

Soon, Belisarius's brilliant Italian victories were nothing but a memory, and the "Romans" of Constantinople began to seem like for-eigners, while the Goths unexpectedly seemed "Italic." Territories slip-ping into the hands of the Goths meant less tax revenue for the empire, and revenue suddenly seemed more important than winning the consensus of the population. Even though consensus in Italy was the reason Justinian had sacrificed a definitive rapprochement with the Eastern Monophysites in the spring of 536.

Justinian wasn't losing sleep only because of news about the valiant Totila or the sardonic Khosrow. If he was wandering the halls of the palace like a blind ghost or a robot, it was partly because of unex-pected news that delayed the plan for security and unity based on squeezing North Africa and Italy militarily and fiscally. The news came from the north, from the area near the Danube, where the emperors had traditionally set the nomadic tribes of the Asiatic plains and the steppes against one another, buying their loyalty and nonbelligerence with gold. But even this custom was about to end.

In 540, the Huns had broken through the empire's defenses with an invasion into Macedonia, Thrace, and Greece. Then the Bulgars, a nomadic tribe of Turkish stock, had crossed the Danube and invaded the Balkans, setting fires and devastating the region. They had taken tens of thousands of prisoners, all subjects of the empire. They had even hit Tauresium, the emperor's birthplace.

The social fabric around Constantinople was disintegrating. With so many men dead or deported, the survivors had to be taxed more heavily, in part to guarantee their military defense. After years of build-ing excellent fortifications along the distant eastern and African fron-tiers, suddenly the very outskirts of the capital needed protection. With diligence and application, Justinian proposed new building works, called for his engineers and studied the waterways, the contour lines, the lay of the land, and the construction materials needed. He was preparing what would become future archaeological ruins.

At the start of the 540s it must have looked like the restoration would never be completed, given the resources that were available. Constantinople had issued a clear, inflexible message in solemn proclamations of principle formulated in both Latin and Greek by the imperial chancery, and the message was emphasized by the swords and arrows of its armies. But it got an equally clear and inflexible reply, both military and political. For the Goths were a proud people, the Moors of Africa were ungovernable, and the popes were lofty. The Persians sought conflict, the Armenians had rebellion in their blood, and the nomad tribes in North Africa were volatile. So the emperor's actions got equal but opposite reactions. Only the Vandals of Africa had truly succumbed to his might. (When some criticized the Vandals for their "effeminacy,"[2] it seemed less a justification of their defeat than an attempt to belittle the emperor's victory.)

At that point, Justinian must have reflected on the many emperors who had preceded him and had revealed so little of themselves, starting with his uncle, the illiterate Justin, who was almost reticent before his people in the Hippodrome. Justinian must have intuited that all his proclamations made people perceive him as a "disturbance" or an element of "confusion." He must have asked himself whether his uncle Justin had better grasped the essential secret of imperial power. His reign was pervaded with incoherence, especially regarding the Monophysite issue. The law said that the Monophysites were heretics banished from the capital and from most other cities, but in fact they were protected by the empress Theodora: they had their headquarters in the palace of Hormisdas and they worshipped in the nearby church of Saints Sergius and Bacchus. So they lived in the very heart of the Sacred Palace.

A cursory look at the empire and the Ecumene would have shown that the principle of unity to which Justinian clung as tightly as a suppliant clutches an altar for sanctuary was being denied or thwarted everywhere. And yet the emperor did not change his beliefs. Divinity lay in the One. He even wrote about it in solemn words: "Nothing pleases merciful God more than the unanimity of belief on the part of all Christians on the matter of the true, immaculate faith."[3] The communion of the Church was a communion in *one* Church. There was no space for anyone else.

Justinian had a softer side. Some sources say that he was "gentle."[4]

He felt affection for the unknown masses, in their unknown regions, who contributed to the treasury, supporting the empire's various initiatives. Theodora, who had fewer illusions, must have repeated a verse from the *Psalms* to him: "Do not place your faith in the children of men, for in them there is no salvation."[5] For Theodora, only power counted. The citizens would have to pay in any case—if not to them, then to others, and not out of respect or admiration, but out of fear, custom, or indolence. Only action would prove that their dominion was more than nominal.

Or the building of public works. Everything is impermanent, but at least monuments would survive. Human beings were unwilling to be molded by the enlightened emperor and empress. But the pale Proconnese marble, the rosy marble from Istria, the porphyry columns, ivory, silver, mosaic tiles—all the materials used by the latest generation of artists and craftsmen who had inherited the classical tradition of workmanship (*technê*)—were like putty in their hands. The monograms, the inscriptions bearing the signature of the Augusti, and the descriptions celebrating their excellence were carved into mute stone, offering silent satisfaction. The Augusti would leave this mark for future generations.

Like a meridian, Easter Day, 542, marked fifteen years of Justinian and Theodora's reign. They must have reviewed a list of their accomplishments and of the other initiatives still in the planning stage or already under construction, from the most remote borders of the empire to the heart of Constantinople. After the destruction wrought by the Nika rebellion, they had completely rebuilt Constantinople in just ten years, transforming it from a city of late antiquity into an imperial capital. A jewel of the Byzantine age, it was to be admired by medieval visitors from both West and East (the Slavs called it Tsargrad), raided by invaders in the second millennium (the Crusaders first, then the Ottoman Turks), and celebrated by poets such as W. B. Yeats. All of this made Constantinople a universal city of the soul. None of this would have transpired without Theodora's unforgettable speech on that bloody Sunday in 532, in the midst of the raging rebellion.

27. Basilike Cistern, c. 530–40, Istanbul.

The emperors' architectural and urban planning policy did not aim
to revive the art of previous centuries. Constantine's and Theodosius's
achievements inspired Justinian's politics, but their art and architecture
did not inspire his. The Augusti leaned toward the new and the
grandiose, fusing classical elements with oriental seduction, three-
dimensional naturalism with geometric abstraction, urban tradition
with Christian touches; they even indulged in personal whims. They rediscovered the daring, insouciant, lighthearted quality that had blessed
their early years together, the boldness of those intricate laws that
seemed to be written for everyone but were really conceived only for

the two of them. They were inimitable. There were no other comparable patrons of art and architecture until the Renaissance.

After the Nika—which was a political phenomenon that impacted the urban fabric—Justinian and Theodora focused on secular architecture, starting with a redefinition of the facade of power: the facade of the palace. They totally redesigned the vestibule, the Chalkê or "bronze house" (a little building with a golden bronze roof). From the palace, the Chalkê opened onto the imperial square (the Augustaeum), with access to the basilica of the Holy Wisdom—the celebrated Hagia Sophia. The Chalkê was the visual threshold of power, its projection upon the city. After the fires of the rebellion, Justinian and Theodora set out to make the new incarnation of the Chalkê more splendid and precious. So the interior of the new dome was decorated with mosaics celebrating Belisarius's victories over the Vandals and the Goths. Nearby were the baths of Zeuxippus and the Senate palace; they were also destroyed in the flames of 532. Now they were rebuilt "in more beautiful form" than before.[6]

But the emperor and empress did not stop here. They had inherited a complex metropolis with an urban administration and police force of more than a thousand men. This required premises for the supply and management of food staples and the channeling of water through aqueducts that still astonish us fifteen hundred years later. Like the ancient provincial benefactors of the earliest pagan tradition (the "Euergeti"), the two emperors undertook other initiatives "for the welfare of their subjects." Some, like the hospitals and almshouses, were Christian institutions; but the porticoed streets, roads, and cisterns were secular public works that stand to this day as masterpieces of ancient architecture (the Basilike Cistern [fig. 27] is one shining example). The rulers who commissioned them, and the skilled engineers and architects, both knew how to "enhance the monumental significance even of those buildings that had a purely functional purpose."[7] Edward Gibbon was wrong to disparage this period: it was not a time dominated simply "by the darkest shadows of shame."[8]

The Augusti didn't leave only their imprint on the city; they left actual portraits, too. Theodora's features could be seen and admired in the Chalkê mosaics, in a mosaic in the Holy Wisdom, in a statue near the baths of Zeuxippus, and in the enchanting red porphyry statue of "superior beauty" dedicated to her near the Arcadian baths.[9] Justinian's great ego required works on a monumental scale. A statue of him, called "gigantic . . . a very noteworthy sight," dominated the Augustaeum square [fig. 28] but was unfortunately lost centuries ago.[10] This equestrian statue of the emperor stood atop a bronze column and represented him in "heroic" fashion "like Achilles"; contemporary praise said that the statue glittered like Sirius, "the evening star."

28. Drawing of the lost equestrian statue of Justinian from Constantinople's Augustaeum square, 15th century, Ms. Ital. 3, University Library, Budapest.

The statue looked eastward: perhaps the horse was galloping toward the Persians. In his left hand, the emperor held a globe, "by which the sculptor signified that the whole earth and sea were subject to him," and the globe carried a cross because with the cross Justinian, like a new Constantine, "had obtained both his empire and his victory in war." His open right hand pointed eastward, perhaps "to command the barbarians from that quarter to remain at home and to advance no further," or to greet the daily miracle of the sunrise, so that the emperor of the sleepless nights could evoke the ancient worship of the sun (even Jesus Christ had been called "the Sun of Justice").[11]

29. The "Barberini ivory," first half of the 6th century, Louvre, Paris.

The lost statue of the emperor in the Augustaeum begs to be compared to other ancient monuments that have survived, such as the
famous "Barberini ivory" showing the emperor on horseback [fig. 29]
and the porphyry group sculpture from the end of the third century
A.D., known as the "Tetrarchs," which adorns a corner of Saint Mark's
basilica in Venice [fig. 30]. In that sculpture, power was signified by
the Caesars and Augusti of East and West embracing and exchanging

the kiss of peace, their hands on each other's shoulders. They are linked by their shared rank and by simple physical contact—but each has one hand poised on the basic sign of power, the sword, ready to be drawn from its gem-studded sheath. Other surviving examples—the fourth- and fifth-century imperial torsos in the Berlin Museum and in Ravenna [figs. 31, 32]—also show a hand on the pommel of a sword; but Justinian's equestrian statue represented him under one shield only, that of the cross: *Romanus, ergo Christianus* (Roman, therefore Christian).

30. The "Tetrarchs," porphyry group sculpture, end of the 3rd century, basilica of Saint Mark, Venice.

Just as the empire was ideally based on an autocratic form of Christianity, religion became the structuring element of the city. The visitor who approached it by land or by sea saw a skyline dominated by a daring edifice [fig. 33], the dome of the basilica dedicated to God's Holy Wisdom. It was the crowning achievement of a frenzied period of building

31. LEFT: Porphyry statue, emperor's torso, Alexandria, 4th century. Staatliche Museen, Berlin.

32. RIGHT:Porphyry statue, emperor's torso, Alexandria, 5th century. Museo Arcivescovile, Ravenna.

religious edifices: in the capital alone, about thirty churches were constructed, some brand-new and some restored after the Nika revolt.

Justinian and Theodora had at least one precedent with which to compare themselves, since the ancient artistic tradition was marked by competitive emulation. That precedent was the church of Saint Polyeuktos, commissioned by Lady Juliana Anicia (mentioned above) and built in 524–27 during the last years of Justin's life. When Justin's nephew Justinian took the throne, he asked the wealthy lady to contribute generously to the imperial coffers. In reply, she pointed to the richly decorated church, with its "colored marbles, columns inlaid with glass and amethysts, and floor and wall mosaics,"[12] and with aristocratic and womanly disdain, she said: "Here is my wealth." Still, not wanting the emperor to leave empty-handed, she pulled one of her rings from her finger and offered it to him.[13]

The new Augusti replied to her biting provocation by building churches for Saint Euphemia and Saint Irene, and then the church of

33. ABOVE:Exterior of the basilica of the Holy Wisdom (Hagia Sophia), 532–37 (with later additions), Istanbul.

34. RIGHT: Marble impost capital with Justinian's monogram, 532–37(?), basilica of the Holy Wisdom (Hagia Sophia), Istanbul.

Saints Sergius and Bacchus, next to the palace of Hormisdas (which became a Monophysite center under Theodora's protection [fig. 25]). Known as the "Little Holy Wisdom" for its structural similarity to the great basilica, it has an enchanting central-plan structure. Inside, marble columns streaked with green and pink are surmounted by impost capitals. These inverted cone shapes [fig. 34] bear the structural weight of the vaults: they are the most functional and rational, and yet the most abstract of all capitals—and they are also triumphantly decorative. Constantinople's craftsmen carved these openwork capitals with an infinite number of volutes, and today they still pull the visitor into an embroidered marble labyrinth of effects, preparing him for the imperial propaganda enunciated in the frieze and then in the great dome above.

Theodora pushed most for the reconstruction, along the northern branch of the Mesê (Constantinople's central avenue), of the basilica of the Holy Apostles. In ancient times the basilica had been used as a tomb-mausoleum of the emperors and their consorts, and this function was preserved, in an extraordinary instance of both the loss and the conservation of artistic heritage.

A new building replaced the former basilica, which dated back to the age of Constantine and was set on fire by the Nika rebels; the new buiding was very popular in the Byzantine age, and was celebrated by intellectuals and poets. (When the Turks later conquered Constantinople, a mosque was erected on the site, but that too suffered the ravages of time.) Few traces survive of the basilica archetype so dear to Theodora: the basilica of Saint Mark's in Venice is one; another is the collection of ruins of the basilica of Saint John in Ephesus (near present-day Kusadasi, Turkey). They stand as enduring evidence of the timeless prestige of the Holy Apostles church, and they permit us to reconstruct it in our mind's eye.

One architectural element made the church of the Holy Apostles famous: the daring cruciform plan, with each arm covered by a dome. The central cupola was located at the point where the arms joined. This "five-dome" structure also became very popular in Slavic Christendom, which owes so much to Constantinople. Under the great dome—almost like the lofty bed canopy of an alcove for eternal sleep—Theodora and Justinian hoped to rest together in their imperial sarcophagi [Fig. 35] until the end of time.

The Augusti intended the church of the Holy Apostles to be their final resting place; they poured their deepest feelings into the church of Saints Sergius and Bacchus; but their pride and joy—especially the emperor's—was the Holy Wisdom. Fifteen hundred years after it was built, after acting as a mosque and then a museum, it is still among the most famous and admired buildings in the world—though, paradoxically, it is famous for what it was *not* meant to be: an architectural space, a temple of light, the final wonder of Christian antiquity.

Medieval visitors might have come closest to the spirit of the place, since they recognized Constantinople as the Mother of all Cities. Admiring the Holy Wisdom, they found renewed faith in Paradise; they were surrounded by objects, colors, visions, and scents (lost to us now) that they perceived as promises and prefigurations. If the city rebuilt by the emperor and the empress in the light of Christianity was a sacred shell, then the Holy Wisdom was its pearl. It was the most visible, most flaunted treasure of Justinian and Theodora.

35. Justinian's sarcophagus, 565, Topkapi Saray, Istanbul.

The two rulers used the Holy Wisdom to express their power fully. They were not building but *re*building a city that had risen against them. They wanted the result to be a total redemption, a gesture of great daring that would fully display their personal and institutional arrogance. Perhaps because of this, there is no great church less mystical than the Holy Wisdom. It was not meant to be the church of a monastic order or a district or a guild, nor was it built by an individual suppliant. It was the basilica where the emperor of Constantinople, the thirteenth apostle, the Viceroy of Christ on Earth, the highest, noblest man of all, attended sacred ceremonies. In the symmetrical, inverted projection of roles between imperial Constantinople and papal Rome, the only worthy comparison is the basilica of Saint Peter's at the time of the universalist popes of the Renaissance.[14]

If the insult of the Nika riots had marked a moment in time, then the imperial basilica would erase time. The unquestionably victorious, triumphant emperor demanded a shape that was tranquil and perfect, a shape as close as possible to a sphere (the image of the eternal). This extraordinary request was born of a "genuine oneiric revelation,"[15] and the engineers responded with extraordinary skill. The engineers were Anthemius of Tralles and Isidore of Miletus; mathematicians proud of their name and their caste, they had inherited a great eastern Mediterranean tradition and belonged to the select cultural and scientific circles of the time.

In their discussions with the Augusti who commissioned the building, the rectilinear plan of the basilica that had burned in the 532 fire was replaced with a central-plan structure. In early Christendom, the *martyria*—places of worship erected atop the tombs of saints or martyrs—followed a central plan, as did the more recent church of Saints Sergius and Bacchus. The engineers extended the dimensions of that small masterpiece for the new Holy Wisdom, so that Christianity and power were expressed monumentally. The basilica would represent an expanding empire protected by the Almighty.

For years, Justinian must have stepped out of his offices in the palace with only one purpose in mind: to visit the basilica under construction. It was being built for the emperor's eye: this was the eye that was invited to appreciate its structure, the eye that could trace the marble embroidery or the curving waves of the capitals, and then fly freely across the immense dome that appeared "suspended from Heaven"[16] by a golden chain and even "under the direct custody of angels";[17] the eye that was suddenly bathed in light, as if the light "did not come from the outside, but was produced inside."[18]

But what he saw then, as he inspected the works with his retinue, was not what we see today. The central cupola was twenty-one feet lower than it is now, making the effect of the ceiling curvature even bolder. The nave was punctuated with windows that were later walled up; the now-empty aisles were filled with rich liturgical furnishings that shone "with gold and silver."[19] The Augustus could observe crafts-men working on gilded mosaics. For the most part, these mosaics (now lost) were "entirely non-figural and imitated the effect of shim-mering silks enlivened by abstract patterns."[20] The lack of iconic repre-sentation has been linked to the anti-figurative tendencies that were latent in the eastern Mediterranean (including in Monophysitism) and that were to flourish in the Byzantine iconoclastic movement. The in-scription on the altar, however, leaves no doubt as to Justinian and Theodora's belief in *one* faith and *one* Church:

> WE, YOUR SERVANTS JUSTINIAN AND THEODORA, OFFER TO YOU, OH CHRIST, WHAT IS YOURS FROM WHAT IS YOURS. MAY YOU ACCEPT IT BENEVOLENTLY, OH SON AND WORD OF GOD WHO BECAME INCARNATED AND WERE CRUCIFIED FOR US. KEEP US IN YOUR TRUE FAITH, AND INCREASE AND PROTECT THIS EMPIRE THAT YOU HAVE ENTRUSTED TO US FOR YOUR GLORY, WITH THE INTERCESSION OF THE HOLY MOTHER OF GOD, THE EVER-VIRGIN MARY.[21]

A visitor at the Holy Wisdom nowadays can try to see the building as the emperor did. Just as the emperor solemnly proceeded down the nave and took his place on the imperial throne, the visitor can walk the nave and scan the succession of spaces, trying to imagine the lost color scheme from the emperor's point of view [fig. 36].

How does this building show humility, affliction, contrition? Every-thing in the Holy Wisdom bespeaks majesty. Earthly and divine majesty both; the court was conceived as a model of Paradise, and the basilica had all the more reason to mirror the heavenly kingdom. At the same time, everything in the Holy Wisdom was a gift, both to the emperor and from the emperor. Not so much to his people as to the Divinity from whom he derived his power, and who in turn affirmed and con-tinued His own power through the emperor's. For this reason, Justinian acquired the most precious materials to celebrate the Godhead, bring-ing them from the Mediterranean nearby and from the remote Atlantic

36. Interior of the basilica of the Holy Wisdom (Hagia Sophia), 532–37
(with later additions), Istanbul.

coasts of Gallia. The amount of money that went into the construction
of the church might have sufficed to support two million families for a
whole year (for example, the entire Aramaic-speaking population of
the Near East).

The legends about the construction of the basilica tell of hidden
treasures, messenger angels, and arks overflowing with gold dropping

from Heaven. This was considered an extraordinary building. Still, while only a heavenly vision or supernatural help could justify such a daring feat of architecture, the necessary economic and financial support was provided by the rigorous fiscal policy of John the Cappadocian.

The minarets and other extraneous structures that were added later to the building's exterior, and the changes to the interior decoration, distort the viewer's perception of the structure as originally intended by the architects, as approved by Justinian and Theodora, and as it was subsequently built. The point of departure of the edifice is a great square almost one hundred feet per side. At each corner an enormous pier rises [fig. 37]. About sixty-eight feet up, four connecting arches

37. Plan of the basilica of the Holy Wisdom (Hagia Sophia).

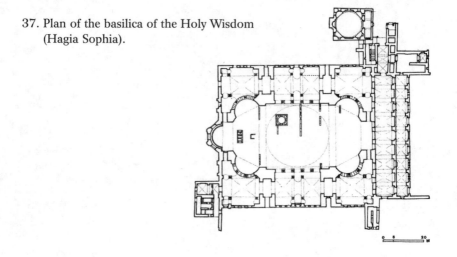

38. Longitudinal section of the basilica of the Holy Wisdom (Hagia Sophia).

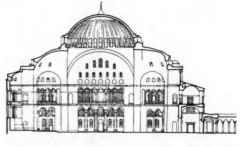

branch off from the piers: two of these are absorbed into the walls, while the other two stretch up into semicircles in the central space. The arches are connected by four pendentives. From the top of the arches and the top of the connecting pendentives (more than 130 feet up) an extraordinary, surprisingly light dome rises up, a giant shell one hundred feet in diameter. Other half-domes and small shells cover the structural spaces [fig. 38].

39. Marble impost capital with Theodora's monogram, c. 540–50(?), basilica of Saint John, Ephesus.

The central section and its appendages are enclosed by a large, nearly square wall (232 by 253 feet) with connecting aisles, a loggia story (with the throne for the empress), and a narthex. The supporting walls and the surrounding volumes create an interplay of gigantic spaces, so the whole structure feels suspended: the building seems not to sit on the earth but to be poised lightly on it.

From his vantage point on the throne, Justinian's eye could roam across impossibly wide spaces, or trace convoluted designs where each form receded into another and each shell recalled another, with the candlelight flickering across the golden mosaics on the walls and the

40, 41. Graphic renderings of Justinian's (left) and Theodora's monograms.

dome, the silver highlights of the furnishings, and the greenish cast of the floor marbles. That enormous space pulsed with its own visual rhythm. It was the powerful sequence of the impost capitals, their embroideries and flower clusters deeply carved into the marble in a continuous wave. The center of each capital bore the imprint of the imperial presence and the imperial will—the carved monograms of the Augusti: Justinian's intricate one [figs. 34, 40] and Theodora's more graphic and linear one [figs. 39, 41].

Justinian's persona was two-sided: his specific, individual identity was complemented by an imperial identity, and the unbreakable bond between the two was clear for all to see when the basilica was officially consecrated.

The Holy Wisdom is the temple of that divine wisdom that several passages of the Bible link to the law of God and to awe of Him. More specifically, the book of the Bible dedicated to wisdom—like the *Song of Songs* and *Ecclesiastes*, mentioned earlier—was thought to have been written by Solomon, the Israelite king who had always been Justinian's model and archetype. Whenever he legislated, the emperor followed the wise king's legendary standards of justice; in the Holy Wisdom he was comparing himself to Solomon the great builder of the Temple of Jerusalem, which had won him so much admiration and fame.

In December 537, a little less than six years after the Nika insurrection, Justinian entered the completed church for its consecration. When he alighted from his imperial coach, he was received by the patriarch, and led a procession into the spectacular basilica; he gave thanks to God and immediately added: "Solomon, I have defeated you!" (*enikêsa se*).[22] The ruler of the Romans, leader of the "new Christian Israel," believed that he had surpassed his ancient model; this was no rhetorical cliché: he considered his succession both real and ideal, a succession that would secure a place in sacred history for The Emperor Justinian.

There is also a hint of the individual, private voice of Flavius Petrus Sabbatius, the man behind the emperor Justinian, who had a

42. Mosaic depicting Constantine offering the city of Constantinople to the Mother of God, and Justinian offering the basilica of the Holy Wisdom, 10th century, basilica of the Holy Wisdom (Hagia Sophia), Istanbul.

competitive, smaller soul. His *enikêsa* ("I won") uses the same root as *nika*, the term that gave voice to the insurrection that had destroyed the earlier basilica in 532. (In that year the rebels had translated the Latin *tu vincas*—may you win!—and used it against him; now he used the profane shout against Solomon.) Justinian lacked the open mind that would have allowed him to comprehend historical cycles broader than his individual fate, or to see "another self"[23] in a defeated person. Indeed, he had been deaf to the (equally Solomonic) refrain "Vanity of vanities, all is vanity," that Belisarius's prisoner Gelimer had repeated (for himself and for the emperor) during the scene of triumph and prostration in the Hippodrome.

The theme of victory and defeat, of continuity and metamorphosis, is inextricable from the construction of the basilica and its history. The basilica was always marked by insecurity: it was damaged by several earthquakes, and each time it was repaired and reconsecrated. More to the point, it is marked by perseverance, not only because the outer structure has survived through the centuries, but because, like the Coliseum or Saint Peter's in Rome, oral tradition and prophecies have identified the survival of the edifice with the duration of history itself: its end will also mark the end of all time.

So the basilica of Justinian became a myth—the myth of Constantinople, the last great ancient city as well as the first major city of the Christian Middle Ages. The architectural miracle of the Holy Wisdom made it unique in each of several diverse cultural traditions: Western and "Latin," Slavic, Scandinavian, Arab, Turkish. Those of the Byzantine Middle Ages were especially cognizant of this, as we can see from a celebrated mosaic in the basilica that showed two emperors offering gifts to the Mother of God: Constantine, the city's founder, offers the city itself, and Justinian offers the Holy Wisdom, the symbolic heart of the city [fig. 42].

Almost one thousand years—an eon—later, in 1453, the city was stormed by the Ottoman Turks of Mohammed II Fatih. It was not the end of all time, but it was the end of a world: the world of the Christian basilica, of the idea of the city that it mirrored and crowned. The conqueror, Mohammed II, entered the temple of the defeated people, the temple that he would later turn into a mosque. He looked, he admired, but he did not speak; he was filled with a spirit of regret rather than triumph. Later, he recited the following Persian verses:

> The spider is a watchman in the palace of Khosrow.
> The owl plays its watch music in the fort of Afrâsijâb.[24]

In his victory, he also saw defeat; in his dominance, he saw the enemy's end. Not like Flavius Petrus Sabbatius Justinianus, but like Publius Cornelius Scipio Emilianus, who wept on seeing the enemy city of Carthage in flames, because it prefigured the destruction of his own Rome.

For the emperor and empress who *refounded* them, Constantinople and the Holy Wisdom, no matter how precious or ostentatious, were still part of a greater plan wherein a unitary, shared Christian faith was expressed in ideas and laws, *and* in urban planning. It was important to affirm and maintain their program, their dream, in cities ravaged by the wrath of God or the fury of enemies or of the elements. In Antioch, the third-largest city of the Ecumene, the Augusti sponsored intense reconstruction after the earthquakes of 526 and 528 and the sack by the Persians in 540. The town plan was revised, and although the traditional colonnaded streets, porticoes, and squares were kept, the famous main boulevard was now studded with churches. Right outside the city rose the monastery of Saint Simeon Stylite the Younger: it was no faraway anchorite retreat, but a visible call to virtue for the city's residents.

In another eastern metropolis, Jerusalem, a church dedicated to the Virgin called the New Church (or "Nea") was famously huge: it was 300 feet long and 156 feet wide. The town plan was reworked around a central artery sixty-six feet wide, flanked by porticoes and colonnades as a sort of monumental stage set for the new city center characterized by a network of Christian elements. Something similar was done in Apamea (now the village of Qal'at al Mudīk) which was capital of the province of Syria Secunda. The great central artery and its columns were restored, and wide sidewalks were built along the porticoes. It was an ideal setting for city life in late antiquity, a sort of perpetual agora filled with churches instead of forums and theaters.

All this rebuilding followed a standard town plan that called for a number of structures to be adapted and modulated in accordance with local preferences. First there had to be fortified walls, then an adequate supply of food staples and water. The urban centers were concentrated around the headquarters of the authorities, which were sometimes both civilian and religious (for example, when the bishoprics were also involved in city administration). The old baths survived and sometimes new ones were built, as were hippodromes, but the theaters and amphitheaters were becoming extinct. All this was happening at a time when new social opportunities were being created for "repentant" actresses. Justinian and Theodora had freed them not only from their sins but also from their vocations and their jobs. The only necessary "show" took place in the city's churches, and it dealt with eternal salvation.

As in any absolute autocracy, ideal cities were built; one such

43. View of the 5th/6th-century fortifications of the city of Zenobia on the Euphrates.

example was Justiniana Prima—now Caricin Grad, the "imperial city" near Justinian's native birthplace of Tauresium in the district of Naissus (now Nis, Serbia). Originally planned to replace the ancient Sirmium (now Sremska Mitrovica, Serbia) as an Illyrian military and administrative stronghold, Justiniana Prima was established to celebrate the emperor, as were the archaic cities of Asia. A profusion of churches rose amid monumental structures, and a great statue of the local hero, Justinian, blessed and protected the city. (This ambitious place can be compared to the quintessential ideal city of the Italian Renaissance, Pienza, founded by Pope Pius II in Tuscany in 1462. Paradoxically, tiny Pienza has survived intact for five centuries, while Justiniana Prima declined after just a few decades, suffering from epidemics, drought, earthquakes, and, worst of all, Slavic invasions from the Danube. It was part of a progressive decline in urban life in the realm that had once been the "empire of the thousand cities.")

The masterpieces of military fortifications and structures in the East—Dara at the Persian border; Zenobia along the Euphrates [fig. 43]; the former caravan capital, Palmyra; and Resafa-Sergiopolis, a strategic crossroads in north-central Syria—combined defensive and religious functions, welcoming pilgrims who worshipped thaumaturgic cults. Resafa-Sergiopolis was dedicated to Sergius, the martyr-soldier and the favorite saint of the Syrians. Empress Theodora honored its beloved church by donating a splendid cross of precious stones.

In Italy, Ravenna was the Byzantine pearl. When it was conquered for Constantinople in 540 by the cunning Belisarius, it had already been thriving for over a century. From 402, it had been the seat of the Western empire. Later it became the Ostrogothic capital: King Theodoric had changed the town plan by constructing numerous secular and religious buildings, and had reclaimed the port of Classe, beautifully portrayed in the mosaics of the church of Sant'Apollinare Nuovo [fig. 44].

44. Mosaic depicting the port of Classe, beginning of the 6th century, church of Sant'Apollinare Nuovo, Ravenna.

Justinian and Theodora never reached Ravenna; they never set foot anywhere in Italy, the place that was so pregnant with meaning for them—for the emperor in particular. But they were careful to project their power there: they left their mark on the city by restructuring it. Political and economic buildings were clustered in the port area, dominated by the church of Sant'Apollinare in Classe, and several monuments were built in the city center, along with the usual large number of churches.

The most imposing of these was the basilica of San Vitale, which had been begun under Ostrogothic rule. Financed by Julianus Argentarius, a banker, construction of the basilica was completed only under Bishop Maximianus (bishop from 546 to 556). In the extraordinary mosaics of the presbytery, the gaunt-faced bishop is the only person identified by an inscription, as if to underline his importance [fig. 2]. The figure of Justinian at his side, and that of Theodora on the opposite wall, are among the greatest visual epiphanies in the entire Mediterranean, but we should not forget that the mosaic had probably not yet been commissioned on Easter Day of 542, the fifteenth anniversary of the imperial couple's coronation. At the time, work was being done only on the bright, spacious brick and marble structure.

But another important artistic work had been completed by then. The mosaic floor of a church in North Africa, west of Cyrene, depicted the human experience as a symbolic navigation from the sea of life to the haven that is the Church, and it has always delighted art historians, partly on account of its "most daring" use of pagan elements to express Christian concepts. This mosaic is even more meaningful when we consider that it was the pride of the ancient city of Olbia, which had just been renovated and renamed for Theodora (539–40): it was another Theodorias, right near Pentapolis, the place that had posed the gravest threat to young Theodora.[25]

SIXTEEN

"God . . . Entrusted These Lands to the Demons of Violence"

Constantinople, Eastern Front, 542

C OLONNADED STREETS and monumental squares dotted with shops and churches, all safeguarded by majestic imperial statues: these were the grand urban spaces created by the imperial couple for their subjects as generous tokens of their benevolence. These cities, and the long inscriptions carved in robust characters on marble slabs, testified to their care for the "Romans" of Africa and Illyria, of Syria and Egypt, and of Italy. Of course, the subjects were always paying taxes, which went for more pomp, more buildings, and more wars of "salvation and glory." This was the well-ordered country that Justinian and Theodora, protagonists of the last great passionate love story of antiquity, dreamed up for their people.

In their vision of the empire, everything good descended from the imperial throne to the new society's basic building block—the Christian family—through the mediation of the Church. Vitality was drained out of all previous forms of association, such as the Blue and Green factions in their world of shows, theaters, and circuses that had played such a central role in the meeting of the two rulers and had strengthened their power on the throne.

The author Agathias Scholasticus produced epigrams that spoke of small kisses stolen or yearned for, but no illicit acts before or outside of marriage; his poetry reflected the imperial couple's predilection for what we might call "the family in the shadow of power."[1] Soon, no poet-functionary cited in the *Greek Anthology* would dream of new flirtations with enchanting singers and dancers, since there was no room these days for a young woman like Theodora to have a career: the laws that allowed her Christian repentance and rehabilitation had eliminated the very reasons she might have to repent.

The former actress on the throne had certainly not forgotten her femininity: her looks were apparently the topic of two poems in the *Greek Anthology* (XVI 77 and 78) by Paul the Silentiary. In one of them, Paul respectfully celebrates the "brilliance" and "glow" of a Theodorias of the "supreme head": this is probably Theodora, with her name adapted to the needs of metric verse. Now over forty years old, she was still blinding like "the sun's brilliance," and she still seduced with her "extremely pale complexion." He laments the fact that her hair was covered by a bonnet, but bonnets were a necessary ornament for the elite women of the time. What is unexpected, though, is the reference to her "golden curls." "Curls" could be a poetic term for "hair," but the "golden" color is surprising: the most scholarly Germanic encyclopedia of the time describes Theodora as a "brunette."[2] If she was indeed a blonde at that time, then she had dyed her hair or was wearing a fanciful "Western-style" wig, like the one that the Frankish ambassador Caribertus offered as a gift in the opening scenes of Sardou's *Theodora*.

Christian and imperial virtues were much celebrated, and imperial propaganda insisted on the throne's example: Justinian was "the sleepless emperor," and Theodora was "merciful" and "inexhaustible." Yet some people pointed to the earthquakes and other natural catastrophes, and the series of difficult wars against too many enemies of the empire, and suggested that the divinity that sanctioned their power, Justinian's especially, was keeping them at a distance. And worse was in store for the empire and its ruler. In those years, even the most perceptive critics stopped referring to fate generically, and instead ascribed the calamities directly to God's anger: "The Deity, detesting his [Justinian's] works, turned away from the Roman empire and gave way to the abominable demons, for the bringing of these things to pass in this fashion."[3]

Whether or not it was truly God's wrath, in 542 the abominable "things" were not huge and terrible and majestic events evoked by the visionaries or the fiery preachers who chastised the Christians for their sins. In 542, the land was not ripped by great earthquakes or drenched by great tidal waves or wild storms. The punishment that came down from Heaven was infinitely tiny: it looked like "a strange sort of carbuncle."[4] Attentive physicians and scientists found the carbuncles inside those "bubonic-like swellings"[5] seen on corpses; and the corpses began piling up in the spring of that year in the cities and the countryside. But the researchers could not identify the cause.

People died everywhere, in every season, with no distinction as to age, sex, diet, or social class. Paradoxically, the people responsible for carrying and burying the corpses were not affected by the contagion, nor were the physicians who came into close contact with the sick. But others who led healthy and secluded lives died quickly. It was left to the survivors to count the victims, to act quickly to dispose of the enormous number of corpses, and describe the phenomena—the course of the illness in an individual, or the development of the sickness from one Mediterranean region to the other, and then beyond. The disease spread all across Europe, and as late as the second half of the seventh century it plagued the British Isles.

The source of the disease was in Egypt, the birthplace of almost everything in antiquity that was destined to spread widely (beliefs in immortality and life after death came from Eygpt; so did wheat, the staple food of the Mediterranean basin.)

The disease had spread from Pelusium, an ancient Egyptian center of temples dedicated to Zeus, a town that was later the cradle of erudite Christian monks. From there, it traveled east-northeast, invading Palestine, Syria, and Anatolia. It first appeared along the coast, in ports and exchange posts, then moved inland. Finally, it reached the capital of the empire.

The sickness was heralded by premonitory dreams that were believed to be supernatural. First the victim had a vision that made him restless; then he experienced a low fever; then carbuncles as big as lentils appeared in several spots. From here the prognosis differed.

Some fell into a deep coma; others suffered delirium, insomnia, or hal-
lucinations. Some leaped from their beds screaming, trying to drink,
or to leave the house; some even threw themselves from rooftops or
from high cliffs. Some bled. It was the bubonic plague, the most severe
epidemic in centuries, and the most lethal for many centuries to come.
It was the saddest of the many records set during the time of Justinian
and Theodora.

This plague happened 1,450 years ago; one millennium before had
come the most infamous similar event, a plague that devastated
Athens during the time of Pericles, in 429 B.C. Little had been learned
in the intervening centuries. So it's no coincidence that Procopius, the
leading historical witness of this plague, based his account in his *Wars*
on that account of the Athenian plague found in Thucydides' *Pelopon-
nesian Wars*.

Modern scientific and medical discoveries give a different perspective on the phenomenon. The culprit is a lethal bacterium, *Pasteurella
pestis*, found in the stomach of the *Xenopsylla* flea (less than a mil-
limeter long), which hides in the fur of black rats. The rats with their
bacterial fleas had left their habitat (probably Ethiopia or Arabia) and
traveled by boat to Egypt. From there they had spread across the
Mediterranean and to the East; everywhere they went, sewers and large
mounds of trash left outdoors—just outside the city walls, and even
inside cities—served as an ideal medium for the lethal bacterium
to grow.

The plague reached Constantinople around Easter of 542, as the
imperial couple was assessing the accomplishments of their fifteen
years of joint power. It became pandemic, and continued to plague the
city and other places for decades. In the sixth century, Antioch was hit
four times, at regular intervals: every fifteen years. The face of historian
Evagrius Scholasticus (536–c. 600), a resident of Antioch, was disfigured by the infection when he was a child in 542, and then the plague
took his wife, children, relatives, and domestics, in the city and in
the country.[6]

The emperor and empress put a high official named Theodore in charge of the emergency. His task was to ensure a dignified burial for the corpses found in the streets and houses. He had the authority, financial resources, and personnel needed for the task, but soon he lacked space. There were often as many as five thousand victims a day; some days the dead reached ten thousand or more. Ultimately, the plague took about half of the population of the Roman Empire, which had recently been expanded by the military campaigns in Africa and Italy.

Rough estimates suggest that no less than twenty million men and women died, most of them in the cities. These high numbers, and the widespread nature of the epidemic, make it similar to the Black Death in the time of Boccaccio and Chaucer, though on a far greater scale: Paris, the largest European city in 1348, had about 200,000 inhabitants, while Constantinople and Alexandria in the mid-sixth century each had perhaps three times that number.

Ancient death rituals had required that burial sites lie outside the cities, but early Christianity, with its urban worship of martyrs, had brought some cemeteries back inside the city walls. The emergency caused by the plague fully justified a return to the ancient custom: the cemeteries of Constantinople, capital of the civilized world, were soon full anyway. Theodore began to bury the dead in the suburbs, but even that space was soon filled by the waves of corpses. Finally he saw that his workers had no time even to leave the city or dig new graves. At that point, Theodore began to use the towers that punctuated the walls of Sykae (now Galata) beyond the Golden Horn. The towers were put to use not against an external enemy but against an even more formidable, internal enemy. The roofs of the towers were removed and the corpses thrown inside. As each tower was filled, its roof was mortared back into place. The people still living in the city breathed air filled with death, "especially when the wind blew fresh from that quarter."[7]

In those terrible days, the moral climate shifted. People devoutly offered pious resolutions and words of repentance. Perhaps some were preparing for the Apocalypse, the anticipated end of the world.

Expecting to die was a distraction from evil thoughts, especially for the Greens and the Blues, who were changed by this tragedy. They began contributing to public health, helping to remove the corpses and attending to the burial rites, regardless of the faction to which the dead had belonged. Years before, in 524, when Justinian had openly displayed his preference for the Blues, the hostility between the two factions had led to a deterioration of social life: people had given up going out in the evening or wearing jewels or sumptuous, official garments. During the epidemic, social life contracted again, but the factions renewed their friendship.

It was extremely rare to find someone in the street without a corpse on his shoulders. Since there were no more burial grounds, the corpses were often dragged to the legendary shores of the Bosphorus and the Propontis. The conventional distinction between Asia and Europe was lost in the common pall of death. Mounds of corpses were loaded into small boats to be dumped randomly on less congested shores, or perhaps dropped into the deep water. It was not uncommon to see disfigured corpses tossed back on shore by the waves, as had happened ten years earlier to the corpse of a usurper to the throne. This sort of disposal helped the epidemic to spread wildly.

It was difficult to replenish supplies, especially food staples, in the city that had once been accustomed to receiving great quantities of all sorts of goods. The business of the administration and the military slowed to a crawl and ultimately stopped altogether. Even Khosrow—who was fighting Belisarius along the Persian border—and other enemies of the empire hesitated to move into lands devastated by a disease that would eventually strike even the palace of Constantinople. Great figures who had molded history for decades died in a just few short weeks: among them were Tribonian, the minister and jurist who had coordinated the writing of the Justinian *Corpus*, and Mār the Solitary, the violent champion of Monophysitism who had dared to reproach the emperor and empress—the one person who had received their apologies.

Finally, the unthinkable happened, and—even worse—the unthinkable rumor spread. Justinian contracted the disease and fell seriously ill.

The fact that this most Christian ruler had been stricken, like an ordinary mortal, truly seemed to be a sign of divine anger. People reflected on what the emperor might be guilty of, and the empire as well. It was a time of sadness, repentance, sickness, and conversion. The fiercest of Justinian's enemies noted that other rulers before him had fallen ill, regardless of whether the gods had favored them. They were referring to the most stoic and upright of all emperors, Marcus Aurelius, who died of the plague in A.D. 180. But he had died on the battlefield, fighting the "barbarians," not shut up inside the palace fiddling with the laws.

These rumors did not escape Theodora's sophisticated espionage and control system. In this time of emergency, the demands of power forced her to take on a most difficult role. She was personally anxious about her sixty-year-old husband; she beseeched the court physicians to help, and she placed her trust in prayers and vigils. But she also had to find extra energy to put into everything official. It was her duty to perform as empress, even more than as a wife, and to take the reins of command. It no longer sufficed to develop *her own* policies (aligned with Justinian's policies, or complementary or alternative to them). Now she had to take action on issues—legislative and even military—where her expertise was not as strong, and where there was a greater risk of falling into traps.

She spent hours by her husband's bedside, out of piety and pure affection. In those hours, she must have bitterly pondered that he, who had given her the gift of purple when it had seemed so impossible, looked like he was close to losing it. He had almost lost it ten years before, during the Nika riots; now history repeated itself. She had to help him as she had done then, hoping at the same time that he could help her. She prayed that he might have lucid intervals so that she could ask his advice and encourage him to survive.

She spent less time on leisure—on sleeping, perfecting her makeup, or taking baths (water was thought to transmit the contagion). And above all, she reduced her expectations. She did not abuse her position of absolute, unshared power; she took no measures that might be interpreted as rejections of Justinian's wishes, decisions, or decrees, not even about the issue closest to her heart: the fate of the Mono-physites. Theodora prayed publicly for her husband's recovery and the safety of the empire "in the communion of the One, Holy, Catholic, and Apostolic Church"—the very church of the characters she disliked: Pope Vigilius in Rome and Patriarch Menas in Constantinople. In this terrible predicament, she transcended all Monophysite and Dyophysite discord. She played the impartial, merciful ruler. She visited churches and hospices, she prayed over tombs and relics, and she listened to holy monks.

In her efforts to propitiate God and make her husband recover, she probably sought the right prayers and tried to sound out God's inten-tions by having intense, frequent meetings with Anthimus. He was the Monophysite patriarch who had been deposed during Pope Agape-tus's visit to Constantinople in 536. Everyone had lost track of him except Theodora. She had saved him by hiding him in the innermost chambers of the palace, and she had visited him regularly. (Paradoxi-cally, Anthimus was kept safe in those same recesses that had meant only hardship to so many of her real or presumed adversaries.) He had become her spiritual "precious pearl" in the years after 536, which were so difficult for Monophysitism.

Theodora must have asked the gentle, stoic Anthimus for prayers of recovery. Eleven years earlier, when she and Justinian had felt invin-cible, she had prayed for grace from Sabas, who was no less worthy of veneration because he was a Dyophysite. At the time, she had asked for a child for her and Justinian; now she was asking for help only for Justinian.

There had been disagreements between Theodora and her hus-band, yet "they never did anything without the other." The Nika rebel-lion; the relationship with the Monophysites and Dyophysites; the problems with Belisarius, Agapetus, Severus, Vigilius, and especially John the Cappadocian had sometimes set them on different sides but never pitted them against each other. If the unity that Justinian dreamed of existed anywhere in the empire, perhaps it existed in the covenant that these two had made on their wedding day in 525—they were so different but they were bound together, with each partner acting as "another self."

Theodora prayed for her husband as someone who did not deserve such suffering. She thought of him and prayed for him with Anthimus, with the other Monophysites hidden in the capital, and in the basilica of the Holy Wisdom, where she was bathed in "an otherwordly light." She even prayed during the official and operational meetings at the palace. Justinian had triumphantly thought of himself as a new Solomon, but the empress was thinking of another, more appropriate Biblical reference. For her, Justinian had become Job, the upright man who suffers the inscrutable silence or holy wisdom of God.

As Theodora suffered, she did not neglect the continuity and the image of the power she embodied. Her royal banner was still held high, and she continued to carefully assess the men and women to whom she entrusted her projects, scrutinizing them closely and asking others to monitor the movements of courtiers and functionaries at the palace and elsewhere. Of all the important characters from the early Justinianean period—the men who had listened to her in silence during the Nika revolt—only the faithful eunuch Narses had remained in Constantinople. Belisarius, whom she found suspiciously enigmatic, was at the Persian front with his troops. And the up-and-coming Syrian functionary Peter Barsymes, who was busy drawing up plans for an imperial monopoly on silk production and trade, did not yet seem ready for high office.

Justinian and Theodora had so personalized their autocracy—power was so completely centralized in the two of them—that they ended up dismantling the delicate structure of the imperial magistra cies of late antiquity. So there were serious consequences when one of the Augusti dropped out of the mechanism. In a reversal worthy of a theatrical *coup-de-scène*, they had become irreplaceable: the masters of the empire had become its slaves. Theodora's sleep may have been troubled by nightmares for the first time; her splendid purple shroud metamorphosed into rough brown sackcloth.

✦ ✦ ✦

In addition to her many everyday responsibilities, Theodora also had to address the discomfort of the military chiefs of staff, which was new for her. They were engaged on three continents, not only fighting enemies but trying to prevent the plague from striking their soldiers, all the while calming the troops' exasperation over the delays in their payments, which were slowed by the raging epidemic.

The generals were aware of Theodora's total lack of experience when it came to war. With the emperor ill and believed to be near death, with the Italian and Persian fronts open, the endemic North African revolts, and the invasions from the Balkans, the chiefs of staff felt that they could and ought to assume more power. If Justinian were to die, they would not tolerate a successor from inside the palace, such as Anastasius in 491 or Justin in 518. Not since Zeno in 474—almost seventy years earlier—had there been an emperor who could lead an army in battle. Several times General Vitalian had almost seized the throne, but he was finally betrayed and murdered—by Justinian, to boot. Maybe it was no coincidence that a nephew of Vitalian named John was the most active of the warriors conferring about the situation. Rumors, plans for secret correspondence, and denials ran rampant.

The difficulties were felt especially severely in Italy, where lack of coordination and authority was allowing the Goths to regain their territories. With his military skills and his popular anti-aristocratic policy, Totila had taken back almost the entire Italian peninsula. He held everything but a few isolated fortresses and the two most illustrious capital cities—Ravenna, the operational seat where the Senate was located, and Rome, which had immense symbolic value.

The battles that were being fought were no longer devastating massacres that left mounds of dead men on the field. Instead, cities surrendered with few victims, because the imperial generals were experienced in defense. As they saw it, the time for great heroic feats was over; the more soldiers they could keep alive, the more negotiating power they had at the palace. Nevertheless, Italy was a bitter lesson. Belisarius had returned to Constantinople in the fall of 540, less than two years earlier, with Italy in his hands and Witigis, the Gothic king, in chains. Now everything had to be done again.

Well-informed courtiers were gossiping about possible candidates for emperor, and Theodora's faithful informers intercepted the gossip. She regularly held brief meetings with the leading ministers of the empire on purely technical matters, so that nothing would leak out. She investigated behind the scenes, and her suspicions were confirmed.

Germanus's name sometimes came up, for he was a blood relative of Justinian, and he had shown valor on the battlefield against the Balkan and African barbarians, as well as the usual Persian enemies. Although he was a cousin of the emperor, his differences with Theodora were too deeply rooted. She had pushed him into a comfortable but distant isolation, and he would not take the first step to come out of it. The same could not be said of Belisarius. Many people looked to him: he was the only Roman general in recent centuries to have been granted a triumph (albeit an anomalous one). Belisarius looked good not only because of his victories but also because he had refused to become king of the Western empire. It was well known that he had chosen to remain a "slave" and keep the oath he had sworn to Justinian of not seeking the crown while the latter was alive. If the emperor died, many believed that Belisarius could immediately grasp what they perceived was his destined position, especially because the masses loved him as much as they feared Theodora.

The lucid empress saw clearly that in an empire without Justinian, a Belisarius supported by the military would constitute the gravest danger to the continuity of her own power. She would never withdraw the words she had spoken ten years earlier, the words that this very general had backed up with force in the Hippodrome: someone who has worn the purple cannot live without it.

What was she to do? She could not open the door to him by abdicating to become a nun, giving up her glittering power for a dull, dark, rough habit—she would be the first empress to take such a step! She

could not choose exile like Athenais-Eudocia—the fifth-century empress
and poetess with whom she shared her Monophysite sympathies and
a rumored whiff of scandalous "paganism"—for she loved the capital
and her Hieron palace too much. Had she had a child with Justinian,
the husband would live on in the son; she could keep the purple and
rule as regent, teaching her heir how to exercise power. But that was
not the case.

Only a miracle would let her continue to wear the purple: only a
miraculous recovery by Justinian. But if he were to die, she could
choose to marry again, as other empresses had. This idea she found
unbearable: no one truly deserved to possess her, or Justinian's
throne. Besides, the hypothesis was even more loathsome because it
would certainly be a forced marriage. A civil war would erupt, and she
would lose, unless she married one of the generals. The one general
she would have to marry to avoid it was Belisarius.

This was truly unfortunate because it would cost her dearly:
Theodora would have to give up Antonina, the only person who in all
this time had proved capable of handling important confidential matters. In 542, after what had transpired with her son Photius, Antonina
probably had not followed Belisarius to the eastern front. If she was in
the capital now, she was the only person Theodora would want to consult, but also the only one that she ought not to consult. Perhaps
Theodora could marry another military man—some lesser general—
and once again use Antonina to act against Belisarius? The reactions
of the other generals would be unpredictable and risky.

With Justinian on the throne, the empire was a series of problems
to be solved. Without Justinian, the empire became unbearable to her.

Theodora prayed; she did not speak; she waited. Of all the ancient
mythological images that have been superimposed on the empress
(and once-promiscuous actress), perhaps the most appropriate one
for this period is the image of Penelope, the least promiscuous of
wives, who stayed faithful to her husband despite the growing violence of her suitors. It was a paradox of history. Like Penelope,
Theodora did not betray any preference; Ulysses's wife had a piece
of cloth to weave and unweave, and Justinian's wife wove her

complex fabric of prayers. But there were no signs that Justinian's health was improving.

Finally, Theodora might have added a vow. If so, it was a personal, intimate vow, not a promise to build churches or cities. In January 532, Theodora had publicly gambled her life for her purple mantle. Ten years later, in the confines of her soul, perhaps she repeated the gamble, offering her own survival in exchange for the emperor's. It would be another secret, another reversal of hers. And if God took her life in exchange for Justinian's, at least she would end her days wearing the purple. Perhaps such a vow gave her new strength to face the idea that Justinian might not survive.

Her secrets and her personal mysticism did not cause her to loosen her total control of everyday situations. Theodora continued to weave her fabric of prayers, and ordered numerous liturgies and orations for the recovery of the emperor in churches and monasteries, including those that she had founded or supported. She kept up with the network of informers who "kept reporting to her what was said and done both in the market-place and in the homes of the people."[8] Among her spies were two officers assigned to the eastern front, John "the Glutton" and a strategist named Peter, who swore to having heard from Belisarius and Bouzes—a high-ranking Thracian officer—that they would never accept another emperor "like Justinian."

We don't know if these words were actually spoken, and in what form; we don't know if it was a repudiation of Justinian's work, or if it referred to an agreement about the appointment of the next emperor, or if it was a formal understanding. It may have been a well-crafted fake rumor, spread for personal profit or commissioned by the empress herself. With such stories she could proceed to eliminate the most dangerous, and certainly the most popular, of the possible claimants to the throne. Teaching Belisarius a lesson would serve as due notice to other officers that in spite of all their secret pacts, in the end they would have to settle accounts with her and her alone.

An investigation was needed to find out if these rumors were fabricated or genuine. If true, they meant high treason, a crime that

Theodora was inflexible about, a crime that had brought down Hypatius, Pompeius, and John the Cappadocian. For the third time in less than two years, Belisarius was recalled to Constantinople.

We can easily imagine what this general who had triumphed over the Vandals and the Goths thought when he got the summons. Yet, once more, he obeyed and returned. More than the Augusta's orders, he was probably honoring the loyalty that bound him to his emperor. And if indeed he was plotting against the Augusti, now would have been the time to disobey the summons and challenge Theodora openly. Historical hindsight, therefore, seems to put him above suspicion. On the other hand, we know that Antonina, his wife and the manager of his wealth, was probably in the capital. An open rebellion could trigger Theodora's reprisal and the confiscation of his wealth, to his detriment and Antonina's (or even to his detriment alone, given the intimacy between the two women). So he did well to return.

In Constantinople, the two "plotters" met different fates. Belisarius was free to move about as he pleased during the investigation, but Bouzes was called before Theodora and disappeared in the recesses of the palace: not the inner rooms reserved for the empress's sorrowful conversations and intense prayers with Anthimus, the deposed patriarch, but the suites "where she usually kept in confinement those who had given her offense."[9] Like Photius and so many others before, Bouzes, "[a] man sprung from a line of consuls, remained, forever unaware of time. For as he sat there in the darkness, he could not distinguish whether it was day or night. . . . For the man who threw him his food each day met him in silence, one as dumb as the other, as one beast meets another."[10]

Perhaps this passage from the *Secret History* is alluding to Acacius, Theodora's father, the keeper of the ferocious bears in the cages of the Kynêgion. Everyone believed that Bouzes was dead. Fear of the empress's wrath, coupled with the awareness that a throng of spies was ready to take down any remark, buried the issue and created a conspiracy of silence: "For if it was her wish to conceal anything that was being done, that thing remained unspoken of and unmentioned by all, and it was thenceforth not permitted either for any man who had knowledge of the matter to report the fact to any of his kinsmen, or for anyone who wished to learn the truth about him to make enquiry, even though he were very curious."[11]

When in 545 Bouzes finally resurfaced "as one who had returned from the dead,"[12] he was broken by years of imprisonment. Was he released because generals were needed, or had the empress been "moved to pity"?[13] In any case, his release from prison was a discretionary decision on the part of the empress. It partially revised the judgment of "inhuman cruelty" that many of Theodora's contemporaries perceived as being the "foundation of her soul." After the troubles with Pope Silverius and John the Cappadocian, Theodora interpreted each and every event in the light of a personal dispute or confrontation. Everything ricocheted off her like a test of strength.

Finally, miraculously, Justinian recovered from the plague. People wondered if he recovered because of his natural strength, or because he had not contracted an acute form of the illness, or because of the concentrated waves of innumerable thaumaturgic energies, prayers, and vows on his behalf. Only Theodora saw the emperor's recovery as her own personal victory as well as a very great relief. (She also might have known that her vow meant that she could pay a very high price for that victory: she could pay with her life.)

Just as in 532 she was able to capitalize on her speech about power, now her husband's recovery gave her renewed strength and energy. She had new energy to move against Belisarius, because the investigation that she had conducted had not erased all her suspicions. The emperor, who had been so close to death, preached indulgence. He reminded Theodora of the punishment they had inflicted on John the Cappadocian when he had, after all, been caught in the act; the charges against Belisarius were not comparable. Eliminating him would be counterproductive.

To placate Theodora, who continued to suspect him of plotting high treason, Belisarius was removed from his post as chief strategist for the East. It was an unexpected and serious humiliation, but not the first one for the general—and it was just the first in a new series of humiliations. Next his personal retinue, which had grown to seven thousand soldiers who marched with him when he appeared before the admiring citizens of Constantinople, was disbanded and sent to replenish the armies decimated by the plague.

This man, so often acclaimed as the light of salvation, now faced a gray future of isolation. Formerly a living symbol of health, energy, and pride, Belisarius now looked "always pensive and gloomy, and dreading a death by violence."[14] His proud list of victories was suddenly worthless. And it seemed that his legendary accumulated wealth was to be confiscated. Paradoxically, this was exactly what Antonina had been trying to avoid when she had redirected Theodora's anger toward John the Cappadocian.

Justinian's face, healthy and florid once more, and Theodora's usual pale and ethereal face appeared to Belisarius as heralds of his own death sentence.

Despite the wounds to his career, his property, and his friendships, Belisarius did not give up. Theodora understood that she had to push harder if she was to break him. She had to properly mark the chasm between masters and slaves. The chasm had already been emphasized during Belisarius's triumph, when he—the winner of so many battles— had been forced to kneel and bow before the emperor on the throne. Now she was sharpening her prod, while continuing to use the most efficient of her accomplices, Antonina, the general's wife. One day, when Belisarius appeared at the palace with the small retinue he was permitted in his diminished condition, Justinian and Theodora brusquely sent him off; they seemed irritated. As he left, "some men of the base and common sort,"[15] insulted and slandered him on the street (perhaps the men had been engaged on purpose). Back in his mansion, he lay on his bed, certain that the hired assassins were approaching.

A messenger from the empress appeared. Belisarius readied himself to die like an ancient hero. But the messenger carried no swords or knives—only a letter from the Augusta: "You know, noble Sir, how you have treated us. But I, for my part, since I am greatly indebted to your wife, have decided to dismiss all these charges against you, giving to her the gift of your life. For the future, then, you may be confident concerning both your life and your property; and we shall know concerning your attitude towards her from your future behavior."[16]

The "noble Sir" was Theodora's way of deriding him. In insisting on the opposition between Belisarius and the Augusti ("how you have treated us"), Theodora was rejecting the general's protestations of innocence. To her and to the emperor, Belisarius's life and his victories for the public "glory of the Romans" had no value. Still, Theodora cared for Antonina; she acknowledged only that she was indebted to the wife for her stratagems against the empress's enemies. So the empress entrusted Belisarius to Antonina, with much less enthusiasm than she had shown when she had entrusted Antonina with "her precious pearl"—the lover, Theodosius. Antonina's private, personal rewards for serving Theodora were worth more than Belisarius's reward for serving the empire. The general was subordinated to the "patrician lady."

As the *Secret History* tells it, at this point Belisarius fell on his knees before his wife, who had become his mistress, his *domina*, like a lesser Theodora. He now welcomed the bowing and kneeling that he had found so bitter in the Hippodrome. "He was . . . constantly shifting his tongue from one of the woman's ankles to the other,"[17] calling her the cause of his life and his salvation, and promising thenceforth to be not her husband, but her faithful slave. He no longer seemed like a disgraced general; it was as if he had abdicated his status as a Roman man—as a man at all. When Pope Silverius was deposed in Rome, Belisarius had sat on the floor, with Antonina reclining higher up, on the triclinium. At that time Belisarius had wanted to stress his separation from her, to remain unsullied by Severus's blood, for which "the empress would have to answer to Jesus Christ." Now, just five years later, he kneeled before his wife, to show not that he was separate but that he was dependent.

This scene marked the decline of the most brilliant general of late antiquity, a decline that was perhaps foreshadowed when he neglected the solemn oaths he had taken with Photius, a decline that began when Photius revealed Antonina's behavior. Belisarius had paid for his invincibility and his series of conquests with his private blindness.

His decline was perhaps his punishment for having refused Witigis's offer, for not becoming king of Ravenna and of Italy, for not grasping and reviving the remnant of the Western empire that he had been offered. (Justinian would have had a hard time removing him.) Belisarius kneeling before Antonina confirmed the sinister prophecy inherent in the question that the citizens of Ravenna had asked in 540: Why would he want to be a slave when he could be a master?

His humiliation was twofold. In a perverted role reversal, the greatest craftsman of Justinian and Theodora's dominion became their servant: once because he was reduced to the status of simple subject, and again because Antonina, in a further irony of history, had become the solicitous guarantor of her husband's salvation. Theodora again proved herself a shrewd, skilled manipulator, turning Justinian's benevolence toward Belisarius to her own specific ends. The general was saved, just as the emperor wished; and yet he had been humiliated, just as the empress wanted.

The year 543 of the Christian era dawned on an exhausted, diminished world with a population smaller in ambition and numbers, in strength and in spirit. The Augusti had tried to tame the world with theoretical constructs and military might. They had placed the world on the pedestal of Christianity, as if it were a mannequin, and draped it with the garments and fabric they had cut to fit laws of *their own* making. But the world had not stood still like a mannequin. It had taken them with it, not the other way around. It had opened their eyes to a wider perspective—the world was perhaps even too vast, so vast that it had seemed emptied of individuals and values. Now it behooved them to reflect and to repent, because the public and private misfortunes that had befallen them in the plague year of 542 required contrition and repentance. The time was past when their victory over the African Vandals was presented by the imperial propaganda machine as "the greatest of God's prodigies on earth."[18]

They also had to reconsider religious issues and attempt to understand how far they were responsible before God for what had happened to them and their people. Once again they had to face the situation of the Monophysites and of Christian unity. Once again, the operational strategies the two rulers would choose would be different: Justinian would work toward theological clarification, while Theodora would consider primarily her authority over people.

Although they used their usual strategies, it seemed like much more than a year had elapsed since 541, when the last Roman consul was appointed.[19] Perhaps we ought to consider the year 542 not only as a watershed in the life of Justinian and Theodora, but as a great watershed between two historical eras.

SEVENTEEN

"Loyal to Her Family"

Constantinople, North Africa, 543–47

FROM 532 to 541 Justinian's world had seemed infinitely expandable, but in 542 it ran up against its limitations. The economic and financial burdens of the restoration project had brought it to its knees, and the "Roman" expansion in Africa and Italy had come to a halt. In the East, the Persian empire refused to be dominated. The dome of the Holy Wisdom, perceived as linked to Heaven and protected by angels, seemed architecturally unsurpassable. The emperors had meant to transform their world; now they had to come to terms with it as it was.

The one person who did effectuate radical changes was Belisarius, who had led the armies of the great transformation; but he was altered forever. The humiliation he had suffered in Theodora's investigation had been further exacerbated by the events that followed.

The empress and Antonina made a pact that served both their interests: they decided to marry off Antonina and Belisarius's only daughter, Joannina. She was perhaps twelve years old and was destined to inherit what was rumored to be a legendary dowry. The two women betrothed her to Anastasius, a son of the daughter born to Theodora during her controversial acting career. The guarantee that his daughter would play a major role in the future of the empire did not soothe the general's wounded pride, for he would be forced to become a relative of the woman who had seized every chance to hurt him.

That was not all. In 544, Belisarius was again dispatched to Italy, not as supreme commander but with the diminished title of "chief of the imperial grooms." What is more, he was asked to finance the military expedition out of his own pocket. Rumor had it that Belisarius accepted this further insult so that he could finally take revenge on the imperial couple, pulling off a move *against* the palace (the plot that Antonina had perfidiously suggested to John the Cappadocian in 541). But that was not Belisarius's plan. He did set sail for Italy, though he was unable to contribute effectively to the military operations because he lacked resources and had frequent disagreements with the other generals, particularly Vitalian's nephew John.

It was only in the summer of 545 that Belisarius was restored to the position of supreme commander[1] of the military expedition. At this point, he dispatched John to Constantinople with a request for fresh troops and money. The new troops were to assemble in Dyrrachium (now Durrës, Albania), where the Egnatia Road ended at the Adriatic Sea; from there they would reach Italy and move to reinforce the imperial garrison in Rome. But events took a different turn.

John stayed longer than planned in the capital, thereby endangering the military situation, and took this opportunity to forge a family bond with Justinian's cousin Germanus, whom Theodora loathed. In fact, he married Germanus's daughter Justina (who was still single "although already eighteen," as some unkind gossips noted). Given his blood ties to the throne, Germanus held a much higher position than his future son-in-law, but he could no longer bear the isolation he had been driven into by Theodora's hostility. He married off his children in order to disperse his wealth among them, for he feared that a pretext might be found to confiscate it for the imperial coffers.

He must really have been in a difficult spot if he betrothed his daughter to John: the imperial couple had reason to distrust John as the nephew of the Vitalian whose murder Justinian had arranged in 520. But John was extremely clever: he married Germanus's daughter and her wealth without falling out of favor with the court; on the contrary, the court granted his requests. He also began a campaign to mend his father-in-law's reputation in upper ministerial and military circles, which would have a positive effect in the long term.

It might seem that John won over Theodora and Justinian, but in fact he harmed their program. Instead of acting for the "glory of the Romans," on returning to Italy he and his men did not rejoin Belisarius, preferring to capture isolated Gothic strongholds in the southern part of the peninsula. He feared that at the chief commander's side he would be exposed to Antonina's wrath, and that Theodora might push her to treat him as she had treated John the Cappadocian and Pope Silverius.

In this situation, Belisarius was unable to rescue Rome from its siege by the Goths; even Pope Vigilius had fled the town (as we will see later). The Gothic king Totila spent Christmas Day, 546, in the Eternal City, which had been abandoned even by the last of the despised imperial troops. From his position of strength, the Gothic king proposed to Justinian that they return to the prewar status quo, in the spirit of the relationship between Anastasius and Theodoric. But the Augustus, already suspicious of Totila's social innovations and unwilling to concede that he had wasted money, time, and soldiers' lives, referred Totila's envoys to Belisarius; this delay irritated the Goths, who were seeking real peace.

Totila was also troubled by the demeanor of the great Roman families who had taken Constantinople's side in an effort to save their caste privileges from the social reforms he promoted. Enraged, he decided to punish the city, so he ordered that the fortified walls of Rome be dismantled.

From his camp in Portus (now Ostia, near Rome), Belisarius sent Totila a letter: a masterpiece of astute rhetoric, it is Byzantine in style rather than late antique. Belisarius replied gently to Totila's wild fury, pointing out that it's difficult to create new beauty but very easy to destroy something beautiful. Such destruction, he wrote, is typical of "men who lack understanding, and who are not ashamed to leave to posterity this token of their character."[2] Whatever the outcome of the war between Goths and Romans, destroying the walls of Rome would not only turn the city back into a "sheeppasture,"[3] it would also earn Totila the scorn of future generations. Is this what Totila was fighting for?

The Goth king, forever worried about his "immortal" glory, "after reading [the letter] over many times and coming to realize accurately the significance of the advice, was convinced."[4] The walls of Rome were spared, and when, in the spring of 547, Totila and his army left the city to put pressure on the enemy forces in southern Italy, Belisarius was able to reenter the Eternal City and send the city keys to Justinian. The fortifications were almost intact, exactly as he had hoped.

In 540 Belisarius had marched into Ravenna and captured king Witigis; this taking of Rome was the second great trick he played on the Goths. Totila was dazzled by the ancient vision of glory that endured in history: the name of Rome, the impalpable value of classical tradition. The Byzantine "Romans" savored their victory: it was like a fruit that had not been picked too hastily or forcibly, but that had been allowed to ripen with patience, experience, and care—all these were Belisarius's virtues.

They might not be the Christian virtues of faith, hope, and charity, but they were positive qualities nonetheless. They could be valuable in other situations as well, since military developments could segue into family strategies and marital politics, as we saw in the case of Germanus and Vitalian's nephew John. No one knew this better than Theodora, since she herself had orchestrated the betrothal of Anastasius and Joannina. For that reason, she kept a close eye on the imperial grandees, from Belisarius to Germanus, and on their offspring, imitators, and successors—for they too could either reinforce her power or block it.

Once upon a time Theodora herself had been scrutinized closely by the audience as she acted out the amorous trysts of Zeus and Leda; now it was her turn to scrutinize the audience with her attentive eyes. The court was a great theater where there were always new claimants popping up, each with their own strategies that Theodora read only too well. She was watchful, as she had always been, because she knew that marriage alliances meant not only a turnover in generations, but also continuity of power—beginning with *her own* power, without which her life had no purpose.

Irritated, the empress's enemies compared her to a matchmaker who "regulated all marriages with . . . authority."[5] This comment merely proves that her critics refused to concede that this daughter of the theater and the Hippodrome, and her family, could do what was permitted to older, more established houses. In her twenty-odd years on the throne, Theodora absorbed the practical wisdom and the skills that were the heritage of the old families. For centuries, they had used familial ties to protect their superior position and their grandiose political, economic, and military ventures in the Mediterranean. Theodora was attentive and considerate to her relatives; she acted on their behalf and against others. She even acted against the family of Justinian, as we shall see in the story of Praejecta, his sister's daughter.

Military and conjugal elements are intertwined in this tale, just as they were in the story of John and Germanus's daughter. In North Africa in the spring of 545, the imperial troops were, as usual, fighting off Berber raids from inland. To support and reinforce the supreme commander—the pretentious and incompetent Sergius—the throne had dispatched Areobindus, a patrician from the senatorial ranks who was the scion of an excellent family. He brought along his wife, the much sought-after Praejecta.

Sergius was recalled to Constantinople for insubordination, and Areobindus was left in charge. Although he possessed many great personal qualities and was the highest military officer in the area,[6] Areobindus had no experience in war. He incited Gontharis, a warrior of Germanic origin who was the imperial commander under him,[7] to move against the Moors, but he failed to realize that Gontharis was conspiring with the enemy against the empire. When on the battlefield he saw that Gontharis had betrayed him, and the blood began to flow, Areobindus fled. He retreated to a fortified monastery, where he thought he could be safe. His wife and sister were there too, to comfort and advise him.

When it was time to confront the "barbaric" and victorious traitor, the Roman patrician went to the meeting not in military uniform, but in a monk's habit, his head and shoulders covered by a scapular to make him look harmless. Instead of displaying Roman virtues, he offered Gontharis an olive branch; Bible in hand, he prostrated himself before the traitor and begged for Christian salvation. Gontharis agreed, swearing sacred oaths, and offered Areobindus all possible guarantees. He invited him to dinner, ostensibly to celebrate their pact, but in reality intending to have him killed that very night. Thus, Areobindus's sacred sanctuary became a mortal trap.

Areobindus was not only killed but beheaded, and his severed head was put on display. Praejecta fell into the hands of the foul traitor, who forced her to write to her uncle Justinian that Gontharis was not responsible for Areobindus's death. Gontharis wanted to marry Praejecta to seal his rule over the territory: he believed that the imperial couple could no longer efficiently control it directly.

He had forgotten or, more probably, did not know, that North Africa, especially Carthage, had long been the ancient backdrop of both vile and cruel acts and lofty thoughts and valiant deeds, with the myth of Dido and Aeneas, the exploits of Hannibal and the Scipios, and, most recently, the victories of Belisarius. Meanwhile, another "Roman" general (who was actually Armenian-born) dreamed of making a name for himself in Carthage. Artabanes had come to Carthage in the retinue of the patrician Areobindus, and he wished to avenge his slain leader. With a clever ruse, he turned an official banquet into a massacre, and personally thrust his blade into the breast of Gontharis, who had collapsed drunkenly on the triclinium next to him. Praejecta was avenged, and she was spared a loathsome marriage. Emperor Justinian rewarded Artabanes by appointing him to Areobindus's post. It was 546, and the new hero, like Gontharis before him, was now eyeing the emperor's niece. No doubt Artabanes was proud of having saved her from marriage with her husband's murderer and usurper, but he also reckoned that marrying her would bring him very close to the throne.

Praejecta was summoned to Constantinople, and then Artabanes was too. His ambition was uncontrollable. In the words of Procopius, "For when men lay hold upon prosperity unexpectedly, their minds cannot remain stable, but in their hopes they ever keep going forward, until they are deprived even of the felicity that has been undeservedly theirs."[8] Still, at the time it seemed as if Artabanes was entitled to everything he wanted: "For he was both tall of stature and handsome, of a noble character and little given to speech."[9] Honored by the emperor with important positions, he seemed to be blessed by the stars, just as Belisarius had briefly seemed to be. (The only person who was consistently blessed by the stars was the diamond-bright empress.)

Artabanes was already married. He was estranged from his wife, and had repudiated her, so he rightly considered himself free. But his wife did not: she left her home and went to the palace, asking to be received by the Augusta. She could not bear the dishonor of being cast aside while her husband's name was on everyone's lips.

It was Theodora's "nature always . . . to assist unfortunate women." As we know, she had even influenced legislation on women's status and on the family. But most important right now was that she saw Artabanes as an intruder approaching the throne from Justinian's side of the family, an intruder who could be an impediment to *her own* family. Should he succeed, her family might be cut out of any transfer of power. Theodora and her close relatives had other reasons for suspecting Artabanes: he was the same soldier who, according to a reliable reconstruction of events, had killed Sittas (Comito's husband, Theodora's brother-in-law) with a cowardly spear-thrust in his back. Sittas had died in 538 during the wars in Armenia, when Artabanes was fighting alongside the Persians and was not yet an ally of the Romans.

Theodora ultimately exposed Artabanes as an opportunist and an unfaithful husband; he was forced to reunite with his wife. He protested uselessly that the new Rome punished him—the best and most trustworthy of its servants, he claimed—by making him "share the bed of the one woman in the world that he hated most."[10]

What about poor Praejecta? Instead of Artabanes, the widow of faint-hearted Areobindus was married off (with Theodora's consent) to a man named John, son of the Pompeius who—with his brother Hypatius—had paid with his blood for the Nika rebellion. Now the families on both sides of the imperial couple were ennobled by links to the great house of old Emperor Anastasius. The Dyophysite wing of Pompeius and Hypatius married into Justinian's family through Praejecta, while Theodora's illegitimate daughter had already been accepted by the Monophysite wing of Probus and his sons. All the parties in Praejecta's marriage had great expectations for the future, but they turned out to be short-lived: Praejecta's new husband, John, died in 549 or 550.

In the *Greek Anthology* Julian the Egyptian, who had already recounted the death of Hypatius, also eulogized John:

> "Famous was John."
> "Mortal, say."
> "The son-in-law of an empress."
> "Yes, but mortal."
> "The flower of the family of Anastasius."
> "And mortal too was he."
> "Righteous in his life."
> "That is no longer mortal. Virtue is stronger than death."[11]

John's virtues are recalled in this Greek verse; but only a sad, uncertain echo remains of Praejecta, who was the wife of Areobindus and John and merely an apparition for Gontharis and Artabanes. Her echo is as uncertain as her pen must have been as she sat, a prisoner in Africa, forced to write to her uncle the emperor under threat of drunken violence from Gontharis.

In acting on the complaint of Artabanes' wife, Theodora did much more than "assist unfortunate women": the empress believed that she had a specific calling as an arbitrator. She projected the message that anyone approaching the throne would have to deal with her whole family. She gave her sister Comito revenge against the traitor who had made her a widow. And so what if her action indirectly made Praejecta unhappy? Justinian's young niece could go on to marry John of the great house of Anastasius, the emperor who was "piously remembered," and Justinian's family would benefit from the arrangement. Once again, the Augusta's moves were based on a winning calculation of the balance between risk and opportunity.

+ + +

Around the year 545, Theodora's experience was making her every move increasingly calculated. The speedy reactions that had brought her fame and victory in extreme situations (dealing with the Nika rebellion or Pope Silverius or John the Cappadocian) might have been faltering in the face of the new military and papal emergencies in Italy. In a world changed by the plague and Justinian's illness, however, her consciousness of her role and of the purple had not changed, nor had her concern for the fate of the empire.

She and Justinian pondered the numerous unresolved issues in the Mediterranean. On their stage, there was no predetermined cast of characters, and no set moment when the curtain would fall: Theodora exhorted the emperor to face the most important issue of all, the question of the succession. Who would rule when their bodies lay in the church of the Holy Apostles?

It was an unwelcome subject for her husband. The sleepless Justinian could not bear the idea that his eyes would close one day in eternal sleep. He was past sixty and he had looked death in the face, but like old Emperor Anastasius he was unwilling to consider the issue of the succession. In the privacy of their apartments, Theodora must have reminded him that they sat on the throne precisely because one reckless action by that "most provident and . . . most prudent administrator of all emperors"[12] had finally paved the way for his uncle Justin's accession to the throne. Theodora understood that the time had come to work out, if not impose, a solution that might meet the needs of both houses (the immigrants from Illyricum and the daughters of the theater and the Hippodrome).

But while Justinian's keen political mind was quick to grasp Theodora's arguments, his private persona was reluctant. He wasn't afraid of being brought down to size, but he believed that if any part of him was destined to last, it would last through what he could imprint on lifeless matter. He sought immortality through what could be written on parchment or papyrus rolls, or carved in ivory, or depicted in mosaics, or built with marble. With the exception of Theodora, to Justinian human beings were remote creatures that evoked no feelings in him. He liked the idea of transforming his efforts into glorious objects, but the idea of securing his immortality or that of his family through future generations was foreign to him. Of course, things might have been different if his marriage to Theodora had produced a child.

The Augusta had a natural genius for command, and because there are no commands without people, people were fundamental to her. Nature had given her offspring, and her daughter and grandchildren secured their place in history. Several sources mention Theodora's daughter as the mother of Athanasius, a complex, controversial monk and theologian. The same sources speak of an "illustrious John" who descended from Emperor Anastasius and whose maternal grand-mother was Empress Theodora: he was honorary consul, patrician, ambassador to Persia in 576–77, and a staunch Monophysite.[13] Fur-thermore, the *Secret History* speaks at length of an Anastasius whose history is indicative of his grandmother Theodora's strong character and aspirations. It's worth taking a closer look at him.

Theodora's daughter had been born around 515 or 516; in 530 or 531, most likely, she was given in marriage to a son of Probus, a nephew of Emperor Anastasius and cousin of Pompeius and Hypatius, the "usurpers" in the Nika rebellion. She soon gave birth to an Anastasius of her own. Around 543, at the time of Belisarius's humiliating treason investigation, Theodora and Antonina arranged for this Anastasius to be betrothed to Joannina, mentioned earlier. The boy and the girl were about the same age—twelve or thirteen. Anasta-sius next appears on our stage as an adolescent of about seventeen. In the *Secret History*, we read that in the summer of 548 he and Joannina "found themselves held by an ardent love for one another, and a space of no less than eight months [had] passed in this way."[14] They had been living together at least since the fall of 547. How could such shameless behavior have been allowed, behavior that is often frowned on even today, in a society that valued marital virtue (as personified by the most Christian rulers Theodora and Justinian)?

In 543 Theodora had decided that a male member of her family—our Anastasius (our nephew)—would get Joannina and her coveted wealth, but no steps were taken for some years; there was no sense in rushing the immature couple. But by the second half of 547 Theodora must have felt the first symptoms of the illness that would soon kill her. She dutifully hid them, for she could not allow the slightest rumor of imperfection to circulate about her or about her power. She quickly wrote to Belisarius and Antonina, summoning them to return so that together they could end the betrothal with a marriage. But the demands of war prevented Belisarius from moving. Besides, the empress's insistence made them suspicious: a summons to Constantinople had never been a good sign for the couple, especially not for the general.

At that point, Theodora felt that she had to intervene personally, forcing Anastasius and Joannina together. The empress seems to have prodded her nephew with very frank language, urging him to use force on the girl, "and thus after the girl had been compromised,"[15] arranging for a hasty marriage to remedy the situation (an age-old Mediterranean custom). In any case, the forced intimacy produced the desired effect, for the two fell in love.[16]

Theodora's radical decision was proof of her strong belief in the continuity of her power but also—and for the first time—proof of her fears. The Augusta suspected that she had only a few months to live and that she had to act quickly, as she had done so often in the past. But on the other hand, she had to deal with Antonina. Theodora must have perceived that the memory of their past collusion and their reciprocal support in dire situations might carry no weight with Belisarius's wife, who had always tended to act only in her own interests. Fearing that after her death Antonina "would not shew herself faithful to her house,"[17] Theodora forced the situation.

There was more. Theodora wanted to act immediately so that "the emperor might not put a stop to her machinations."[18] Perhaps she planned to find Justinian's successor in her own family, forming an alliance linking her people to the houses of Emperor Anastasius and Belisarius. In this way the wealthy and glorious family of Belisarius and the noble family of Anastasius would be joined to her family in a regime of power and Monophysitism. It would be another metamorphosis, though not Theodora's last. She would create a sort of dynasty, which in a miraculous (though all too human) parthenogenesis would be born of Theodora's now imperial loins from an unknown father. Ultimately, *she* would be the founder of the dynasty.

The only person excluded from this hypothetical succession was—paradoxically enough—the emperor who sat on the throne and was to outlive Theodora. But he wasn't the one to put a stop to the project. Antonina was solely responsible for the failed marriage. She set off for the capital, not because she was caving in to Theodora's insistent letters, but to request money and soldiers for the war, as Belisarius's envoy. But when she reached the capital in the summer of 548, Theodora was already dead. Antonina wept at the empress's tomb, but then she did only what she herself wanted.

The woman who had been Theodora's "favorite Patrician" disregarded the childhood betrothal and the forced cohabitation of Joannina and Anastasius, even though it meant censure for her teenage daughter. With Theodora dead, Antonina believed that she could reshuffle all the cards, and she refused to allow her daughter to marry into Theodora's family. She separated Joannina from her beloved and took her home. In spite of all that had happened, Antonina still believed that she could round up a *genuine* blueblood for her daughter.

We do not know who Joannina and Anastasius finally married. Theodora had forced the teenagers' situation, and Antonina heaped wrong upon wrong by forbidding her daughter a wedding that would have made her respectable and that remained the only realistic option. Belisarius could not intervene, though he suffered, sources report, as "misfortune fell upon his own house."[19]

At Theodora's death in June 548, no one foresaw that the young lovers Joannina and Anastasius would end up apart. The empress probably also considered that her family's future would be ensured by the daughter born to her sister Comito and the late general Sittas, and here she was right. In 548 this niece, Sophia ("wisdom"), was eighteen. By this age, girls from good families like hers—and power had made Theodora's into an excellent family—had had their marriages arranged already. The perfect choice had been made for her: she was betrothed to a nephew of Justinian, son of the emperor's sister Vigilantia Secunda.

Born around the year 520, the groom was about thirty years old in 548. His name was Justin, like the unpolished founder of the dynasty, but unlike his namesake he was a reluctant warrior. On the other hand, he had a passion and a talent for palace procedures; by modern standards, we would call him an enlightened bureaucrat. The imperial couple must have considered him trustworthy, and they agreed to his marriage with Sophia, fancying it a sequel to the alliance between their respective houses. And indeed, after Justinian's death in 565, the throne passed to his man, Justin II, and his wife, Sophia.

This second imperial couple was to be less famous than Justinian and Theodora, but their representation *as a couple* was far more emphatic than that of their illustrious predecessors. Sophia's portrait appeared on coins, an honor Theodora had never had. Shown sitting on the throne next to her husband, Sophia was a symbol and a personification of wisdom. In his propaganda, Justin II could in all honesty say that wisdom inspired his rule (although he turned out to have a devastating psychological disorder).

The imperial couple was also portrayed together on a work of art known as the Vatican Cross [fig. 45], a masterpiece in gilt silver enriched with embossing and precious stones that the couple donated to Rome at the time of Pope John III (pope from 561 to 574). The piece, which contains a relic said to be part of the true cross, is designed as a symbolic representation of salvation. In the center is the lamb, on the vertical arm are two images of Christ Pantocrator, and at both ends of the cross arms are portraits of Justin and Sophia, their palms open in a typical gesture of prayer. Christ the Judge and Pantocrator is aligned with the sacrificial lamb, so that Justin and Sophia, earthly potentates, are shown giving tribute to the most high and yet most humble miracle of divine power.

In the Vatican Cross, imperial, secular authority is set below religious authority; it marks a big step toward the medieval cult of relics. This is confirmed by a poet of the time, the African Flavius Cresconius Corippus, who describes Sophia as she wove the funeral robe of

Justinian in 565.[20] Like one of the saintly women at the tomb of Jesus—
a favorite theme in the ivory diptychs of late antiquity—Sophia/
Wisdom prepares the ritual celebrations for another person. She doesn't
make history or make the ritual; she is not a creator but merely a less
distinguished descendant of an illustrious family.

45. Reliquary cross of Justin II and
Sophia in embossed gilt silver with
gemstones, c. 570, Treasury of Saint
Peter, Vatican City.

That funeral robe actually emphasizes the difference between the triumphant patriarchs and the epigones who merely celebrated them. The
robe wrapping Justinian's body when it went into the limestone sarcophagus [fig. 35] was decorated with scenes of his victories, perhaps
recalling the brilliant Chalkê mosaic where he and Theodora were
shown rejoicing at the victories over the Goth and Vandal "barbarians."
Now the Chalkê mosaic is gone and in 1204 the "most Christian"
Western crusaders stole Justinian's wonderful funeral garment and lost
it. They entered the church of the Holy Apostles—the model for

St. Mark's basilica in Venice—and despoiled the tombs. How much of the glory of the West is nothing but the glory of followers?

Sophia was a ruler of great character, and some historians have claimed that she held more real power than her famous aunt. Certainly, as Justin's mental health began to weaken around 574, she held on to the reins of the empire, preparing the transition to Tiberius that formally took place in 578. Justin II was a man of the palace, but his successor was an army man; the idea of a warrior on the throne had seemed like an ominous threat to Theodora at the time of the plague in 542, but Sophia eventually made it happen. Sophia may have planned to marry Tiberius, not for love but out of devotion to her aunt Theodora's lesson that marriage was the key to continuity of power. She succeeded in maintaining part of her power, at least, in a world that continued to evolve toward the Middle Ages, with the decline of theaters, hippodromes, and factions, with the breaking up of the mosaic "of the thousand cities," with the progressive loss of the Justinianean ideal of restoration.

Ironically, the imperial throne of Constantinople—which had stood for brilliant glory, sleepless responsibility, and stubborn continuity—became a sickness: overwhelmed by his duties, or perhaps by the unbearable heritage of his past, Justin II suffered repeated nervous breakdowns and lost his mind. Justin II is remembered not so much for his deeds on the throne as for the words he spoke when he said farewell to it. He expressed a new, medieval version of the concept of imperial excellence: "Do not rejoice for the shedding of blood. . . . Do not return evil for evil. . . . Be thou before everyone what you are before thyself. . . . May whoever has wealth rejoice in it; as to thyself, give to those who have not."

It was his farewell to his Byzantine successors and to the great tradition of power, a tradition that would live on only in the Slavic cultures.[21]

"Her Next Stage"

Constantinople, 543–48

*S*ENESCIT MUNDUS, "the world grows old," wrote Saint Augustine[1] more than a century before Theodora lived. His words have often been taken out of context, as if they applied to the whole late-ancient world. But if the aging had been real, that world would have been dying or even extinct by the year 550. Instead, this period marked not only the end of the old world—the one that had allowed Theodora to follow her unique and stunning career—but something more: the new concepts that she fostered, and the generations that she launched, show the first glimmers of the new.

Further proof of this can be found in the life of the great Cassiodorus, an intellectual and statesman in Italy. After King Witigis was deceived by Belisarius and surrendered to him, Cassiodorus left the court of Ravenna and stepped away from political life. It was the end of one world for him, but it was also a new beginning, because he could finally devote all of his time to leisurely intellectual pursuits. He retired not to some idyllic or idealized countryside, but to a Christian monastery he himself founded in Vivarium, near his native town of Squillace (in Calabria). It was around 550, and Cassiodorus was about sixty years old. He lived on for almost four further decades, time that he spent in contemplation, reading, and writing. He remained famous down through the centuries for his *Institutiones* (Institutions), a clear, in-depth study and comparison of the Holy Scriptures and the liberal arts that became the basic text for intellectual speculation throughout the Middle Ages.

The world grew old, but Theodora's matrimonial strategies kept it fresh, just as the imperial couple had renewed Constantinople by rebuilding it. The city might have seemed too grandiose and sumptuous a setting for the remaining population—the 542 plague had wiped out almost half the empire—but Constantinople was to remain a jewel of the Mediterranean for centuries to come. New strategies also came from Emperor Justinian after he recovered from his bout with the plague. In 543, at the age of sixty, he began the "second term" of his very long autocratic rule. He governed from 527 to 565, so his second term lasted twenty-two years—longer than the first. As he had in 527, he inaugurated his new term with religion, but otherwise this fresh start had very little in common with his first inauguration.

In 527 he had had many adversaries to subdue, but in 543 Monophysitism was the only problem left. The emperor seemed to be seeking reconciliation at a higher level now, instead of simply making statements to please his own Dyophysite group. This was partly because the evasive behavior of Pope Vigilius in Rome showed that the deposition and the humiliation inflicted on Silverius had been in vain. In the end, the imperial couple must have acknowledged that they themselves were at fault, and perhaps they connected their guilt to the emergence of the plague, which many had perceived as divine punishment for their despotism. One wonders whether the ghost of Silverius haunted Justinian's sleepless nights, just as the ghost of the Roman senators Simmacus and Boetius—executed in a fit of rage—had tormented the last years of the Ostrogoth king Theodoric in Ravenna. The Constantinopolitan rulers must have pledged to avoid despotic and violent action in the future. The emptier, slower world where they now lived called for study and patience as they grew older.

Justinian and his contemporaries believed that the good was to be found in the One, but which One *was* the good? A single solution had to be found for this problem, a solution that could be valid for the whole Ecumene, from the remote bishoprics of Sardinia to the lively theological schools of Africa or the Levant. Unfortunately, Justinian had only a few good thinkers around him in 543 (that was another difference from 527); the only solid theological thinker he had to help him was Theodore Askidas, metropolitan of Caesarea in Cappadocia. So the emperor himself studied this problem, piling tomes and rolls of religious writings atop other documents in his study regarding tax collection, the military, and the legislative work of the empire—management of the empire was neglected in favor of the theological enterprise.

Finally, Justinian told Theodora that he had developed a new strategy. He thought it would resolve the problem, but it turned out to be the start of a complex chain of actions and reactions, the bitterness of which would be so problematic that within ten years another ecumenical council, the fifth, would be called in Constantinople to address it.

Justinian's solution was the publication of the *Edict of the Three Chapters,* issued in the winter of 543–44, condemning three theologians. The men in question had all died peacefully, years earlier, in the embrace of the Church. Yet it appeared that they were infected with Nestorianism, a doctrine condemned at the Third Council of Ephesus (431) and opposed particularly strongly by the Eastern Monophysites for its rationalistic approach to the issue of Christ.

The anathemized authors were Theodore (350–428), who had been bishop of Mopsuestia in Cilicia and was considered Nestorius's teacher; Ibas, bishop of Edessa from 435–39 to 457; and Theodoretus (393–458), who had been bishop of Cyrus in northern Syria from 423 until his death (he was a well-known writer of tracts and a clear-eyed chronicler in an extreme camp of Syrian asceticism). Although he had been one of Nestorius's early sympathizers, he had later condemned him before the fathers of the Fourth Council of Chalcedon.

Justinian was convinced that he could undermine the credibility of the Chalcedon Council by attacking the three theologians; even though one of them (Theodore of Mopsuestia) had not been at issue in Chalcedon, the other two had been rehabilitated at the council. He hoped to undermine it and thus support Monophysitism without attacking the council directly (which might have led the Dyophysites to abandon their support for him). It was a move partially inspired by the old *Edict of the Union* of 482, because it sought to align Monophysites and Dyophysites against their common enemy, Nestorianism. But that "enemy" had already long since faded from the empire; it was expanding only outside, along the great commercial routes that linked the Mediterranean to Asia.

Menas, patriarch of the second Rome, approved of Justinian's edict, but other reactions were uncertain, lukewarm, or outright negative. The attack on Chalcedon was not strong enough to satisfy the Eastern Monophysites. Other critics recalled that the three theologians were in the bosom of the Church when they died. Many wondered about the emperor's interference with the Church, especially in the Western bishoprics who considered the Roman pope, not the secular Augustus of Constantinople, to be the successor of Christ on Earth.

Although he owed his position as pope to the imperial couple's scheming, Vigilius refused to accept the edict. The papal nuncio in Constantinople excommunicated Menas—the patriarch who had been appointed because he was a Dyophysite—for supporting Justinian's document. In spite of everything, the emperor's latest move in favor of reconciliation and unity created only opposition and fragmentation.

In keeping with the new spirit of the time, Justinian avoided an instinctive, irritated reaction. He and Theodora had learned from their experience with Silverius: they continued to be patient and, despite their theological differences and disappointments, they kept showing Pope Vigilius great formal deference. This was particularly important given the military situation in Italy, where the Gothic king Totila was preparing his siege on Rome, and the papal seat (discussed in the preceding chapter), and the generals Belisarius and John—Vitalian's nephew— were failing to collaborate.

Then, on November 22, 545, Constantinople scored a masterful diplomatic success. Under the pretense of protecting the pope from an imminent enemy attack, imperial soldiers kidnapped Vigilius as he was celebrating mass before the faithful in the church of Saint Cecilia in the Trastevere section of Rome. The pope suddenly saw soldiers marching in; then an officer handed him an imperial order summoning him to Constantinople. Vigilius interrupted the mass, hurried to the banks of the Tiber, and boarded a ship for Portus (Rome's ancient port, now Ostia). He blessed the crowd from aboard the ship, but the Roman citizens immediately understood that the pope's kidnapping meant that the other "Romans" (in Constantinople) were abandoning them to the Gothic siege. Instead of answering him with prayers of their own, they shouted insults and hurled stones at the representatives of that empire and that Church.

Pope Vigilius did not reach Constantinople until January 547, more than a year after his hasty kidnapping. Perhaps Justinian wanted to give him ample time to prepare for their confrontation, but some sources say that the entire episode was a cover-up designed to waste time and save face. Finally, the ship carrying Vigilius docked at the port of the second Rome. Sixty-five-year-old Justinian, in person, gave the pope an official welcome, as he had done with his predecessors. (At the time, the popes visited Constantinople more often than the emperors traveled to Rome.) The two men discussed the past. They talked of the fact that in 536 Pope Agapetus had excommunicated Anthimus, patriarch of Constantinople, and replaced him with Menas because the pope preferred his Dyophysite views. Now the *Edict of the Three Chapters* had made the current pope, Vigilius, excommunicate Menas, too. Moreover, Vigilius had promised Theodora years before that he would rehabilitate Anthimus, but he hadn't done so. There's no doubt that Theodora suggested the heavy pressure that was brought to bear on Vigilius: the pressure was a shrewd mix of formal honors and unbudging firmness about principles. The empress knew that Vigilius was easily influenced by his surroundings and circumstances, and too attached to his office to forcefully defend theoretical positions that perhaps he did not fully comprehend.

Finally, the pope seemed to give in to Justinian and Theodora's pressure. In May 547, he reconciled with Patriarch Menas, and in April 548 he sent to him a judgment—called *Iudicatum*—on the Three Chapters. In keeping with Justinian's edict, it roundly condemned the three theologians. But in a contradictory move, Vigilius reiterated his faith in the Council of Chalcedon. The ambiguous document forever undermined Vigilius's prestige, even in the West that he cherished so much.

The empress was finally getting her revenge, albeit indirectly. Although her body was growing weak, she didn't weaken her struggle against her enemies, and she was no more indulgent in her treatment of traitors. Vigilius had been deceiving her for more than ten years now, since the spring of 537: despite all his promises he had yet to rehabilitate Anthimus the Monophysite. Finally, the Augusta managed to wound Vigilius's treasured self-respect and his honor as a Western aristocrat, not just as pope.

While this was happening, a new situation was emerging that would represent a radical antithesis to Justinian's ideal of one empire united and at peace under one Church. Although it was emerging thousands of miles from the diatribes in the capital, and people were talking of it in a language other than the pope's Latin or the Greek used by the Mediterranean urban elite, still it all led back to imperial power—more precisely, it led back to Theodora.

Immediately after the plague (in 542 or 543), an important Eastern authority appealed to the empress. Byzantine sources refer to him as Arethas (al-Harith in Arabic), a *phylarch* or one of the chiefs of the Arab auxiliary forces allied with the empire. More precisely, he was the king of the Christianized Arabs, the Ghassanids, who inhabited the northwestern Arabian peninsula and did lively trade in both the Red Sea and the Mediterranean with close political and military ties to the Roman Empire of Constantinople. This Ghassanid *phylarkhos*, decorated with the highest court titles, was an ardent Monophysite Christian. He had come to inform the merciful empress that the local authorities were persecuting his coreligionists in the outer territories of the empire. Justinian was probably in the midst of revising his authoritarian Dyophysitism (as the Three Chapters would show), but his harsh anti-Monophysite measures were still in force, and were still applied energetically at the local level. The most observant Monophysites, especially the monks, were dying in the imperial prisons as "confessors." The rest of the faithful Monophysites were left without sacraments, without new clergy being ordained, without priests, in lands that had been devastated by the plague. In the words of the prophet, it was the "horrible abomination . . . of desolation."[2] How could the devout empress tolerate such a situation?

Justinian devoted much of his energy to intellectual research in the hope that it might lead to unity, albeit a theoretical and speculative unity; but Theodora felt that an immediate signal of support had to be sent to Arethas and his kingdom, and in general to the Monophysite subjects of the distant imperial provinces. She felt obligated to them not just because their beliefs about Christ coincided with her own, but because she had seen the whole Levant, the outpost defending the empire against the Persian enemy, in her early travels. Even before ascending the throne, she had understood that the survival of the empire in the East would depend not only on military fortifications and the valor of soldiers, but also on the survival of Christianity in its Monophysite version. Without bishops to ordain priests and to proselytize, a precious heritage and a long-established reality would crumble.

Such a state of emergency called for someone who was willing to live dangerously and talk convincingly. A monk named Jacob was in the city at the time, an exceptional individual who epitomized the two faces of Monophysitism. He combined Timothy's, Severus's, and Anthimus's proper, official styles with the rigor of the radical ascetics who were strengthened rather than weakened by renunciation. These were men of moral strength such as Mār the Solitary, the monk "athlete of God" who was stronger than "ten criminals,"[3] the same one who had refused to accept money from the empress. These were men who knew how to mobilize the faithful in the East; they were heroes such as Simeon the Stylite, the fifth-century Syrian saint who had lived for thirty-seven years atop a column (the pilgrimage site is now the tourist attraction of Qal'at Sim'ān).

For a long time, Theodora had followed the development of Jacob's great theological mind, which was housed in a body that had the strength of an adventurer and the resistance of a fakir. After the anti-Monophysite measures of 536, the Augusta had duly sent him into hiding, but she continued to hear reports of his ascetic exploits and of his ease with languages, especially Syriac. It was crucial that he spoke

Syriac, for his future interlocutors were not literary sophisticates; in those deserts, some past bishops had even boasted of not knowing any Greek at all. Classical, "Roman," or imperial virtues were needed less than what we might simply call ethnic, local virtues. The same was true of Egypt, where the people choosing Monophysitism were increasingly Coptic-speakers from deep inside Egypt. Conversely, the official (imperial or melkite) Dyophysite version of Christianity was already shrinking down to include only an elite network in Alexandria and a few other Hellenized cities, a network that would not resist the impending onslaught of Islamic expansionism.

In that year, 543, Jacob was secretly ordained bishop against all canon rules; he was probably ordained by Theodosius, the exiled Monophysite patriarch of Alexandria (he can be considered a Copt) who lived under Theodora's protection in a country villa in Thrace.

While Arethas's specific request was satisfied by ordaining an Arab bishop (his name was Theodore), Jacob was formally appointed to a nominal office as bishop of Edessa on the empire's border with Persia, in the heart of Syrian Christendom and of the agricultural Fertile Crescent (the town is now Urfa, in southeast Turkey). Edessa held precious relics of Christ, including a sacred image that some have identified as being the Holy Shroud of Turin. The ordination reaffirmed and institutionalized the Monophysite presence in the Near East, which, along with Egypt, had been its historical cradle and the heart of its resistance. At the same time, the new bishop had a supraregional dimension that made him a sort of patriarchal vicar.

There was already a bishop in Edessa, and he was a strict Orthodox Catholic who espoused Dyophysitism. Jacob never attempted to undermine him. Was this a contradiction? For Theodora, it was part of a providential design acting through her. She might have believed that in time the opposition would be settled, especially when she considered the parallel developments regarding Vigilius and the Roman papacy. According to the earliest Christian sources, the bishop represents the unity of the Church. But Bishop Jacob, appointed under the auspices of the imperial couple, embodied duplicity, if not outright deceit, a deceit that tainted not only the Church but the empire as well, the very center of power that so forcefully preached for and demanded unity.

In the Syriac language, Jacob was called the "Baradeus" or "beggar"; since he had no real seat, the only way for him to preach freely was to disguise himself in rags like a wandering beggar. The imperial soldiers were chasing him, and if he was identified they would have to arrest him, for they had undoubtedly sworn to serve "the divine and most devout rulers Justinian and Theodora his consort." In keeping with this oath, they pursued a man who paradoxically was protected by the very rulers in whose name he was being persecuted.

Reports say that Jacob used to hide during the day and walk dozens of miles each night. His theological conviction was as strong as his migratory spirit. A circle of acolytes served as his bodyguards, preparing the ground in Arabia, Asia Minor, Armenia, Syria, Mesopotamia, and Egypt. We read that he consecrated eighty-nine bishops and two patriarchs, and ordained eighty thousand priests; these are doubtless exaggerated figures, but he was undeniably responsible for the birth and organization of the "Syrian Orthodox" Church; to this day, it is called "Jacobite" in his honor.

A vast number of anecdotes describe Jacob as a healer and a performer of miracles. These powers were accepted and interpreted as the proof and the result of his true faith, yet a historian would say the miracle he performed was quite different. He was responsible for the persistence of a strong Christian identity in the region: it survived the decline of the imperial Orthodox presence, especially in the wake of Islam's spectacular successes, and it lives on today despite all sorts of nationalistic and fundamentalist intolerance. For more than sixteen centuries now, millions of the faithful have been members of the Jacobite Church (they are known as "old Syrians" or Orthodox Syrians); their spiritual fortresses are the monasteries that they built on the parched hills of Tur Abdin (in present-day southeast Turkey).

None of these developments would have been possible without Theodora. She also deserves recognition for her successful effort on behalf of the Coptic churches in Egypt, Ethiopia, and Nubia, which have welcomed millions of believers. In different ways they all inherited the Monophysite tradition developed by the patriarchate of Alexandria, the institution that had had such a momentous effect on Theodora; she always defended that part of the world as a spiritual Promised Land.

Was Justinian, a Dyophysite, informed of Jacob's investiture? Did he give his consent? Did he feign indifference? We do know that in the same period he entrusted the still semipagan regions of interior Anatolia, Caria, and Lycia to John of Amida (better known as John, bishop of Ephesus). Despite the latter's Monophysite beliefs, converts were accepted into the Dyophysite Church, which could be called the "state Church." On the other hand, it would be incorrect to attribute the appointment of Bishop Jacob to a whim or a secret plan of Theodora's. In this and other matters, she could have achieved much more during the emperor's illness, but she chose not to act then. So we must presume that she informed her husband of the appointment of Jacob, putting "reasons of state" ahead of reasons of dogma. Justinian, who was deeply indebted to her not only for all the years during which they shared power but also for the long months of his illness, might have consented unofficially.

The events of recent years had made Justinian more flexible about the popes' ecumenical and universalist expectations for the deserts and the tells of the non-Latin-speaking Near East, lands that Theodora knew so well. Perhaps the emperor believed that when the moment was right he could heal the split with some sophisticated theology. Certainly ambiguously Monophysite subjects were preferable to no subjects at all: he would have lost his subjects altogether if the followers of Monophysitism, exhausted by war and plague, had been forced to migrate to Persia.

Senescit mundus?—was the world growing old? Certainly Eastern Christendom showed no signs of aging, of pathetic senility, or nostalgia for the past: it was theologically and ethnically vital. We must look elsewhere for a gloomy antiquarian stubbornness: for example, in Justinian's 547 welcome to Khosrow's ambassador, Isdigousnas Zich (Yazd-Gushnap).

Constantinople and Ctesiphon had signed a new truce in 545 that cost the Romans dearly. The Persians had no intention of respecting the agreement; they intended only to exploit it in order to reinforce their position in the Black Sea. Khosrow had sent Isdigousnas to the new Rome with a series of cavils and pretexts that might divert Justinian's attention from his real aims. The ambassador had come to the palace with his wife and children and an entourage of five hundred. All the pomp was a facade with very little substance behind it: apart from the gifts, the only message that Khosrow sent to Justinian concerned the state of his health. He even teased him playfully about his recovery after the epidemic.

No ambassador was ever treated with greater honors by Justinian, who considered that his only "noble" opponent was his historical enemy, Persia. Just a short time before, he had dismissed Totila's Gothic messengers abruptly and sent them back to Belisarius: he could not foresee that the future of the empire would depend as much on relations with the Goths and the other northern "barbarians" as on a confrontation with the illustrious Persian adversary. Once again he was misled by the spell of antiquity and its traditions.

At the same time, the high cost of maintaining peace with Persia jeopardized the initiatives in the West that were at the very heart of Justinian's restoration project. Consequently, he continued to begrudge Belisarius supplies in Italy. This looks even more paradoxical when we consider that the two great empires of the Ecumene—so intent on celebrating each other's greatness in banquets and feasts— would survive for only a few more decades. (Each aiming to finally vanquish the other, the two empires were to clash again at the beginning of the seventh century; the struggle weakened and impoverished them both and left the field open for the Islamic Arabs.)

The receptions and banquets of 547 planted the seed of at least one sad death, a result of Justinian's informality leading to what became known as the "Bradukios incident." Justinian had an elevated sense of his imperial persona but was nevertheless unwilling to create barriers between himself and his collaborators, so in one meeting he invited not only Isdigousnas but also Bradukios, the interpreter in the ambassador's retinue, to share his triclinium. Observers already irritated by the emperor's expenditure of time and money noted that "no one ever saw an interpreter become a table companion of even one of the more humble officials, not to speak of a king."[4] Justinian granted this liberty as an instance of his personal benevolence, but it was repugnant to the rigid protocol of the Persians. When in 550 Isdigousnas appeared in the city again for more summit meetings, Bradukios was no longer with him. Khosrow, the Persian king, had explained that "as a mere interpreter, [Bradukios] would not have achieved such high honour from the emperor unless he had betrayed the cause of the Persians."[5] Other sources hint that Isdigousnas himself killed the interpreter. However Bradukios died, it's certain that few people paid more for the ephemeral honor of sitting next to the powerful emperor.

For Bradukios, power turned out to be a subtle perfume that wafted over him for the length of a single banquet dinner. For Hypatius, power had been the mirage of one single Sunday in the Hippodrome. For John the Cappadocian, power was the dream of his whole career. For Theodora, power was a discipline that she honed every day for twenty years as Augusta (527–48). But in the summer of 547 she began to live daily with another, equally solemn, kind of discipline: the discipline of pain, which she endured and dutifully disguised.

This pain was among the first symptoms of her fatal illness; she may have had a tumor, but the terminology is imprecise in the only source that mentions it—and the source is a hostile one. She never got a chance to grow old in her world, the world that she was helping to transform. She weakened over the course of the year, and on June 28, 548, Theodora died. Chroniclers report that her death was attended by earthquakes, thunder, and lightning bolts, together with the "universal inauspicious omen," the shattering of a column.[6]

In that final year, she let no word of her sickness get out to the public. Perhaps she recognized it not as a calamity but as a sign. Perhaps the Almighty had come to collect on the vow she had made in 542, sacrificing her own life in exchange for Justinian's recovery (and for the continuity of his power). Authority and power had to be maintained, and so physicians and chamber servants were sworn to silence. Of course, Monophysites came more often to her bedside in the women's quarters. Among other things, they brought her updates on the latest developments: the successes of Jacob Baradeus in the East and Pope Vigilius's yielding in his *Iudicatum*, which seemed to open up favorable possibilities.

Theodora died in the comfort of the sacraments and according to the rites of the one Church, the Catholic and Orthodox Church of Vigilius and of the Dyophysite patriarch Menas. There was no contradiction, because Theodora, insofar as she was empress of the new Rome, certainly did not and could not follow deviant, ethnic beliefs. She wanted to remain in communion with the "One Holy Catholic and Apostolic" Church that was celebrated in all professions of faith and in the oath of the magistrates. It was the same Church that Justinian had built up with so many laws, the Church that, liberally interpreted, could and should have accepted Theodora's favorite holy men, the deceased (Timothy of Alexandria and Severus of Antioch) and the living (Patriarch Theodosius, confined to his villa outside the city; Jacob, who wandered the Near Eastern and Middle Eastern deserts; and Anthimus, who was to see the light of day again only after long years spent in the recesses of the palace).

No one felt so abandoned and grief-stricken as Justinian. Theodora's illness and death deprived him of the only person he had ever loved. And in addition to this private, personal suffering, he was now burdened with the problems that Theodora had handled with such superior skill for so many years; suddenly they fell on the shoulders of the sixty-five-year-old Justinian.

Just as when disease had struck Justinian in 542, the long course of Theodora's illness gave the couple time to exchange information about managing their estate, the problem of the Monophysites and the East, and their family strategies. It is most unlikely that the imperial couple discussed whether it would be appropriate for another woman to be at Justinian's side; neither one mentioned Lady Anastasia, who, years before, had allegedly been driven by Theodora's jealousy to seek refuge in an Egyptian convent. One hagiographer of Anastasia tells us that the widowed emperor searched for her but failed to find her. Anastasia hid her identity and remained faithful to her religious seclusion, never returning to the court where she had briefly shone like a bright meteor.[7] She never fully realized her destiny in the secular world, as Theodora did.

On the day of her death, the Augusta may have recognized the moment her life slipped away; but if so, she probably didn't grab someone's hand for comfort, and try to stave off death. She had said it already, sixteen years earlier, in her Nika speech: it is impossible for someone who has seen the light of this world not to die. She did not rebuke life because it was leaving her. Rather, she trusted that she was leaving something of herself to life, for Justinian was surviving her; the prestige of the purple had not been diminished; her power had not been separated from his; her protégés would continue to receive support even in the most remote lands of the empire;[8] and her family could look forward to bright prospects and high ambitions.

She shut her eyes on an infinitely greater stage than the one she saw when her father, Acacius the bear keeper in the arena, had died. She perceived that her next stage would be even vaster once the bars that kept her inside were lifted, once the gates of the Hippodrome chute were flung open so she could race forward, once the gilded ceilings that still shielded her became the domes that imitate Heaven with their gentle curve, once everything opened up to a single, everlasting, brilliant light.

Epilogue

66 THEODORA! Theodora! Theodora! The Lord of Lords cal-
leth thee!" repeated the chanters in the official funeral rite.
Amid the smoke of the incense, candlelight flickered over
the multitude of subjects, functionaries, and courtiers who had so
feared her, and the one man who had loved her. The words had a special meaning, because Theodora had aspired to a place among the
lords and ladies, and Justinian had worked to expand the range of her
domain.

The corpse with the funeral accoutrements of the deceased lady
(who had long prevented other women from using the title of "lady")
was finally lowered by devout hands into the waiting sarcophagus.
The great chest was made of the prized marble (referred to as "golden"
or "rosy alabaster") from Hierapolis (now Pamukkale, Turkey). The sarcophagus was placed in the imperial mausoleum of the Holy Apostles
that she had so treasured; the building was completed and consecrated on the second anniversary of her death, June 28, 550.

Justinian often returned to the church of the Holy Apostles to pray
intensely. His visit on August 11, 559, had special significance, for he
recited prayers and lit candles on Theodora's tomb that day after having repelled an attack near Constantinople by the Kutrigur Huns. It
was the first and only battle he himself directed during his long reign.
He was seventy-seven years old, and his consort had become a holy
relic; her very name was a magic spell,[1] and she was invoked and
thanked after any lucky military or civilian event. (Although the term

civilian did not mean what it means to us today.) Though now out of sight, Theodora's body—once the object of so much desire, controversy, and inquiry—was still quite present: it became a vessel for collective salvation rather than individual, personal fulfillment. This was a medieval approach, which is all the more significant for having appeared during the reign of Justinian, the last emperor of antiquity. This great change can be seen as yet another metamorphosis of Theodora's.

So Justinian was projected into the Middle Ages by the cult of Theodora, and bound to sacred Judeo-Christian history by his cherished model Solomon; but he had not lost touch with the older Roman imperial tradition. He had always cherished the memory of Julius Caesar, and when in 552 he annexed the southern part of the Iberian peninsula the Augustus felt even closer to his ancient paragon. The annexation marked the greatest expansion that the Christian empire was to have in its thousand years of existence.

In the same year, Narses the eunuch (who was older than seventy) and John, Vitalian's nephew, took the "Roman" troops into battle in Italy. The army finally had adequate resources, and it dealt a fatal blow to the Gothic resistance: the indomitable, "immortal" Totila perished. In 553 the leader of the last Gothic effort, the bellicose Teia, also died. And although Procopius admired their valor and paid them homage in his *Wars*, in 554 Justinian published the *Pragmatic Sanction*, in which he equated Totila with a tyrant and abolished all the laws that the Goth had instituted for Italy's social renewal. He then placed the Italian peninsula under the supervision of the local landed aristocracy and the clergy.

The second Rome had won its war against the Goths and reannexed the first Rome. But it had won *to the detriment of Italy*: the war had lasted eighteen years (with a lull during the plague) and had led to a dramatic deterioration of urban and civilian life. Sources likened the Italy of those years to a desert. In the words of Procopius, "Italy . . . [had] become everywhere even more destitute of men than

Libya," it was a such a "wilderness"[2] that an epigram commissioned by the "most glorious" Narses in 565 rings particularly false and sinister. Almost ninety years old by this time, Narses was celebrating the restoration of a bridge near Rome, in the "thirty-ninth year of the empire of the most pious and always triumphant our Lord Justinian, father of our Fatherland, the August." The elegiac couplets of the epigraph contain the following exhortation:

> Go agreeably to your pleasures, O Quirites [Roman citizens]
> and let resounding applause cheer the name of Narses,
> everywhere.[3]

But how many Roman citizens were left? What pleasures were to be had, and what was there to cheer about, when the second Rome had destroyed the first Rome under the pretext of defending it?

The fruits of victory—of the extraordinary patience that characterized the second phase of Justinian's rule—would prove bitter and disappointing. Justinian died in 565 (the year of Narses' epigram), and as early as 568 the Longobards left their lands in Pannonia (a Roman province roughly corresponding to Hungary) to cross the Julian Alps and enter the Italian peninsula. Over time, Italy's territory came to be fragmented, permitting the eventual rise of the papal state, an unequalled union of Rome and Ravenna, of the Church and temporal power. The heritage of Byzantium in southern Italy would endure for centuries, but the same cannot be said of Justinian's conquest of the Iberian peninsula. And at the opposite frontier of the empire, in the northeast, the Danube was to be crossed often by Slavic people who would change many aspects of the Balkans, from geographic boundaries to governmental administration to the ethnic makeup of its inhabitants.

In Africa, Egypt, and the Near East, the issues of "national" and religious identity—the issues that Theodora had been able to keep under control for so many years—would continue to be explosive. In the course of a few generations there was to be a frontal clash with Persia, and then the area would be invaded by Islamic Arabs. The living space of the Christian empire of Constantinople would shrink, and its center would shift to the Balkans and to Anatolia; ultimately the Greek language would prevail over Latin. Only then—in the middle of the seventh century—could one properly refer to it as the Byzantine empire.

So Justinian turned out to be unable to use his armies to reach his lifelong goal of lasting geopolitical and religious unity in the Mediterranean. The strength of the second Rome in his lifetime lay elsewhere: in his immense juridical opus, in the quality of his arts and architecture, and in the introduction of silkworm cultivation to the Mediterranean basin. (The silk industry was the work of enterprising monks who in 552 succeeded in importing the eggs from Sogdiana—now Uzbekistan and Tajikistan—to Constantinople, bypassing the Persian monopoly.)

Finally, then, Justinian's achievement was not so much a restoration of antiquity as a realization of the new: he established a sophisticated, opulent paradigm that was already medieval and Byzantine.

From a historical perspective, these developments would not have been possible without the Nika resistance—without Theodora. But the Augusta, with her background in the theater, had left much more to the throne and to the future style of medieval Byzantium: above all, she bequeathed the use of Christian preaching for political purposes. As late as the mid-Byzantine period, the Slavic peoples were evangelized by two brothers, Constantine-Cyril and Methodius; this push, now considered to be one of the major elements in the Christianization of Europe, was the continuation of a plan launched in the sixth century. It emulated the evangelical work of the Monophysites John of Tella in Bithynia, John of Amida in Caria and Phrygia, Jacob Baradeus throughout the Near East, and Julian in remote African Nubia. Nubia had been drawn into the second Rome through a sleight of hand by Monophysite missionaries—Theodora had played on a parallel Dyophysite mission to achieve her aim.

On two continents—Asia and Africa—Theodora had promoted versions of Christianity that endured in part because the local churches were solicitous of their specific environments and their peoples' needs.

Her constant attention to the human element was the perfect corrective to the theorizing that characterized Justinian's thinking—theorizing that twisted and undid what he intended to do, and sometimes backfired completely.

A letter by Gregory the Great, Roman pope from 590 to 603, speaks of an otherwise unknown excommunication of Theodora by Pope Vigilius;[4] but the Sixth Ecumenical Council, held in Constantinople in 680–81, spoke of her "most devout memory." That council proclaimed that Christ had a double will and a double energy: this was as far from Monophysitism as it was possible to be. Nor was this the only paradox or mystery of the Christian faith, of the story of this empire, or of the psychology of these people: without Theodora in the last years of his life, Justinian moved further away from his original Dyophysitism and turned decisively toward an extreme version of Monophysitism. He warmed to Aphthartodocetism (from the Greek *aphthartos*, "incorruptible"), a heretical doctrine possibly inspired by ancient Gnosticism, according to which the earthly body of Jesus Christ was divine and therefore naturally incorruptible: it was nothing but an illusion. This was just what Julian of Halicarnassus had taught. Julian was an adversary of Severus and the historical leader of those "visionaries" that Justinian and Theodora had ordered expelled by force from Alexandria in 535.

Whatever his reasons, the emperor issued an edict on the subject (perhaps in 564), but instead of reestablishing unity it ignited more controversy. In the past, his forays into the field of theology had moved at the same pace as his concrete political, legislative, and administrative activity. Now the equation between Roman and Christian had become increasingly problematic, for the former term referred to civilian matters that he no longer took into consideration, while the latter brought confrontation and strife instead of unity.

Theodora's originality and passion, and her protean skill in self-transformation, made her the last woman of antiquity. The new Aphthartodocetism insisted on the incorruptibility of God made man, whereas earlier Christian orientations had stressed the persistence of human nature, celebrating it and sublimating it in myth and above all in art, and one of the most celebrated people of the time had been Theodora. For this reason we might even call her archaic—a final echo of Medea, Dido, and Antigone. She rose from the depths and she ultimately became a legend, but not because she was revered by the Monophysite historians who wrote in Syriac or because she was briefly mentioned in Procopius's *Wars* and *Buildings*. Her modern fame was inspired by the rhetoric of vituperation that pervades the *Secret History*, and by the visual arts (which had been important to her even at an early age).

Her miraculously enduring fame and her metamorphosis was ensured by the celebrated mosaic in the presbytery of the basilica of San Vitale in Ravenna, one of the most extraordinary and most controversial representations of imperial splendor and womanly power ever produced.

On the wall to the left of the altar is a vigorous but not friendly interpretation of the theme of "Church and empire" [fig. 2]. Justinian is surrounded by prelates (including Maximianus, bishop of Ravenna) and military officers, including one who may be Belisarius and another whom recent studies identify as Anastasius, Theodora's grandson. On the opposite wall, to the right of the altar, is Theodora [fig. 1]. She advances majestically toward the onlooker, flanked by two courtiers (probably eunuchs) on her right and on her left a cortège of seven ladies, whom scholars have tried to identify as Antonina and her daughter Joannina (Anastasius's beloved) and other specific women. The enigma of those faces is seductive enough, and then the artist undeniably used all sorts of techniques (in both draftsmanship and composition) to stress and exalt the dignity of the empress.

Theodora is at the center of the mosaic, her crowned head surrounded by the halo of the elect; her figure is inscribed within a niche that probably holds a throne. The image includes every single attribute of sovereignty and of the pomp of Constantinople's court: Theodora wears the purple chlamys and the imperial *maniakon* (a bejeweled collar), and *praependulia* ornaments dangle from her crown. She bears a precious chalice, which she is offering to the basilica of San Vitale. The artist stressed that the very construction of the church was also a sign of imperial munificence. The concept of the offering—more subtly, an offering from the East—is strengthened by a detail of Theodora's robe: embroidery on the lower hem of her chlamys represents the three Magi from the East bearing gifts for the Savior. The Augusta's gesture is as elegant as it is laconic, and her huge eyes (under the knitted brow that Procopius remarked on) gaze off into the distance, beyond the onlookers. Her presence is both oneiric and hieratic: dreamlike and formally stylized.

Theodora never visited Ravenna; it doesn't appear that she ever intended to. But those who see the empress as a blind champion of the Eastern Monophysite cause should consider that she was pictured with unequalled splendor in the basilica of the political and administrative capital of the West. The most important thing about her was that she was the Augusta. She sympathized with the Monophysites in the East, but she clung tightly to her purple as if it were an altar of asylum—she was enfolded by it as if it were a shroud.

When the sponsors of the Ravenna basilica mosaics asked Constantinople for models or sketches of the imperial couple, Justinian and Theodora must have posed in the positions that we see today in San Vitale. Thus the mosaic is a snapshot of the Augusta and her court in the palace of Constantinople around 545 or 546, when the artwork was commissioned. The commission may have come from Belisarius, chief commander of the army in Italy at the time. The general and Antonina may have wanted to stress their closeness to the emperor and empress, a closeness that Joannina's marriage to Anastasius would have reinforced. If that is the case, the mosaic expresses a project that did not materialize—one of the many paradoxes of history.[5]

Others have suggested that the portrait in Ravenna depicts Theodora's otherworldly destiny. Her unusual pallor, which the literary sources also stressed, has been interpreted as an allusion to her being already deceased when the colored tesserae were set on the wall. The water of the fountain to her right has been interpreted as the "water of life" for baptismal regeneration in the afterlife. The niche above Theodora could be a distinctive sign that denotes the presence of a deceased person. And the curtain pulled aside by a eunuch in one corner of the mosaic gives a glimpse of a dark room and has been read as the curtain that rises in the final moment of life, disclosing the world beyond. In early Christian iconography, furthermore, eunuchs and angels often had similar features, so the eunuch opening the curtain supports an otherworldly interpretation.

Yet what the artist who made the sketch in Constantinople actually *saw* was simply a procession in the palace, led by the Augusta who was offering a gift. The cortège advances from the observer's right, and the eunuch pulls aside the curtain to allow Theodora to pass freely to another hall. The palace had many fountains: they were among the rulers' main delights. For the artist, the eunuch's gesture and the jets of water were lively, exquisite details that were simply realistic.

The artist who worked on the mosaics in San Vitale was not the same artist who drew the sketch. He infused the mosaics with a spirit that makes him "one of the great artists of the first Christian millennium," and the mosaic is filled with apocalyptic elements. It is a cosmic recapitulation of sacred history interpreted as a unitary flow that leads to the lamb of salvation.[6] He gave the realistic palace scene a tint of prophecy that was certainly specific to *his* art. Such a prophetic quality would also be typical of the so-called figural method of the poetry of Dante Alighieri (who was to die in Ravenna in 1321). It is almost as if the artist had been physiologically predestined to spiritualize the "real" image, independent of whether he knew about the empress's illness and later her death.

✠ ✠ ✠

Careful observation of the ritual procession in the Ravenna basilica (our closing recessional that takes us out of this story) reveals that it has all the elements typical of a stage. The eunuch who raises the curtain can be seen, metaphorically, as the man who closes the curtain on the mime actress who became a lady and an empress.

So, *exit Theodora*.

She made an offering—a splendid chalice—in the temple of a capital that she never visited; and here she also played her last, secret performance: in that temple, she underwent her final metamorphosis and became a sacred icon.

Notes

Introduction

1. Since the times of the Greek historian Herodotus of Halicarnassus (c. 485–425 B.C.), ancient historiography has insisted on the importance of "direct vision" (*autopsia* in Greek; see Glossary), seeing for oneself, being an eyewitness to events.
2. Procopius, *The Anecdota or Secret History*, trans. H. B. Dewing (London and Cambridge, Mass.: Loeb Classical Library, 1935).
3. The earliest reference to the text is found in a Byzantine encyclopedia of the tenth century, which uses the Greek term *Anekdota* (literally, "unpublished items"); this continued to be the prevalent term in philological and specialist literature. But most translations into modern languages lean instead toward the concept of a "secret history."
4. It is the *psogos* ("blame" in Greek) genre, a critical deformation of "reality," antithetical to the encomiastic genre (from the Greek *enkômion*, "praise").
5. *Secret History* 1.10; 10.1–3.
6. We are applying the terminology used by Hans-Georg Beck in his memorable *Kaiserin Theodora und Prokop: Der Historiker und sein Opfer* (Empress Theodora and Procopius: The Historian and His Victim) (Munich: Piper, 1986).
7. *Secret History* 10.1.
8. With the sole exception of Ammianus Marcellinus (c. A.D. 330–400).
9. *Paideia* in Greek (see Glossary).
10. Procopius, *History of the Wars*, 6 vols., trans. H. B. Dewing (London and New York: Loeb Classical Library, 1914–28), I, 24.33.

ONE: "Keeper of the Bears"

1. *Secret History* 9.2.
2. *Canti di Pianto e d'amore dall'antico Salento* (Songs of Love and Woe from Ancient Salento), ed. B. Montinaro (Milan: Bompiani, 1994), p. 45.

3. *The Life of St. Andrew the Fool,* ed. L. Rydén (Uppsala: Almgrist & Wiksell, 1995), vol. II, 204 (l. 2954 foll.); cf. *I Santi Folli di Bisanzio* (The Holy Fools of Byzantium), Italian trans. (Milan: Mondadori, 1990), p. 204.
4. As in the salvation acronym *ichthys* ("fish"), *Iêsous Christos Theou Hyos. Sôtêr, Sybilline Oracles* 8.217.
5. Plato, *Phaedo* 109b.
6. For Constantinople as the "new Jerusalem" and "second Rome," see Gilbert Dagron, *Naissance d'une capitale. Constantinople et ses institutions de 333 à 451* (Paris: PUF, 1974).
7. *Life of St. Andrew*, op. cit., II, p. 260 (l. 3820 foll.); cf. *I Santi Folli*, op. cit., p. 237.
8. Seneca, *Moral Letters* III, 2.4. What Romans called *res severa*, "the weighty matter" of life. See Glossary.
9. Palladius, *Dialogus de vita S. Joannis Chrysostomi*, 5 (Migne, *Patrologia Graeca*, vol. XLVII, col. 20).
10. For sources, see F. Halkin, *Bibliotheca Hagiographica Graeca*, II (Brussels, 1957), p. 1743.
11. *Secret History* 9.4.
12. See, for example, St. John Chrysostom, *In Matthaeum Homilia* VI (Migne, *Patrologia Graeca*, vol. LVII, col. 71 foll.), XXXVII (ibid., col. 427).
13. *The Greek Anthology*, trans. W. R. Paton (Cambridge, Mass.: Loeb Classical Library, 1916–18; reprint 1993–98), XV 47.

TWO: **"He Removed These Persons from That Office. . . . They Conferred This Position . . . upon Them"**

1. The *curia* in Latin (see Glossary).
2. For this purpose see Theophylactus Simocatta; *Historiae* IV 11.2 foll. (p. 169, 19 foll. De Boor-Wirth).
3. Gregory of Nyssa, *De deitate Filii et Spiritus Sancti* (Migne, *Patrologia Graeca*, vol. XLVI, col. 557).
4. The emperor's absolute power was expressed by the Greek word *autokratôr* (see Glossary).
5. Cf., for example, Eustathios of Thessalonica, *Oratio* III, p. 49, 18 Regel.
6. *Deuteronomy* 32.10; *Psalms* 16(17).8.
7. Cf. *Secret History* 14.14. Also Pollux, *Onomasticon* IX 110; Suvetonius, *Nero* 35.9.
8. *Acts of the Apostles* 22.25–27.
9. *Secret History* 9.5.
10. Ibid.
11. Ibid. 7.4.
12. Homer, *The Odyssey* XIX 547, passim. Homer made a distinction between *onar* (a mere dream) and *hypar* (a nocturnal vision foreshadowing

a reality that later comes true). The notion of these two different types was still current in the Byzantine world.

13. *Matthew* 20.23.

14. Late antiquity disdained the special arrogance of the powerful, which was identified by the Greek term *hybris* (see Glossary). For *hubris*, see Glossary.

15. *Secret History* 9.7.

16. *Matthew* 7.7; *Luke* 11.9.

17. In Greek, *metabolê* (see Glossary).

18. *Métal du coeur*, as in Proust's *Jean Santeuil*.

19. *Secret History* 30.26.

THREE: **"As Each One Seemed to Her to Be Ripe for This Calling"**

1. See Glossary (*curia, curialis*).

2. Proclus, *Comment to Plato's Alcibiades*, 248C Creuzer.

3. *Greek Anthology* XVI 283.1 (Leontius Scholasticus): "Rhodoclea is the tenth Muse and fourth Grace."

4. Homer, *The Odyssey* XII 246.

5. *Secret History* 9.8.

6. Ibid.

7. Ibid. 9.9. Here I depart from Dewing's Loeb Classical Library translation (otherwise used throughout, for the convenience of my readers); the Greek text has "slave boy," but Dewing translated it as "slave girl" in 1935.

8. Cassiodorus, *Variae* IV 51.

9. Coricius, *Apologia Mimorum* I (p. 345, 8 foll. Foerster).

10. *Greek Anthology* XVI 283.3 foll. (Leontius Scholasticus).

11. Ibid. V 250 (Paulus Silentiarius).

12. Ibid. V 258 (Paulus Silentiarius).

13. St. John Chrysostom, *De Lazaro*, II (Migne, *Patrologia Graeca*, vol. XLVIII, col. 986); VI (ibid., col. 1034 foll.).

14. Legend has it that Plato died with his head lying on a mime text by Sophron of Syracuse (fifth century B.C.).

15. M. Bonaria, in *Dizionario degli scrittori greci e latini* (Dictionary of Greek and Latin Authors), vol. II, ed. F. Della Corte (Settimo Milanese: Marzorati, 1987), under entry "Mimografi" (Mimes), p. 1363.

16. Aristophanes, *Clouds* 2.

17. *Secret History* 9.10.

18. See H.-G. Beck, op. cit., and note supra, in introduction.

19. Cf. Saint Augustine, *De Ordine* II, 4.12 (Migne, *Patrologia Latina*, vol. XXXII, col. 1000).

20. For *vir romanus*, see Glossary.

21. For the other-/inner-directed opposition as applied to Byzantine art by

Ernst Kitzinger especially, see David Riesman, Nathan Glazer, and Reuel Denney, *The Lonely Crowd* (New Haven, Conn.: Yale University Press, 1950).

FOUR: **"She Immediately Became Admired for This Sort of Thing"**

1. *Secret History* 9.10.
2. Ibid. 9.9.
3. See F. Bornmann, "Su alcuni passi di Procopio" (On Selected Procopius Passages), *Studi Italiani di Filologia Classica* (N.S. 50, 1978), p. 34.
4. *Secret History* 9.13 foll.
5. H.-G. Beck, op. cit. Beck has brought out some affinities between Eva Perón's career and that of Theodora.
6. Gabriele D'Annunzio, *La nave* (The Ship) (Rome, 1943), p. 121.
7. *Secret History* 9.15 foll.
8. See Maria Bellonci, *Lucrezia Borgia: La sua vita e i suoi tempi* (The Life and Times of Lucrezia Borgia) (Milan, 1940), p. 171.
9. *Daimon* in Greek (see Glossary).
10. *Secret History* 9.17.
11. Ibid. 9.26.
12. *Thymos* in Greek, the soul's emotional function, the "seat of joy, of pleasure, of love, of compassion, of anger." See Bruno Snell, *The Discovery of the Mind*, trans. T. G. Rosenmeyer (Cambridge, Mass.: Harvard University Press, 1953).
13. *Secret History* 9.17.
14. Ibid. 9.25.
15. Ibid. 9.24.

FIVE: **"Contriver of Shameless Deeds Above All Others"**

1. I am indebted to Andrea Ferrari for the *Anna Christie* quotation.
2. *Secret History* 9.18.
3. *Auxêsis* in Greek.
4. See F. Bornmann, op. cit., p. 32.
5. Edward Gibbon, *The Decline and Fall of the Roman Empire*, vol. 4 (London: Methuen, 1909), chap. 40, p. 228, n. 26.
6. Baronio, *Annales ecclesiastici*, anno 535, LXIII. The "names given to the Furies in Hell" were Alecto, Megaera, and Tisiphone: this is a remarkable anachronistic use of pagan netherworld mythology in a Catholic Counter-Reformation tract.
7. *Secret History* 9.15
8. Ibid. 10.11.
9. See Fernanda de' Maffei, "La mimesi dal tardoantico al bizantino nei ritratti imperiali" (Mimesis from Late Antiquity to the Byzantine Period in Imperial Portraits), in *La mimesi bizantina* (Byzantine Mimesis), ed. F. Conca and R. Maisano (Naples, 1998), pp. 81–84.

10. *Secret History* 15.8.
11. Ibid. 9.20–23.
12. F. Bornmann, op. cit., p. 31.
13. *Secret History* 10.3; 9.19.
14. Ibid. 17.16–18.
15. Ibid. 17.21.
16. Ibid. 5.9.
17. It's Saint Thomaides of Lesbos (tenth century). See *Acta Sanctorum, Novembris*, IV, ed. by H. Delehaye and P. Peeters (Brussels, 1925), p. 235 E.
18. Alice-Mary Talbot, "La donna" (Woman), in *L'uomo bizantino* (Byzantine Man), ed. G. Cavallo (Rome and Bari: Laterza, 1992), p. 180.

SIX: **"She Was at a Loss for the Necessities of Life"**

1. Joseph Conrad, *The Shadow Line* I.
2. *Secret History* 9.27.
3. *Hecebolus* is from the Greek *Hekebolos*, maybe derived from *hekôn ballein*, "to reach one's goal," or perhaps from *hekas ballein*, "to throw (an arrow) at a great distance." In either case, the two destinies prophesied in his name came true, for he obtained the beautiful Theodora and he went far away, to remote Pentapolis, on the Mediterranean shores of Africa.
4. See Herocles, *Synekdemos*, V.631.3 (935 city); see Cyril Mango, *Byzantium: The Empire of New Rome* (London: Weidenfeld and Nicolson, 1980).
5. The *dux* (see Glossary), *Lybiae Pentapoleos*.
6. S. Ellis, "The 'Palace of the Dux' at Apollonia, and Related Houses," in *Cyrenaica in Antiquity*, ed. G. Barker, J. Lloyd, and J. Reynolds (Oxford: B.A.R. International Series, 1985), pp. 15–25.
7. *Parrhêsia* in Greek (see Glossary).
8. *Secret History* 12.30.
9. Theodora's peregrinations through the Levant from Pentapolis to Constantinople can also be read as a late-antiquity, Christianized, female version of the ancient returning-home narratives (*nostoi*) of the Homeric heroes of Troy, which loomed so large in the collective imagination of antiquity and late antiquity.
10. Immortalized in a short story by Arno Schmidt in *Kosmas, oder vom Berg des Nordens* (Krefeld: Agis, 1955). He may have reached the Indies, and for that reason was called "Indicopleustes."
11. See supra, introduction, note 1 (*autopsia*) and Glossary.
12. As in the earliest Greek etymology of the verb forms *eidon* ("I saw") and *oida* ("I have seen," therefore "I know").
13. *Secret History* 9.27 foll. Here again I depart from Dewing's Loeb Classical Library translation: the Greek text allows interpretation as "the devil" or as "Heaven" (Dewing's choice).

SEVEN: **"The Pious . . . the Saintly . . . the Devout"**

1. Authors such as Zacharias Scholasticus; John of Amida, bishop of Ephesus in the sixth century; and Michael the Syrian, patriarch of Antioch in the twelfth century.
2. A very clear statement of Saint Cyril of Alexandria's belief about the resolution of two natures into one in the Incarnated Word is in *Epist. XL, Ad Acacium Melitinae* (Migne, *Patrologia Graeca*, vol. LXXVII, coll. 192 foll.).
3. *Gospel according to Matthew* 19.6.
4. Copt (see Glossary).
5. *Secret History* 12.28.
6. Ibid. 12.30.
7. Baronio, op. cit.

EIGHT: **"I, Consul"**

1. *Secret History* 12.28.
2. Ibid. 12.27. Dewing's translation says he was "passionately devoted to the joys of Aphrodite," but the Greek text allows my interpretation.
3. Ibid. 12.18 foll.
4. George Ostrogorsky, *History of the Byzantine State* (New Brunswick, NJ: Rutgers University Press, 1969).
5. *Secret History* 12.24–26.
6. Ibid. 12.20–22.
7. Ibid. 12.23.
8. *Testamentum Salomonis* 9.
9. *Secret History* 12.14; cf. Homer, *The Iliad* V 31.
10. *Secret History* 30.34.
11. *Wars* I 17.37.
12. *Secret History* 12.29.
13. *Secret History* 12.30.
14. Ibid.
15. Ibid. 12.31 foll.
16. If, as we think, this happened in the year A.D. 521, the message was probably dated 570, since it was the custom in Antioch to consider that year 1 was our B.C. 49, the date of Julius Caesar's victory at Pharsalus. (In reality, the battle took place in 48 B.C.)
17. *Secret History* 27.6.
18. Ibid. 8.12.
19. Or *excubitor*; see Glossary.
20. Ibid. 6.9.
21. See Constantine VII Porphyrogenitus (tenth century), *De Cerimoniis Aulae Byzantinae*, I, pp. 429 foll. Reiske.

22. Robert Browning, *Justinian and Theodora* (London: Weidenfeld and Nicolson, 1971), p. 39.

23. *Secret History* 6.27.

24. Ibid.

25. Ibid. 6.20.

26. See *Novella* 30.11 (*usque ad utriusque oceani fines*).

27. Dante Alighieri, *Paradiso* VI 10.

28. A church was later built on the "foundations of Theodora's house": the church of Saint Panteleëmon ("the All Merciful").

29. On this issue see Raymond Janin, *La géographie ecclésiastique de l'empire byzantin, I, Le siège de Constantinople et le patriarcat oecuménique, III, Les églises et les monastères* (The Ecclesiastical Geography of the Byzantine Empire, I, The See of Constantinople and the Ecumenical Patriarchate, III, The Churches and the Monasteries) (Paris: Publications de l'Institut Francais d'études Byzantines, 1969), 387 foll.

30. *Isaiah* 34.4; *Apocalypse* 6.14.

31. *Song of Songs* (King James version) 1.2–4.

32. Ibid.

NINE: **"They Received Imperial Power"**

1. The reference to Pietro Aretino (see also above, p. 21) is not only to his notorious 1534–36 work, which is called "Playful and Pleasing Conversations"; in him, as in Procopius, we find different literary veins that are sometimes at variance with each other, but nonetheless all "authentic."

2. *Secret History* 9.30; *Wars* I 25.4.

3. *Secret History* 9.15.

4. Homer, *The Odyssey* XVII 218, now a proverb.

5. *Secret History* 9.32.

6. Marcus Aurelius, *Meditations*, XI 12.

7. Philostratus, *Lives of the Sophists* 561 (p. 68.30 foll. Kayser).

8. Ammianus Marcellinus, *Rerum gestarum libri* XVI 10.10.

9. Horace, *Odes* III 30.1.

10. *Secret History* 4.44 foll.; *Wars* VIII 12.34.

11. *Secret History* 9.51.

12. Ibid. 10.2 foll.

13. The Roman poet Tibullus captured the feeling in an elegy: "Quisquis amore tenetur, eat tutusque sacerque / Qualibet, insidias non timuisse decet ("He who is a slave of love can walk as assuredly as a god, / Go everywhere, and have nothing to fear"). *Tibullus* I 2.29 foll.

14. *Secret History* 9.33.

15. Ibid. 7.9 foll.

16. Ibid. 7.15.

17. Ibid. 7.23.

18. Ibid. 17.35.
19. Ernst Kitzinger, *Byzantine Art in the Making: Main Lines of Stylistic Development in Mediterranean Art, 3rd–7th Century* (Cambridge, Mass.: Harvard University Press, 1977).
20. See the life of Saint Samson Hospitaler in *Acta Sanctorum, Iunii,* V (Antwerp, 1709), pp. 267, line 5 foll.
21. *Secret History* 10.13.
22. It is, therefore, unlikely that their private conversations as lovers, later as husband and wife, and finally as emperor and empress, were as long and elaborate as Harold Lamb imagined them in his psychological portrait *Theodora and the Emperor* (Garden City, N.Y.: Doubleday, 1952).
23. *Novella* 30 (536), pref.
24. Browning, op. cit., p. 69.
25. Giorgio Ravegnani, *La corte di Giustiniano* (Justinian's Court) (Rome: Jouvence, 1989), p. 48.
26. *Secret History* 9.53. Dewing read the Greek as "They took over the Roman Empire," but I read it as "received."

TEN: **"Harmonious Movement"**

1. Constantine VII Porphyrogenitus, op. cit., I, proem (p. 5 Reiske).
2. *Secret History* 7.7.
3. Ibid. 19.1–3.
4. See *The Oxford Dictionary of Byzantium*, ed. A. P. Kazhdan et al. (New York and Oxford: Oxford University Press, 1991), vol. I, p. 364 foll., under entry "Caesaropapism"; Gilbert Dagron, *Empereur et prêtre: Étude sur le "césaropapism" byzantin* (Emperor and Priest: Study on Byzantine "Caesaropapism") (Paris: Gallimard, 1996).
5. "De haereticis et Manichaeis et Samaritis," in *Codex Justinianus* I 5.12.
6. Ibid. I 5 12.3.
7. *Secret History* 11.23.
8. Ibid.
9. *Codex Justinianus* I 27 1.1.
10. *Secret History* 11.29.
11. See Averil Cameron, "The Last Days of the Academy at Athens," *Proceedings of the Cambridge Philological Society*, 195, New Series 15 (1969): 7–30.
12. Mango, op. cit., chapter 4.
13. *Collectio Avellana* 125, 11.
14. Theodoric died plagued with nightmares that have become legendary in literature. See *Wars* V 1.35 foll.
15. *Secret History* 15.25–35.
16. *Wars* II 3.26.
17. Ibid. III 11.21. He was described as coming from a sort of Balkan "Germany," halfway between "Thrace and Illyricum."

18. *Secret History* 1.11.
19. Ibid. 1.12.
20. Ibid. 1.19 foll.
21. Ibid. 1.13.
22. *Wars* V 3.30.
23. *Secret History* 16.5.
24. Ibid. 16.1–5.
25. Ibid. 30.21–6.
26. Cyril of Scythopolis, *Vita S. Sabae* 71 (pp. 173.28–174.12, ed. Schwartz).
27. John of Ephesus, *Lives of the Eastern Saints*, ed. E. W. Brooks, II, pp. 630 foll. (*Patrologia Orientalis* XVIII 4).
28. *Matthew* 27.54; *Mark* 15.39; *Luke* 23.47.

ELEVEN: "Royalty Is a Good Burial-Shroud"

1. *Secret History* 8.5
2. *Wars* I 24.16.
3. *Praefectus praetorio per Orientem* (see Glossary).
4. The *res publica* (see Glossary).
5. *Secret History* 30.11.
6. Ibid. 30.6; 30.11.
7. *Civis romani* (see Glossary entry for *cives romanus*).
8. Theophanes Confessor, *Chronographia,* p. 183.9 De Boor.
9. *Wars* I 24.6.
10. Ibid. I 24.3 foll.
11. Aristotle, *Politics* 1728 b 19 passim, now a proverb.
12. Cf. *Secret History* 8.3.
13. Epicurus, fr. 551 Usener, now a proverb.
14. Homer, *The Iliad* XXII 305.
15. *Wars* I 24.33–37.
16. *Apocalypse* 2.11 passim.
17. Isocrates, *Archidamus* 45. See on this matter B. Baldwin, "An Aphorism in Procopius," *Rheinisches Museum für Philologie*, 125 (1982): 309–11.
18. *Wars* I 24.58.
19. *Greek Anthology* VII 591.
20. Ibid. VII 592.
21. There was a tradition of women's *parrhêsia* in Byzantium after Theodora: her niece Sophia was a particularly good example. Another example, hundreds of years later, was a sophisticated historian who was "born to the purple," Anna Comnena.
22. *Magister militum* (see Glossary).

TWELVE: **"The Victories That Heaven Has Granted Us"**

1. Anthony the Hermit, the father of all monks, lived to the age of 105 (he died in A.D. 356) and was told by God when he was to die. *Life of Antony* 89.2.
2. *Psalms* 129(130).1.
3. *Secret History* 10.14. Even the famous passage from Evagrius, *History of the Church* IV 10, about the different theological views of the two rulers, does not attack the idea of a deep cooperation, for which reason the twelfth-century chronicler John Zonaras wrote of a paradoxical "double monarchy."
4. Ibid. 18.21. The passage calls it "a Scythian wilderness."
5. Winston Churchill; see Martin Gilbert, *Churchill: A Life*, (London: Heinemann, 1991), p. 33.
6. *Secret History* 3.21.
7. Ibid. 3.12.
8. Ibid. 16.18.
9. Ibid. 16.21.
10. *Codex Justinianius* VII 37.3 (Nov. 27, 531), *titl.*, where the text mentions a Peter, "vir inlustris, curator divinae domus serenissimae Augustae" ("an excellent man, administrator of the private treasury of the most serene Augusta"). See *domus divina* in Glossary. See also, for ex., *Novellae* 38, 5 (Pontus), XXIX, 4 (Paphlagonia), XXX, 6 (Cappadocia).
11. *Secret History* 2.35.
12. Gregory of Nazianzus, *Epithalamium ad Olympiadem*, vols. 23, 12, 40 (Migne, *Patrologia Graeca*, vol. XXXVII, cols. 1543–45).
13. Procopius, *Buildings* I 11.9.
14. Had Theodora been a literary person, to the prospect of a cure she might have added seductions such as those inspired by the famous poem of Catullus (No. 46) about spring in Bithynia, "Now spring brings back balmy warmth" ("Iam ver egelidos refert tepores"), trans. Francis Warre Cornish, in *Catullus, Tibullus, Pervigilium Veneris*, 2nd ed. (Cambridge, Mass.: Loeb Classical Library, 1995). Here I am not the first to follow Theophanes Confessor, p. 168.8 ff. De Boor instead of John Malalas, p. 368.49 ff. Thurn.
15. *Codex Justinianus* I 1 6.6.
16. *Wars* III 10.20.
17. *Secret History* 1.15
18. Ibid. 1.17.
19. *Imperator Caesar Flavius Justinianus Alamannicus Gothicus Francicus Germanicus Anticus Alanicus Vandalicus Africanus pius felix inclitus victor ac triumphator semper Augustus.*
20. *Institutiones*, proem 1.
21. *Digest, Tanta/Dedôken*, pref.
22. *Ecclesiastes* 1.2 passim.

23. *Wars* IV 9.11.
24. *Ecclesiastes*, 3.6.
25. Ibid. 2.9.
26. Ibid. 1.14.
27. Procopius's audience also caught several delightful literary allusions, including the famous passage in Polybius about Scipio Emilianus weeping over Carthage after he himself had set it ablaze in 146 B.C. See Polybius, *The Histories* XXXVIII 21–22 (22 = Appianus, *Punica* 132).
28. *Secret History* 1.18.

THIRTEEN: **"Our Most Pious Consort Given Us by God"**

1. *Wars* VII 31.14.
2. Dido in Virgil, *Aeneid* I 630.
3. *Digesto* XXIV 1 32.13 (Ulpianus).
4. John Malalas, *Chronographia* XVIII 214 (p. 368 Thurn).
5. *Buildings* I 9.6.
6. *Secret History* 17.36.
7. See Ibid. 17.24.
8. See in any case the important G. E. M. de Ste. Croix, *The Class Struggle in the Ancient Greek World, 2nd ed.* (London: Duckworth, 1983), where there is a curious mention of Theodora at p. 391 and p. 631 (n. 52). Marxism has always been more concerned with the dialectic between slaves and free men, and with mythologizing the Spartans and the Gracchi.
9. *Novella* 8, *Iusiurandum*.
10. Ibid. pref.
11. Ibid. 8.1.
12. *Corpus Inscriptionum Graecarum* IV 8639 (read *akteanôn* for *kteanôn*). I wish to mention here the essay by S. G. Mercati, "Sulla tradizione manoscritta dell'iscrizione nel fregio dei SS. Sergio e Bacco a Costantinopoli" (On the Handwriting Tradition of the Inscription in the Frieze of Sts. Sergius and Bacchus in Constantinople), *Rendiconti della Pontificia Accademia Romana di Archeologia* 3 (1925): 197–205.
13. *Secret History* 16.11. Dewing read the Greek as "maltreat," but I read it as "torture."
14. *Daimoniôs erôsa*, ibid.; *erastheisa ektopôs* (Antonina), ibid. 1.17; *êrasthê erôta exaision* (Justinian), ibid. 9.30.
15. Ferdinand Gregorovious, *Athenaïs. Geschichte einer byzantinischen kaiserin,* (Leipzig: F. A. Brockhaus, 1882).
16. See *The Chronicle of John, Bishop of Nikiu*, trans. by R.-H. Charles (London and Oxford, 1916), p. 144.
17. *Secret History* 16.1. Dewing read the Greek as "schemed to lie in wait for the woman even unto her death," but I read it as "schemed to lay a fatal trap for her."

18. Ibid. 9.26.
19. The *Life* of the "patrician" Anastasia can be read in *Propylaeum ad Acta Sanctorum Novembris, Synaxarium Ecclesiae Constantinopolitanae,* ed. H. Delehaye (Brussels, 1902), c. 565.8 foll.
20. *Liber Pontificalis* LVIII 3 (Agapitus).
21. *Matthew* 10:16.
22. John of Ephesus, op. cit., II, p. 677.
23. Ibid. I, pp. 26 foll. (*Patrologia Orientalis* XVII I).
24. *Secret History* 13.12.
25. *Liber Pontificalis* LX 6 (Silverius).

FOURTEEN: **"Inhuman cruelty"**

1. Cf. *Liber Pontificalis* LX 7 (Silverius).
2. Ibid. LX 8.
3. *Wars* I 25.13.
4. "Ex duabus naturis compositum unum," Liberatus, *Breviarium causae Nestorianorum et Eutychianorum* 22 (p. 138.8 Schwartz).
5. *Wars* VI 21.6.
6. Ibid. VI 22.15.
7. Ibid. I 26.3.
8. Ibid. II 14.1 foll.
9. Ibid. II 4.1 foll.
10. Ibid. VI 29.11.
11. Ibid. VI 29.34.
12. Ibid. VI 29.32.
13. *Buildings* I 10.17.
14. *Wars* III 13.12 foll.
15. Cf. *Sappho* 1.2.
16. *Wars* I 25.16.
17. Ibid. VI 4.20 foll.
18. Ibid. I 25.27.
19. *Secret History* 15.1.
20. Ibid. 15.5.
21. *Res publica* and *res privata* (see Glossary).
22. *Secret History* 3.2.
23. Ibid. 2.13.
24. Ibid. 2.11.
25. *Wars* II 19.36.
26. *Secret History* 2.21.
27. Ibid., 3.6.
28. Ibid. 3.2.
29. Ibid. 3.15–18.
30. Ibid. 3.26.

31. Ibid. 3.20.
32. *Liber Pontificalis* LXI 3 (Vigilius).

FIFTEEN: **"Solomon, I Have Conquered You!"**

1. John the Lydian, *De magistratibus populi romani* III 69 (p. 263.14 Bekker).
2. Cf. *Wars* IV 6.5–9.
3. Cf. Justinian's *Confessio rectae fidei* (Migne, *Patrologia Graeca*, vol. LXXXVI, col. 993).
4. Cf., for ex., Paul the Silentiary, *Descriptio Sanctae Sophiae* 56.
5. *Psalms* 145(146).3.
6. *Buildings* I 10.2.
7. Enrico Zanini, *Introduzione all'archeologia bizantina* (Introduction to Byzantine Archaeology) (Rome: Nuova Italia scientifica, 1994), p. 95.
8. Gibbon, op. cit., vol. 2.
9. *Buildings* I 11.9.
10. Ibid. I 2.5–12.
11. Following Malachi 3.20.
12. Cyril Mango, *Byzantine Architecture*, (London: Faber & Faber, 1986), p. 98.
13. Gregory of Tours, *Libri Miraculorum* I, *De gloria martyrum* 103 (Migne, *Patrologia Latina*, vol. LXXI, cols. 793–95).
14. See Robert Byron, *The Byzantine Achievement* (London: G. Routledge & Sons, 1929), where the comparison is more a confrontation, all in favor of Holy Wisdom.
15. *Kat'onar: Narratio de Sancta Sophia* 8 (p. 83.1 foll. Praeger).
16. *Buildings* I 1.46.
17. *Narratio de Sancta Sophia* 10 (pp. 86.19–24; 87.19–21; 88.4 foll. Praeger).
18. *Buildings* I 1.30.
19. *Narratio de Sancta Sophia* 26 (p. 102.10 foll. Praeger).
20. Cyril Mango, *Byzantium: The Empire of New Rome* (London: Weidenfeld and Nicolson, 1980), p. 262.
21. *Corpus Inscriptionum Graecarum* IV 8643.
22. *Narratio de Sancta Sophia* 27 (p. 105.4 foll. Praeger).
23. Cf. Aristotle, *Nicomachean Ethics* 1166a 31, now a proverb.
24. See Tursun Beg and Ibn Kemâl, "Storia del signore della conquista" (History of the Conquering Lord), in *La caduta di Costantinopoli* (The Fall of Constantinople), ed. A. Pertusi, vol. I. *Le testimonianze dei contemporanei* (Contemporary Witnesses) (Milan: Mondadori-Fondazione Lorenzo Valla, 1976), pp. 330, 466.
25. See Margherita Guarducci, *La più antica catechesi figurata: Il grande musaico della Basilica di Gasr Elbia in Cirenaica* (The Oldest Figured

Catechesis: The Great Mosaic of the Gasr Elbia Basilica in Cyrenaica), "Atti della Accademia Nazionale dei Lincei," year 372, Remembrances of the Class of Moral, Historical and Philological Sciences, series VIII, XVIII (1975), fascimile 7, pp. 659–86.

SIXTEEN: **"God . . . Entrusted These Lands to the Demons of Violence"**

1. For Agathias's poetry see R. C. McCail, "The Erotic and Ascetic Poetry of Agathias Scholasticus" *Byzantion* 41 (1971): 205–267. "Romance in the shadow of power," was a favorite theme of Georg Lukács (1885–1971).
2. See Assunta Nagl, entry "Theodora," in *Paulys Real-Encyclopädie der Classischen Altertumswissenschaft*, Neue Bearbeitung, begonnen von G. Wissowa . . . hsgb. Von W. Kroll–K. Mittelhaus, Zweite Reihe, V 2 (Stuttgart: Meltzer Verlag, 1934), col. 1790.
3. *Secret History* 18.37.
4. *Wars* II 22.29.
5. Ibid. II 22.17.
6. Evagrius Scholasticus, *Church History* IV 29 (p. 178.2 foll. Bidez-Parmentier).
7. *Wars* II 23.11.
8. *Secret History* 16.14.
9. Ibid. 4.7.
10. Ibid. 4.8–10.
11. Ibid. 16.12.
12. Ibid. 4.12.
13. Ibid. 4.11.
14. Ibid. 4.16.
15. Ibid. 4.21.
16. Ibid. 4.27 foll.
17. Ibid. 4.30.
18. *Codex Justinianus* I 27 1.1.
19. The solemn majesty of the term "Consul Romanus" inspired a great passage in Thomas de Quincey's *Confessions of an English Opium-Eater*.

SEVENTEEN: **"Loyal to Her Family"**

1. *Autokratôr* (see Glossary).
2. *Wars* VII 22.8.
3. Ibid. VII 22.7.
4. Ibid. VII 22.17.
5. *Secret History* 17.28.
6. *Magister militum* (see Glossary).
7. In his role as *dux* (see Glossary), Gontharis reported directly to Areobindus.

8. *Wars* VII 31.6.
9. Ibid. VII 31.9.
10. Ibid. VII 31.15.
11. *Greek Anthology* VII 590.
12. *Secret History* 19.5.
13. See "Ioannes 90," in *The Prosopography of the Later Roman Empire*, ed. J. R. Martindale, III A (Cambridge, 1992), pp. 676 foll.
14. *Secret History* 5.22.
15. Ibid. 5.21.
16. Ibid. 5.22. Dewing's translation was "Ioannes," but I prefer "John" here.
17. Ibid.5.20.
18. Ibid. 5.21.
19. Ibid. 5.17.
20. Corippus, *In laudem Iustini* I 272 foll.
21. See Averil Cameron, *An Emperor's Abdication, Byzantinoslavica* 37 (1976): 161–67.

EIGHTEEN: **"Her Next Stage"**

1. Augustine, *Sermo 81* (Migne, *Patrologia Latina*, vol. XXXVIII, col. 505).
2. *Daniel* 9.27 passim.
3. John of Ephesus, op. cit., II, pp. 626, 635 foll.
4. *Wars* II 28.41 foll.
5. Ibid. VIII 11.9.
6. John Malalas, *Chronographia* XVIII 103 (p. 410 Thurn).
7. See the *Life* of the "patrician" Anastasia, op. cit., c. 565.16 foll.
8. On the specific issue of the Egyptian village of Aphroditos, which had "entrusted itself" to Theodora, see R. G. Salomon, "A Papyrus from Constantinople," *The Journal of Egyptian Archaeology* 34 (1948): 98–108.

Epilogue

1. Paul the Silentiary, *Descriptio Sanctae Sophiae* 59 foll.: "for the good of the surviving ruler and his subjects" (v. 64).
2. *Secret History* 18.13; 18.21 (this is the passage that calls it "a Scythian wilderness").
3. The original text is "Ite igitur faciles per gaudia vestra, Quirites / et Narsim resonans plausus ubique canat." From *Corpus Inscriptionum Latinarum* VI (1199).
4. Gregory the Great, *Epistulae* II 47.
5. For the interpretation and identification of the Ravenna mosaics, see also Irina Andreescu-Treadgold and W. Treadgold, "Procopius and the Imperial Panels of S. Vitale," *Art Bulletin* 69 (1997): 708–23.
6. Kitzinger, op. cit, p. 88.

Glossary

AGNOETS. From the Greek *agnoêtês* ("he who knows not"). Name given to the followers of the Monophysite (see Glossary) doctrine of Themistius, a sixth-century deacon in Alexandria, Egypt. They believed that Jesus' human soul could not know the future.

APHTHARTODOCETISM. From the Greek *aphtartos* ("incorruptible") and *dokeô* ("I appear"). It is one of the names given to the doctrine put forth by Julian, sixth-century bishop of Halicarnassus (now Bodrum, Turkey), that evolved from Monophysitism (see Glossary). Aphthartodocetism teaches that the body of Jesus Christ was incorruptible, impassible, and immortal from the first instant of the incarnation. Its adversaries claimed that such a doctrine was incompatible with the concept of the full humanity of Jesus.

ARIANISM. From Arius (c. 250–336), founder of this heretical sect that denied full humanity to Jesus because they believed that out of the three persons of the Trinity only the Father ought to be considered truly God, uncreated and ungenerated, eternal and immutable. Although condemned at the First Ecumenical Council held at Nicaea (now Iznik, Turkey) in 325, in the fourth century Arianism still had a large following in high imperial circles. It survived even longer among Christianized Teutonic tribes such as the Ostrogoths, the Vandals, and the Visigoths.

AUGUSTUS (fem. AUGUSTA). A Latin noun. An honorific appellation given to Roman emperors starting with Octavian in the first century B.C. Often used as a synonym for "emperor" (Augustus) and "empress" (Augusta). As an adjective, it signifies "imperial," "majestic," "noble," and "solemn."

AUTOKRATÔR. From the Greek *autos* ("by himself") and *kratêo* ("lord"), it designates he who exercises or holds absolute power, imperial power first of all. In its negative meaning it signifies "despot," "tyrant."

AUTOPSIA. From the Greek *autos* ("by himself") and *opsis* ("sight"). It refers to what is observed or investigated firsthand, not through third-party experience or authority.

BASILEUS. A Greek noun designating a "king," "sovereign," or "lord." Starting in the seventh century it became the official title of the emperor of Byzantium.

BLUES. Also called "Venetians," one of the two "parties" or "factions" (see Glossary) of the Hippodrome.

BYZANTIUM. Ancient name (from the Greek *Byzantion*) of the city founded at the eastern tip of Europe by Hellene settlers around the seventh century B.C. In the early part of the fourth century A.D., Emperor Constantine elected Byzantium to be the center of the Roman Empire, changing its name to Constantinople (see Glossary). Since then, the term has been used to refer to Constantinople in scholarly, archaizing texts. Today, broadly speaking, Byzantium also refers to the empire as such, especially from the seventh century forward, when its Eastern characteristics intensified.

CASTRUM. A Latin noun (*kastron* in Greek) that originally meant a military camp, later a fortified city.

CIVES ROMANUS. A Latin expression denoting a Roman citizen, with all his rights and duties with respect to the state.

COMES. A Latin noun (from which the English noun *count* is derived). Initially it referred to a comrade or companion of the emperor or his family; later it became an honorific title or the official appellation of imperial ministers. Militarily, a *comes* was a lower-rank officer.

CONSTANTINOPLE. Literally, "the city of Constantine," from the emperor (r. 306–37) who named after himself the ancient city of Byzantium (see Glossary) which he chose in 324 and inaugurated in 330 as the capital of the eastern part of the Roman Empire. After the fall of Rome and the western empire, it became capital of the entire empire. Later, as a result of the growing orientalization of the empire and the emergence in western Europe of the Holy Roman Empire, Constantinople was the capital of the medieval empire that we call Byzantine. In 1453, the Ottoman Turks seized the city and changed its name to Istanbul (perhaps from the Greek expression *eis tên polin*, "in the city").

COPT. Appellation given to the Christians of Egypt, a contraction of the Greek *aigyptioi* and the Arabic *qibt*. The term *Copt* is often applied to followers of Monophysitism (see Glossary) and to those who speak the Coptic language derived from ancient Egyptian.

CUBICULUM. A Latin noun from the verb *cubo* ("I lay, I rest"), it initially referred to a bedroom other than that of the master or mistress of the house. Later, it signified an apartment. *Sacrum cubiculum* is the apartment par excellence, that of the emperors.

CURIA. A Latin noun. In late antiquity, it referred to the city council that managed the administrative, financial, and logistic (but not political) responsibilities of a city (*polis*; see Glossary) and its territory (*chora*). Starting at about the close of the fifth and the beginning of the sixth century A.D., the relevance of the *curia* declined as a result of the growing centralization of the empire.

CURIALIS. From *curia* (see Glossary). In the period under consideration, it referred to the *decurion* (a local councilor) who was a member of the city's elite.

DAIMON. A Greek noun with many nuances. Initially it referred to a deity, later to a demon, a being intermediate between gods and men, then to the soul freed from the body, and still later to one's individual destiny or deepest vocation. In its negative meaning it signified an evil spirit or devil.

DESPOTÊS (fem. DESPOINA). A Greek noun meaning "master" (mistress), "owner," or "absolute lord" (lady).

DOMINUS (fem. DOMINA). A Latin noun with analogous meaning to that of the Greek *despotês* (fem. *despoina*) (see Glossary).

DOMUS. A Latin noun that means "home," "seat," "family," also "fatherland."

DOMUS DIVINA. A Latin technical expression (literally, "divine house") designating those landholdings whose rent was specifically assigned to the emperor's liberality or to the maintenance of the emperor's apartments.

DUX. A Latin noun. In late antiquity, this technical term referred to the military commander of frontier troops in a given province. In some rare cases, the *dux* also filled civilian posts and performed nonmilitary duties.

DYNATOS. A Greek term meaning "powerful," a person invested with formal authority.

DYOPHYSITE (also spelled DUOPHYSITE). From the Greek *dyo* ("two") and *physis* ("nature"), it designated those who saw in the triune person of Jesus Christ, the Incarnate Word, both a divine and a human nature in a state of permanent union but without intermingling or fusion. The Dyophysite doctrine was formulated by Pope Leo the Great in 449 and prevailed at the Council of Chalcedon (451) over the Monophysite (see Glossary) interpretation of the nature of Jesus. The opposition to Dyophysitism was long-lasting, especially in the eastern Mediterranean regions, until the birth of Islam at the close of the seventh century.

ECUMENE. From the Greek *oikoumene*, or "the inhabited [lands]," (in Greek, *gê* means "land" or "earth"). The universalistic tendency of the Byzantine empire meant that all the inhabited lands were in principle subject to the emperor's power, just as the Christian "message"—which the empire promoted—was directed at all the people of those lands.

EON. From the Greek term *aiôn*, which means a "long period of time" such as a century, a millennium, an age, or similar. In Gnosticism (see Glossary) it is an emanation of the supreme Divine Being.

EXCUBITOR. A Latin noun whose literal meaning is "sentry." It designated a military man with a superior physique, member of a choice unit of the Imperial Palace Guard in Constantinople.

FACTIONS. Descended from the four *factiones* of the Rome Circus, in Constantinople there were two factions, as the Whites gradually came to identify with the Blues and the Reds with the Greens. The names originated from the colors of the tunic worn by the charioteers during the chariot races in the Hippodrome, the most popular spectator sport of city life. The factions did more than cheer the charioteers; they managed enormous sums of money that they received from the city government to organize the shows and compensate the athletes and the service personnel. Since the emperor and the highest authorities were customary spectators at the races, the factions were also empowered to submit political or administrative issues to them, although they are not comparable to modern political parties.

GNOSTICISM. From the Greek noun *gnôsis* ("knowledge"), it designates a set of ideas and trends that arose within Christianity, starting especially in the second century, and reappeared in many forms at various times in history. Central to all the forms of Gnosticism is the belief in a supreme, unknowable Divine Being from whom, through a series of emanations (eons; see Glossary) the Demiurge is derived. The Demiurge is the creator and ruler of our earthly world, which is intrinsically evil. In Gnosticism, Jesus is an emissary of the Divine Being and a bearer of knowledge (*gnôsis*) to a restricted circle of "spiritual," not "carnal," men.

GREENS. Also known as "Prasini," they were one of the two "parties" or "factions" (see Glossary) attached to the Hippodrome.

HIPPODROME. The leading monumental public building of Constantinople and its entertainment center. It was connected to the imperial palace through a loge or gallery called the Kathisma, where the emperor appeared in order to be acclaimed or to watch the games and the chariot races. The Hippodrome could house up to a fifth of the city's population at its highest demographic density (more than 100,000 spectators out of a total population of 500,000 to 600,000). The succession of columns and obelisks that separated the tracks made this circus a sort of outdoor museum.

HUBRIS. From the Greek *hybris*, a noun signifying "violence," "arrogance," "smugness," "insolence," or "excessive pride," manifested as a challenge to the law (whether divine, natural, or political) and as such invoking the gods' revenge.

IMPERIUM. A Latin noun that signifies an order or command, therefore the power to give it, hence "authority." It also refers to the territory where authority is exercised, and therefore to the "state" or "empire."

INFAMIS. A Latin adjective signifying "without honor," "discredited," and thus "dishonorable," "infamous," or "shameful."

KYRIOS (fem. KYRIA). A Greek noun. See *despotês* (fem. *despoina*).

LOCUS AMOENUS. A Latin expression meaning "pleasant place," "agreeable location," an ideal or idyllic setting.

MAGISTER MILITUM. The army's highest rank (literally, master of soldiers).

MANIAKION. A Greek noun designating a fabric collar embroidered with pearls and gems that was part of the imperial garb.

MANICHEISM. A religious doctrine preached by Mani (A.D. 216?–276). Born in the region of Persia, it spread to the Mediterranean and the whole of Asia. Taking its cue from elements of early Christianity and Gnosticism (see Glossary), Manicheism saw the world as a clash between light and darkness, devalued all earthly experience, and recommended a strict asceticism. In Manicheism, Jesus Christ is one of many "enlightened" human beings (Mani is another) who are called upon to free the tiny particles of light that are present in each man and woman.

METABOLÊ. A Greek noun that means "mutation," "variation," "transformation," as well as (in ancient Greek tragedy especially) the "reversal of a situation."

MONOPHYSITISM. From the Greek *monos* ("single" or "one") and *physis* ("nature"), it designated the doctrine that saw in Jesus, the Incarnate Word, only one nature, divine, instead of two natures, divine and human (Dyophysitism; see Glossary). An extreme formulation of Monophysitism was put forth by Eutyches and condemned at the Fourth Ecumenical Council, held at Chalcedon in 451, since it seemed to negate the humanity of Jesus that was instead accepted by other versions of Monophysitism. The doctrine gained a wide following in Egypt and among Syrian monastic groups.

NESTORIANISM. From the name of the heretical leader Nestorius (patriarch of Constantinople in 428, deposed in 430, died after 451), it refers to a doctrine that refused to call the Virgin Mary *Theotokos*, "Mother of God," preferring to call her *Christotokos* or "Mother of Christ." Nestorianism also taught that in Christ two persons coexist, one divine, the other human, a violation of the dogma of the unity of each of the three persons of the Trinity.

NOMISMA. A Greek noun, equivalent to *solidus* (see Glossary).

NOVELLAE. The "new" laws, promulgated by Justinian after he published the *Codex Iustinianus* in 534.

PAIDEIA. A Greek noun with layered meanings. Originally it meant "children's education," later it came to signify their teaching through an adequate course of study that led to identifying *paideia* with "culture," and later, metaphorically, with "individual experience." It may also mean "art," "discipline."

PARRHÊSIA. A Greek term with a double meaning: in the positive sense it means "freedom of speech," "power of speaking." In the negative sense it means "unrestrained speech," "speaking recklessly."

PATRIARCH. An ecclesiastical title reserved in antiquity for the bishops of the five major Christian centers: Rome, Alexandria, and Antioch since the First Ecumenical Council (Nicaea, 325), and Constantinople and Jerusalem since the Fourth Council (Chalcedon, 451).

PHANTASIAST. See Aphthartodocetism.

PLEBS. A Latin noun that initially referred to the mass of Roman citizens (as distinguished from the patricians, who enjoyed special privileges). Later it came to signify the "common people," or the poorest population of large cities in general.

POLIS. A Greek noun signifying "city."

PRAEFECTUS PRAETORIO. In the late ancient empire, the highest civilian functionary in a given territory. Among his duties was collecting the main tax in the province, the so-called *annona*.

PRAEPENDULIA. Long pendants that were part of the crown of an Augusta (see Glossary).

RES PRIVATA. A Latin expression meaning "personal matter" as opposed to *res publica* (see Glossary). In late antiquity, *res privatae* were also the assets owned by the imperial crown, as separate from those owned by the empire (*fiscus*).

RES PUBLICA. A Latin expression meaning "public matter," and therefore, metaphorically, the "state" or its "government."

RES SEVERA. A Latin expression meaning "serious matter," "weighty issue."

RESTITUTIO. A Latin expression meaning "restitution"; metaphorically, "restoration."

SAMARITANS. An unorthodox Jewish sect that recognized only the authority of the Pentateuch in the Bible. It had its temple not in Jerusalem but on Mount Gerizim in northern Palestine.

SILENTIUM. A Latin technical term designating the council meetings the emperor held with his ministers (the term clarifies how the ministers were to behave).

SOLIDUS. Also called *nomisma* (see Glossary) in Greek, it was the basic coin of the monetary system of the late-ancient, later Byzantine, empire. It was 4.48 grams of solid gold.

TECHNÊ. A Greek noun meaning "art," "skill," "artifice," "technique," or "trade."

TELL. A technical term (*tell* is Arabic for "hill," mount") for the mounds that indicate the superimposition of sites of possible archaeological interest in the eastern Mediterranean.

THYMOS. A Greek noun signifying "mind," "life," "vital principle," "courage," "ardor," "rage," "ire."

TORQUES. A Latin noun equivalent to the Greek *maniakion* (see Glossary).

VELUM. A fabric curtain that separated rooms, whose lifting or lowering had important meaning in ceremonies and in hearings in the imperial palace and other official locales.

VENATIO (VENATOR). A Latin noun that originally designated the "hunt," later the wild-animal-hunting shows performed in the circuses of the Empire, with the participation of specialized gladiators called *venatores*.

VIR ROMANUS. A Latin expression meaning "Roman man," with the ensemble of all the virtues and duties connected to Roman citizenship.

About the Sources

Procopius of Caesarea

There are several Italian translations of the primary source for Theodora, Procipius's *Secret History* or *Anekdota*. The first, all-important edition is by D. Comparetti and D. Bassi and is also renowned for its critical text (*Le inedite*; Rome, 1928). Among modern editions, *Storia segreta*, ed. F. M. Pontani (Rome, 1972); *Carte segrete*, 2nd ed., ed. by Lia Raffaella Cresci Sacchini (Milan, 1981); and, most recently, with a profusion of notes and with parallel Greek text, *Storie segrete*, with an introduction, critical revision of the text, and notes by F. Conca, Italian trans. P. Cesaretti (Milan, 1996), from which the quotations in this *Teodora: Ascesa di una imperatrice* have been generally taken.

The most recent French edition of the *Secret History*, by P. Maraval, *Procope: Histoire secrète* (Paris, 1990), has numerous notes but no critical text.

The other works of Procopius are currently unavailable in Italian translation, although there have been renowned versions of the *Wars*, *Le guerre persiana vandalica gotica* (The Persian, Vandal, and Gothic Wars), ed. M. Craveri (Turin, 1977); but especially *La guerra gotica* (The Gothic War), 3 vols., ed. and trans. by D. Comparetti (Rome, 1895–99).

English-language readers may read all of Procopius's opus with parallel Greek text in the Loeb edition that has been generally used for the quotations in this English-language translation of *Theodora*. *Procopius*, 7 vols., ed. H. B. Dewing (individual volumes published by several publishers from 1914–40), has been reprinted numerous times.

German-language readers may read the German translation with parallel Greek text by O. Veh published by Tusculum, Prokopios, *Werke*, 5 vols. (Munich, 1966–77).

The reference critical edition for the works of Procopius is still Teubner's, by J. Haury, *Procopii Caesariensis Opera Omnia*, 4 vols. (Leipzig, 1905–13), revised by G. Wirth in 1963–64.

For the text of the *Secret History* the edition by H. Mihăescu, *Historia arcana* (Bucharest, 1972), is important.

SELECTED ADDITIONAL SOURCES IN GREEK

Antologia Palatina (*Greek Anthology*) Ed. F. M. Pontani, 4 vols. (Turin, 1978–81).

Quotations in this *Theodora* are from *The Greek Anthology*, English trans. W. R. Paton (Cambridge, Mass.: Loeb Classical Library, 1916–18; repr. 1993–98), English version with parallel Greek text.

Agapetus

Agapetus Diaconus. *Expositio capitum admonitoriorum*, in Migne, *Patrologia Graeca*, vol. LXVI 1, cols. 1164 foll.

Corpus Iuris Civilis

Vol. I, *Institutiones—Digesta*, 16th ed., ed. P. Krueger and Th. Mommsen. Berlin, 1954.

Vol. II, *Codex Iustinianus*, 11th ed., ed. P. Krueger. Berlin, 1954.

Vol. III, *Novellae*, 6th ed., ed. R. Schoell and G. Kroll. Berlin, 1954.

Dialogus de Scientia Politica

Menae patricii cum Thoma referendario De scientia politica dialogus, ed. C. M. Mazzucchi. Milan, 1982.

Evagrius Scholasticus

The Ecclesiastical History of Evagrius, ed. J. Bidez and L. Parmentier. London, 1898.

John Lydus

Lydus, Iohannes. *De magistratibus populi romani*, ed. R. Wuensch. Leipzig, 1903.

John Malalas

Malalae, Iohannis. *Chronographia*, ed. I. Thurn. Berlin and New York, 2000.

Narratio de Sancta Sophia

In *Scriptores Originum Constantinopolitanarum*, ed. Th. Preger. Leipzig, 1901. Vol. I, pp. 74–108.

Theophanes

Theophanes Confessor, *Chronographia*, 2 vols., ed. C. de Boor. Leipzig, 1883–85.

Vita Sancti Sabae

In E. Schwartz, "Kyrillos von Skythopolis," *Texte und Untersuchungen* XLIX 2. Leipzig, 1939, pp. 85–200.

Selected Sources in Latin
Collectio Avellana
Epistulae Imperatorum, pontificum, aliorum inde ab a. CCCLXVII usque ad a. DLIII datae, 2 vols., ed. O. Guenther, *Corpus Scriptorum Ecclesiasticorum Latinorum* XXXV. Vienna, 1895–98.

Liber Pontificalis
Le Liber Pontificalis, 2nd ed., ed. L. Duchesne. Paris, 1955, vol. I.

LIBERATO
Liberati
"Breviarium causae Nestorianorum et Euthychianorum," in *Acta Conciliorum Oecumenicorum*, ed. E. Schwartz. Concilium Universale Chalcedonense V 2. Berlin and Leipzig, 1936, pp. 98–141.

Victorinus of Tonnennae
Victorinus Tonnennensis, *Chronica*, ed. Th. Mommsen, in "Monumenta Germaniae Historica," Auctores Antiquisissimi XI. Berlin, 1894, pp. 184–206.

Selected Eastern Sources
John of Ephesus
Lives of the Eastern Saints, 3 vols., ed. E. W. Brooks. Paris, 1923–25. (*Patrologia Orientalis* XVII 1; XVIII 4; XIX 2).
Iohannis Ephesini Historia Ecclesiastica Pars Tertia, ed. E. W. Brooks, in *Corpus Scriptorum Christianorum Orientalium: Scriptores Syri* (henceforth CSCO.SS), LV. Louvain, 1936.

Zacharias Scholasticus
Historia Ecclesiastica Zachariae Rhetori vulgo adscripta, 2 vols., ed. E. W. Brooks, CSCO.SS, XLI and XLII. Louvain, 1924.
La vie de Sévère par Zacharie le Scholastique, ed. M.-A. Kugener. (*Patrologia Orientalis* II 1). Paris, 1907.

Michael the Syrian
Michel le Syrien. *Chronique*, 4 vols., ed. J.-B. Chabot. Paris, 1899–1924. (esp. vol. 2; Paris, 1901).

Other Sources
Vitae virorum apud Monophysitas celeberrimorum, vol. I, ed. E. W. Brooks. CSCO.SS, VIII. Louvain, 1907.
The Chronicle of John, Bishop of Nikiu, trans. R.-H. Charles. London and Oxford, 1916.
Documenta ad origines Monophysitarum illustrandas, ed. J.-B. Chabot. CSCO.SS, LII. Louvain, 1933.

History of the Patriarchs of the Coptic Church of Alexandria, ed. B. Evetts. (*Patrologia Orientalis* I 4). Paris, 1907.

ABOUT THE MODERN MYTH OF THEODORA

Baronii, C. *Annales Ecclesiastici* cum *Critica Historico-chronologica* Antonii Pagi, etc., 38 vols. J. D. Mansi. Lucca, 1738–59, vol. IX.

Gibbon, Edward. *The History of the Decline and Fall of the Roman Empire*, 7 vols. London: Methuen & Co., 1909.

de Sade, D.-A.-F. *La filosofia nel boudoir,* (Italian translation of *La Philosophie dans le boudoir*, 1795) Rome, 1993.

Sardou, Victorien. *Théodora: Drame en cinq actes et sept tableaux* (Theodora: A Five-Act, Seven-Scene Play). Paris, 1884.

D'Annunzio, Gabriele. *La nave: Tragedia* (The Ship: A Tragedy). Milan, 1908.

Graves, Robert. *Count Belisarius*. New York: Farrar, Straus, & Giroux, 1982.

In general, pages 255–60 of Browning's *Justinian and Theodora* serve as a good introduction. But it is less well known that Theodora appears in *Upravda*, a *récit dramatique* (1912) by one of the more significant Russian authors of the early twentieth century, Velimir Chlebnikov (a sort of modern "mad saint" and "baradeus" whose portrait by Angelo Maria Ripellino is unforgettable). The text, chock-full of pathos and lacking critical accuracy, indulged an ancient and undocumented tradition according to which Justinian was of Slavic origin and named, appropriately, "Upravda." In the play, during the Nika riots Theodora is likened to an oriental tiger that incites the Russian ruler of Constantinople to fight back, because "only with strength can strength be subdued."

By virtue of an ironic historical coincidence, precise even at a distance of centuries, Chlebnikov died in 1922 after a brief life, in Novgorod, that most Byzantine of Russian cities, and on the same day, June 28, of Theodora's death.

Silvia Ronchey wrote an essay that is rich with information (although some readers, including myself, may not subscribe to her overall interpretation) which depicts Theodora as a Byzantine *femme fatale* of a decadentist European culture; the essay is "Teodora Femme Fatale," in S. Ronchey, ed., *La decadenza* (Palermo: Sellerio Editore, 2002), pp. 19–43.

Film

Leopoldo Carlucci, *Teodora* (1922); see M. Musumeci, "Fra decadenza e restauro. Un film degli anni Venti," in S. Ronchey, *La decadenza*, pp. 131–153.

Riccardo Freda, with Gianna-Maria Canale, *Theodora, imperatrice di Bisanzio* (Theodora, Empress of Byzantium) (1953).

Theater

Theodora's theater popularity is not limited to Sardou's play. In Averil Cameron, *Procopius and the Sixth Century*, p. 77 and n. 63, we read of a 1956 Arabic-language play, translated into Syriac in 1977. Additionally, Maria

Luisa Bigai has kindly reported about *Teodora,* a theatrical version in fourteen "frames" of Procopius's *Secret History,* by Andrea Camilleri, which was successfully performed at the Teatro Tordinona in Rome in 1975. Federica Giulietta played the part of Theodora.

Justinian, not Theodora, appears on pp. 26 foll. of the "dramatic *satura*" by G. Giudici, *Il Paradiso: Perché mi vinse il lume d'esta stella* (The Paradiso: Why I Was Captured by the Light of This Star) (Genoa, 1991), performed at the Petruzzelli Theater in Bari in 1991. Finally, despite the efforts of Maria Luisa Agati, to whom I am thankful, I could not find more details about a *Teodora* that was recently staged in Rome, with the Greek actress Irene Papas in the leading role.

Music

Sardou's *Théodora* was performed in 1883 with incidental music by Jules Massenet. An opera evolved from the play: *Théodora,* music by Xavier-H. N. Leroux, lyrics by V. Sardou and P. Ferrier, first performed at the Monte Carlo Casino in 1907 (also staged at the Teatro alla Scala in 1909), and a ballet, *Teodora,* music by Romualdo Marenco, choreography by Raffaele Grassi, performed at the Scala in 1889.

Visual Arts

I cannot add anything to what Browning has written in *Justinian and Theodora,* except to note Theodora's presence in an installation that has been called an "icon of feminist art": *The Dinner Party,* by American artist Judy Chicago. The work was first shown in 1979 and is expected to be on permanent display at the Brooklyn Museum of Art in New York in 2004.

Selected Bibliography

The present book was originally published in Italian in 2001. Thus I was unable to consider Clive Foss's remarkable essay "The Empress Theodora," published in *Byzantion* LXXII (2002): 141–176. Foss's interpretation of Theodora coincides with mine on several points, even though we pursued independent and different paths in our research.

I was, however, able to avail myself for this English-language edition of the information presented in a review by Carmelo Capizzi of the first Italian edition, as well as other foreign-language editions. The observations presented in his "Un nuovo ritratto–icona dell'imperatrice Teodora," in *La Civiltà Cattolica* CLIII 2, no. 3644 (April 20, 2002): 165–171, were very helpful.

ON THE EMPIRE OF THE SECOND ROME
Ostrogorsky, George. *History of the Byzantine State.* New Brunswick, NJ: Rutgers University Press, 1969.
Mango, Cyril. *Byzantium: The Empire of New Rome.* London: Weidenfeld and Nicolson, 1980.

ON THE WORLD OF LATE ANTIQUITY IN GENERAL
Stein, Ernst. *Histoire du Bas Empire,* vol. II, *De la disparition de l'Empire d'Occident à la mort de Justinien* (History of the Late Empire, II, From the Disappearance of the Western Empire to the Death of Justinian). Paris, Brussels, and Amsterdam: Desclée de Brouwer, 1949.
Jones, A. H. M. *The Later Roman Empire, 284–602.* 3 vols. London: Blackwell, 1964.
Brown, Peter Robert Lamont. *The World of Late Antiquity: From Marcus Aurelius to Mohammed.* London: Thames & Hudson, 1971.
Cameron, Averil. *The Mediterranean World in Late Antiquity A.D. 395–600* (Routledge History of the Ancient World). New York and London: Routledge, 1993.

ON SOCIETY IN GENERAL
Cavallo, Guglielmo, ed. *L'uomo bizantino* (Byzantine Man). Rome and Bari: Laterza, 1992.
Gallina, M. *Potere e società a Bisanzio* (Power and Society in Byzantium). Turin, 1995.

ON THE AGE OF JUSTINIAN AND THEODORA IN PARTICULAR
Diehl, Charles. *Justinien et la civilisation byzantine au VIe siècle* (Justinian and Byzantine Civilization in the Sixth Century). Paris: E. Leroux, 1901.
Vasiliev, A. A. *Justin the First: An Introduction to the Epoch of Justinian the Great*. Cambridge, Mass.: Harvard University Press, 1950.
Rubin, Berthold, and Carmelo Capizzi. *Das Zeitalter Justinians* (The Age of Justinian), 2 vols. Berlin: De Gruyter, 1960–95.
Browning, Robert. *Justinian and Theodora*. London: Weidenfeld and Nicolson, 1971.
Ravegnani, Giorgio. *Giustiniano* (Justinian). Teramo: Giunti e Lisciani, 1993.

BIOGRAPHIES AND NARRATIVES OF THEODORA AND HER WORLD
Diehl, Charles. *Théodora, impératrice de Byzance* (Theodora, Empress of Byzantium.) Paris: E. de Boccard, 1937.
———. *Figures Byzantines* (Byzantine Figures), 2nd ed., vol. I. Paris: A. Collin, 1908, pp. 51–75.
Stadelman, H. *Theodora von Byzanz* (Theodora of Byzantium). 2 vols. Dresden, 1927.
Nagl, A. Entry "Theodora," in *Paulys Real: Encyclopädie der Classischen Altertumswissenschaft* (Paulys Real: Encyclopaedia of Classical Antiquity), new version begun by G. Wissowa, ed. W. Kroll and K. Mittelhaus, Zweite Reihe, vol. 2. Stuttgart: Meltzer Verlag, 1934, cols. 1776–91.
Graves, Robert. *Count Belisarius*. New York: Farrar, Straus, & Giroux, 1982.
Lamb, Harold. *Theodora and the Emperor*. Garden City, NY: Doubleday, 1952.
D'Anna, G. *Teodora: L'imperatrice dal passato equivoco* (Theodora: The Empress with the Shady Past). Milan, 1967.
Bridge, Anthony. *Theodora: Portrait in a Byzantine Landscape*. London: Cassel, 1978.
Fèvre, Francis. *Théodora: Impératrice de Byzance* (Theodora: Empress of Byzantium). Paris: Presses de la Renaissance, 1984.
Garland, Linda. *Byzantine Empresses: Women and Power in Byzantium* A.D. *527–1204*. London and New York: Routledge, 1991.

ON PROCOPIUS
Cameron, Averil. *Procopius and the Sixth Century*. London: Duckworth, 1985.

ON PROCOPIUS AND THEODORA
Beck, H.-G. *Kaiserin Theodora und Prokop: Der Historiker und sein Opfer* (Empress Theodora and Procopius: The Historian and His Victim). Munich: Piper, 1986.

Bornmann, F. "Su alcuni passi di Procopio" (On Selected Procopius Passages). *Studi Italiani di Filologia Classica*, New Series 50 (1978): 27–37.

Angold, M. "Procopius's Portrait of Theodora," in *Philellēn: Studies in Honour of Robert Browning*, ed. C. N. Constantinides et al. Venice, 1996, pp. 21–34.

For specific topics, in addition to the entries in *The Oxford Dictionary of Byzantium*, 3 vols., ed. A. P. Kazhdan et al. (Oxford and New York, 1991), and *The Prosopography of the Later Roman Empire*, 3 vols. in 4 tomes., ed. A. H. M. Jones, J. R. Martindale, and J. Morris (Cambridge, Mass.: Cambridge University Press, 1971–92), the following are noteworthy:

ON ARCHAEOLOGY
Zanini, Enrico. *Introduzione all'archeologia bizantina* (Introduction to Byzantine Archaeology). Rome: Nuova Italia Scientifica, 1995.

ON ARCHITECTURE
Mango, Cyril. *Byzantine Architecture*. London: Faber & Faber, 1986.

Krautheimer, Richard. *Early Christian and Byzantine Architecture* (The Pelican History of Art Series). Harmondsworth, England and Baltimore, Maryland: Penguin Books, 1975.

ON ART
Grabar, A. *The Golden Age of Justinian's Golden Age: From the Death of Theodosius to the Rise of Islam*. Translated by Stuart Gilbert and James Emmons. New York: Odyssey Press, 1967.

Kitzinger, Ernst. *Byzantine Art in the Making: Main Lines of Stylistic Development in Mediterranean Art, 3rd–7th Century*. Cambridge, Mass.: Harvard University Press, 1977.

ON THE CEREMONIAL
McCormick, Michael. *Eternal Victory: Triumphal Rulership in Late Antiquity, Byzantium, and the Early Medieval West*. Cambridge and New York: Cambridge University Press, 1986.

Ravegnani, Giorgio. *La corte di Giustiniano* (Justinian's Court). Rome: Jouvence, 1989.

MacCormack, Sabine. *Art and Ceremony in Late Antiquity*. Berkeley: University of California Press, 1981.

ON CONSTANTINOPLE
Janin, Raymond. *Constantinople byzantine: Développement urbain et répertoire topographique* (Byzantine Constantinople: Urban Development and Topography). Paris: Institut francais d'études byzantines, 1964.

Beck, H.-G. "Konstantinopel: Zur Sozialgeschichte einer frühmittelalterlichen Haupstadt," *Byzantinishe Zeitschrift* LVIII (1965):11–45.

Dagron, Gilbert. *Naissance d'une capitale. Constantinople et ses institutions de 333 à 451.* Paris: PUF, 1974.

——.*Constantinople imaginaire* (Imaginary Constantinople). Paris: PUF, 1984.

ON LITERATURE

McCail, R. C. "The Erotic and Ascetic Poetry of Agathias Scholasticus," *Byzantion* XLI (1971): 205–67.

Cameron, Averil. *Literature and Society in the Early Byzantine World.* London, 1985.

ON RELIGION

Beck, H.-G. "Actus Fidei. Wege zum Autodafé," in *Sitzungsberichte der Bayerischen Akademie der Wissenschaften: Phil.-Hist. Klasse* (1987).

Jedin, Hubert, and John Dolan. *Handbook of Church History.* New York: Herder and Herder, 1965.

Capizzi, Carmelo. *Giustiniano I tra politica e religione.* Soveria Mannelli: Rubbetino, 1994.

ON FACTIONS

Cameron, Averil. *Circus Factions: Blues and Greens at Rome and Byzantium.* Oxford: Clarendon Press, 1976.

ON THE ROLE OF THE AUGUSTI

St. Maslev, "Die staatsrechtliche Stellung des byzantinischen Kaiserinnen," *Byzantinoslavica* XXVII (1966): 308–43 (on Theodora specifically, pp. 312 foll.).

ON THE MILITARY

Ravegnani, Giorgio. *Soldati di Bisanzio in età giustinianea* (Soldiers of Byzantium in the Age of Justinian). Rome: Jouvence, 1988.

ON MONOPHYSITISM

Frend, W. H. C. *The Rise of the Monophysite Movement: Chapters in the History of the Church in the Fifth and Sixth Centuries.* Cambridge: Cambridge University Press, 1972.

Duchesne, L. "Les protégés de Théodora" (Theodora's Protégés), *Mélanges d'archéologie et d'histoire de l'École Française de Rome* XXXV (1915): 57–79.

ON THE IDEOLOGY OF POWER

Ahrweiler, Hélène. *L'idéologie politique de l'empire byzantin* (The Political Ideology of the Byzantine Empire). Paris: PUF, 1975.

ON THE CROWN PROPERTIES

Kaplan, M. *Les propriétés de la Couronne et de l'Église dans l'Empire byzantin* (Crown and Church Property in the Byzantine Empire). Paris: Publications de la Sorbonne, 1975.

Photo Credits

16 Marble head of an empress ("Theodora"). Museum of Ancient Art in the Castello Sforzesco, Milan. Photo Scala.

22 Gold marriage ring, 6th century. Courtesy Dumbarton Oaks, Byzantine Collection, Washington, D.C.

23 Gold marriage belt, late 6th to 7th century. Courtesy Dumbarton Oaks, Byzantine Collection, Washington, D.C.

25 Dome of the church of Saints Sergius and Bacchus, Istanbul. Photo Werner Forman Archive.

33 Exterior of the basilica of the Holy Wisdom (Hagia Sophia), Istanbul. From Cyril Mango, *Byzantine Architecture* (London: Faber & Faber, 1986).

36 Interior of the basilica of the Holy Wisdom. Photo Werner Forman Archive.

38 Longitudinal section of the basilica of the Holy Wisdom, Istanbul. *Byzantine Architecture*.

40, 41 Stylized renderings of the monograms of Justinian and Theodora. From H. Swainson, "Monograms on the Capitals of St. Sergius in Constantinople," *Byzantinische Zeitschrift* IV (1895).

The Publisher has made all reasonable efforts to identify the owners of photographic rights and is at their disposal to fulfill all rightful obligations.

Acknowledgments

The idea for this work arose casually in 1995, after the systematic research and readings I did for the Italian edition of Procopius, *Storie segrete* (Milan: Rizzoli, 1996), published with Fabrizio Conca. I wrote the first draft of parts of this work in 1996, and made little progress in 1997. In 1999, after a two-year hiatus, I began to work regularly at the text; it took me a little over a year to finalize it.

I am indebted to many for encouragement, advice, and corrections. I apologize if I have left anyone out. I cannot thank enough those who saved me from mistakes (I am solely responsible for any still left) and opened new horizons to me.

First I wish to thank the troika that patiently tackled the various versions of this work: Laura Grandi, who was always ready to advise me on the publishing world's expectations; Elisabetta Matelli, always ready to warn me about convoluted or rough writing; and Gino Cesaretti, my formidable personal narrative trainer (together with my mother, Iris).

The following also offered recommendations and corrections in addition to exquisite attention and friendship as they were faced with not-quite-final versions: Antonio Aimi, Valentino Baldacci, Amilcare Bardi, Pino Bardi, Mariella De Battisti, Piera Detassis, Maria Falla Castelfranchi, Paola Lovato, Andrea Martano, Carlo Maria Mazzucchi, Giustina Ostuni, Lorella Pagnucco Salvemini, Bruno Pedretti, Luigi Pellegrini, Giorgio Ravegnani, Eileen Romano, and Giorgio Taborelli. A special thanks to Amilcare and Giorgio.

Guido and Clelia Matelli allowed me to invade their lovely Milan home with all my papers and books while my own house was unavailable. Therefore, a large part of this work was written away from my usual residence, but never really away from home: thank you.

I am especially grateful to the library of the Università Cattolica del Sacro Cuore of Milan and to the courtesy and skill of its library personnel, who greatly facilitated my work of research and verification.

At Mondadori, Marco Vigevani, Carlo Alberto Brioschi, Nicoletta Lazzari, Margherita Leardi, and Renato Curti (in chronological order) were patient traveling companions in this adventure.

How much I owe my friend—my reader—my spouse—Clara, I cannot even begin to say. And how could I ever thank you? The volume that I offer you, here, is already yours.

Index

"Roman" in quotations is used when referring to what was officially and institutionally connected to the empire of Constantinople as the second Rome.